THE CRYPTO GENIUS

'*The Crypto Genius* delves into the enigma of Bitcoin's creator, Satoshi Nakamoto, and the quest to unmask the figure behind the revolutionary cryptocurrency. Combining deep research and gripping storytelling, Benjamin Wallace unravels the mystery of Nakamoto's identity while exploring the cultural and financial impact of Bitcoin on the modern world. It's a thrilling, illuminating read.' Bradley Hope, *New York Times* bestselling author of *Billion-Dollar Whale*

'Benjamin Wallace's astonishingly obsessive deep dive into the financial world's greatest modern mystery will leave you amazed, enlightened, and utterly breathless.' Robert Kolker, #1 *New York Times* bestselling author of *Hidden Valley Road*

'*The Crypto Genius* takes us on a wild adventure among the oddballs, geniuses, longevity fanatics, and anarchists of crypto in search of one of the most elusive and consequential figures of our time.' Sheelah Kolhatkar, *New Yorker* staff writer and bestselling author of *Black Edge*

'I have long relished Ben Wallace's storytelling talents, and in *The Crypto Genius*, he delivers a tale that is somehow a blend of Agatha Christie and Soren Kierkegaard, unraveling a mystery while also exploring the nature of mystery itself. His search leads us into many dark corners of the nation-state of Bitcoin, a world and its people I was surprised, as a reader who willfully never gave much thought to crypto, to find absolutely mesmerizing.' Adam Moss, author of *The Work of Art: How Something Comes from Nothing*

ALSO BY BENJAMIN WALLACE:

The Billionaire's Vinegar

THE CRYPTO GENIUS

A Quest to Unmask the Mysterious Mr Nakamoto

BENJAMIN WALLACE

Atlantic Books
London

First published in hardback in Great Britain as *The Mysterious Mr Nakamoto* in 2025 by Atlantic Books, an imprint of Atlantic Books Ltd, by arrangement with Crown, an imprint of the Crown Publishing Group, a division of Penguin Random House LLC, New York.

This paperback edition published in 2026 by Atlantic Books.

10 9 8 7 6 5 4 3 2 1

A CIP catalogue record for this book is available from the British Library.

Paperback ISBN: 978 1 80546 438 9
E-book ISBN: 978 1 80546 437 2

Printed and bound by CPI (UK) Ltd, Croydon CR0 4YY

Atlantic Books
An imprint of Atlantic Books Ltd
Ormond House
26–27 Boswell Street
London
WC1N 3JZ

www.atlantic-books.co.uk

Product safety EU representative: Authorised Rep Compliance Ltd., Ground Floor, 71 Lower Baggot Street, Dublin, D02 P593, Ireland. www.arccompliance.com

MIX
Paper | Supporting responsible forestry
FSC® C013604

For Nicole and Lucinda

Contents

It's Him

If Satoshi Nakamoto, the pseudonymous inventor of Bitcoin, was who I believed him to be, he was not going to acknowledge it. He probably wouldn't talk to me. And seeing him was going to mean sitting on a plane for twenty hours and driving another eight. But I needed to try to have a conversation with him, and it had to be face to face.

Nakamoto had disappeared in the spring of 2011. I learned about him that summer, when I wrote *Wired*'s first feature article about Bitcoin, the internet-based currency that operated beyond the control of a government or bank. Twelve years later, Bitcoin's creator remained unknown and his enormous fortune untouched. His anonymity and restraint were a confounding rebuttal to the acclaim and riches that would be his were he only to step out of the shadows. The modern history of science supplied no precedent for someone who conceived a revolutionary technology and brought it into the world without taking credit.

Acolytes of Bitcoin, denied a flesh-and-blood human to venerate, had conferred on the pseudonym the halo of legend. In 2022, you could see Kanye West, as he stepped from an Escalade in Beverly Hills, wearing a Satoshi Nakamoto baseball hat. In Budapest, adherents had unveiled the first statue of Nakamoto, a depiction in bronze of a hooded, spectral figure. In the Vanuatu archipelago in the South

Pacific Ocean, real estate developers sold shares in a utopian paradise named Satoshi Island. A trio of libertarians bought a decommissioned cruise ship, christened it the MS *Satoshi,* and recruited settlers for the world's first sovereign Bitcoin-powered society. More than one fellow technologist lobbied for Satoshi Nakamoto to receive a Nobel Prize.

But the riddle of Nakamoto's identity stubbornly defied solution. Elon Musk and Peter Thiel, among others, speculated about it. Obsessed Nakamoto hunters strove to unearth new clues or remix existing ones in a more convincing way. By this point, more than one hundred different suspects had been fingered.

The intrigue transcended technology. In a world where the internet shone a pervasive light into every corner, there were vanishingly few unanswered questions of this kind. We'd learned who Bob Woodward's secret source was. We finally knew the proof of Fermat's Last Theorem. We'd been informed that Thomas Pynchon likely copped his bagels at Zabar's.

When I first set out to write about Nakamoto, I couldn't have foreseen that more than a decade later his identity would be the last big mystery. It would have been still more ludicrous to imagine that the ghost behind the world's first cryptocurrency, and the drive to decipher him, would bring with them lawsuits, a car chase, a bounty, a $75 billion fortune, extortion attempts, death threats, a SWAT team, a suicide, a fugitive arms dealer, a serial forger, a hidden society of paranoiacs known only by pseudonyms, a big-hearted genius trapped by disease in his own body, a nuclear bunker in Europe, frozen corpses in the Arizona desert, and a British spy in a locked duffel bag.

Prior attempts to unmask Nakamoto had failed, sometimes spectacularly. Even *60 Minutes,* with untold resources and a deep bench of seasoned investigative journalists, had thrown up its hands and declared the challenge "mission impossible." Yet now, against all odds, I believed I had cracked it.

I was nervous about what this might mean. The Bitcoin world was hostile toward projects like mine. But that wasn't my main concern. When I'd locked in on Nakamoto's real identity, I'd been surprised that he wasn't a usual suspect. This was someone who'd gone to great lengths to be unfindable. And what I learned about him was disturbing. He was nothing like how people had imagined Satoshi Nakamoto. He may have been talking himself up but he repeatedly described himself as dangerous. He had guns.

Before I flew around the world to meet him, I needed to be certain that I knew where he was. He owned at least four properties on two continents. I'd initially thought he was hiding out in a remote part of Hawaii's Big Island. More recently, I'd come to believe that he lived on the east coast of Australia, in a small beach community north of Brisbane. It was dawning on me that I'd have to hire private investigators to surveil the property and confirm his presence.

I was in the midst of fretting about all this when I met my sister for dinner at a Mexican restaurant in Manhattan and told her what I'd learned.

"It's him," she said, with a certainty I didn't feel.

She coolly sipped her margarita while I made doubtful noises.

"It's him," she repeated.

I told her my anxieties, but she had more experience with this sort of thing. She'd been a TV news producer for twenty years. During a period when she worked at *48 Hours,* she'd been onsite in Montana after the FBI raided the Unabomber's property and arrested him.

She suggested I take professional security people with me. And that I wear a bulletproof vest. And give local police a heads-up.

"Thanks," I mumbled.

I felt a little better. This was a plan. TV news people did this all the time. She wasn't worried. I needn't worry.

Later that night, she texted me.

"Couldn't sleep not sure why."

It was 4:09 a.m.

"Two thoughts. Maybe doorstep him in a public place if he ever leaves the house. Also might be worth having someone video the encounter (from a safe distance) for evidence."

A Straight-Up Legend

Eighteen months earlier, on New Year's Eve 2021, an email had arrived in my inbox.

"Subject: New information re Satoshi."

Ever since writing the *Wired* article, I'd periodically received emails like this. Bitcoin, and the broader cryptocurrency industry it begat, was still young enough that if you'd bought some as recently as 2017, you were an "OG"; journalists who'd covered the story in its earliest years were graybeards, and natural targets for anyone with a Satoshi theory to sell. Someone was always shopping a new Satoshi theory.

Usually, I paid little heed to these emails. Nakamoto news would rekindle a fleeting hope of learning something fresh and inevitably prove unconvincing. I was inured to the likelihood that the mystery would persist. This particular email hardly inspired confidence, being unsigned. I clicked it open anyway. There was no text, but a link led to a blog post titled "I'm the SpaceX Intern Who Speculated Satoshi Is Elon Musk. There Is More to the Story." The author, Sahil Gupta, had briefly produced a ripple on the internet four years earlier with another post making the case that Musk was "probably" Nakamoto. Now he presented further evidence: an account of an interaction he'd had with Musk's chief of staff, Sam Teller. It seemed slight and ambiguous, and I didn't respond.

Two days later, I received another unsigned email from the same address. This one contained a link to a page on GitHub, a website where software programmers share their work, featuring a detailed breakdown of Gupta's case for Musk as Nakamoto. Maybe because Musk was by then a fixture in the news, over the next few weeks I found myself mulling over Gupta's theory. I didn't know what to make of his arguments, which ranged from vague to highly technical. Finally, I wrote back to Gupta, who'd clearly sent the emails. He had, after all, in looking for someone to amplify his theory, singled me out.

"Thanks for taking the call," Sahil began. "I've emailed hundreds of reporters."

He was at home near San Jose, and we were on a video call. He wore a magenta T-shirt and silver can headphones and the shadow of a beard.

"It's remarkable how negative a caricature of Musk they have," Sahil continued, with an antsy energy. "They think he built a rocket and a car company by a fluke."

Sahil then described how he'd come to discover Nakamoto's real identity.

In 2015, when Sahil was an undergraduate at Yale University, he'd been impressed by what SpaceX was doing and had scored a summer internship writing inventory management software at its rocket factory in Hawthorne, California. "It was an amazing experience," Sahil recalled. Musk was in the office maybe three days a week, and Sahil would see him now and then in the hallways. After a "rapid unscheduled disassembly," the company's term for one of its rockets blowing up, Sahil was present as Musk gave a speech about how SpaceX was going to improve the technology and fix the problem. "It was very inspiring," Sahil said.

It was after his internship ended that he made the connection to Bitcoin. Sahil was majoring in computer science, and for a senior thesis he collaborated with two other students to propose a central bank digital currency called Fedcoin. "What if the U.S. could improve the dollar, taking the best aspects of Bitcoin?" he explained later. The paper's acknowledgments ended by thanking "Satoshi Nakamoto for being a straight up legend."

While researching the thesis, Sahil steeped himself in cryptocurrency literature, starting with the nine-page white paper where Nakamoto first described Bitcoin. Sahil had learned only recently that Nakamoto's true identity was a famous mystery. Reading the Bitcoin creator's writing, he was struck by similarities to Musk's language. Both spoke of "order of magnitude" reasoning and used the word *bloody*. Both argued from first principles. Nakamoto talked about money in a conceptual way, as Musk had done when he was an executive at PayPal in the early 2000s. Sahil learned that Musk, like Nakamoto, had a history of programming in the C++ language and was knowledgeable about economics and cryptography. Nakamoto also had demonstrated a mission-driven selflessness of a sort. "That's Musk," Sahil told me. He began to wonder: Might the inventor of Bitcoin have been in front of us all along, hiding in the dazzle of his own celebrity?

When Sahil graduated from college, he decided he wanted to work directly for Musk, in the office of the CEO. After emailing Musk several times, he got a phone interview with Teller, the chief of staff. Sahil told Teller about his background, but Teller said that he wasn't a good fit. Teller was looking for an administrative assistant; Sahil would be better off starting his own company.

"It was good advice," Sahil said.

As the call with Teller drew to a close, Sahil took a chance:

"Is Elon Satoshi?"

"Teller didn't say anything for fifteen seconds," Sahil told me. "Then he said, 'Well, what can I say?'"

"That was another big clue," Sahil said. "It's pretty clear what's going on. Like, I surprised him. The answer I got is pretty telling."

Later that year, Sahil wrote his "Elon Musk Probably Invented Bitcoin" blog post. He omitted what had been a private conversation with Teller, but he described the other parallels he'd found. And he argued that the Bitcoin community, which had been riven by strife over how and whether to mainstream the technology, would benefit from the return of its founder to guide it. A few cryptocurrency blogs picked up Sahil's theory, and Bloomberg News covered it. Musk himself tweeted: "Not true. A friend sent me part of a [bitcoin]* a few years [ago], but I don't know where it is."

Sahil eventually did go to work for Musk, getting hired in 2018 to help code Tesla's cloud software. He found it thrilling and fascinating how Musk, defying industry norms, located software engineers under the same roof as production workers. This was during the Model 3 ramp-up, and Sahil saw firsthand how Musk persevered through skepticism. Sahil told me that his Elon-is-Satoshi advocacy hadn't been a problem for his work at Tesla. "I admitted my attitude toward it. I really think Elon is Ben Franklin. I think my manager asked me about it once."

In time, Sahil left to start his own company, doing 3D virtual modeling for sites like Shopify. But as the years passed, and he connected more dots, his belief that Musk was Nakamoto became a conviction. He came across something Luke Nosek, a cofounder of PayPal, had once said while speaking on a panel at Davos: the company's original goal was to develop a currency free from banks. Sahil got a tip that Musk, like Nakamoto, had a history of using two spaces after a period in his writing. A colleague mentioned that Musk regularly flew in and out of Van Nuys Airport, which matched up eerily with perhaps the only security lapse Nakamoto had ever made: early in Bitcoin's history, an email from Nakamoto to another software developer inadvertently betrayed an IP address in North Los Angeles. Sahil learned that early Bitcoin coders had considered Satoshi "bossy"; Musk was certainly that. And what was Musk's brand,

* Bitcoin is capitalized when referring to the system and lowercased when referring to the currency.

in those pre-Twitter days? Doing difficult things: making electric cars cool; landing a rocket *on a barge*.

In late 2021, Sahil decided that the moment was ripe to make another public push. Nakamoto was now seen almost universally as a benevolent genius, and Sahil felt that a rare window had opened when the media might finally accept that Nakamoto and Musk were the same person. SpaceX had successfully docked a capsule at the International Space Station, and Musk had recently been named *Time*'s Person of the Year. He had even tweeted playfully about Dogecoin, a meme cryptocurrency. When Sahil published his new blog post, the one that prompted his email to me and hundreds of other reporters, he recounted the story of his interaction with Musk's chief of staff for the first time.

Now, on my computer screen, Sahil was saying he was "99 percent sure" about his theory. He chalked up others' doubts to prejudice against Musk. "I'm surprised people are skeptical of Musk's capabilities. That tells me there's a deep rut in society where people are not able to look at objective facts."

I had a few questions. Musk was an unusually capable person, but he had once described 2008—when he went into debt, got a divorce, and saw the third Falcon rocket in a row fail to launch—as the worst year of his life. Nakamoto had released the Bitcoin white paper in 2008. Could Musk possibly have had the bandwidth to create the world's first viable cryptocurrency, and then personally manage the software project for nearly two years, all while he was willing into existence an e-car industry and a successful private space company?

Sahil was ready with answers. He said he'd seen an interview in which Musk recalled that in 2007 he was spending only three days a month on Tesla. And hadn't Musk shown a prodigious ability to work on several unrelated projects at the same time? He even had a history of releasing a bold product idea in a white paper: in 2013, without fanfare, Musk had published fifty-eight pages online detailing a new kind of transportation system he called a hyperloop.

Okay, but Musk had done that under his own name, and he wasn't humble, so why, if he was Bitcoin's creator, would he deny being Nakamoto? To Sahil, this was no contradiction; it was further evidence of Musk's savvy. "Unlike a company that needs marketing, Bitcoin was stronger and could grow faster, in the early days, when it had the aura of an anonymous founder."

And why did Sahil think it important to share Musk's secret with the world? "It's an amazing story," Sahil said. He wanted Musk to receive the glory he was due. Sahil's goal was to help spur "sufficient public will, asking Musk to take credit."

Whether Sahil was right or not, I couldn't say, but I could relate to his fixation. Bitcoin had recently hit an all-time high of nearly $70,000 for a single coin, and the market value of all bitcoins in circulation had passed $1 trillion. El Salvador had recognized bitcoin as legal tender. In 2011, it hadn't seemed like such a big deal that no one knew who Nakamoto was. But how was it possible that even now no one knew?

Six months later, I quit my job to devote myself full-time to unraveling the mystery that had first beguiled me a decade earlier.

Pretend Internet Money

"Have you heard of Bitcoin?" Jason Tanz asked.

I had not.

"Do you know about Silk Road?"

I did not.

Jason was an editor at *Wired*. It was June 2011.

Jason mentioned a recent Gawker story about Silk Road, the dark web marketplace where bitcoin, described as an "untraceable digital currency," was the coin of the realm. Not yet three years old, Bitcoin had already traced a three-act arc from utopian software project to improbable $130 million-a-day market to shady network beset by crime, scandal, and a price crash. But with Occupy Wall Street only a few months in the future it felt timely. And Jason explained how Bitcoin was truly new. Past attempts at creating digital cash had failed because the same feature that made the internet revolutionary—instantaneous, borderless distribution with no central authority—had also led to something called the double-spending problem. If the internet was a Xerox machine, and digital cash just a string of bits, what was to stop a person from copy-pasting the same one over and over again? Bitcoin's architect, Satoshi Nakamoto, had ingeniously solved this problem.

"Are you interested?" Jason asked.

I was a former English major, knew nothing about computer science, and was an egregiously late adopter. When the internet started becoming popular in the 1990s, I'd been mystified: Why was everyone treating what was merely the latest in a long line of incremental human inventions like some kind of paradigm-shifting technology? "It's a *toaster,*" I'd scoff.

"That sounds amazing," I told Jason.

The Economist had published a detailed breakdown of how Bitcoin worked. Fred Wilson, a prominent venture capitalist, had likened it to WikiLeaks and the Arab Spring in its world-changing potential. And the story was irresistible. The idea of a rogue, parallel money system evoked the underground postal service in Thomas Pynchon's novel *The Crying of Lot 49*. Bitcoin's staunchest backers were a vivid cyberpunk mélange of hackers, goldbugs, anarchists, and Ayn Rand freaks. And I was captivated by the enigma of Satoshi Nakamoto.

The idea that no matter how detailed our maps became there were still blank, unaccounted-for spots had an enduring hold over me. When I was a kid, I'd kept, beneath my bedside table, a large-format book, rich with wild illustrations and grainy black-and-white photos, that was a collection of unexplained mysteries like the Loch Ness Monster and the Bermuda Triangle. Eventually my interest in these legends, with their whiff of unreality, gave way to a fascination with a species of public figure that abounded in the late 1970s and early 1980s, the iconic fugitive or recluse: On-the-lam members of the Weather Underground and the Baader-Meinhof Gang. Third Reich alums holed up in the Paraguayan jungle. Blue-blooded kidnap victim turned machine-gun-toting bank robber Patty Hearst. Footloose terrorist Carlos the Jackal. Media-allergic writers like Pynchon and J. D. Salinger. We were surrounded by and imprinted with these stories. Maybe, as a devoted young reader of each new Robert Ludlum novel, I'd been overly susceptible. But to my mind now, Satoshi Nakamoto, this elusive figure who might or might not exist, had done something more extreme than any of them.

I began calling around to Bitcoin people and subwaying from Brooklyn, where I lived, to meetups. Some took place in a dingy fifth-floor office suite in midtown Manhattan that housed a small web video production company whose owner was obsessed with Bitcoin, others at a bubble-tea cafe near Union Square.

I learned that three years earlier, on Halloween 2008, Nakamoto had posted a short write-up outlining "a peer-to-peer electronic cash system" on an obscure, moderated email list about cryptography that was informally known as Metzdowd. He described a new kind of money. It would run on a network of volunteers' computers, which anyone could join or leave at will. It would solve the double-spending problem by using a transparent public ledger collectively maintained by the network, rather than relying on a bank's or government's database of debits and credits. Nakamoto included a link to a more detailed formal description that would come to be known as "the Bitcoin white paper," but that was the high-level idea.

Nakamoto's timing for launching an alternative money was canny. Plenty of people, just then, were mad at banks: the prior month, Lehman Brothers had filed for the largest bankruptcy in U.S. history, and the Federal Reserve had used taxpayer money to bail out AIG, one of the world's biggest insurance companies. Decentralization, or not putting all your eggs in one basket, was more attractive than ever.

Nakamoto's choice of forum to announce Bitcoin was also adroit. Technically astute libertarians—people both good at computer science and hostile to authority—were amply represented on Metzdowd, with its cryptography focus. That none of its subscribers had heard of Satoshi Nakamoto didn't strike anyone as odd. Metzdowd was frequented by people devoted to the mathematics of secrecy. They were used to aliases.

A few members of the list who were particularly interested in the promise of digital cash gave Nakamoto feedback on the software he was writing, and he gamely welcomed it. "Thanks for bringing up that point," he told one person. "I appreciate your questions," he told another in a private email, before adding, "I actually did this kind of backwards. I had to write all the code before I could convince myself that I could solve every problem, then I wrote the paper." In early January of 2009, Nakamoto released an alpha version on SourceForge. At the time, it was a popular site for open-source software projects, collaborative endeavors that welcome any programmers who want to take part. The first day, according to one early Bitcoiner, 127 people downloaded the Bitcoin software.

A lot of the first participants were programmers who thought money was overdue for a product update. Paper bills and coins faded, wrinkled, tore, wore down, got dirty, spread germs. They were available only in fixed denominations, could be counterfeited, and were hard to move in any significant quantity. Bitcoin was money 2.0: durable, unforgeable, almost infinitely divisible. It might finally realize the internet commerce dream of microtransactions. You could send any amount of it, anywhere, instantly.

Many people in that initial wave held especially strong feelings about their personal autonomy. Bitcoin, as a currency based on 0s and 1s in a cloud maintained by far-flung, ordinary individuals, was immune to meddling by central powers. Unlike bars of gold, bitcoin couldn't be seized. Unlike a bank account, it couldn't be frozen. Unlike a national currency, it couldn't be devalued at the whim of a central bank or subjected to capital controls by a dictator. Unlike credit cards and bank wires, it didn't impose excessive transaction fees.

The earliest adopters tended to have an idiosyncratic mix of motives and beliefs. A typically atypical example was Dustin Trammell, who went by Druid online. Dustin was a thirty-year-old hacker who liked to learn by participating; away from his computer, he was a cosplay enthusiast. He'd dabbled in metal-backed alt-currencies, such as one called the Liberty Dollar, and donated his computers' spare processing cycles to SETI@home, a long-running UC Berkeley experiment in crowdsourcing analysis of radio-telescope data as part of a search for extraterrestrial intelligence. After learning about Bitcoin, Dustin diverted half of those computers to run its software, just because he saw it as a cool tech project. Later, he'd become interested in libertarian monetary ideas. Dustin exchanged a few emails with Nakamoto, letting Bitcoin's creator know that "electronic currency and cryptography are two things that I am very interested in" and offering to help with the project. "We definitely have similar interests!," Nakamoto responded. "You know, I think there were a lot more people interested in the 90's, but after more than a decade of failed Trusted Third Party based systems (Digicash, etc), they see it as a lost cause. I hope they can make the distinction, that this is the first time I know of that we're trying a non-trust based system."

At the heart of Nakamoto's creation was something called the blockchain, an ever-lengthening record of all transactions (buy, sell, etc.) that had occurred in the system. Approximately every ten minutes, the latest batch of transaction records were bundled into a "block," and the block was "chained" onto the block that had preceded it using some clever math that made it impractical for anyone to go back and tamper with the block's contents. This record, or ledger, which in traditional finance would be maintained by an institution such as a government or bank, was in Bitcoin maintained by a network of volunteers' computers, each of which ran the Bitcoin software, communicated with the other computers in the network, and stored more or less identical, constantly updating copies of the ledger. The price of entry to this network, for a computer, was to try to solve a math puzzle generated by the system every ten minutes. Much as websites distinguish humans from bots by asking computer users how many bridges are in a grid of landscape photos, this requirement, called "proof of work," deterred bad actors from taking over the system. Why would anyone bother wasting his computer power on this strange activity? Nakamoto cleverly engineered the system so that the first computer to solve each puzzle received a multibitcoin reward. In a stroke, he'd found a way to both attract sincere participants and dissuade insincere ones, while also creating a predictable mechanism for releasing new bitcoins into the money supply. Though the main purpose of the puzzle-solving race was to ensure the integrity of the system, it came to be called "mining" because of the multibitcoin reward. (The enormous energy used by hundreds of thousands of computers constantly working to solve these puzzles is also what gives Bitcoin its bad reputation among environmentalists.)

All this could sound arcane to civilians, but a centerless money was something the world had never seen. Its invention was an intellectual tour de force. Zooko Wilcox, whose obsession with the idea of decentralized money began when he was a politically inclined nineteen-year-old coder attending the University of Colorado Boulder, had been thinking of little else in the decade before Bitcoin appeared. "It was one of my favorite bedtime activities for twelve years, or whatever it was, to try to figure it out," he told me. "My instinct of Nakamoto consensus, and its integration with the incentive mechanisms, is it wouldn't have been discovered by anyone else. It would have taken another hundred years."

Whether you mined bitcoins or bought them from someone who had, there was an allure to getting in early. Nakamoto's software included a cap on how many bitcoins would ever be minted, 21 million, which the system was projected to hit around the year 2140. Instead of being at risk of inflation or hyperinflation, Bitcoin was deflationary: if the technology spread, you were holding an asset that would appreciate. "I love the idea," Nakamoto wrote in a post to the P2P Foundation's social network, "of virtual, non-geographic communities experimenting with new economic paradigms."

I found Bitcoin mind-bending, like a portal to a world, or a worldview, that I hadn't realized existed. Alienated libertarians already saw everyday money as mere *fiat*—they pronounced the word with audible, contemptuous italics—valuable only by decree of government. But for the rest of us, to encounter a currency that existed outside of a familiar context was to be like David Foster Wallace's fish who don't know they're in water—and then to be yanked gasping from it and, for the first time, *see*.

What made bitcoin worth anything? The U.S. dollar was legal tender backed by one of the world's most stable governments. You could use it to pay your taxes. Merchants were required to accept it. But what could possibly give a string of numbers and letters value? When a bitcoin exchange named New Liberty Standard launched in October 2009, it priced a single bitcoin (BTC) at less than a tenth of a penny, based on the cost of the electricity required to mine it. But bitcoin's price took on a life of its own. In early 2011, the market rate passed $1, and by the time Jason called me, a bitcoin cost more than $17. Much of the value, in those early days, seemed to derive from a belief in bitcoin's potential as a kind of digital gold with a worldwide market, and from rank financial speculation.

I was drawn to the frontier fizz. "It's fascinating to bootstrap a new currency," Jeff Garzik, a Bitcoin programmer who lived and worked in a 1984 Fleetwood Southwind RV in North Carolina, told me. "It's arguably the world's first global currency." In Brooklyn, I met Mark Suppes, a tinkerer who was building a bitcoin ATM in his Bedford-Stuyvesant loft, feet away from the DIY nuclear fusion reactor he was also building. A bearded, bandanna'd anarchist who posted to YouTube as The Real Plato was driving from Connecticut to California, Jack Kerouac-style, and attempting to fund the trip solely with bitcoin. Rare-coin enthusiasts spoke of a time years hence when people would trade unusual bitcoins—like those from the so-called Genesis Block, the first in the chain—as eagerly as if they were 1933 Double Eagles.

Even as I got caught up in the excitement, certain aspects escaped me. I could see how this new money might be attractive in a place like Argentina, where hyperinflation and currency controls were real. Likewise in Mexico or the Philippines or much of Africa, where more than 60 percent of the population didn't have bank accounts. But I didn't understand the beef the American Bitcoiners had with traditional financial institutions. Federal deposit insurance worked well enough. ATMs were convenient. What did these people have against banks?

I also struggled to fathom Bitcoin's technical underpinnings and how the system's parts interacted. At the meetups, I'd nod along as people talked about "one-way hash functions" and "Nash equilibria" and then go home and spend hours, until my eyes hurt, reading up on them. I'd think I finally understood it all, only to watch my newfound clarity slip away when I tried to explain it to someone else a few days later. I felt slightly less dim after Garzik, one of the project's main software developers, told me, "Bitcoin is really, really difficult to understand."

Bitcoin was also difficult to buy, to store, to use, and to hold onto. It was extremely volatile: the month I learned about it, it briefly lost more than 99 percent of its value, dropping from $17 to $0.01. Online exchanges, unregulated and unaccountable, often turned out to be fly-by-night operations, with anonymous owners who'd take in customer deposits and then, one day, simply abscond with them. Even Mt. Gox, the biggest exchange, had had 25,000 BTC, worth $500,000 at the time, stolen by hackers; this was what had precipitated the flash crash in bitcoin's price.

The alternative to storing your bitcoin on an exchange was "self-custody"-ing a private key, typically a fifty-one-character string of numbers and letters that was the cryptographic equivalent of a password, in a bitcoin "wallet," which was really more like a keyring. You could scribble your key on a piece of paper, etch it on a steel plate you buried in your backyard, save it on a virgin computer, or simply memorize it. That was the ultimate in self-sovereignty, and there was something thrilling about the idea that you could walk across an international border, key in brain, and you'd effectively just moved your money.

Not that anyone would advise doing this, given that a single misremembered digit could cost you your assets. Self-custody, an ideal that would come to be enshrined in the crypto-head mantra "Not your keys, not your coins," carried its own set of problems. Stefan Thomas, a Swiss programmer, had stored copies of the keys to 7,002 bitcoins in three places, putting his main wallet on a "virtual machine" air-gapped from the internet and backing it up both with TrueCrypt software and on an IronKey, a secure piece of hardware resembling a thumb drive. But then, while updating his operating system, he accidentally deleted the virtual machine. And when he logged into his TrueCrypt, which was stored in Dropbox, it, too, was deleted; it turned out that it could be overwritten if more than two machines were logged in at the same time. As for his IronKey, he'd simply misplaced the password. The value of the lost coins at the time was $140,000. "I spent a week trying to recover it," unsuccessfully, Stefan told me. "It was pretty painful."

In late 2021, the coins would be worth $473 million. But Stefan wasn't alone in his misfortune. The data firm Chainalysis estimated that 20 percent of all outstanding bitcoins had been lost.

I found Gavin Andresen to be a likable first guide to this esoteric world. Approaching forty-one, he wore his brown hair plastered across his forehead and the label "Geek" literally on his chest, as a patch on a short-sleeve button-down shirt he owned. He was a soft-spoken suburban father of two. Where someone else deprecating his own powers of recall might say, "My wife can tell you all about how poor my memory tends to be," and leave it at that, Gavin would elaborate with "I've seen the research on how fallible our memories are" and proceed to detail it for you. He rode a unicycle.

Bitcoin had shown up in Gavin's life at an opportune time. In 2009, his wife Michele, a geology professor at the University of Massachusetts, went on sabbatical, Gavin left a salaried position working on machine learning at the university, and the family moved to Australia. Gavin spent the next six months in Queensland juggling coconuts, running on the beach, snorkeling, being bitten by sand flies, rescuing a beaked sea snake, drinking XXXX beer, and shaving off the goatee he'd worn for the past seventeen years, among other pastimes. He planned to launch a start-up when the family returned to the United States, but in May 2010 he still hadn't found an idea that stuck.

Then he read a tech-blog post about a handful of open-source software projects, including Bitcoin. Gavin had graduated from Princeton University and worked for Silicon Graphics. He sat on the legislative body in his small New England town, took an active interest in local school politics, and had volunteered to help with the Amherst

League of Women Voters' website. But the idea of money not controlled by an elite group at the Federal Reserve appealed to him. He liked individual freedom, the wisdom of crowds, organic grassroots processes instead of top-down control. He believed in evolution over revolution, "small steps toward a better world."

His main reaction to Bitcoin, though, as he told me later, was *How could this possibly work?* He puzzled over how the system created new coins and how it prevented double-spending. He googled "Bitcoin" and got just four pages of results. Then he downloaded the code and started reading. It was clear that the programmer knew what he was doing. Gavin ran the software and mined some coins. Still, "I had to really think hard about it to convince myself that I can't see holes in the scheme." By the time we spoke, he was "pretty darn confident there's no fundamental flaw."

A month after learning about Bitcoin, Gavin created the Bitcoin Faucet. A bitcoin cost half a penny then, and Gavin spent $50 to buy 10,000 and set up a website to give them away. Anyone could solve a CAPTCHA and receive five bitcoins for free. The idea was to make this experiment welcoming to newcomers. Gavin understood that the only way a money became valuable was if people used it.

The Bitcoin Faucet was well suited to Bitcoin's cottage industry quaintness in those early days. One time, Gavin had lunch with David Forster, a farmer who lived near him in Massachusetts and was selling alpaca socks for bitcoin. Bitcoiners became positively giddy after Laszlo Hanyecz, who lived in Florida, paid 10,000 bitcoins for two large pizzas from Papa John's. In later years, people would never tire of revaluing those pies at whatever the current bitcoin price was—$690 million pizza! "I don't feel bad about it," Laszlo told me when those bitcoins were worth a mere $85,000 or so. "The pizza was really good."

Soon Gavin was asking and answering questions on the Bitcoin forum and sending off bits of code to Nakamoto to patch the inevitable holes present in any new software. He knew little about Nakamoto. They'd never met in person or talked on the phone. Gavin's sense of his main work collaborator drew solely from their written correspondence. In emails and private messages, Gavin found Nakamoto businesslike and prickly and self-sufficient and brilliant. Gavin worried about legal issues. The government had prosecuted previous creators of alternative currencies. Could he be arrested? Michele enjoyed teasing him about this "pretend Internet money," but soon Gavin was spending all his time on it.

He was working on the project because it interested him, but he also admired how well Nakamoto had tailored Bitcoin to human nature. As soon as you had some bitcoin, you wanted to help the system, whether by mining bitcoin, or using it, or promoting it, or working on the code, so that your bitcoin would be worth more tomorrow than it was yesterday. As the price went up, Gavin was being materially rewarded in real time. His involvement was "enlightened self-interest." Gavin thought bitcoin could become a major world currency and in time possibly even replace the dollar as the global reserve currency.

Although Bitcoin was an open-source project, an it-takes-a-village group effort notionally immune to individual agendas, someone needed to be in charge, and for the first twenty months that had been Satoshi Nakamoto. He would release code, other developers would suggest patches, and he would integrate the ones he liked.

Four months after Gavin began contributing, his dedication, computer science chops, and community-minded earnestness seemed to have won Nakamoto's trust. First, Nakamoto gave Gavin direct access to the source code. Then, around September of 2010, Nakamoto told Gavin that he was getting busy with other projects, and over the coming months he would hand over control of both the code repository on SourceForge and the project's "alert key," which allowed the broadcasting of urgent messages to all machines running the Bitcoin software. For an open-source project, these were the closest things to a leadership badge, and at that point Gavin effectively became the project's head developer, guiding a team of five other volunteer coders.

Over the next few months, Nakamoto continued to chime in occasionally on technical questions, but his reclusive tendencies chafed against Gavin's openness. After PayPal and Visa froze WikiLeaks' accounts, a faction of Bitcoiners argued that Bitcoin could be helpful to the controversial organization and that the association might help promote Bitcoin. "Bring it on," someone wrote on a forum called BitcoinTalk. But Nakamoto bristled. "No," he replied. "Don't 'bring it on.' The project needs to grow gradually so the software can be strengthened along the way. I make this appeal to WikiLeaks not to try to use Bitcoin. . . . The heat you would bring would likely destroy us at this stage."

The idea of WikiLeaks accepting bitcoin donations prompted an article in *PC Magazine*. Some Bitcoiners welcomed the spotlight, but Nakamoto did not. "It would have been nice to get this attention in any other context," he wrote. "WikiLeaks has kicked the hornet's nest, and the swarm is headed towards us."

For journalists covering Bitcoin, Gavin had become the natural person to call first. He had a mild, reasonable manner, a capacity for political moderation, and a tolerance for working under his real name, making him the Bitcoin ambassador Nakamoto had never been. But Nakamoto seemed increasingly uncomfortable with Gavin's interactions with media. In late April of 2011, Nakamoto emailed Gavin: "I wish you wouldn't keep talking about me as a mysterious shadowy figure, the press just turns that into a pirate currency angle."

This turned out to be the last time Gavin heard from Nakamoto. When I first spoke with Gavin that July, he said he hadn't communicated with Nakamoto "in a couple months." After Gavin ingenuously told Nakamoto in an email on April 26 that he'd agreed to give a talk on Bitcoin to the crypto-curious CIA at its headquarters in Langley, Virginia, Nakamoto never responded. Around the same date, he wrote emails to at least one other programmer who'd worked on the project.

Then he went silent.

Shiny Pony

"So," I said, "do you know who Satoshi is?"

If anyone knew, it would be Gavin.

"I don't know his real name," Gavin said. "I'm hoping one day he decides not to be anonymous anymore, and I'll meet him, but I expect not."

Gavin and the other developers agreed on a few things. The second place Nakamoto had announced his white paper was the website of the P2P Foundation, an idealistic nonprofit dedicated to peer-to-peer networks of all kinds. In his profile on the site, Nakamoto gave his residence as Japan. But no one really believed he was Japanese. His English was flawless, with the supple confidence of a native speaker. He sounded British, or at least from a Commonwealth country. The Genesis Block had had embedded within it a headline from the London *Times,* and in both the Bitcoin source code and his posts to the BitcoinTalk forum, Nakamoto favored Anglo spellings like *colour* and *optimise*. The *Times* headline hinted at Nakamoto's motivation: "Chancellor on Brink of Second Bailout for Banks."

It was also striking how closely Nakamoto guarded his identity. When registering the domain bitcoin.org, he had done so through a masking service called anonymousspeech.com, which itself had been registered from a temporary-housing broker in Tokyo. That service gave him an email address at vistomail.com, which offered the option of manipulating the date and time an email was sent. A third email address Nakamoto used was from gmx.com, another free webmail provider. Michael Marquardt, who ran BitcoinTalk under the name Theymos, was convinced that Nakamoto was hiding his IP address by using TOR, the same browser-anonymizing software required to reach dark web sites like Silk Road. And Nakamoto expressed himself with a practiced opacity. He'd answer technical questions, according to Gavin, like "one programming geek talking to another programming geek." Any attempts to draw Nakamoto out on personal matters were ignored.

Nakamoto's code told its own story. Gavin felt that programmers had authorial styles as distinct as Kurt Vonnegut's was from Jackie Collins's. There were some indications that Nakamoto might be a bit older. His coding style struck Gavin as slightly dated, and an Irish developer named Mike Hearn, who worked for Google in Switzerland, observed that Nakamoto used Hungarian notation, a convention of variable naming popular among Windows programmers in the 1990s. It was also a bit unusual to see a Windows person running an open-source project; the open-source movement had arisen largely in reaction to closed systems like Windows.

The Bitcoin programmers disagreed on other points. Gavin thought Nakamoto was in the top 10 percent of programmers, in terms of ability. But Amir Taaki, an early Bitcoin dev and anarchist hacker—he lived in a squat in London and would later become an activist for 3D-printed guns and fight alongside the Kurds on the front lines of Syria's civil war—told me he didn't think Nakamoto even had a computer science background. While Amir found the concept of Bitcoin solid, he thought the code was poorly written, with everything globbed together into two unwieldy files instead of broken into modular components, the way a pro would organize it. It made him think that Nakamoto might be a professor. "When you do programming for many years, if you're working with a team of people, you start thinking, How can I write this source code so it's understandable by many people? You learn to abstract things in a way that makes it obvious and understandable—you learn basic design patterns, standard ways of doing things—but these are things that academics don't learn. Engineers are concerned with: *How can I build this bug-free and easy to understand?*" Amir had a math background, and what he sensed when he read the white paper was a surehandedness with mathematical and statistical tools.

Gavin had the impression that the Bitcoin code had been written by a small group or even just one person. When programmers collaborate, they tend to insert regular comments in their code, telling one another what this or that block of instructions is supposed to accomplish. The Bitcoin software contained few of these. Others felt that Bitcoin was too clever, and worked too smoothly from the moment it launched, to be the product of a single brain. The white paper used "we." Satoshi Nakamoto must be the catch-all for a group of people or an institution.

By the time I learned about Bitcoin, members of its young community had begun asking who Nakamoto might be. Speculation predated his disappearance. By January 2011, even before Nakamoto evaporated, he was coming to be revered. When it became clear that Bitcoin needed smaller units, the community took to calling a hundredth of a bitcoin "a Satoshi."* The same month, someone noticed that Nakamoto's last BitcoinTalk post had been on December 13. There was a panic. Had Nakamoto left the project? Had he died? Who would lead them? A few people openly wondered, for the first time, about Nakamoto's true identity.

Someone floated the idea that Nakamoto was "along the lines of Nicolas Bourbaki," referring to a small group of French mathematicians who'd begun publishing papers in the 1930s using a collective

---

* ultimately, "a Satoshi" would come to mean one hundredth of a millionth of a bitcoin.

pseudonym. Someone else pointed out that the mystery lent Bitcoin a useful glamor. Another person suggested that "the guy just wants some privacy. And this is good, because that shows clearly that it's not the fame he is after, but ideals. IMHO we should respect that and leave his identity alone." But people couldn't help throwing names around: Could Nakamoto be Neal Stephenson, the novelist whose *Cryptonomicon* had anticipated digital money? Julian Assange, the Australian founder of WikiLeaks? Grigori Perelman, a hermitic Russian genius who'd turned down a million-dollar math prize?

The freakout proved unwarranted. On January 13, Gavin reassured the community: Nakamoto had emailed him that day "about a tricky bug. . . . He's just busy." But on April 16, 2011, a BitcoinTalker named Wobber, noting that a "long time [had] passed since he last posted in here," started a new thread: "Who is Satoshi Nakamoto?"

Wobber pointed out how varied Nakamoto's expertise was, and how unusual his behavior—to come up with something so innovative, not take credit for it or exploit his stature, and leave without telling anyone. Someone likened Nakamoto to Zorro, or a masked David who'd aimed his slingshot at the Goliath of banks and governments. Someone else wondered whether Nakamoto might be Gavin Andresen. Gavin did have an Australia connection, having been born there before moving to America as a child—which would explain Nakamoto's distinctive use of both American and Commonwealth spellings. Another person questioned whether Nakamoto would go to the length of creating a fake persona to interact with himself.

With so little to go on, sleuths seized on the smallest details. Might the name contain a clue? Satoshi Nakamoto, roughly translated from Japanese, could mean "central intelligence." Perhaps this pointed to the role of spies in Bitcoin's creation. Maybe the National Security Agency was playing a long game, launching an off-the-books financial network it could use either to pay assets in the field, anywhere in the world, or as a honeypot where adversaries would transact with a false sense of security, while the spooks at Fort Meade monitored their every move.

It wasn't a totally crazy idea. The U.S. Naval Research Laboratory had birthed The Onion Router, the anonymizing software known as TOR that enabled the dark web. The FBI would later secretly create its own line of encrypted phones and a messaging service, ANOM, that were unwittingly adopted by organized criminals, resulting in more than eight hundred arrests. And in the summer of 1996, three researchers in the Cryptology Division of the NSA's Office of Information Security Research and Technology had internally published a lengthy paper, later made public, titled "How to Make a Mint: The Cryptography of Anonymous Electronic Cash."

You could also read Nakamoto's name as a portmanteau of big tech-company names—SAmsung, TOSHIba, NAKAmichi, MOTOrola—so maybe a corporate cabal was behind it. Redditors pooled their deciphering skills, eventually finding Satoshi Nakamoto to be an anagram of, among other phrases, "Ma, I took NSA's oath" and "So a man took a shit."

For the first time, people scrutinized why Nakamoto had used a pseudonym. Was it because of the hassle of celebrity? The history of governments going after cryptographers? A desire to avoid bullying? "The enemies Bitcoin could make?" "Maybe he just wanted to be anonymous." Maybe he didn't want to mix this venture with other businesses he had.

In May, Gwern Branwen, himself a pseudonymous coder and writer with a following on certain blogs popular in Silicon Valley, sketched his own idea of Nakamoto. "Satoshi could be *anybody,*" he wrote. Bitcoin required "no major intellectual breakthroughs of a mathematical/cryptographic kind"; it was more a clever bundling of existing technologies, he argued, so "Satoshi need have no credentials in cryptography or be anything but a self-taught programmer!"

Stefan Thomas, the Swiss Bitcoiner who'd lost more than 7,000 coins, approached the question methodically, graphing the time stamps of every one of Nakamoto's five-hundred-plus forum posts. These revealed a pronounced dip in posting activity during hours corresponding to nighttime in North America. "Mike swears he has a British accent," Stefan told me, referring to Mike Hearn, the Bitcoin dev. Stefan had a vague profile of Nakamoto in mind: a single person living in the U.S., even if not an American. "Occam's razor," he said. A simple explanation trumped a complicated one.

When Stefan posted his graph to BitcoinTalk, it was greeted with a chorus of dissent: Wouldn't Nakamoto have been most likely to spend time on Bitcoin when he *wasn't* working? In that case, his posting hours could correspond to western Europe. "Since when does a hacker sleep at night?" someone protested. Someone else noted that the pattern should change for weekends but didn't.

Dan Kaminsky, a thirty-two-year-old computer security researcher who'd shot to prominence three years earlier when he discovered a technical glitch that could have undermined the entire internet, thought Nakamoto might be a group at a bank. "I suspect Satoshi is a small team at a financial institution," Dan told me. "I just get that feeling."

Nakamoto's identity was "a shiny pony," Dan added. "But I don't think it's that critical to what Bitcoin is. Bitcoin is larger than Satoshi." This jibed with a sentiment I'd heard voiced more than once: the whole idea of Nakamoto as an unknown pseudonymous entity who'd dematerialized was an integral part of Bitcoin's design.

I couldn't stop thinking about Bitcoin. I couldn't stop thinking about its creator. Maybe this didn't have to be so hard. The internet sometimes seemed to consist largely of recirculated air. The laptop Sherlocks graphing time stamps and scrutinizing variable names hadn't bothered to pick up the phone. Beliefs considered fact online often dissolved when they made contact with reality. Perhaps Nakamoto was twiddling his keyboard-callused thumbs in an ergonomic gaming chair, just waiting for someone like me to call. I wrote to him at satoshin@gmx.com, the address Gavin said he'd used, and requested an interview.

While I waited for a response, I reached out to a couple of plausible Nakamoto candidates. One was Adam Back, a British cryptographer who in the 1990s had written Hashcash, spam-prevention software that used computational puzzles—so-called proof of work—to force machines to show they were "honest." This was the same technology that Nakamoto later incorporated into Bitcoin. In fact, Back was the first person publicly known to have been contacted by Nakamoto, whom he'd never heard of and who had written to him in August of 2008 to ask how to properly cite Hashcash in the Bitcoin white paper, as Back later revealed.

We exchanged emails, but I found myself convinced by what Amir Taaki had told me: "Adam has a consistent style across his projects. His style does not match Satoshi's." Amir elaborated that Back followed standard programming conventions, wrote in C, and was a Unix/Linux programmer, while Nakamoto was stylistically erratic, wrote in C++, and was a Windows guy. Back was also known at the time as a privacy absolutist, someone likely to balk at Bitcoin's anonymity trade-offs; the point and pitfall of a blockchain was that everyone could see everything that happened on it. I also thought it implausibly clumsy for someone trying to elude detection, who'd cited only a handful of precedents, to include his own work among them.

The most obvious potential Nakamoto was David Chaum, a girthsome, Birkenstock-wearing e-cash entrepreneur who'd had one of his first eureka moments while driving a Volkswagen van in Northern California, and another while sitting in a hot tub. Chaum had designed the cryptographic protocols that made anonymous transactions possible, held several patents for untraceable digital money, and through his company DigiCash, in the Netherlands, had come as close as anyone to making it a reality. He also seemed like a pseudonym kind of guy. When a *Wired* reporter, years earlier, had innocently asked how old he was, Chaum said, "I don't tell that to people." When I emailed Chaum, he wrote back, "Kind of tied up," and didn't reply to further emails.

But when I phoned Stefan Brands, a Dutch cryptographer who'd worked closely with Chaum for many years, he was confident that

Bitcoin was not Chaum's. "He will not do anything that does not truly have strong anonymity," Stefan said. He also noted that Chaum had a PhD and "stellar academic credentials," while in Stefan's judgment whoever created Bitcoin was "probably a security engineer at the bachelor's level." Stefan thought Bitcoin showed a knack for high-level design, but he was most impressed by the marketing incentives baked into the system. He did wonder whether Gavin Andresen might be Nakamoto. Gavin denied it, I said. "Obviously whoever did this made a deliberate effort to hide their identity," Stefan replied, "so if it is him, he's not going to say 'Yes.'"

One thing clear to Stefan was that, because Bitcoin required a basic knowledge of cryptography and was apparently motivated by the libertarian economic idea of decentralization, whoever authored it was almost certainly tied to a radical group that had been active in the early 1990s. Stefan wasn't the only person who pointed me toward the group, which a former member described as "mathematicians with guns."

Mathematicians with Guns

At noon on a Saturday in September 1992, twenty revolutionaries gathered in a living room in Oakland, California. It belonged to Eric Hughes, a long-haired, Mormon-raised grad student in mathematics who was partial to fringed suede jackets. Hughes had only recently bought the house and not yet furnished it, so people brought pillows to sit on.

Tim May, a friend of Hughes, addressed the gathering. May was a tall, bearded physicist who as an early employee at Intel had solved a critical problem that led to a redesign of its chips; with stock options, he was able to retire when he was thirty-four, which gave him a lot of time to read and write. Among the inspirations that swirled in his brain were two works of fiction. One was Ayn Rand's novel *Atlas Shrugged,* with its elitist libertarian fantasy of a mountain enclave named Galt's Gulch where the world's intellectuals could shrug the humdrum atlas and its populace of mediocrities. The other was Vernor Vinge's science fiction novella *True Names,* which told the story of a group of hackers who had to operate under the cloak of "nyms" (pseudonyms) in virtual reality, against a variety of adversaries including the True Enemy (the government), in order to protect themselves in the physical world. May became convinced that the technology now existed to make these visions real: the anonymous digital cash devised by David Chaum, and the breakthroughs in cryptography that had made Chaum's dream possible.

For more than two thousand years, cryptography, the science of secret writing, had been symmetric: the secret key used to scramble a message was the same as the secret key used to unscramble it. This meant that the key had to be transmitted between the communicating parties, which presented both a vulnerability and a limitation: interception of the key was a risk, and sender and receiver had to know each other in advance. This had worked imperfectly for centuries, when the parties were, say, an emperor communicating with one of his military commanders.

But at the dawn of the internet, far-sighted technologists began imagining a world when billions of strangers would want to encrypt their online communications, and symmetric cryptography wouldn't be sufficient. In the 1970s, Whitfield Diffie and Martin Hellman at Stanford, and Ralph Merkle at Berkeley, separately made a remarkable discovery: a way to generate pairs of mathematically related keys. You'd keep the first one private. The second, which was derived from the first but from which you couldn't figure out what the first was, would be distributed publicly. Anyone else could then encrypt a message with the public key, and the message would be decipherable only by the private key. For the first time, strangers would be able to communicate securely. You could also reverse the process. You could "sign" (scramble, really) a document with your private key, and anyone could then prove you were the one who'd signed it by testing whether it could be unscrambled using your public key. Thus were born digital signatures, or the ability to prove your identity online.

May synthesized these ideas in a manifesto, and now, in Hughes's living room, he read it aloud. "A specter is haunting the modern world," he told the crowd sitting cross-legged on the floor, "the specter of crypto anarchy." May meant this in a positive way. He described a future with secure, untraceable email and online payments, impervious to government scrutiny or intervention. He imagined criminal misuses of this—most of which didn't seem to trouble him—but considered public-key cryptography as revolutionary as the printing press had been in disrupting medieval institutions or barbed wire had been in changing the American frontier. "So too," he declared, "will the seemingly minor discovery out of an arcane branch of mathematics come to be the wire clippers which dismantle the barbed wire around intellectual property."

Beyond his imagined utopia, which May called "Libertaria in Cyberspace," he was motivated by an imminent threat. Phil Zimmermann, a bearded former antinuclear activist, had released PGP, which stood for Pretty Good Privacy and was freeware that made public-key crypto available to anyone. Just load a copy onto your computer, and you could encrypt your emails before sending them. And the U.S. government, which deemed strong cryptography a munition in the same class as Tomahawk cruise missiles, was pursuing possible legal action against him. May, Hughes, and John Gilmore, an early employee of Sun Microsystems who'd also been able to retire early and then cofounded the Electronic Frontier Foundation, wanted to put cryptography in the hands of the masses.

After May read his manifesto, a rare female attendee named Jude Milhon, who was known as St. Jude, proposed that the group be called "cypherpunks." They would focus on real action in the real world: "Cypherpunks write code," in Hughes's words.

Then everyone spent hours playing the Crypto-Anarchy Game, an exercise May and Hughes had designed to make math protocols and abstractions like anonymity and digital money tangible and stimulate fresh thinking. Everyone was assigned a role: some people played drug dealers looking to conduct business and evade scrutiny, others counterintelligence agents hunting moles, others information brokers. May and Hughes passed out fake currency representing "e-money," and empty envelopes inside of other empty envelopes to simulate remailers, services that stripped away identifying information from email and made it harder for outsiders to track senders and recipients. The event was chaotic, with many messages misrouted and people putting the wrong postage on their envelopes, but the group had fun.

Those drawn to the cypherpunks were nearly all men but otherwise eclectic. One member claimed to be a prince of Liechtenstein. Another came to meetings in full leathers. A cypherpunk named John Draper was better known as Captain Crunch, because in the 1970s he'd figured out how to make free long-distance phone calls when he'd discovered that the giveaway whistles in Cap'n Crunch cereal boxes happened to emit the precise frequency, 2,600 hertz, needed to spoof AT&T's call-routing system. (For this, Draper served time in federal prison.) The group would also come to include BitTorrent inventor Bram Cohen, Grateful Dead lyricist and Electronic Frontier Foundation cofounder John Perry Barlow, Signal creator Moxie Marlinspike, and Julian Assange.

Though the Bay Area cypherpunks met in person once a month, their main gathering spot was an email list anyone could join. Many posters went by their real names, but there were also well-respected regulars known only by handles like Black Unicorn and Pr0duct Cypher. Using nyms to post to the list under multiple identities became a game for some and a tool for others. The internet was still an unsettled frontier, ripe for exploring the new kinds of relationships with strangers it made possible. Nyms also stood for an idea: being judged for your ideas instead of your credentials.

The cypherpunks were decidedly not people who beheld the embryonic web and thought: *pffft*. Instead, they saw vast opportunity and had in common both a piercing foresight about how a digitally networked world would endanger personal privacy and the conviction that only cryptography could safeguard it. This mattered whether you were a leave-me-alone antistatist, a civil rights activist concerned about the safety of dissidents in autocratic countries, or a regular person who just wanted to write emails without prying eyes reading them. Cryptography, as Hughes liked to say, was "the mathematical consequence of paranoid assumptions." (Hughes himself, according to a cypherpunk named Jim McCoy, "was keeping his car immaculately clean, so if he got pulled over, the police would have no excuse to search it.")

Since a core cypherpunk tenet held that "code is speech," any restrictions on it were seen as infringements of the First Amendment. The government wanted to criminalize *a computer program*? Adam Back started selling a T-shirt printed with an export-banned encryption formula; any self-respecting cypherpunk could blithely wear it as he boarded an international flight. Other cypherpunks, to the same end, got tattoos of the outlaw algorithms. When a grand jury was considering indicting PGP's Zimmermann, cypherpunks helped disseminate his software, exporting printed and digital versions to make it so widespread abroad that the U.S. government would have no recourse. After the Clinton administration in 1993 pressed phone makers to equip their products with the Clipper Chip, a backdoor to enable government surveillance, cypherpunks marched into electronics stores and slapped stickers reading "Big Brother Inside" on compromised machines.

Some cypherpunks also had more personal reasons for their interest in privacy. Gene Hoffman, a onetime executive at PGP, told me the group wasn't united solely by abstract ideals. Privacy rights are "a hard thing to care about," Hoffman said. "A lot of people in the cypherpunks movement had some part of their life they did want to shield. The overlap between cypherpunks and BDSM is not low." When I bounced this off a cypherpunk named Doug Barnes, whom Neal Stephenson has credited with coining the term *meatspace,* he disagreed: "Most of the cypherpunks I know are kind of chronic oversharers," he said, acknowledging the irony. "There were a lot of people who were notoriously polyamorous."

Mixing revolution and technology sometimes made for an unstable compound, and there was a hard-edged faction among the cypherpunks who styled themselves crypto-anarchists. They were more radical than libertarians, believing that technology could eliminate the need for any government at all. Tim May imagined an anonymous information market he called BlackNet, where corporate secrets could be illicitly sold and insider trading abetted. Other cypherpunks spoke hopefully about using digital cash to evade taxes. A cypherpunk named Jim Bell wrote an essay called "Assassination Politics," in which he proposed a website where people using anonymous digital cash could fund a large reward for anyone who correctly guessed the date of death of a particular public official; this would presumably incentivize someone else to "guess" a date and try to make the death happen then, while theoretically keeping the original funder(s) free from criminal culpability. Bell later spent years in federal prison, first for tax evasion and then for stalking and harassing IRS agents.

PGP's Phil Zimmermann, a gentle man facing the threat of criminal prosecution, had worn a suit every day for the past three years to present a respectable image in the court of public opinion. He was shocked when, at a cypherpunks meeting hosted by PGP, a member who went by the name Lucky Green reached into his duffel bag, announced that "the Cypherpunks Gun Club is going shooting next Saturday, and you're all invited," and proceeded to pull out an AR-15 assault rifle with an ammo clip. "PGP's offices were in a bank building," Phil recalled.

Some cypherpunks were dogmatic, and a certain amount of their activity tended toward windy quarrels that irritated professional cryptographers and working programmers and hackers. "I know at the time, there was this saying, 'Cypherpunks write code,'" recalls Jon Callas, who worked for PGP and later Apple and who attended many of the early meetings. "I was like, 'I'm too busy coding to be a cypherpunk.'" When Bram Cohen later ran a hacker convention, he announced that it would explicitly exclude topics like "mathematical cryptography lacking practical implementation" and "political debate about key escrow." But the sense of living in a time and place where you were shaping history was inescapable. To be a cypherpunk was to feel a covered-wagon thrill. You were leading the charge into a brave new future, propelled by a righteous cause.

Given the focus on pseudonyms, decentralization, and libertarian economics, there were obvious ways in which Satoshi Nakamoto had an air of cypherpunk about him. But the main reason Stefan Brands and others had pointed me toward the rebel technologists was that they had been consistently vocal about the need for digital cash. Many cypherpunks considered it their ultimate goal, the capstone to May's Libertaria in Cyberspace. While serial numbers and bankers made old money traceable, future money would be anonymous. While old money was connected to politics and governments, future money would stand on its own. Private digital currency became a fixation for the more radical cypherpunks, because it represented a threat to governments, with their monopolies on money issuance and the power of taxation.

These cypherpunks felt ambivalently toward David Chaum. His 1982 paper "Blind Signatures for Untraceable Payments," which laid a computer science foundation for digital money, verged on holy writ. Eric Hughes worked at DigiCash for a time. But many cypherpunks bristled at Chaum's commercial orientation. He wasn't shy about enforcing his patents. And Chaumian cash, viewed through a cypherpunk lens, had a critical flaw: it required a mint to issue currency and prevent double-spending by validating transactions; Chaum convinced Mark Twain Bank, in St. Louis, Missouri, to provide this service in the U.S. But to cypherpunks, a mint was a trusted third party, a single point of failure, a target. The government might shut it down for fear of tax evasion; criminals might harm the holder of the keys to any virtual Fort Knox. "Recall Nero's wish that Rome had a single throat that he could cut," a cypherpunk named James Donald wrote much later. "If we provide them with such a throat, it will be cut."

As it turned out, digital cash was a dream the cypherpunks never attained. By the late '90s, early cypherpunks had begun to leave the group. Some got bored. Others got busy with jobs and families. Others tired of the spam flood and general chaos that inevitably afflicted a mailing list populated by anarchists who'd decry the slightest moderation effort as "censorship." The group further dispersed after 9/11, when internal political differences that had been masked by a shared belief in cryptography-enabled privacy became more apparent.

Cypherpunks would still get together for patent-expiration parties, like the Saturday afternoon gathering at a beer garden in Portola Valley, California, in July 2005 to toast the end of Chaum's seventeen-year patent for blind signatures. And there was a glorious if shortlived burst of cypherpunk energy that year when a handful of cypherpunks tried to launch an offshore data haven on a wind-whipped antiaircraft platform in the North Sea. But from the late 1990s until 2008, there was a digital cash dark age, caused in part by a post-9/11 War on Terror crackdown on alternative moneys; the most successful of these, e-gold, ended in asset seizures, civil suits, and criminal indictments. Some of the most committed cypherpunks began to lose hope. "Tim May has succumbed to terminal grumps," James Donald wrote to the now-degraded cypherpunks list, "on discovering that the crypto transcendence is not coming soon." Others, Donald among them, were more sanguine. "We have a long way to go," Donald insisted, "but we are going." A handful of cypherpunks never let go of the e-money dream. And as I delved into the group's history, I kept hearing the same names.

Wei

Wei Dai was an amateur cryptographer who'd created Crypto++, a library of software tools that Bitcoin used, and Dai still maintained it, but the main reason some people thought he might be Nakamoto was a concept Dai had written about in 1998.

B-money, as he called it, combined several ideas that would later show up in Bitcoin: these included a peer-to-peer network that collectively maintained a common record of all transactions; a money-minting mechanism that depended on solving computational puzzles; and the use of public-key cryptography to shield users' identities. And Dai's b-money, like Back's Hashcash, was among the handful of precursors Nakamoto credited by name at the end of the Bitcoin white paper.

Dai was also, like Nakamoto, a ghostly figure. He'd graduated from the University of Washington in the late 1990s, but beyond that, little was known about him. There didn't seem to be any photos of him on the internet. Such a person clearly necessitated the most delicate, circumspect approach.

"Are you Satoshi Nakamoto?" I blurted in an email that summer of 2011.

"Satoshi is not me," Wei responded.

Long before Bitcoin appeared, Wei, after many years' interest in cryptography, had concluded that it wouldn't be as important to the future as he'd initially thought, and had become more interested in philosophy, he told me. He now spent much of his time in conversation on *LessWrong,* a blog popular among Silicon Valley futurists, which was focused on "refining the art of human rationality."

"I don't think it's anyone I know," Wei continued, regarding Nakamoto, "since he apparently invented Bitcoin independently and was not aware of my b-money article until Adam Back pointed it out to him. I do agree with gwern's guess that he's probably not a professional/academic cryptographer. I think he's probably a single student or programmer. (I was a student when I started working on Crypto++ and wrote about b-money.)"

Wei forwarded me some emails Nakamoto had sent him. In the first, from August 2008, Nakamoto said he wanted to cite b-money in the white paper and needed to know when Wei had published it. The second, from early 2009, contained a link to the Bitcoin software that Nakamoto sent Wei the day after releasing it. "I think it achieves nearly all the goals you set out to solve in your b-money paper," Nakamoto wrote.

Boom Boom

Another recurring person of interest among BitcoinTalkers was Nick Szabo, and I reached out to him next. Szabo was only slightly less reclusive than Wei, with a largely invisible job history. He would later say that he believed in "security through obscurity."

Szabo had been naturally drawn to the cypherpunks, with their commitment to real-world action. Cryptography enabled what he called "libertarian realpolitik"—"practical engineering" instead of "intellectual masturbation." In April 1993, when he'd been living in Oregon (where he'd worked for the computer maker Sequent), he wrote a pamphlet on "how to protect your electronic privacy" and handed it out at a meeting of Portland libertarians. He also went on a Portland-area TV forum to talk about how he was switching from AT&T to another provider to protest the telecom giant's support of the Clipper Chip, and he offered $200 as an advance order for whoever was first to make high-quality "Big Brother Inside" stickers. He proposed ideas for thwarting the incipient technology of face recognition by "'encrypting' one's image," suggesting an avoidance of overly obvious disguises (ski masks, sunglasses at night) in favor of a variety of hats, hairstyles, and makeup.

Tall and soft-bodied and not visibly concerned with fashion, Szabo had grown up in Washington State and had inherited a contempt for socialism from his father, Julius, whose Hungarian parents had watched Communists expropriate their farm. As a university student in Hungary, Julius had taken part in the 1956 revolt against the Soviet-puppet government, then fled to the United States, where he became a plant scientist. Nick's mother, Mary, also had a quantitative bent, working as an accountant and bringing home an Apple II from the office for her children to use.

When Szabo was a young man, his favorite science fiction novel was Robert Heinlein's *The Moon Is a Harsh Mistress,* which fused his two great interests: libertarian philosophy and outer space. While studying computer science at the University of Washington, a decade before Wei, he got an internship at the Jet Propulsion Laboratory in Pasadena, working on the Deep Space Network to help schedule communications for projects like Voyager, Galileo, and Magellan. The experience changed his life. Seeing the dynamism of smaller projects underway there and at nearby CalTech—ranging from the Mars Rover to neural nets—he became disillusioned with the American space program, with its focus not on long-term space colonization but on headline-grabbing space stations and space shuttles. He came to consider these "sacraments of the astronaut cult" a short-sighted affront—publicity stunts inflicted on taxpayers by a bloated NASA bureaucracy populated by "overhead-slide artists."

Szabo could be intellectualizing to the point of regarding his own bodily sensations as if they were data obtained using someone else's scientific instruments. Even his sexual arousal became a metric: of the more than one hundred women he'd asked out, "over half" of the times "I have had an erection." "Dust in the Wind," by Kansas, made him feel depressed: "Some kinds of music . . . can have a very strong impact on the emotions, in my experience."

Maybe the slights of youth—in junior high, he'd been bullied until he started punching back—had made him combative. He could be withering to those whose arguments he didn't respect, telling one, "Thanks for the memories, Gramps," another, "I assumed you were halfway intelligent," and a third, "Here's a reform proposal: Wake the fuck up to the real world out there." Antagonists variously suggested he needed lithium or was "desperately lonely," or asked, "Did someone . . . molest you as a child?"

Soon after subscribing to the cypherpunks list, Szabo had moved from Oregon to the San Francisco Bay Area in order to be near the group's physical meetings. He still found his online interactions at least as stimulating as in-person ones, but he basked in his heady new life. After midnight, one night that August, he drove south of Los Gatos, past the worst of the city glow to the foothills of the Santa Cruz Mountains, set up a lounge chair, covered himself with blankets and sweaters, and gazed up at the clear night sky. For the next two hours, he daydreamed about comet mining and space colonies and "Jupiter-sized brains" and watched dozens of dazzling meteors streak across the heavens, including "a spectacular bursting fireball." Two days after that, he was at a cypherpunks meeting with all the big names—John Gilmore, Eric Hughes, Tim May, Whit Diffie (co-inventor of public-key cryptography!). At the meeting, Romana Machado, who was both a software developer for Apple's handheld Newton device and a "glamor model" who went by Cypherella (*Playboy,* November 1985), debuted Stego, a piece of free software she'd written that let you hide a message in an image.

Machado was also a member of a group called the extropians, with which Szabo became deeply involved too. Extropians were devoted to transhumanism, or extreme life extension. This encompassed everything from smart drugs to artificial intelligence to the Singularity, that moment in the future when humans could be uploaded to the cloud. Szabo called it "Future Rapture."

Extropianism stood for expansion of all sorts. The extropian T-shirt read, "Forward, Upward, Outward," and a number of group members took sunny, techno-optimist nicknames like Jay Prime Positive, Tom Morrow, Max More, and David Victor de Transcend. Tim May's extropian "nom de humor," as he called it, was Klaus! von Future Prime, and Szabo sometimes went by !Boom!Boom or !Boom!Boom von Past Primeval.

The extropians merged future positivity with a libertarian allergy to constriction, whether by government, gravity, or aging. A typical extropian had read reams of science fiction and was an atheist who'd made a religion of tech. Though the group shared many members with the cypherpunks, the extropians were more hedonistic. Why live longer if you weren't having a good time? "They had better drugs, no question," Doug Barnes, who belonged to both groups, recalled, and "were certainly better looking, more fit." The chance for geeks to hang out with pretty girls "was part of our brand," Tom "Morrow" Bell, one of the group's cofounders, echoed.

The list of group interests was a syllabus for the future leaders of twenty-first-century Silicon Valley: life extension, space colonization, homeschooling, biohacking, consciousness-uploading, AI, self-sovereignty, seasteading, digital money, antistatism, transhumanism, polycentric law, prediction markets, digital nomads (their term was *tech nomads*), and memetics, among other things.

A remarkable number of members were or would become influential. Nick Bostrom was the Oxford philosopher of the so-called simulation hypothesis—the improbably widely held belief, among Elon Musk and his peers, that we are all living in a videogame. Robin Hanson pioneered modern prediction markets. K. Eric Drexler was the foremost proponent of nanotechnology. Hans Moravec, a roboticist, was the visionary of uploading oneself to the cloud. Bart Kosko was a leading popularizer of fuzzy logic. Eliezer Yudkowsky became the best-known AI doomer as well as a leader of the statistics-and-game-theory-fixated Rationalist movement.

When Szabo learned about the extropians, he found people talking seriously, as if they were engineers discussing viable future projects, about ideas he'd previously dismissed as whimsical fictions conjured in the sci-fi stories he loved. Cryonics. Uploading. Nanotech. When he didn't have to get to work early, he liked to lie in bed, barely awake, daydreaming and chewing over his many ideas.

The computer programmer view of the body as just another system to be optimized appealed to him. He joined the Life Extension Foundation, went on a weight loss plan, urinated in a cup to monitor his ketone level, cut his fat intake in favor of boiled or raw low-fat foods, stuck to Diet Coke, and took vitamin and mineral supplements, a mental-clarity nootropic called Deep Thought, and the appetite suppressant Acutrim. Twice a week, he swam a mile. In six months, he dropped from 240 to 180 pounds, and then, for maintenance, ate mainly salads.

He was a young, single man eager to meet women, and some of the extreme regimen was surely vanity. But he was also a proponent of Pascal's Wager. The original version, set forth by the seventeenth-century French philosopher Blaise Pascal, was religious bet-hedging: in case God existed, your best move was to act as if he did, in order to maximize your chances of admission to heaven. The extropian gloss was: you should strive to live as long and as healthily as possible, in order to increase the odds that uploading and/or cryonic reanimation would be ready for prime time before you died.

Szabo was enthusiastic about the extropians' more distant dreams too. He took an interest in nanotech and in definitions of death (extropians sometimes called themselves anti-Deathist). He liked the idea, once uploading became a possibility and sex drive was no longer needed to propagate the species, of redesigning its purpose: "If I got an orgasm on payday, instead of just a dull looking piece of paper with some abstract numbers, I'd probably be more motivated to make money."

He moved into a tan, high-roofed house in Cupertino that was home to an intentional community called Nexus-Lite. His four roommates included Romana Machado, and they sometimes threw parties, like a potluck supper on a Saturday in March 1994 that they billed the Extropaganza. Some guests, upon arriving, gave each other the extropian handshake that group cofounder Max More had devised: after intertwining fingers, you'd shoot them upwards. While Szabo was a bookish personality, his roommates were of like mind politically: Machado would walk around a party in a dominatrix outfit, dressed as "the State" and holding a leash attached to her boyfriend Geoff Dale, who was dressed as "the Taxpayer." The extropian playlist ranged from Alphaville's on-the-nose "Forever Young" to future-ish electronica like the Orb.

As Szabo spent more time among the extropians and cypherpunks, he seemed happier. Gone were the angry rants of the flame-warrior space activist. He was more courteous and empathic. Though he was quiet and reserved and sparing with eye contact, fellow extropians who spent time with him found him "nice" and "mild-mannered," in addition to radiating intelligence. His erudition on such a remarkable variety of subjects led some extropians who hadn't met him in person to believe his name was the pseudonym for a group.

For all his libertarianism, Szabo eschewed Ayn Rand's selfishness and considered himself a "communitarian"—someone who didn't mind volunteering for a greater good—in contrast with his own brother, whom he called "a free rider: absorbed in his own desires and ambitions." By 1993, Szabo had moved away from Libertarian Party politics toward individualist action, "making freedom for myself in an unfree world."

Around this time, Szabo became especially interested in cryptography-enabled "smart contracts," as he called them, self-executing computer code that could, like a vending machine that dispensed a candy bar for your quarter, operate free of human interference. His other great interest was digital cash and its ability to support online markets. For a brief time, he worked, as Eric Hughes had, for Chaum's DigiCash in the Netherlands.

It was on lib-tech, a private mailing list Szabo created to focus on freedom-promoting technologies, that Wei Dai first wrote about b-money, in 1998. It was also there, the same year, that Szabo floated his own idea for bit gold, which he described as "trust independent digital money." Like b-money, bit gold foreshadowed Bitcoin: it was motivated by a desire to do away with a so-called trusted third party and to replicate in cyberspace the "unforgeable scarcity" of precious metals. Like bitcoins, bit gold would be minted through the solving of a computational puzzle, the solution would be confirmed by a network of computers, and each solution would be cryptographically linked to both its predecessor and its successor. Like bitcoins, bit gold would have "miners."

After Nakamoto announced Bitcoin in October 2008, Szabo showed a light hand in drawing the connection, reposting a 2005 bit gold blog post that December without mentioning the bit gold-esque newcomer. The first time Szabo acknowledged Bitcoin by name, the following May, he noted that it worked "very similarly" to bit gold. He'd later describe Bitcoin as "an implementation of the bit gold idea."

When Gwern Branwen suggested that there was nothing technologically new in Bitcoin, Szabo came to Bitcoin's defense, calling it "not a list of cryptographic features, it's a very complex system of interacting mathematics and protocols in pursuit of what was a very unpopular goal." "By far the biggest stumbling block" to something like Bitcoin arriving earlier, Szabo wrote, was "the 'why'"—"Nearly everybody who heard the general idea thought it was a very bad idea. Myself, Wei Dai, and Hal Finney [another cypherpunk] were the only people I know of who liked the idea (or in Dai's case his related idea) enough to pursue it to any significant extent until Nakamoto (assuming Nakamoto is not really Finney or Dai). . . . The overlap between cryptographic experts and libertarians who might sympathize with such a 'gold bug' idea is already rather small."

When I asked Nick in the summer of 2011 about his experience with Bitcoin, he replied, "I haven't used it. There's nothing for sale with it I want to buy, a common problem with starting a currency. I've read the paper, some of the online descriptions, and some of the source code."

As I had with Wei, I tried the direct approach with Nick. I still didn't rule out the possibility that Nakamoto was frustrated no one had bothered to simply ask him.

"Are you Satoshi Nakamoto?" I asked.

"No," Nick replied.

When I asked him about his remark "assuming Nakamoto is not

really Finney or Dai," he replied: "They're just logical possibilities." He added that he'd always found Wei's description of b-money to be "hopelessly vague."

I floated a few other Nakamoto candidates past him.

"I'm not going to speculate on this further," Nick responded. "I think he has made a great contribution to the world and in return I want to respect his privacy."

Nick did make a point of mentioning Finney, though. He was "very disabled like Stephen Hawking," Nick cautioned, but he thought I should try to interview him. Nick wasn't the first person to suggest I contact Finney. Mike Hearn had said he'd be good for "hard-core insight." And Nick described Finney to me as "the first person to implement this kind of scheme."

An Evening of Pseudonymous Socializing

I was no closer to an answer when, a few weeks after my correspondence with Nick, I attended the world's first Bitcoin conference. Just getting a ticket was cumbersome. One cost $26, and you had to pay in bitcoin. I decided to buy $200 worth of the currency. It seemed loony, paying $14 a coin for something I couldn't touch, see, or even use for anything I really needed.

I wasn't going to make the same mistake as poor Stefan Thomas, so first I created an account with Mt. Gox, which was based in Tokyo and which everyone said was the most reliable bitcoin exchange. Then I registered with Dwolla, a payment-processing company in Iowa, which had to verify my bank account before it would accept money from me. This took four days. Then I had to wire money from my bank to Dwolla, which took another day to clear. Then I had to transfer the money from Dwolla to Tradehill, an exchange in San Francisco, to convert my dollars into 14 bitcoins. Then I had to withdraw four of them from Tradehill to an address controlled by my computer and send around two and a third of those to the conference organizer (the price of a bitcoin had dropped below $11 at that moment). The rest I withdrew from Tradehill to Mt. Gox, for safekeeping.

This was the money of the future?

Registration took place in the offices of Bruce Wagner's Only-OneTV, which produced *The Bitcoin Show* on YouTube, on a utilitarian stretch of Fifth Avenue in midtown Manhattan. It was late August, and people—almost all of them male people—had traveled from far-flung places to talk about invisible money that was backed by nothing and that hardly anybody understood, yet was trading at $15 a coin, up from less than a dollar six months earlier. Gavin Andresen had traveled from Massachusetts. Jeff Garzik had come up from North Carolina. Stefan Thomas had flown in from Switzerland, and Roger Ver, an energetic booster known as "Bitcoin Jesus," from Japan. In line ahead of me, as we waited to pick up our conference badges, I saw Jed McCaleb, future founder of Ripple, who'd originally created Mt. Gox as a site to trade cards from his favorite game (it stood for *Magic: The Gathering* Online eXchange) and later sold it. Although there were only around sixty-five of us, Bruce had branded the event "Bitcoin Conference & World Expo 2011 NYC."

Later, we gathered at a restaurant in Hell's Kitchen named Hudson Eatery, one of a few places Bruce had convinced to accept bitcoin as payment, for "an evening of pseudonymous socializing." The next day, in keynote talks at the Roosevelt Hotel on East Forty-Fifth Street, Gavin envisioned the day when Bitcoin would be mainstream and "boring"; Jeff spoke of the need for Bitcoin to step up its PR game, given how easily it could be misunderstood; and Stefan talked about coding applications for Bitcoin, which were sorely needed.

It didn't feel exactly like a revolution. One evening during the conference, Stefan found it such a hassle to pay with bitcoin at the bitcoin-accepting restaurants that he ended up paying with dollars. But there was a scrappy energy to the proceedings. In between airy musings about a Bitcoin-dominated future and networking by entrepreneurs who had Bitcoin-related start-ups, attendees traded theories about Nakamoto, who had never responded to my email. Religious overtones had already begun to creep into the way Bitcoiners spoke. The first block mined by Nakamoto was, after all, known as the Genesis Block. The event merch was a T-shirt that read I AM SATOSHI. The question loomed over the conference. Might he be here among us?

Not, I thought, if he was someone who was incapable of making the trip.

Mr. Rogers

Hal Finney, the digital-cash buff toward whom Nick Szabo had pointed me, had a radiant smile and, for a time, a pencil mustache of such lush breadth and Euclidean straightness it could have been cast in *Anchorman: The Legend of Ron Burgundy.* Exuberantly nerdy, Finney once posted an ad in a free newspaper offering to answer anyone's scientific or technical question for a dollar, and he approached mental hurdles with a roving enthusiasm. When he was working in the nascent videogame industry in the late 1970s, programming Intellivision's *Space Battle* and Atari's *Adventures of Tron,* he set out to create sound effects for Intellivision's *Major League Baseball.*

The Intellivision hardware included a programmable sound chip, and David Rolfe, a housemate and coworker from that period, recalls Finney "delving into wave patterns" to meet the ballpark-sonics challenge: "If you lived in an era in which computers had never made sounds, and you were given this tool, how would you make a 'crowd sound'? What does a crowd even sound like, anyway? There was a sports movie out around this time, *Heaven Can Wait,* and Hal paid particular attention to the stadium scenes in which the crowd cheered, and then carefully recreated the roar and the whistles and the air horn effects." He even came up with a "Yer out!" that mimicked human speech reasonably well.

Finney had always liked puzzles. Even as a child, in a family that moved from California to Louisiana to Texas following his father's work as a petroleum engineer, he jotted his own secret codes of letters and numbers in paper booklets. He was an imaginative boy with a taste for science fiction. He took out books from the public library about flying-saucer sightings and read them in bed at night, getting "a deliciously scary thrill imagining aliens hiding in the shadows." Often he found himself wondering, "Why was I born here and now, instead of at some other time throughout the whole sweep of history?"

Back in California for high school, he learned to program in FORTRAN and helped the Arcadia High administrators calculate student data, storing it on punch cards. He graduated in 1974 as class valedictorian and attended the California Institute of Technology, where even there he was seen as exceptionally bright, someone who could crack a textbook for the first time the night before a big test and crush it. Rarer still, for someone with his IQ, he was known equally for his kind and upbeat personality. A fraternity brother would recall that "he'd stuff as many as would fit into his VW bug and take us all out to Tommy's at 3 am for burgers."

Finney embraced science and technology, and he and his wife Fran, who'd been his college sweetheart, named their children and pets after astronomical objects: Arky, the name of their Rhodesian ridgeback, came from a star in the Boötes constellation. After learning about the extropians, Finney became a regular contributor to its email list. He already avoided alcohol, because he'd experienced seizures in college and there was a history of alcoholism in his family, and now he started experimenting with different approaches to being healthy: he went vegetarian for less than a year, tried a ketogenic diet, took antioxidant vitamin supplements, and joined Weight Watchers, among other things.

He also took a more extreme step popular among extropians. In October 1992, he and Fran drove from Santa Barbara, where they'd recently moved, to Riverside, southeast of LA, to sign the paperwork needed to enroll with Alcor, a cryonics organization. Alcor offered both a less expensive, head-only "neuro" package and a more expensive, full-body package, which the Finneys chose. When they died, their bodies would be frozen, in the hope that eventually technology could reanimate them. Alcor gave them each an emergency ID tag that could be worn as a pendant or on a chain-link bracelet. Hal wore the densely engraved steel plate from that day forward. It included a phone number manned 24/7; mention of a reward for calling it; "biostasis protocol" instructions; and the injunction "No embalming/no autopsy." This would announce to first responders, in the event of his "de-animation," that he was a paid-up cryonics patient, and whom to call so that his cryopreservation could begin without interference or delay. "He did not believe in God," Fran said later. "He believed in the future."

It was also through the extropians that Hal Finney learned about the project that would become his life's work. When he read that a guy named Phil Zimmermann had invented the world's first DIY cryptography program—software anyone could run on his personal computer to send and receive emails unreadable by interlopers—and that the government considered it a threat to national security, Finney downloaded it, experimented with it, and was impressed. This sent him to the library for further research, where he encountered David Chaum's papers showing conceptually and mathematically how the new cryptography could be used to ensure personal privacy online. "It just blew me away," Finney later recalled.

He was taken with "the mystery and the paradox" of cryptography. "The thing I always love is when there's an intellectual challenge that when you master it gives you practical abilities." Whenever he found something like that, he recognized his own tendency to develop an obsessive interest. "It's completely uncontrollable when it happens."

Cryptography was magic to him. Finney, like Tim May, had been inspired by *True Names* and its "untraceable identities." As he'd read the novella, he'd found himself picking out flaws in the technical aspects of Vinge's fantasy. Also like May, Finney immediately saw how cryptography, the grown-up version of his youthful puzzling, could be the means to make the future imagined in *True Names* real. Take nyms: anyone could use the name Secret Squirrel, Finney observed, but only one person could prove ownership of a private key connected to a public key. "It seemed so obvious to me. Here we are faced with the problems of loss of privacy, creeping computerization, massive databases, more centralization—and Chaum offers a completely different direction to go in, one which puts power into the hands of individuals rather than governments and corporations. The computer can be used as a tool to liberate and protect people, rather than to control them."

He volunteered to help Phil Zimmermann, and for the next several years he worked full-time at his day job, then went home and spent his evenings as a volunteer in the trenches, albeit in the lovely environs of California's Central Coast, grinding out lines of code for PGP. Later, after PGP overcame its legal troubles and became a for-profit company, Finney signed on as one of its first two employees. It was an ideal job for him, combining his love of brainteasers with a zeal for privacy.

In a field that skewed paranoid and autistic, Finney stood out for his amiable normality. Will Price, who worked with Finney at PGP, contrasts him with another cryptographer, a "Stephen Hawking–level genius" who also worked for PGP in the 1990s. This cryptographer eschewed bathing, would write only code that would be given away for free, and refused to accept money for his work because he didn't have a bank account. "We had to pay him with computers. I don't want to use the word *psycho*. No one has seen him since 2000. I think he lives in the woods somewhere."

Finney was outwardly more conventional. He liked spending time with his family. He was "such a centered person," Will told me, describing Finney as "serene" and "never angry." "Sometimes people that are super smart pay a price for that," Phil Zimmermann echoed. "There's something about their personality that doesn't work exactly right. Hal never paid that price. He preserved his humanity and kindness and grace. I saw Tom Hanks in a movie about Mr. Rogers. That's the kind of soul I'm talking about."

Finney was in many ways a quintessential cypherpunk. He really did write code. But though he held strong beliefs about freedom, he was more prosocial than some of his fellow travelers. He'd talk about how cryptography could have helped abolitionists working to liberate slaves on the Underground Railroad. "Big-L libertarians tend to be less compassionate," Phil said, "and I think Hal was a compassionate person."

Finney concluded that anonymity and pseudonymity, despite their drawbacks, would provide "real benefits to all members of society." He'd point to *The Federalist Papers,* "published anonymously due to fear of political retribution." And how about whistleblowers and dissidents? He had himself used multiple pseudonyms online. "For me, crypto anarchy is a way to oppose the constantly growing databases of information about each person, a way for individuals to take control of information about their own lives." He'd talk about *True Names,* in which "having your true name discovered was the worst disaster that could occur, as it made you vulnerable to many kinds of attacks, both from other hackers and from the government."

It wasn't a tweedy abstraction for Finney either. He'd get emotional thinking about how nonanonymous emails might land his boss Phil Zimmermann in prison. Finney had already spent $1,000 of his own money to retain a lawyer to advise on his risk of prosecution for the volunteer work he'd done for PGP, and he warned other cypherpunks that if the government found them guilty of violating the Arms Export Control Act, it could result in a fine of up to $1 million and ten years in prison. "It's sickening, but you can't be too careful these days. You can certainly see where Pr0duct Cypher and our other anonymous/pseudonymous posters are coming from."

After a remailer service hosted on the computer of a man in Finland was raided at the behest of the Church of Scientology, which was hunting an anonymous leaker of internal documents, Finney coded and ran one of the first encrypted, anonymous remailers; it bounced messages through multiple servers, with no server ever knowing more than the prior stop and next stop on the message's route. When the U.S. government started requiring export versions of popular software packages to employ weaker cryptography than the domestic versions, Finney, as a way of drawing attention to the absurdity and commercial disadvantages of the policy, posted a challenge to fellow cypherpunks to break the new export version of the Netscape browser. After a team succeeded in breaking it in one month, Finney posted a second Netscape-cracking challenge, and this time cypherpunks broke it in under thirty-two hours.

Remailers were just the ground floor of the privacy-respecting world Finney wanted to help build. What consumed him was the second floor: digital money. That dream had receded during the wars over the public's right to strong cryptography, but once that right was secured, Finney became increasingly focused on e-cash. He'd hint at both practical reasons for his interest—credit cards couldn't handle micropayments, didn't work for people who didn't have them, and were weak on privacy—and a more ideological one, referring to bankers printing money and causing inflation.

And Finney did the hard work of thinking through the details necessary to make digital cash real. How might the government view it, or any alternative money for that matter? Finney read up on the history of private banknotes and learned that they'd been subject to a heavy tax by a Civil War–era law that was still on the books. He learned that scrip and barter had been subject to oversight by the Internal Revenue Service. He studied workarounds to Chaum's patents. He foresaw that even in a system that bypassed the government, the conversion of paper money to digital money was a "choke point" where the government could exercise control.

In the near term, Finney thought that one path through the legal thicket might be to create "an educational game" and suggested that "anyone who proposes to implement such a game might want to consider releasing it anonymously (actually, pseudonymously). . . . This way there won't be a single-point target for anyone wishing to punish users of the game."

With a few like-minded cypherpunks, Finney bandied about possible names for the new currency: "cryps," "crydets," "emoney," "ecash," or, he wryly suggested, "Chaums. That way he'd be less likely to sue us for infringing on his patent." After another brainstorm, he proposed "CRASH," short for CRypto cASH.

Whenever this or that cypherpunk proposed a new digital-cash system, Finney reliably responded, offering encouragement or pointing out a vulnerability. He thought Chaum's idea of using tamperproof cryptographic hardware, installed on one's computer to prevent double-spending, was "the wrong direction," but he was also quick to take Chaum's e-cash product for a spin. After Pr0duct Cypher posted software he'd written for a "Magic Money" system, Finney patted him on the back: "Wow! Hot stuff!" Two days later, Finney reported that Magic Money might have a security flaw.

He also mused about the aesthetics of digital currency. Reading an old book on American paper money, he found some of the archaic bills depicted to be "startlingly beautiful." Was it possible, he wondered in a reply to Pr0duct Cypher, to create digital money that was beautiful and rare? He imagined discrete quantities of it, timestamped to prove their vintage. Digital money would be bits adrift in the ether, but Finney suggested ways that particular units of the currency could be made visible, such as "attractive fractal-looking patterns for many bills. . . . With a little more thought I hope to come up with a viewer for your Magic Money that will bring out its natural beauty and rarity. This will be a must for all serious collectors of digicash."

During the e-cash doldrums of the early '00s, Finney was one of the few who remained focused on solving the problem. He was obsessed enough to throw much of his free time at it. In 2004, he released his own implementation of Nick Szabo's bit gold. RPOW (Reusable Proofs of Work) used the same computational-puzzles method proposed for bit gold, employed cryptography to secure the system and ensure scarcity, and aimed to be decentralized, replacing a trusted third party with specialized hardware that participating computers would have.

RPOW never got much traction, but when Nakamoto announced Bitcoin four years later, Finney was the first person on Metzdowd to praise it. He gave Nakamoto feedback on the source code, and when Nakamoto launched the software on January 9, 2009, Finney's computer became the second node in the network. "Running Bitcoin," Finney tweeted.

This doubled as a nod to his new hobby. Given the sedentary nature of Finney's work, in middle age his weight had gone from 170 to around 250, and after his doctor told him he was obese, he began dieting and competing in half-marathons. Eventually he'd get down to 160. At the start of 2009, Finney was at a personal fitness peak and in training for his first full marathon.

Always Look on the Bright Side

The month after he tweeted about Bitcoin, Finney noticed that his running times weren't getting faster. He was tiring sooner and cramping more often. Fran noticed that when she and Hal ran together, he couldn't talk and run at the same time, as he had in the past. When she mentioned this, he said, with uncharacteristic impatience, "No one can talk and run at the same time."

Finney started to notice that his speech occasionally ran together, almost like he'd been drinking. His right hand began to feel shaky. Fran, a physical therapist, knew something was wrong. "I kept saying, 'Hal, you need to get tested, you need to go to the doctor.' I didn't want to be right." In May, when Hal ran the Los Angeles Marathon, the cramps and twitching in his right leg grew so intense that he stopped on the Sunset Strip around mile 13.

Every anniversary since their wedding in 1979, he and Fran had gone on a bike ride, a mile for each year they'd been married. This year was their thirtieth anniversary, and starting from an inn in San Luis Obispo, they set out on a tandem bicycle for a thirty-mile ride. For the first time, Hal was too tired to finish. A week later, he was diagnosed with ALS, the neurodegenerative condition also known as Lou Gehrig's disease.

His voice became softer. He slurred more. His hands weakened. "It is annoying and worrisome that my initial symptoms are showing up in my voice and hands, the two most used and highest bandwidth sources of output available," he told his friends on *LessWrong* in terms the technologist-heavy crowd could appreciate.

He'd been surprised to learn that more than 90 percent of people afflicted with ALS chose to die when they could no longer breathe on their own. Hal had no such plans. He intended to go on mechanical ventilation. A free voice-banking service at the University of Delaware's Speech Research Lab was modeling his voice, which he'd later be able to play through a synthesizer. He'd read that Stephen Hawking, who'd survived forty years with ALS, could type ten words per minute by twitching a cheek muscle. "I may even still be able to write code," Hal told *LessWrong* readers, "and my dream is to contribute to open source software projects even from within an immobile body. That will be a life very much worth living."

That December, raising money to fight ALS as part of a relay team in the Santa Barbara International Marathon, Fran ran the tracking chip to Hal, and they walked the last two-mile leg together, with Hal using a cane. He'd grown up skiing and become an expert on the slopes, tackling double black diamonds and doing aerials, but in December he skied for the last time, sticking to beginner slopes and struggling to get on and off the chairlift.

Hal met his fate with an attitude so upbeat that Phil Zimmermann likened it to Monty Python's "Always Look on the Bright Side of Life." When Phil visited Hal at home, after Hal was far along in the progression of the disease, he said, "Well, I have more time to read now."

"Everybody with ALS talks about how terrible it is, all the things you can't do any more," Hal wrote on *LessWrong*. "But nobody seems to notice that there are all these things you get to do that you've never done before. I've never used a power wheelchair. I've never controlled a computer with my eyes. I've never had a voice synthesizer trained to mimic my natural voice. If I told people on the ALS forums that I was looking forward to some of this, they'd think I was crazy. Maybe people here will understand."

He could no longer get out of a chair? Well, that was nothing a lift chair and a nearby pole couldn't fix. He had always been a fast typist, so when his right hand stopped working he learned to touch-type rapidly using only his left hand. When that hand weakened, he splinted its fingers so he could still do two-fingered typing. When only one finger remained useful, he typed with that. When he lost the use of his hands altogether, he moved to an eye-tracker. As his eye muscles began to go, he switched to screens where he had just four letters to choose from at a time. When his wheelchair started causing painful pressure sores that required other people to constantly adjust his position, he rigged a system that let him control the wheelchair with the eye-gaze software. "He was gleeful about doing this," Fran said later. "That brought him supreme happiness. . . . Every time Hal achieved something that he was excited about, he was so happy."

By the time I contacted Hal in August 2011, he was able to communicate only by using the eye-tracker. But he graciously responded to my emailed questions. He wrote that he anticipated that Bitcoin would be improved upon, and that this "may lead to fragmentation and competition between different versions." He expected the international monetary system to become much more complex, with Bitcoin playing an important part. He foresaw the question of whether, once there were no more coins to mine and Bitcoin's integrity-preserving incentives changed, the system would remain stable. And he was already concerned about the problems that would continue to bedevil Bitcoin and its offspring and scare most people away, telling me that "experience with Bitcoin has graphically demonstrated the sad state of computer security today. Securing digital coins against theft has proven to be unexpectedly difficult."

I asked Hal whether he was Satoshi Nakamoto. "No, I am not," he responded. "I wish I had created something as potentially world-changing as Bitcoin. Under my current circumstances, facing limited life expectancy, I would have little to lose by shedding anonymity. But it was not I."

Did he think Wei Dai might be Nakamoto? "I've known Wei for

many years," Hal replied. "He is a brilliant guy and he would certainly be capable of creating something as imaginative as Bitcoin. However, my impression of Satoshi's writing style is that it is different."

Hal gently demurred at my further queries on the topic, writing, "Not wanting to throw cold water, but I am a bit uncomfortable playing the speculation game too hard. Satoshi clearly values his privacy, and perhaps the best way to show respect and gratitude for his creation is to honor his wishes."

The Pin, Not the Bubble

Eleven years later in Miami, as I walked along Collins Avenue toward my hotel one evening, a balding, ginger-haired man striding briskly in the other direction passed me, and I did a double-take. He was wearing glasses, shorts, a short-sleeve button-down shirt, and black high-top Converse sneakers with socks. I turned to watch his receding figure. *Wasn't that—?*

"That was Adam Back," a guy behind me on the sidewalk said. "I had the same reaction."

A man walking in the other direction with three friends said: "He has a private island in Malta, right?"

It was a Thursday in April, during the Bitcoin 2022 conference. Miami had recently branded itself as America's most cryptocurrency-friendly city, and an estimated twenty-six thousand people were attending. Back, who in 2011 had been an obscure cryptography consultant, now led Blockstream, a $3 billion blockchain-infrastructure company he'd cofounded. The next day, after Back made an onstage presentation, I'd watch the cryptocurrency trade press and fans surround him, seeking answers and selfies. Figures who'd been obscure technical experts a decade earlier were now industry superstars.

Bitcoin had taken some time to escape the narrow confines of computer people. When it did, at first, the attention was not favorable.

On a 2012 episode of *The Good Wife,* the U.S. government was pursuing Bitcoin's creator because of his "illegal online currency." On *The Simpsons,* Krusty the Klown went broke after investing in bitcoin, among other things. In late 2013, Silk Road, the dark web marketplace where bitcoin was the currency of choice, was shut down, its creator Ross Ulbricht arrested. In 2014, Mt. Gox, the safe and reliable exchange where I'd parked my remaining seven bitcoins, declared bankruptcy after 850,000 bitcoins went missing, and its owner Mark Karpelès was arrested; he was cleared of theft but eventually received a suspended prison sentence for "electronic record tampering."

Bitcoin's volatility made it exciting to speculators and terrifying to most people. A 2011 boom and bust, from $1 to $32 to $2, was only the first of many such cycles. In the early months of 2013, bitcoin rose from $13 to $260 before plummeting in less than a week to $50. In the second half of that year, it went from below $100 to over $1,100, then lost half its value in a couple of weeks in December. But despite the extreme ups and downs, and a series of hacks and scams, bitcoin's value unsteadily rose.

There were fitful signs that it was broadening its appeal. In 2014, the U.S. Senate held an unexpectedly hopeful hearing on Bitcoin, titled "Beyond Silk Road: Potential Risks, Threats, and Promises of Virtual Currencies." Richard Branson announced that his Virgin Galactic space travel company would accept bitcoin, which he said was "driving a revolution." Bill Gates called Bitcoin "exciting," "better than currency," and "a techno tour de force." A year later, Marc Andreessen, who had pioneered the web browser before becoming a venture capitalist, said: "We're quite confident that when we're sitting here in twenty years, we'll be talking about Bitcoin the way we talk about the Internet today." And the more time passed, the longer Bitcoin went without itself being successfully hacked, the more solid it felt.

And now, thirteen years after its launch, a single bitcoin was worth more than $65,000, and Bitcoin was just part of a much larger industry. *Crypto,* which had long been shorthand for cryptography, stood, to the chagrin of cryptographers, for cryptocurrency. There were, almost unbelievably, more than sixteen thousand different cryptocurrencies in existence—riffs of one sort or another on the first and only one that had existed in 2011. Collectively, they had recently passed $3 trillion in value. Eighty-six percent of Americans had heard of crypto. Sixteen percent had used, traded, or invested in it.

That didn't mean they understood it. I wasn't sure I did, and I'd been trying for eleven years. People would ask, "What *is* Bitcoin?" and it wasn't a simple question to answer.

"Why is bitcoin worth anything?" my father-in-law asked one day.

"Why is gold worth anything?" I said.

My father-in-law looked at me impatiently. "Why does everyone I ask this question respond with another question?"

On the plane to Florida, I'd sat between a guy who worked in digital assets for Bank of America and a guy who made loans to bitcoin miners. Both called stolid old Bitcoin "boring" compared with the churn and dynamism of newer crypto projects. Experiments with DeFi (decentralized finance) and NFTs (nonfungible tokens) and DAOs (decentralized autonomous organizations) were happening on other blockchains, Ethereum in particular. But being boring had also made Bitcoin the cryptocurrency most likely to get mainstream adoption. In Miami, Wyoming senator Cynthia Lummis was scheduled to do a "fireside chat" on Bitcoin legislation, and Tucker Carlson would be at the convention center with a crew from Fox to interview Michael Saylor, whose company MicroStrategy held more than $5 billion worth of bitcoin. In line for lanyards, I talked to a couple of guys who said they lived in Panama and had a bitcoin-mining operation, powered by hydroelectric energy, in a remote section of Paraguay. I saw a man and woman wearing matching orange, the color of the Bitcoin logo.

The crowd circulating in the building was only slightly less male than the group at the conference I'd attended a decade earlier, but these men seemed more oppositional. I jotted down slogans printed on the T-shirts and hoodies I passed:

FREE SPEECH ABSOLUTIST

BITCOIN VS. THE WORLD

ANTI-FIAT SOCIAL CLUB

BITCOIN IS THE PIN, NOT THE BUBBLE

INTROVERTED BUT WILLING TO DISCUSS CRYPTO

WE WERE BORN TOO LATE TO EXPLORE THE SEAS, TOO EARLY TO EXPLORE THE STARS, JUST RIGHT TO FIX THE MONEY

I AM SATOSHI NAKAMOTO

On a long hallway on the second floor, I crouched to examine what looked like trash on the carpeted ground. It was a five-dollar bill, or what remained of one. Someone had torn it into tiny pieces, in a fit of antidollar pique or as some kind of impromptu art installation.

A large sign, "FREE ROSS!," sought one million signatures for a petition to liberate Ross Ulbricht, the imprisoned creator of Silk Road who'd operated as Dread Pirate Roberts, the *Princess Bride* character who, like some people's conception of Satoshi Nakamoto, wasn't an individual but an identity handed from one person to the next.

Had Bitcoin become more mainstream? Had the mainstream become more Bitcoin? A panel entitled "Becoming a Sovereign Individual" featured a maned crypto-influencer named Robert Breedlove, who had a ₿ tattooed on his bicep; then–Buffalo Bills quarterback Matt Barkley; and Pascal Gauthier, CEO of hardware wallet maker Ledger, who wore rings on six of his fingers.

Self-sovereignty was the ultimate extension of Bitcoin's libertarian ethos. As I listened to the panelists talk, I thought that the ideology had probably been necessary for bootstrapping Bitcoin but that its continuing dominance of Bitcoin culture was a hindrance. Bitcoin had at least as many critics as fans. Hard-edged libertarianism was off-putting to regular people. There was something bleak and disappointed about having so little trust in people that you put your faith in a network of machines. Most people preferred to rely on banks, police, and utilities. They weren't interested in homeschooling their children on a stateless oil rig they defended with semiautomatic weapons.

And it was hard to make the case that crypto was a better mousetrap when it kept snapping on people's fingers. As Hal Finney had worried, many of the problems that afflicted Bitcoin in its earlier years, from price volatility to bad luck to crime, had increased. Now that bitcoin was worth a lot more, the stakes were much higher. A man in Wales who'd accidentally thrown out a hard drive containing the keys to 8,000 bitcoins, worth $320 million by the time of the conference, had spent the past nine years trying to excavate a landfill to search for his lost fortune.

When the only thing protecting your bitcoins was a string of letters and numbers, violence became inevitable. In the Netherlands, a thirty-eight-year-old bitcoin trader was attacked in his home by robbers wearing balaclavas, bulletproof vests, and police coats. They tortured him in front of his four-year-old daughter for more than an hour, he told police, tying his hands behind his back, kicking him, pointing a gun at his head, waterboarding him with a shower hose, using a power tool to drill seven holes in his leg and foot, and hanging him by his neck.

Bitcoin's more fanatical adherents, sometimes called Bitcoin maximalists or maxis, seemed indifferent to how these risks played with normies, even if it doomed them to the fringe.

"Yes!"

The sound came from my right. A man sitting there leaned forward, rapt. Across the aisle, another man wore a Daft Punk–style motorcycle helmet, dark visor lowered. Anonymity transposed to meatspace.

Ledger's Gauthier was saying that 70 percent of the world doesn't live in a democracy.

"Wow!," the guy next to me exclaimed. "Woo!"

Afterward, on the street, I passed a man hoisting a placard bearing the names of libertarian economist icons: Ludwig von Mises, Murray Rothbard, Friedrich Hayek. Nearby, a parallel gathering timed to coincide with this one was hosting gun enthusiasts. I saw rare dissenting graffiti: “Fuck Crypto, it’s an MLM, and not the fun kind.”

After lunch, Peter Thiel, PayPal founder turned venture capitalist, was scheduled to speak. For all the talk of Bitcoin being leaderless, Satoshi Nakamoto was, in absentia, everywhere. The Nakamoto Stage, where the keynotes and most important panels took place, was flanked by illuminated screens featuring a rotating display of snippets from his writings. They had the *Dianetics*-like quality of being banal to outsiders and profound to insiders.

“Imagine if gold turned to lead when stolen.”

“Writing a description for this thing for general audiences is bloody hard. There’s nothing to relate it to.”

“I’m sure that in twenty years there will either be very large Bitcoin transaction volume . . . or no volume.”

“The network is robust in its unstructured simplicity.”

Before Thiel came on stage, a video from 1999 showed a younger, leaner version of him enthusing about the future of online money. When everyone in the middle class had an internet-enabled cellphone, which he predicted would happen in the next five years, countries like China and India would have to either shut down telecom networks or give up their monetary sovereignty.

Thiel then emerged stage right, wearing a white polo shirt. He softballed a wad of hundred-dollar bills into the front rows: “It’s kind of crazy that this stuff still works, you know?” Why, he asked the crowd, hadn’t bitcoin, which was now worth $813 billion, replaced gold, which was worth $12 trillion? Bitcoin was a warning, he said, that the fiat system was over.

He put up a slide that read “BTC vs ETH.” Ether was the second most valuable cryptocurrency. Above the “BTC” was a photograph of a man aiming a machine gun at the camera, while above the “ETH” was a photo of Ethereum founder Vitalik Buterin at his most gawky and wearing purple pants. However technically innovative and superior Bitcoin might be, Thiel said, it was a political movement, and what stood in its way were “the enemies of this movement.”

"And so I want to maybe end with an enemies list," he said, "a list of people who I think are stopping Bitcoin." He wanted to "expose them." He showed a slide of a hater he called "Enemy #1." It was Warren Buffett. I knew that Buffett was famous for his sensible investing strategy, that he had a passion for contract bridge, and that he'd pledged to give away his entire fortune. Apparently, though, Buffett had a dark side. Thiel called him "the sociopathic grandpa from Omaha." (Buffett's crime had been to call Bitcoin "rat poison.") Enemy #2 was JPMorganChase CEO Jamie Dimon, who exemplified what Thiel called "the New York banker bias." (Dimon had made the mistake of dissing Bitcoin as "worthless.") Enemy #3 was BlackRock CEO Larry Fink. (His crime against Bitcoin wasn't immediately clear.) Together, the men were what Thiel, who was fifty-four, called "the gerontocracy." Thiel contrasted these oldsters with a photo of palmy Miami and this "revolutionary youth movement. We have to go out from this conference and take over the world!"

The audience in the cavernous space erupted in cheers. It would later come to light that around the time of this speech, Thiel's investment firm dumped a large bitcoin position it had held for eight years.

In Miami, Thiel concluded his talk by telling the crowd that the "enemies" he'd named were "extensions of the state." Bitcoin, by contrast, wasn't a company and had no board. "We do not know who Satoshi is," Thiel added for emphasis.

I walked outside with my friend Andy, who was also a venture capitalist.

"That was crazy," Andy said, shaking his head.

We do not know who Satoshi is. Back in 2011, he'd been the no-name coder of an experimental money that was of interest mainly to a fringe community. Ten years later, he was the mythic founder of a project with a $1 trillion market capitalization, making it the ninth most valuable asset in the world, just below Tesla and above Meta (Facebook). Nakamoto's success in remaining anonymous in spite of that shift had itself become one of his greatest achievements. And he was fantastically rich.

A computer scientist named Sergio Demian Lerner, through some clever analysis of the early blockchain, had estimated that nearly 1.1 million bitcoins had been mined by the same machines, presumably Nakamoto's. The value of those coins just then was $40 billion. Nakamoto was by far the largest holder of the currency and someone who could significantly affect its price.

When the crypto exchange Coinbase went public in the spring of 2021, giving it an instant market value of $86 billion, one of the risk factors listed in the prospectus the company filed with the SEC was the public identification of Nakamoto or transfer of his bitcoin hoard. It wasn't hard to think of scenarios where who Nakamoto was—what his motives and intentions were—might be relevant. Thiel himself had speculated that Nakamoto was among his fellow attendees at a financial cryptography conference on the island of Anguilla in 2000.

Talking with my friend Andy outside the conference center, where orange-pilled lost boys milled, steeping themselves in the curious brew of revolutionary fervor, Miami hedonism, and accounting, I mentioned my recently reignited Nakamoto quest. Andy asked why I was speaking so quietly. In the Bitcoin realm, I explained without raising my voice, the Nakamoto mystery was seen as necessary—a feature rather than a bug. To be truly decentralized required that Bitcoin have a virgin birth. Depriving it of a human figurehead—a flawed individual with a particular identity that might be palatable to this group but not to that one—gave it the best shot at being received on its own terms and taken up en masse.

And so among Bitcoiners the Nakamoto alias had come to be hallowed, and inquiries into it discouraged. While some people conjectured that the Bitcoin creator had gone to ground mainly for his own protection, lest he be prosecuted for tax evasion or physically attacked for his coin stash, the common view was that he'd acted selflessly. The most zealous Bitcoiners treated Nakamotology as a sort of blasphemy, as if they were Scientologists being asked about Xenu.

There was also a messy history of journalists trying to crack the mystery. Some reporters had been embarrassed by their overconfidence or credulity. Others had been hit: one writer was dragged into a lawsuit that cost him more than $100,000. At least one reporter had received "death threats." A private citizen had had his life blown up by a media mob. There was now an ambient antipathy toward reporters trying to shed light on the secret. This was on top of a general disdain about mainstream coverage of crypto. A site called Bitcoin Obituaries listed more than 440 articles that had prematurely reported Bitcoin's imminent demise. One was my 2011 *Wired* article, with its headline "The Rise and Fall of Bitcoin."

The main reason I'd come to Miami, though, was to attend a talk later that day by Nick Szabo. In midafternoon, Nick loped onto the Nakamoto stage, wearing an untucked button-down shirt, a wireless mike taped to his head, his now-gray hair cropped.

Offline, Nick seemed to shrink from the light of physical society. The rare exception was an occasional slide-heavy stage presentation sans Q&A: an in-person blog post. A year earlier, when a *Harper's* reporter mentioned he planned to attend one, Nick responded: "Please do not try to approach me at the conference."

"I'm going to talk today," Nick said now, "about some of the dreams and ideas that I believe influenced Bitcoin." The people behind these dreams and ideas were "pioneers of the years BB," before Bitcoin, who helped bring "libertarian dreams" to life, things like "depoliticizing money" and "nonviolently enforcing contracts." Nick paid tribute to various computer scientists whose work had paved the way for Bitcoin. It was a decentralized version of Bitcoin's origin story.

Despite the organizers' best stab at glitzing up these talks—meteors streaked across a lunar landscape on the screen behind Nick—his presentation was a skeletal list of names and bullet points that barely hinted at their rich history. Nick became animated only when he talked about the cypherpunks and extropians and his old buddies Tim May and Hal Finney. What I was most interested to hear was how he'd situate himself in this lineage, because I was certain that Nick was Satoshi Nakamoto.

Satoshi Studies

By the time my *Wired* story was published in late 2011, two journalists had already proposed Satoshi Nakamoto candidates. Joshua Davis, reporting for *The New Yorker,* pursued the theory that Nakamoto was an experienced cryptographer and showed up at Crypto, the field's annual conference in Santa Barbara. There, he tracked down a long-haired, twenty-three-year-old Irish attendee named Michael Clear. Clear ticked several Nakamoto boxes: he was a cryptography grad student, a user of British spelling, a guarded personality (his Trinity College profile page, unlike those of his peers, displayed no photos or phone numbers), a student of peer-to-peer networks, and a brilliant mind (as an undergraduate, he'd been top of his class in computer science) who'd worked on currency-trading software.

On the steps in front of the building where lectures were held, Davis was able to elicit a salient fact—Clear knew how to code in C++, the language Bitcoin was written in—but when Davis asked directly whether he was Nakamoto, Clear laughed and didn't answer, instead offering to "review" Bitcoin's design for him. A week later, Clear emailed Davis to say he thought he could identify Nakamoto. Clear had evidently been bitten by the who-is-Satoshi bug, but he seemed ambivalent, advising Davis that "it would be unfair to publish an identity when the person or persons has/have taken major steps to remain anonymous," while also offering the name of "a certain individual who matches the profile of the author on many levels."

That person, a Finnish virtual-currency researcher named Vili Lehdonvirta, also laughed when Davis asked whether he was Nakamoto, responding that he didn't have the requisite C++ skills or any experience with cryptography. Davis found the denial convincing and went back to Clear, suggesting that maybe Clear was Nakamoto after all. This time Clear said, "I'm not Satoshi," then added, "But even if I was, I wouldn't tell you." And Clear made the point that was becoming a refrain among Bitcoiners: Nakamoto's identity shouldn't matter. That was the essence of a decentralized currency. Being headless was its greatest attribute. After Davis's article came out, Clear vehemently denied being Nakamoto. He'd been speaking "jokingly" when he played coy with Davis. "I could never allow myself to be even remotely given credit for someone else's creativity and hard work."

Meanwhile, a *Fast Company* reporter named Adam Penenberg, who had previously exposed the journalistic frauds of Stephen Glass, came upon a striking similarity. Penenberg, too, had been enthralled by the Nakamoto mystery, and he googled distinctive phrases from Nakamoto's writing. When he searched for one of these, "computationally impractical to reverse," he got an intriguing hit: a patent application for a secure-communications method containing that very phrase had been filed on August 15, 2008, three days before Nakamoto registered bitcoin.org. "Now that is one hell of a coincidence," Penenberg wrote. The patent listed three authors: Neal King and Charles Bry, who both lived in Munich, and Vladimir Oksman, who lived in New Jersey. Penenberg found other coincidences: Bry had visited Finland six months before bitcoin.org was registered through a *Finnish internet company*. King's Facebook page abounded with anti–Wall Street messages, and Amazon reviews King had written were, in Penenberg's view, reminiscent of Nakamoto's forum posts.

Although King didn't use British spellings, Penenberg had already come to believe that Nakamoto used Anglicisms as "red herrings, placed there to throw pursuers off the scent."

When Penenberg contacted Bry, the computer scientist replied: "I hope I do not disappoint you too much by saying that I am not Satoshi"; he could say "with absolute certainty" that neither of his co-inventors was either. King told Penenberg that the focus of the patent was very different from Bitcoin, he'd never heard of Bitcoin "until this question came up," and now that he'd read up on it, he thought it was "a solution in search of a problem."

Penenberg found King's arguments unpersuasive. Without claiming to have identified Nakamoto, Penenberg believed that his circumstantial evidence was "far more compelling" than Davis's. I had to agree with him, and I was kicking myself for not having thought to use his googling-unique-phrases method.

For the next two years, little happened in the infant field of Satoshi studies. Then, on December 1, 2013, someone using the Nakamoto-esque nym Skye Grey published an argument, on a newly created blog called *LikeInAMirror,* titled "Satoshi Nakamoto Is (Probably) Nick Szabo."

Grey, like Penenberg, had sifted through the white paper for unusual phrases and searched the web for them. These included terms like *timestamp server* and *trusted third party,* which led him to a series of articles by Nick about bit gold. Grey acknowledged that Nakamoto would likely have digested Nick's work, and might naturally express himself similarly, so he also looked at what he called "content-neutral expressions."

There, too, the match was close. Comparing a handful of white-paper-isms that also popped up in Nick Szabo articles with their appearance in the academic cryptography literature, Grey highlighted "repeated use of 'of course' without isolating commas, contrary to convention ('the problem of course is')"; the "expression 'can be characterized,' frequent in Nick's blog (found in 1% of crypto papers)"; and the "use of 'for our purposes' when describing hypotheses (found in 1.5% of crypto papers)," among others.

"[E]ither Nick wrote the white paper, or it was written by somebody imitating Nick's writing style," Grey argued. He also acknowledged that the spelling *favour,* used by Nakamoto, wasn't used by Nick. This led Grey to conclude that "it is highly probable the paper had several authors," or else, as Penenberg believed, that the Britishism had been included as a fake-out.

Grey thought other evidence pointed to Nick, too. Why had the white paper cited Adam Back and Wei Dai but not Nick, whose work was clearly a direct inspiration? Why had Nick, one of the most consistent proponents of decentralized digital cash, waited until months after Bitcoin's launch to even acknowledge it and then only in passing, as a throwaway line near the end of a longer essay? Grey observed that in April 2008, six months before the white paper was released, Nick had blogged that bit gold "would greatly benefit from a demonstration, an experimental market (with e.g. a trusted third party substituted for the complex security that would be needed for a real system). Anybody want to help me code one up?" And he noted that after Bitcoin launched, the bit gold project, which Nick had been actively interested in just a few months earlier, "became perfectly silent."

Grey posited that, at a minimum, Nick was the dominant author of the white paper. Perhaps Bitcoin was coded by someone else. "[I]t seems much more likely that a Satoshi-like character inventing Bitcoin would first contact the original father of the project, rather than start devoting all of their resources to shipping what was largely somebody else's pet idea."

Grey later explained that he'd been motivated by "simple curiosity . . . I like mysteries." And he defended his investigation, which he acknowledged "has not been received well": "[W]hen one starts having a huge impact on the world, one loses his right to anonymity." He justified the publication of his findings "so as to address people's concerns that a 'bad guy' might have created Bitcoin."

Other gentleman gumshoes came to similar conclusions. Dominic Frisby, an English comedian and financial writer, zeroed in on the combination of expertises Nakamoto would need to have had—"computer coding, mathematics, databases, accounting, peer-to-peer systems, digital ownership, law, smart contracts, cryptography, and monetary history." He believed that the way Bitcoin had launched suggested "experience in open-source tech start-ups." The software's bulletproof defenses indicated a security-savvy hacker, Nakamoto's prose a writer, and his pseudonym someone practiced at secrecy. Nakamoto showed patience, foresight, humility, integrity, and a shrewdness about human psychology. Only a libertarian or cypherpunk would have had the necessary motivation, and the instinct for where to announce his creation. Frisby homed in on the birthdate Nakamoto registered on the P2P Foundation website: April 5, 1975. April 5 was the date in 1933 when President Franklin D. Roosevelt made it illegal for U.S. citizens to own gold, and 1975 was the year when Americans were once again permitted to own gold. Frisby noted that in 2007, Nick, having just graduated from law school at age forty-two, had time for another big project.

Although Frisby built a compelling circumstantial case, when he presented it to Nick, Nick replied: "I'm afraid you got it wrong doxxing me as Satoshi, but I am used to it." *Doxing,* which had previously meant revealing personal details like someone's address or social security number, had clearly loosened in meaning for some people.

Neither Grey's nor Frisby's findings seemed to stick. Both had made much of Nakamoto's decision to launch Bitcoin through an academic-style paper, and of his posting activity, which seemed to spike during the summer. Grey wrote that "Nick is a professor with a significant publication history." But Nick was not and had never been a professor. And while he had blogged extensively and in a learned fashion, he had never published academically. Some of the terms

Grey had interpreted as slam-dunk evidence, like *digital signatures* and *cryptographic proof,* were commonplace in cryptography.

The following year, Nathaniel Popper, a *New York Times* reporter, confronted Nick at an industry gathering at a hedge fund manager's home in Lake Tahoe. Popper had been invited because he covered cryptocurrency, and Nick had come as an employee of a new Bitcoin-related start-up called Vaurum. At predinner cocktails, when the Nakamoto topic came up, Nick told a small group, "Well, I will say this, in the hope of setting the record straight: I'm not Satoshi, and I'm not a college professor." At some point, Popper cornered Nick in the kitchen, and Nick acknowledged, "[T]here are all these parallels, and it looks funny to me, and looks funny to a lot of other people." Nick later emailed Popper a definitive denial: "As I've stated many times before, all this speculation is flattering, but wrong—I am not Satoshi." Soon after, Popper reported that Nick had left Vaurum "after becoming nervous about public exposure."

Grey, Frisby, and Popper all pointed out that Nick had reposted his old bit gold essays after October 2008 and suggested that he'd done so to make it appear that he'd written them post-Bitcoin, in order to direct suspicion away from himself. But even after *The New York Times* named Nick as the person Silicon Valley insiders believed to be Nakamoto, the lack of concrete evidence gave the allegation a hazy status that would remain hazy.

In the spring of 2022, eleven years after I'd asked Nick whether he was Satoshi Nakamoto, and despite his denial then and many times since, it was still impossible to exclude him as a candidate. The world sometimes treated him as if he was Nakamoto, but in weird ways. Universidad Francisco Marroquín in Guatemala, noting his "research in digital contracts and digital currency," awarded him an honorary doctorate and professorship. Podcaster Tim Ferriss spent two and a half hours interviewing him as "the quiet master of cryptocurrency," without once mentioning or asking about an obvious subtext of Nick's presence on the show. Nick drew capacity crowds for colorless, repetitive presentations.

More evidence pointed toward Nick than anyone else, but this fact had somehow been lost in the noise of other Nakamoto guesses. If anything, though, there were now additional reasons to focus on him.

Anonymous

First among my new Nick-as-Nakamoto exhibits was that I no longer gave a lot of weight to his denials. My prior acceptance of them had been naive. This wasn't because of how honest he was or wasn't. I'd just familiarized myself with other cases when someone using a pseudonym was unmasked.

In 1996, an English professor named Donald Foster identified the journalist Joe Klein as Anonymous, author of a bestselling, thinly fictionalized novel about Bill Clinton's 1992 presidential campaign titled *Primary Colors,* based on their similar writing styles. Klein angrily denied he was the author. "For God's sake, definitely, I didn't write it," he shouted at a *New York Times* reporter. He left a sixty-second outgoing voice message denying authorship, denied it on CBS News, where he was a commentator, and denied it to his own colleagues at *Newsweek,* letting the magazine publish speculation pointing toward other Anonymous suspects. Eventually, Klein admitted that he was, in fact, Anonymous.

Mark Felt, a former acting associate director of the FBI, repeatedly and elaborately claimed not to be Deep Throat, the secret source with whose help *Washington Post* reporters Bob Woodward and Carl Bernstein had unraveled Watergate. Felt testified before a grand jury, under penalty of perjury, that he wasn't Deep Throat (before hastily withdrawing the testimony). To *The Wall Street Journal* he proposed a theory that Deep Throat might be "a composite" of multiple people. In his own memoir, Felt stressed that "I never leaked information to Woodward and Bernstein or to anyone else!" Years later, after a summer camp friend of Bernstein's son Jacob told *The Hartford Courant* that Jacob had identified Felt as Deep Throat, Felt told the paper, "No, it's not me. I would have done better. I would have been more effective." Eventually Felt admitted that he was, in fact, Deep Throat.

These people *always* denied it. Felt's denials, Woodward later reflected, "only solidified my sad understanding that anyone in a jam—or [who] believes he is in a jam—will say anything to protect and extricate himself. Over time, we all become committed to a version of the story of our lives. Simplification and repetition solidify the account, and we tend to stick with that identity." (Woodward knew whereof he spoke, having lied about it to his *Washington Post* colleague Richard Cohen, who was going to write a column naming Felt as Deep Throat until Woodward denied it.) If you were motivated to be anonymous in the first place, and to endure the inconvenience of maintaining a cover, it was trivial to lie about it.

The problem was illustrated by Ralph Merkle, co-inventor of public-key cryptography, whose work was one of eight papers cited in the Bitcoin white paper, and who had invented a data structure, Merkle trees, relied on by the Bitcoin software for constructing the blocks in the blockchain. Inevitably, he was on the long list of possible Nakamotos.

Asked about it in an interview, he said: "I deny being Satoshi."

Interviewer: "So I can cross that off the list as well?"

Merkle: "Absolutely. But do you really expect Satoshi is going to say, 'Yes, I'm Satoshi'?"

"If you were Satoshi, would you tell me you were Satoshi?"

"Good heavens, no."

A Spectacular Display of Hindsight

Many further clues pointed toward Nick Szabo. Nakamoto's level of OPSEC, or operational security, indicated someone who had thought deeply about and practiced the art of avoiding all the ways the internet can link your data. "His mastery of not being traceable is pretty much unparalleled," Ray Dillinger, a cryptographer who along with Hal Finney had done code review for Nakamoto before Bitcoin's launch, told me. "I've never met someone who really could remain unknown, when he wanted to, on the internet."

Nick had been thinking about those things for fifteen years before Bitcoin appeared. "In my limited experience creating Internet pseudonyms, I've been quite distracted by the continual need to avoid leaving pointers to my True Name lying around," Nick told fellow cypherpunks in 1993. Everything from shared files to spelling tics could do you in. "The hazards are everywhere. With our current tools it's practically impossible to maintain an active pseudonym for a long period of time against a sufficiently determined opponent, and quite a hassle to maintain even a modicum of decent security."

Nick's denials, when he was asked if he was Nakamoto, had been parsimonious. The failure of the Bitcoin white paper to credit Nick's obvious influence—plus a contrasting later remark on BitcoinTalk, in which Nakamoto wrote that "Bitcoin is an implementation of Wei Dai's b-money proposal . . . on Cypherpunks . . . in 1998 and Nick

Szabo's Bitgold proposal"—remained unexplained. The debt to Nick's work was so obvious that cypherpunk James Donald, the first person to respond to Nakamoto on Metzdowd in late 2008, had referred to bitcoins as "bitgold coins." Hal Finney then responded, in the context of saying the best way to work through questions about Bitcoin might be through a release of its source code: "I found that there is a sourceforge project set up for bitgold, although it does not have any code yet."

Why had Nick never taken offense at the omission of his work from the white paper's citations? If he was being modest, why wouldn't he at least have spoken up on Hal's behalf and said, "Yeah, it's weird that Hal's RPOW wasn't cited in the white paper"? He had never said, "I wish I could take credit, but my C++ skills aren't even close to Satoshi's." He had never said, "I understand why everyone thinks I'm Satoshi, but let's put this rumor to rest: Here's the boss I was working for in 2008 and 2009, and here's who I was dating. They can both confirm that I was working twelve-hour days on something else, and that when Nakamoto succeeded at doing what I'd been trying to do for years, I was crippled by jealousy."

Nick didn't owe anyone clarity, but suspicion followed him precisely because he scarcely acknowledged the many reasons to think he might be Nakamoto. This encouraged people to think that he either was Nakamoto or didn't mind if you thought he was.

Almost as marked as Nick's silence were the prickly exceptions to it. After Gwern Branwen argued that Bitcoin wasn't so novel, Nick wrote a lengthy rejoinder calling Branwen's argument "a spectacular display of hindsight." When a Silicon Valley investor named Balaji Srinivasan exercised his moderation powers in a Telegram channel named for the Bitcoin founder, Nick derided Srinivasan for his "pathetic corporate norms that seem to include treating Nakamoto's name as your property and censoring people under its rubric." And Nick clearly saw himself as the father of crypto, writing: "Knowledge of the long history of non-governmental money was one of the inspirations of the original invention of trust-minimized cryptocurrency."

When in 2022 I deep-dove into Nick's voluminous internet writings, it was easy to hear echoes of Bitcoin's founder. Nakamoto once wrote: "If you don't believe me or don't get it, I don't have time to try to convince you, sorry." Nick once wrote: "If you don't get it I can't help you any further." I went back and looked at a lengthy email Nick had sent me in 2011 and saw that, like Nakamoto, he used two spaces after a period and internet slang including "BTW." Nick was at ease with the same vocabularies and references as Nakamoto, from the work of Austrian economist Carl Menger to game-theory pioneer John Nash's concept of equilibrium.

"The design supports a tremendous variety of possible transaction types that I designed years ago," Nakamoto had written. "Escrow transactions, bonded contracts, third party arbitration, multi-party signatures, etc." Nick, in 1994, wrote, "I'm particularly interested in the art of writing contracts and designing transactions for online data services," and he took a three-year detour in middle age to attend law school.

Lots of people had jawboned about the money of the future, but Bitcoin was the first *working* decentralized digital-money system. Nick had always anchored his dreams with a hardheaded rigor, disdaining wispy utopians as "Hello Kitty people." He filtered every discussion through a pragmatic lens, crunching the numbers on what was doable now. He'd believed space projects should be market-driven—"First we start meeting people's needs, then they will come"—and not "a welfare case." In the early 1990s, he'd put his own money on the line, investing most of what savings he had in companies on the cutting edge of space tech, like Qualcomm and Orbital Sciences. When people used the term *bean counter,* he'd take offense and spreadsheet a cash-flow analysis of, say, moving asteroids to terraform Venus. He wanted to know not just what was scientifically possible but what was economically probable. "Reality does not wreck dreams," he wrote. "It gives us a way of making them come true."

Nick also had made a penetrating study of money's origins. With an archaeologist's feel for physical currency, he reveled in the variety of different objects that had historically served as money, from snail-shell beads to ostrich eggshells to mammoth ivory. He delighted in slang like *clams* and *shelling out*, which came from the clamshell beads known as wampum. He collected banknotes from the free-banking era of the nineteenth century, issued by corporations like Boone County Bank Indiana and the Great Western Railroad Company, which he found beautiful as well as "remarkably free of politicians' faces."

A recurring argument against Nick, whenever someone proposed that he might be Nakamoto, was that he wasn't known as a programmer. But Nick had majored in computer science in college and held several software jobs after graduating. Rummaging through what was left of the early internet, I found that at one point in the early 1990s he'd touted his experience in "software architecture and engineering," his "extensive hacking skills," and his knowledge of C/C++ and Windows/DOS. He mentioned having no fewer than six C/C++ books on his desk. On another occasion, he wrote: "I knit some mean code."

He had also, I learned, studied Japanese and been fascinated by Japanese culture. Nakamoto's initials, SN, were the inverse of Nick's, which fit with the convention in both Japanese and Hungarian of putting surname before given name: In Hungary, Nick's name would be Szabo Nikolas, and in Japan it would be, let's say, Szaboshi Nickamoto.

Then there was Nick's appearance on the Tim Ferriss podcast in 2017. At one point during the interview, Nick slipped: "I designed bitcoi—gold with two layers." When I saw Nick speak in Miami, he again slipped: "In my implement—, or in my design, of bit gold . . ."

How, I thought, could Nick *not* be Nakamoto?

Sniffing Bronze

Soon after the conference in Miami, and before I quit my job, I went to Texas on an assignment and took the opportunity to catch up with Justin Posey. Justin was a young computer scientist working as a director of engineering for Cisco. When I'd last seen him, nearly two years earlier, he was standing in Yellowstone National Park with Tucker, his Vizsla. Justin had spent the better part of the past decade looking for a treasure chest in the Rocky Mountains.

Over dinner at an Italian place in Austin, I told Justin what I was working on. He'd been living in Redmond, Washington, when Bitcoin launched, and he recalled a Microsoft executive who'd been conspicuously interested in it. Our conversation drifted to the treasure. An eccentric art dealer in Santa Fe named Forrest Fenn had filled a bronze chest with rubies, diamonds, gold coins, pre-Columbian artifacts, cash, and jewelry; hidden it; self-published a memoir containing a puzzle poem with nine clues; and set the world loose on a treasure hunt.

Thousands of people took part. Five died, three in rivers, one freezing to death, and one falling off a cliff. Other people got arrested, went bankrupt, or got divorced because of their obsession. Dozens of searchers believed they'd cracked the mystery, despite having no treasure to show for it. They'd explain the discrepancy with baroque theories about the treasure having been moved, or never having been there in the first place. Some of these "solves," as the hunters called their theories, were wild: Fenn had specified that the treasure was buried north of Santa Fe, and one treasure seeker, convinced that it was buried in Fenn's own backyard, insisted that if you started in Santa Fe and went north until you'd gone all the way around the world, you'd end up in the backyard while still being "north of Santa Fe."

Other theories mapped more persuasively to the poem. Michael O'Connell, a career police officer in Boston who had two master's degrees, found that when you put Fenn's poem over graph paper and deleted periods and apostrophes, the two longest sentences each totaled thirty-one characters. Fenn had stayed, while on childhood camping trips to Yellowstone, in cabins across from U.S. Forest Trail 31. On the basis of this finding, Michael deciphered each of the poem's nine clues and fixed on a location. When we spoke, the treasure had already been found by someone else, but the location hadn't been revealed. Michael was convinced it must have been in the place he'd figured out.

Michael's theory was one of several I heard that sounded not merely plausible but almost certainly as if they must be correct. And yet, they were all wrong. "People get so excited about these solves," Matt DeMoss, who'd posted thoughtful YouTube videos about the treasure hunt, told me. "I'll get five emails in one day, each pointing to five different places. But these people are all willing to die for their solve. I don't know what to compare it to but religious devotion. You have to be mindful of the fact that the human brain is great at making connections. We see Orion's Belt in the stars, but if we were on some other planet we wouldn't see that. So it's easy to make connections that aren't there."

Justin, whom I was having dinner with in Austin, had brought both rigor and creativity to his search for the treasure. He'd sharpened his skills by picking intricate locks and cracking a gun safe that cost more than $20,000; trained Tucker to sniff bronze at forty feet in case the chest was underground; and developed a machine-learning algorithm which, by processing video clips of Fenn talking about the treasure hunt and analyzing anomalies in his eye movements, suggested, correctly as it would turn out, that the treasure was in Wyoming. Though someone else had beaten him to the treasure, Justin later got a tip that the successful solve had resided in the poem's homophones: words like "too" and "for," which could also stand for numbers (2, 4). In sequence, they added up to latitude and longitude coordinates inside of Yellowstone. When Justin first told me about this solve, I was utterly convinced. Of the millions of possible coordinates, what were the chances that the single set derivable from words in the poem happened to be within the search area?

Justin found the solve "compelling," but he was more cautious. "What's challenging," he told me at the time, "is hindsight bias and apophenia."

"Apowhatia?"

"The inclination for someone to see patterns in disparate information. There are a lot of ways you can force numbers out of that poem."

And he was right. It turned out that even that statistically persuasive solve was incorrect.

A lesson I'd taken from the Fenn hunt was that rare coincidences don't prove anything and aren't even that rare. Another was never to mistake the strength of someone's conviction for the power of his argument. I'd become resistant to taking fiercely held theories, even the most plausible, at face value.

I thought these lessons would be even more relevant to the Nakamoto mystery. Fenn had said the purpose of his treasure hunt was to get people off their couches, out into nature, away from their digital devices. Nakamoto had lived and died only on the internet, where creatively connecting info-flotsam was an international pastime. Those of us who fell under the spell of the Nakamoto mystery often engaged in pattern recognition not so different from the filter with which conspiracy theorists made sense of the world. The internet had made Keyser Sözes of us all, training us to assemble coherent stories from mismatched shards.

I thought of Sahil Gupta and his Elon Musk crusade. Sahil had continued to bug me about his theory. "Speaking as an outsider here," he suggested helpfully one day, "I think more readers will buy the book, if they first know you as the journalist who first wrote the Satoshi = Musk story."

Later, he sent me a link to an interview with Musk in which podcaster Lex Fridman mentioned that Musk had been suggested as Nakamoto.

"I'm not," Musk replied.

"For sure?" Fridman asked.

"One hundred percent," Musk said.

"Would you tell us if you were?"

"Yeah."

Musk brought a mug of something to his lips and sipped.

"Do you think it's a feature or a bug that he's anonymous?" Fridman asked. "Or she, or they? It's an interesting kind of quirk of human history, that there's a particular technology that has a completely anonymous inventor, or creator."

Thirteen seconds passed before Musk responded.

"Well, you can look at the evolution of ideas before the launch of Bitcoin and see who wrote about those ideas, and obviously I don't know who created Bitcoin for practical purposes. But the evolution of ideas is pretty clear before that. And it seems as though Nick Szabo probably more than anyone else is responsible for the evolution of those ideas. He claims not to be Nakamoto, but I'm not sure, that's neither here nor there."

"So . . . perhaps singular figures aren't even as important as the figures involved in the evolution of ideas that led to a thing."

"Yeah."

"What is a name, anyway?" Musk said a moment later. "A name attached to an idea, what does it even mean?"

"From this video," Sahil informed me, "one can make a binary conclusion. Either he is (1) truthfully denying, or he is (2) falsely denying. Given that he dodged the interviewer's actual question; that he mentioned Nick Szabo as a candidate when Szabo is an easily falsified candidate (Szabo is not a proficient engineer); that he went for the cup of water after his answer—this is a set of actions consistent with false denial."

Had he dodged the question? *Was* it a given that Nick wasn't a proficient engineer?

Sahil clarified that the dodged question concerned whether Nakamoto's anonymity was a feature or a bug and said that the one known publicly viewable sample of Nick-written code was "entry-level Javascript."

"Do you think Musk is telling the truth in the clip?" Sahil pressed me on another occasion.

"My sense is yes," I replied, "but what do I know?"

"You know that there are twenty vectors pointing in the direction that Musk is Satoshi. And you know that there is one vector pointing against, which is a video where he is nervously denying it, then nervously going for a glass of water, then not answering the question the interviewer asked him."

I wasn't as convinced as Sahil was, I said.

Sahil continued to press his case. Finally he wrote, a bit pushily: "Who's gonna buy your book if you weren't the reporter to break the story?"

Slow, Not Furious

When Ryan Nakashima awoke in Los Angeles on March 6, 2014, he scrolled through his phone, scanning headlines. As a media and tech reporter for the Associated Press, it was his job to know what was making news. On this morning, what caught his attention was a feature story in *Newsweek,* already being picked up by media outlets around the world. The cover of the magazine featured a stark black-and-white illustration of a masked man. Laid over that were the words "BITCOIN'S FACE."

The article intersected with both of Ryan's beats. The question of who Satoshi Nakamoto was had recently taken on new urgency after Sergio Demian Lerner published his research showing that Nakamoto had mined 1.1 million coins and never spent them. Suddenly, an obscure and still unknown technologist or group of them was among the richest people in the world. And one of the big stories Ryan had been covering was the decline of newspapers and magazines. *Newsweek* had been sold twice in recent years and in late 2012 had killed its print edition. Its newest owner, IBT Media, had decided to relaunch the print magazine into a brutal media environment where it was harder than ever to break through the noise. In that sense, the 4,500-word *Newsweek* story, which Ryan read quickly on his phone, was a lightning strike.

The mystery man had apparently been hiding in plain sight, right there in LA. Where other reporters had proceeded with the understanding that Satoshi Nakamoto was a pseudonym, *Newsweek* reporter Leah McGrath Goodman had made no such assumption. Combing through a database of naturalization records, she'd found a Japanese-born U.S. citizen named Dorian Prentice Satoshi Nakamoto with a tantalizing background: He was a sixty-four-year-old unemployed engineer who'd studied physics at California State Polytechnic, typed double spaces after periods, and, according to his wife, used both American and British spellings. His estranged brother told Goodman that Dorian, as he was known, was "an asshole" who had worked on classified government projects and whose "life was a complete blank for a while. . . . He'll deny everything." Dorian had had health issues, including prostate cancer and a stroke, which synced with Satoshi Nakamoto's departure from the Bitcoin project.

In early February, after getting Dorian's email address from a model-train company with which he'd placed orders, Goodman emailed and asked him about his hobby. Dorian said he'd been into model trains since his teen years and that he machined parts himself using "manual lathe, mill, surface grinders." In response to questions about his background, he was "evasive," Goodman would write, and after she started asking about Bitcoin, he stopped responding to her altogether. Dorian's son Eric told Goodman that his father wouldn't talk to her about Bitcoin.

Goodman then went to his house in Temple City, a northeastern suburb of LA. Dorian was a father of six who was separated from his wife and lived with his 93-year-old mother. He peeked out the window but wouldn't come to the door. Soon two deputies from the local sheriff's department arrived. Dorian had called them to say a woman he didn't know had been knocking on his door and sitting on his stoop for the past hour. Goodman explained to the officers why she was there, and Dorian emerged from his house wearing jeans, a T-shirt, gym socks, and no shoes. He walked to the end of the driveway, where Goodman stood, and briefly responded to a couple of her questions. "I am no longer involved in that and I cannot discuss it," she would report that he told her, waving a hand in the air dismissively. "It's been turned over to other people. They are in charge of it now. I no longer have any connection." He went back inside. Goodman left, thinking that he'd confirmed her scoop.

Bitcoiners reacted angrily to the story, with its interviews with estranged family members and publication of a photograph of Dorian's home and car, house number and license plate both readable. Gavin Andresen, under whose leadership Bitcoin developers had by now rewritten two-thirds of Nakamoto's original code, tweeted, "I'm disappointed *Newsweek* decided to dox the Nakamoto family, and regret talking to Leah." But all of that was perhaps to be expected.

When Ryan looked up Dorian's address and saw that it was just a few miles from the AP bureau, he pitched his editor on driving over and trying to get an interview. He knew Temple City to be an Asian American suburb southeast of Pasadena. "If you were to look for delicious dumplings," Ryan said later, "you'd head in that direction."

Dorian's house, when Ryan arrived, struck him as having "very Japanese-American landscaping." There was a stone lantern outside and a silver Toyota Corolla, covered by a tarp, in the driveway. The house didn't look like it belonged to someone who was really rich. It was a sweltering morning. Nearly a dozen other reporters were already sitting on neighbors' lawns, looking tired and bored and chatting with each other. Ryan had been on a lot of stakeouts, and he expected this one to proceed like most others: he'd wait around for hours, nothing would happen, and he'd return to the office empty-handed.

Suddenly, the door opened, and an unassuming-looking, slightly disheveled man stepped out. The reporters rushed forward, surrounding him in a scrum and barking questions. "Okay, no questions right now," Dorian Nakamoto said. "I want my free lunch." Ryan was at the back of the pack and expected someone to seize the moment, but "there was a weird silence. For some reason, no one says anything."

Ryan raised his hand. "I'll get you lunch."

"I'm going with this guy," Dorian said.

Ryan pulled Dorian through the crowd, saying, "He's with me," and led Dorian to his aging blue Prius.

In the car, Dorian said he wanted sushi.

"No problem," Ryan said.

"My senses are going off," Ryan recalls. "Why would the founder of Bitcoin need someone to buy him a free lunch?"

Ryan turned on his tape recorder and began asking questions. He later sent me the recording, which captured the next two hours and forty-four minutes.

Dorian immediately denied that he was Bitcoin's inventor.

"I got nothing to do with it, so if you don't want to pay lunch, that's okay."

Ryan started driving east toward the nearest sushi place he knew, in Arcadia. He and Dorian noticed that several of the other reporters were following in their cars.

When Ryan and Dorian entered Mako Sushi, Ryan figured that the other reporters would respect that Dorian had decided to talk to him and leave them alone. Instead, everyone crowded into the narrow restaurant and sat down at the adjacent tables. This wasn't going to work. Ryan and Dorian went back to the car, where Ryan called his boss to say he was bringing Dorian into the office and to order sushi for him there.

Driving west on I-10, Ryan was careful to keep to the speed limit—this would be a terrible time to get pulled over—and couldn't help being reminded of another Los Angeles freeway-chase spectacle. "It was like the white Bronco: super-slow motion." A newspaper editor in one of the trailing cars live-tweeted the action. "After some traffic, and some red lights, we are now again right behind #nakamoto in the #bitcoinchase."

Ryan asked Dorian in several different ways whether he might be Bitcoin's inventor, and Dorian kept saying no. Ryan wasn't sure how to weigh these denials. Dorian had a secretive way about him, which *Newsweek*'s Goodman had picked up on. A defining characteristic of Satoshi Nakamoto was that he didn't want to be known.

Ryan considered whether Dorian's behavior now could be a ruse and whether Dorian, who kept mispronouncing *bitcoin* as "bitcom," might be playing dumb. But Dorian really seemed not to have a grasp of what Bitcoin was. "Even for a faker," Ryan recalls, "you couldn't fake it this bad."

As they approached Figueroa Courtyard, the leafy, low-rise office complex that housed the AP bureau, Ryan explained the plan for avoiding their pursuers and drove into the underground parking garage through the employee entrance. Then he and Dorian got out of the car and ran for the elevator. Ryan pressed 3. He could see Andrea Chang from the *L.A. Times* sprinting toward them. The doors were closing, but then, as in a horror movie, a hand shot through.

Chang followed the hand into the elevator and immediately asked Dorian: "Are you the founder of Bitcoin?"

"No," he said, as the doors closed. "I never was involved."

"When I then asked him why he had gone along with the whole thing and was talking to a reporter," Chang told me much later, "he said, 'It was all for a free lunch.'"

Upstairs, Ryan led Dorian into the AP offices, leaving Chang in the hallway, where she was soon joined by other journalists from the chase.

In the AP conference room, Dorian produced his driver's license, and Ryan photographed it. Then Ryan printed the *Newsweek* article and walked through it line-by-line with Dorian. Dorian continued to deny he had anything to do with Bitcoin. He seemed genuinely confused, and at a loss for why people were treating this like such a big deal. It began to crystallize for Ryan that this had all been a misunderstanding. After interviewing Dorian for two hours, Ryan led him to a back exit, where there was a second staircase, and Dorian left the building without other reporters noticing. Ryan's AP story featuring Dorian's denial posted later that day.

With CNN still broadcasting images of Dorian swarmed by camera-wielding, microphone-thrusting reporters, the real Satoshi Nakamoto broke his silence the next day. For the first and last time since he'd gone poof in 2011, he posted to the P2P Foundation's NING social network using his old gmx email address: "I am not Dorian Nakamoto."

Juola & Associates, a Pennsylvania firm specializing in forensic stylometry, which could match unsigned texts to their true authors using an impressively accurate statistical method, had previously compared some of the Nakamoto candidates proposed by journalists. Using measures such as average word length, word combinations, and use of different parts of speech, the firm had found that Neal J. King was the closest match. But the limitations of the assessment were obvious: it assumed that Satoshi Nakamoto was in that group of candidates. *Forbes* now asked the firm to rerun the test, this time throwing Dorian Nakamoto's writings, such as his public forum posts about model trains, into the mix. King again came out on top, which at a minimum suggested that Dorian Nakamoto was unlikely to be Bitcoin's creator.

Leah Goodman responded online that there was "NOT enough data for good statistical analysis," but Patrick Juola, who did this stuff for a living, was confident that the approximately 1,700 words, and 10,000 characters, of Dorian prose available were more than sufficient to yield reliable results.

Newsweek posted a statement about the magazine's "high editorial and ethical standards," saying that it "stands strongly behind Ms. Goodman and her article" and that "the facts as reported point toward Mr. Nakamoto's role in the founding of Bitcoin. It is natural and expected for a major news revelation such as this to spark debate and controversy. Many of the greatest journalistic scoops have prompted similar reaction."

The next day, reporters were back outside Dorian's house, and the sheriff's department was sending a car to check on Dorian every couple of hours. *Newsweek* would soon be criticized by other publications for its "colossal arrogance" and "half-baked theory." The *Los Angeles Times* gleefully noted that *Newsweek* had also published the forged "Hitler Diaries."

Venture capitalist Marc Andreessen, referring to Goodman's construal of Dorian's failure to answer his phone as a sign of evasiveness, asked, "Is there anyone left on planet earth who does not screen their phone calls? What is this, 1962?" One of his partners noted that "four million people hold top secret security clearances" and that "the first name Satoshi and last name Nakamoto are moderately common in Japan."

Ten days later, a lawyer for Dorian issued a strongly worded statement in which Dorian "unconditionally" denied having anything to do with Bitcoin, which he said he had only heard about for the first time in February, after Goodman contacted his son. He had never worked on cryptography or peer-to-peer networks or alternative currencies, and he revealed that he'd cut off his internet service in 2013 "due to severe financial distress."

The following month, a website appeared: NewsweekLied.com. A photo showed Dorian holding a sign that read "NEWSWEEK'S ARTICLE HURT MY FAMILY." Dorian's mother, according to the site, had been so traumatized by the *Newsweek* article and its aftermath that she "believed the authorities were planning on removing her from her home to put her in a care facility. His estranged wife and children were alienated by the story . . ." The site listed a Bitcoin address* for donations and contact information for a legal defense fund, which would ultimately receive forty-eight bitcoins from two thousand donors, worth $23,000 at the time.

It was starting to look as if Goodman had mistaken Dorian's gripes about money and bank fees, which surely a large percentage of humanity shares, for signs of a fervent antibank ideology. In her article, Goodman had acknowledged numerous inconsistencies between Dorian Nakamoto and Satoshi Nakamoto, but instead of seeing them as clues that she might have the wrong guy, she'd waved them away. She'd dismissed the obvious differences between Dorian's

---

* A Bitcoin address is a shorter, modified version of a public key.

and Satoshi's use of English (from Dorian's Amazon review of Royal Danish Butter Cookies: "it has lots of buttery taste . . . i've had a nice comment from my kids. It's a perfect xmas and I would say, for other occasions"). She'd misread Dorian's evasions and secrecy as confirmation that he was Satoshi, rather than the understandable reaction of a shy person dealing with unwanted attention.

Goodman seemed, also, to have been tripped up by a hazard facing any Nakamotologist: a candidate's denial could be interpreted as evidence that the person either was or wasn't Nakamoto.

Hungarian Brainstorming

As much as I thought Sahil Gupta had succumbed to apophenia with his Elon Musk theory, by the spring of 2022 I worried that I had too. It was obvious, as Musk had noted, that Nick Szabo as much as anyone was Bitcoin's intellectual architect. He seemed to have the rare mix of prerequisite knowledge, skills, and motivation to have invented Bitcoin. His behavior around Bitcoin had been odd. But I knew that I was ignoring anything that muddied the picture.

Lots of California tech people in the 1990s were fascinated by Japan. Vocabulary Nick used that seemed telling to outsiders was part of the standard glossary of the digital-cash world: That might still be a relatively small set of people, but a small set of people was different from a single candidate. Unlike Nakamoto, whose typing was impeccable, Nick's online conversations often showed a hasty sloppiness. And Nakamoto's reference to Wei Dai releasing b-money on the cypherpunks list would be an odd mistake for Nick to have made, given that b-money was first proposed on his own private lib-tech list.

Some of the seeming coincidences, on closer inspection, were misleading. Nick's "re-dated blog posts," which Grey, Frisby, and Popper had all drawn attention to, turned out not to be so suspicious: the original blog post dates were still visible in the URLs, and Nick had announced, before reposting them, that his blog was going into "reruns season." Nick's open-ended invitation to collaborate on a bit gold implementation, "Anybody want to help me code one up?" had appeared six months before Nakamoto announced Bitcoin, whereas Nakamoto spoke of taking a year and a half to write the software. Even in April 2008, half a year before Bitcoin was announced, Nick's bit gold idea was focused on the complicated pricing of coins based on when they were created. Did he really, in the next six months, make the considerable conceptual leap from there to the clarity of Bitcoin?

I wondered also about Nick's personality. To believe he was Nakamoto, you had to buy that someone who'd published hundreds of thousands of words and engaged energetically in scores of internet debates, all under his own name, had decided to forgo credit for his greatest accomplishment. Earlier Nakamoto sleuths had dismissed the Anglo spellings and the time stamps and the quote from the London *Times* as subterfuge, but I had a hard time picturing Nick Szabo wearing Groucho Marx glasses for the better part of two years. Had it all been an elaborate ruse when Nakamoto wrote things like "I am not a lawyer" (Nick by that point had a law degree) and "I'm better with code than with words" (Nick was to all appearances the reverse of this)? Had he really assumed a guise in private emails even before the launch of a project that could easily have gone nowhere? When Nakamoto first emailed Hashcash creator Adam Back in the summer of 2008, he acted as if he'd never heard of Wei Dai's b-money; after Back mentioned it, Nakamoto told Dai, three months before the white paper posted and six months before the software launched, that Bitcoin "expands on your ideas into a complete working system." All of this assumed both an elaborate campaign of misdirection at a time when there was no particular reason to assume Bitcoin would succeed, and a ham-handed impersonation by Nick of someone who wasn't him.

I thought there was a more fundamental inconsistency. Nick had been an instinctive extropian, with a hummingbird mind that could alight anywhere: smart drugs, genetic engineering, the corporation of the future. He was a mad tinkerer with a "spectacularly large list of projects, over 150 of them," as he'd boasted at one point. There was a Play-Doh Fun Factory–designed structure that could, with human assistance, extrude copies of itself; N-Cat (Nick's Catalog), hawking extropian-friendly products including his own essays, remailer software, and digests of the cypherpunks list; a methodology for pricing memes; a game called Hungarian Brainstorming, with points for conceiving original ideas and "destroying" other players' ideas; a mailing list about "comet materials processing"; a "microrobot" cute enough to generate comic strips and other IP; "Operation Desert Blossom," a multipoint plan to end the Gulf War; and a piece of speculative fiction in which "the main character has to make a painful transition from a statist hierarchy of trust to a web of trust in order to solve her problem." (Nick was, perhaps understandably, happier with his settings than with his plots or characters.) Later, Nick became known for abstruse essays on computer security and internet commerce, from "Distributing Authorities and Verifying Their Claims" to "The Mental Accounting Barrier to Micropayments."

Had Nick really spent three and a half years, flannel sleeves rolled up, debugging code and sweating the small stuff, as Nakamoto had needed to do? Nick was first and foremost a Big Thinker, a self-publishing Jared Diamond of libertarian computer science. He had announced ambitious projects: a history of commercial institutions he was writing, a new programming language he was developing. Neither saw the light of day. He'd graduated from law school in his forties, but as far as I could tell, he'd never practiced. Maybe Nick had a vast, secret body of tangible work, but the public face he'd presented was that of an idea person.

Jeremy Clark, a blockchain-focused computer scientist at Concordia University in Montreal, attended a conclave of Bitcoin brains on the campus of Princeton University in 2014 and chatted with Nick at a private workshop the first day. By that point Nick had already denied being Nakamoto several times, and in conversation Clark was further convinced that Nick was telling the truth. "He still seemed to think his bit gold was better" than Bitcoin, Jeremy recalled. "To me that's an indication. And to a nonexpert, when you read the Bitcoin and bit gold proposals, they use a lot of the same words, but they're actually really different ideas." At the workshop, everyone took a turn at the whiteboard for ten minutes, and "Nick's talk was so incoherent, that added to my skepticism, 'cause Satoshi was very lucid."

Finally, I wondered, why wouldn't Nick have admitted it by now? Legal exposure was an understandable concern when Bitcoin launched, but thirteen years later, no one had been arrested for merely using or creating a cryptocurrency. If personal safety was a concern, there were plenty of examples of extremely rich people who managed to go about their lives enjoyably and productively despite being potential targets. And not coming forward as Nakamoto meant forgoing real benefits: Wealth. Glory. And importantly for Nick, I believed, the power to be listened to and have your ideas taken seriously. For years, he'd blogged in the wilderness, hungrily engaging in the comments section with everyone who took the time to read and respond to his thoughts.

I found myself losing faith that Nick was Nakamoto. This meant that I was back to knowing very little, if anything at all. I'd need to start my search over, now without even a hunch about who Nakamoto might be.

"My Father Is an Honest Guy"

The Dorian Nakamoto episode had given emotional weight to the Bitcoiners' mantra to "leave Satoshi alone" and not try to figure out who he was. "Even if it's NOT him, she still painted a 1,000,000BTC target on this man's home," CryptoCobain tweeted. But it also supported the opposite position: it was important to know who the real Nakamoto was so that innocent bystanders like Dorian wouldn't be harassed. And so, despite the *Newsweek* debacle or because of it, the Nakamoto obsession only spread.

Within hours of *Newsweek*'s revelations, a rumor circulated at a Bitcoin conference in Texas that for ten years in the 1980s and early 1990s, Hal Finney had lived not just in the same thirty-one-thousand-population suburb as Dorian but less than two miles away from him. People began to wonder whether Hal and Dorian might know one another or whether Hal was Satoshi Nakamoto and had borrowed his neighbor's name.

Robin Hanson speculated on the statistics-obsessed *LessWrong* blog that there was at least a 15 percent chance that his old co-extropian Hal had been more involved with Bitcoin than he'd let on. A *Forbes* reporter named Andy Greenberg, who'd also heard the rumor, began to entertain a variant theory: perhaps Dorian had invented Bitcoin, but Hal, given Dorian's lackluster English, had communicated the idea to the world.

Greenberg assembled twenty thousand words of Hal's writing and sent them to the stylometrists at Juola & Associates, to add to the samples the firm had considered for his colleague hours before. Then he contacted Fran Finney, who relayed his questions to her husband. Hal was on a ventilator by then and could do little more, using eye and eyebrow movements, than say yes or no. He denied being connected in any way with Dorian or the invention of Bitcoin. When Greenberg still wasn't convinced, Fran suggested he come to the Finney home and ask Hal in person. Before Greenberg went to Santa Barbara, he heard back from Juola's John Noecker, who said Finney's writing was the closest match he'd seen so far to the Bitcoin white paper.

When Greenberg arrived at the Finneys' home and posed his questions, Hal laboriously moved his eyes and eyebrows to indicate that he was not Nakamoto and had nothing to do with Bitcoin's creation. Hal's son Jason showed Greenberg his father's Gmail account, including more than a dozen emails Hal and Satoshi Nakamoto had exchanged. "My father is an honest guy," Jason told Greenberg. "He would have loved to have been part of creating Bitcoin, and he wouldn't have hidden it. But he wasn't involved." Greenberg left, convinced by the Finneys' denials. It really was just a crazy coincidence.

After Greenberg's article came out, Bitcoiners donated twenty-five bitcoins, at the time worth $16,000, to the Finneys, who hoped to spend it on an electrical switch that would read signals from Hal's surface muscles, enabling him to control his keyboard and wheelchair. But the switch proved incompatible with the muscles Hal could still control, so the Finneys put the money toward end-of-life costs instead. Hal's evident lack of wealth only strengthened the consensus that he wasn't Satoshi Nakamoto.

On a Tuesday in late August of 2014, Hal and Fran flew by chartered air ambulance to Scottsdale, Arizona. From the private airport, they were driven to the intensive care unit at Paradise Valley Hospital. The

Alcor Life Extension Foundation, having relocated from California, was nearby, and an Alcor team was already at the hospital awaiting member A-1436's arrival. The hospital had hosted a number of Alcor members before, and its staff was familiar with what was about to happen.

At age fifty-eight, after nearly five years with ALS, Hal had begun to notice that his mind wasn't as quick as it once was, a particularly terrible loss for a person so cerebral, and it was getting worse. He'd made clear that once he could no longer communicate, he didn't want to be kept on life support. After his family said their goodbyes, the hospital administered drugs to ensure he wasn't conscious, and his ventilator was removed.

Doctors expected him to stop breathing within an hour, but it wasn't until thirty-eight hours later, at 8:50 a.m. on August 28, that Hal was declared clinically dead. Only then could the Alcor team spring into action and drive his body to their nearby facility. Speed was essential. The first priority with cryopreservation was "to maintain viability of the tissue."

At Alcor, Hal's body was transferred to a narrow, custom-made, stainless-steel trough called a patient-former. "You don't want the patient to freeze with their arms sticking out," Max More, who'd cofounded the extropians and was now Alcor's CEO, told me later, "'cause it makes them hard to fit in." A circulating ice bath began external cooling. Then the team intubated Hal, a pump restarted his circulation, and a ventilator resumed his breathing.

Through a tube into Hal's heart, the surgical team removed as much blood as possible—blood being susceptible to ice formation—and replaced it with a cocktail of chemical preservatives Alcor called M-22. Fran was in the room as all this happened, and Max kept fellow extropians updated: "Hal Finney is being cryopreserved now."

Once perfusion was complete, Hal's body temperature was rapidly lowered to minus 110 degrees Celsius. The process then slowed to prevent fracturing, as Hal's body went through a phase transition to a solid. After another four days, his body reached minus 160 degrees Celsius. At that point, it was sealed inside a numbered aluminum pod, which was lowered into a ten-foot-tall steel thermos flask called a Dewar and immersed in 450 liters of liquid nitrogen. Hal was Alcor's 128th patient. Like many Alcor members, much of his cryopreservation was covered by life insurance.

Max More eulogized his old extropian friend: "Hal, I know I speak for many when I say that I look forward to speaking to you again sometime in the future and to throwing a party in honor of your revival."

Fran, who took comfort from the knowledge that her husband was being preserved through cryonics, later said, "He just wanted to be able to see what the world turned into, because it was going to be such an amazing, wondrous place."

Some Bitcoiners took to calling one ten-millionth of a coin a Finney.

Bag of Words

When I got back from Austin in May of 2022, I decided I needed to broaden my search. This was a mystery from the realm of computers. Computers should be able to solve it. But stylometry had so far produced a muddle. In the U.K., a professor of computational linguistics had assigned his students to compare the Bitcoin white paper with various Nakamoto candidates' writings. They'd found Nick Szabo to be the closest match. Juola & Associates, which had originally named Neal King, and later Hal Finney, the closest match to Nakamoto, told Dominic Frisby that Szabo and Finney were consistently the best matches. A Georgetown University computer science student, looking at Szabo, Finney, Wei Dai, Tim May, and an Australian cryptographer named Ian Grigg, variously showed Szabo, Dai, or May to have possibly authored the white paper, and Grigg or Finney to have possibly written the emails. Another pair of scholars, looking at a slightly different set of suspects, concluded that Gavin Andresen was the closest match.

On a sticky day in June, I visited Patrick Juola at his lab on a scruffy block in Pittsburgh. We sat at a long table in the basement, which would normally be abuzz with graduate students. Duquesne University, where Patrick was a professor, was on summer break, and we were the only people there.

Patrick, who was fifty-six, had a ponytail and goatee and a jovial way about him. The son of a math professor in Idaho, he'd grown up loving Encyclopedia Brown detective stories, computers, and foreign languages, the three enthusiasms I assumed were most likely to predict a career in stylometry. Patrick had made it his life's work to transform a ragged, variable, questionable craft into a reliable, consistent, authoritative science. The premise of scientific stylometry was, in another stylometrist's expression, the existence of a "human stylome," a unique signature to every person's writing. Stylometry, like cryptanalysis, used frequency anomalies* to crack a code. The pioneering scholars who in the early 1960s took a statistical approach to determining authorship of *The Federalist Papers* had focused on the frequencies of functional words, nuts and bolts like *the*, *an*, *with*, and *but*. These offered the advantage of distinguishing among authors regardless of topic, and were also largely unconscious and hard to obfuscate.

Whatever pride a writer might take in his surgical word choices, deftly turned phrases, and architectural sentences, a computer just looked at numbers: frequencies of words, of parts of words, and of combinations of words, irrespective even of their order. To a machine and the computational linguists who operated it, a writer's cherished opus was merely a "bag of words." That was the phrase they used.

---

* One of the earliest-known instances of cryptography was the Caesar cipher. It was how Julius Caesar sent messages to his generals that enemy interceptors couldn't read. It was also called a shift cipher, because Caesar would choose a number—he preferred 3—and then shift each letter in the original message to the letter three places later in the alphabet. B would become E, C would become F, and so on. The plaintext "Veni Vidi Vici" would become the ciphertext "Yhql Ylgl Ylfl." To unscramble it, the recipient would shift each letter three places in reverse.

This code, amazingly, went uncracked for nine hundred years. Then al-Kindi, an Arab philosopher translating an ancient text from the Greek, had a crucial insight: some of an alphabet's letters are used more often than others. (In modern English, the seven most frequently used letters are E, then T, then A, I, O, N, and S.) By counting the occurrences of letters in an enciphered text and ranking them, al-Kindi could figure out which letters they actually stood for.

Patrick was able to publicly demonstrate stylometry's power in 2013 when he fielded a call from the London *Times,* which was chasing down a tip that Robert Galbraith, author of a novel titled *The Cuckoo's Calling,* was in fact Harry Potter writer J. K. Rowling. The *Times* reporter's evidence was circumstantial: Rowling and Galbraith shared both an agent and an editor; Galbraith wrote with a skill belied by his dust-jacket description as a first-time author; and despite being billed as a male career military officer, he was impressively adept at describing women's clothes. Could Patrick help settle the matter?

To add what he called "distractors," Patrick put novels by three female British crime writers next to Rowling's novel *The Casual Vacancy.* Comparing these with the Galbraith novel, his software assessed four features Patrick had found reliable for author attribution: word lengths, the one hundred most common words, and the most frequent two- and four-character clusters. By each of the measures, Rowling was a very close match. This didn't prove anything, but it suggested that Galbraith was either Rowling or someone who wrote in a style very similar to hers. With this fact in hand, the *Times* reporter approached Rowling's agent, and Rowling admitted that she was, in fact, Galbraith.

Now, in his lab's basement in Pittsburgh, Patrick described the Satoshi Nakamoto attribution problem as "very, very hard to work with." He thought the Nakamoto writings, such as they were, were "not a lot. . . . And half the candidates who have been named have even less available for them."

Patrick felt that the conflicting results from different stylometrists pointed to Nakamoto being a group rather than to deliberate obfuscation by whoever Nakamoto was, which would have left traces. "Kinda like wiping your fingerprints off the murder weapon. If there are no fingerprints, you don't know who did it, but you do know that whoever did it is aware that they did something wrong and tried to hide the evidence." An unfortunate but inescapable feature of Nakamotology was that you ended up using the language of homicide detectives to talk about someone whose only crime, as far as anyone knew, was writing a clever computer program and giving it away for free.

Part of the challenge lay in the specific nature of the Nakamoto mystery. It wasn't what Patrick and his peers called a closed-class problem. "*Death in the Clouds,* Agatha Christie," Patrick said by way of analogy. "Hercule Poirot is flying from France to England, and somebody dies in the air. And it's obviously a case of murder. It has to be somebody on that plane. The question is: Which one?"

I thought the Nakamoto question was more like a police lineup, where you're trying to identify the purse snatcher, but he might not be in the group you're looking at. In the case of Nakamoto, what the mixed stylometry efforts had in common was that they'd all focused on roughly the same handful of cypherpunks. Why should we assume that Nakamoto was one of them? Was it technically possible, I asked, to automate a much broader search, doing a mass stylometric crawl of all the tangentially related forums and email lists and evaluating tens of thousands of candidates?

Leaving aside cost and feasibility, Patrick didn't think a search like the one I was suggesting was relevant to the Nakamoto question. "We're dealing not with a locked-room mystery," he said, "but we are dealing with a country-house mystery." He meant a suspect set that was limited but fuzzy at the edges. "We can be fairly confident that Nakamoto was one of a smaller group of candidates," he said.

I recalled that Nick Szabo had said there was a tiny number of people who had the combination of skills, knowledge, and motivation needed to create Bitcoin. Patrick, similarly, believed Nakamoto was almost certainly connected with the cypherpunks, and in particular with the handful who were developing digital cash in the late '90s. "This is one where I think good old-fashioned detective work is possibly a better step than stylometry," Patrick said. "Could they actually, physically have written it? There are some people who might not have been available for such a project because they were on sabbatical or had died four years previously. In the detective novels that

I was reading a whole bunch of, they talk about method, motive, and opportunity. So opportunity is important in all of this. If the guy was a continent away from the blackboard the document was scribbled on, it doesn't matter what the stylometry says. So stylometry is useful for establishing corroborative evidence. But it's not magic. It's not divination."

This wasn't quite what I'd been hoping to hear. I drove home across Pennsylvania discouraged. I hadn't thought this was going to be easy, but maybe it wasn't even possible. I was no longer sure how to think about the problem. It remained an open question how many people were in on Nakamoto's secret. I was skeptical of Patrick's theory that a group might be involved. But even if Nakamoto was one person, did no one around him know or strongly suspect what he'd been up to?

The identity of Deep Throat—a generation-defining secret, the archetype of a modern mystery—had been, in hindsight, almost comically widely known. H. R. Haldeman, citing his own confidential source, told Richard Nixon that there was a leaker at the FBI, and Haldeman later named him as Mark Felt. A federal prosecutor became aware of Deep Throat's identity during Felt's grand jury testimony. Felt told a girlfriend the secret, and Bob Woodward told his *Washington Post* editors, Ben Bradlee and Leonard Downie, Jr.; his co-byliner, Carl Bernstein; and, "because it was a big part of my past," his future wife Elsa. Bernstein's ex-wife Nora Ephron believed Felt was Deep Throat and apparently shared the news with their son Jacob.

But with Nakamoto, I thought there was a chance the mystery was more like the Unabomber's, where only a single person knew the secret. What were the chances that the world's greatest piece of gossip would remain under wraps for fifteen years? That it could survive the swerves of human relations: a divorce, a business breakup, the irritant of greed or jealousy or resentment? The revelation that Robert Galbraith was really J. K. Rowling was a case in point: The person who'd tipped off the British newspaper was the best friend of the wife of a partner at Rowling's solicitors. Maybe Nakamoto had never told anyone.

I thought of the title of one of Nick Szabo's essays: "Trusted Third Parties Are Security Holes." The more years that passed without a leak, the more likely it seemed that Nakamoto must be either dead or superhumanly discreet. Only a stylometry of sorts had finally unmasked Ted Kaczynski, when his sister-in-law, reading the Unabomber's thirty-five-thousand-word antitechnology manifesto printed in *The Washington Post,* thought it sounded alarmingly like her husband's hermit brother in Montana. I'd thought only stylometry held the hope of cracking the Nakamoto mystery too. But now I wasn't so sure. And I soon spoke with someone who thought the problem was even bigger.

When Aston University announced its stylometry results pointing to Nick Szabo, Jeremy Clark—the Concordia professor who'd been at the 2014 Princeton summit with Nick and others—had rebutted the findings as "grossly insufficient. . . . If you take 13 people, SOMEONE will always be the most close by definition."

When I called him, he sounded almost relieved to talk to me about Nakamoto. "I've tried to talk to a lot of people," Jeremy said. "No one's that interested."

Jeremy made several observations about Nakamoto. One was that he did not behave like a trained academic. Professional scholars were conditioned to thoroughly review and cite precedent literature, the giants on the shoulders of which their paper was standing or which their paper was going to knock down. Nakamoto's citations were anemic; his white paper would have been laughed out of any peer review process. And professional scholars were incentivized to publish under their own names. "Most academics would try to get some credit, not do it anonymously, write it up, submit it to a conference."

Jeremy also echoed remarks others had made to me about Nakamoto's failure to follow software industry norms. "Being a good solo programmer is not the same as being a good software engineer." He pointed out, as others had, that Bitcoin's cryptography, while effective, wasn't sophisticated.

But mainly Jeremy wanted to talk about Bayesian probability, a statistical approach revered by Silicon Valley's influential Rationalists, the contemporary community that came closest to and shared many members with the extropians. "If I give you no evidence, am I Satoshi?" Jeremy said. "The probability is one in seven billion. So things like 'He's from the UK,' or 'He uses Canadian spelling,' or 'He uses two spaces,' or 'He knows about cryptography': These do limit the number of people, but you can't get over the probability" that any single suspect is extremely unlikely to be Nakamoto. To surmount an outright denial by a candidate, "the evidence you'd need would have to be overwhelming. Extraordinary claims require extraordinary evidence." Perhaps sensing the perplexity in my silence, Jeremy added: "This is maybe an overly formal way to think about it."

Jeremy then told the parable of the policeman who finds a drunk looking for his keys under a streetlamp. After the man acknowledges that he lost the keys in some nearby bushes, the cop asks why he's looking under the lamp. "This is where the light is," the drunk says.

Whenever Nakamoto nuts floated names like Szabo and Finney, Jeremy thought of Linus Torvalds, the twenty-something Scandinavian programmer who'd created Linux, a free version of the Unix operating system that catalyzed the open-source software movement. Torvalds did so under his own name, but Jeremy imagined the counterfactual: "What if Linus did that anonymously? Is anyone going to guess it was him? He was a Finnish grad student no one had heard of." If Torvalds hadn't taken credit for Linux, Jeremy argued, people would have assumed its creator was Unix designer Ken Thompson or some other obvious candidate.

"You have all these armchair people who are looking for candidates to be Satoshi," Jeremy said, "and they're looking where the lights are—people who published papers on the internet, or were on a message board. But there are a lot more people in the bushes. Maybe Satoshi never posted on a message board or filed a patent."

Jeremy wasn't the first person to suggest that Nakamoto could turn out to be someone no one had heard of. Stefan Thomas had conjectured that Nakamoto, rather than being Wei or Hal or Nick, could be one of their followers. "Genius is pretty widespread," Stefan said. "There's a lot of people who could come up with a good idea." Patrick Juola had made a similar point: the inventors of public-key cryptography itself were, when they invented it, "people that you'd never heard of."

And Nakamoto had written that he was "better with code than with words." Maybe he was someone who wasn't in the habit of publishing his thoughts. Maybe he had no internet footprint at all.

"How Deep Are You?"

The morning of November 12, 2015, I opened my inbox to find an email sent at 1:39 a.m.

"Subject: I hacked Satoshi Nakamoto."

I wasn't reassured by the parenthetical warning "Not Virus Scanned." But the sender's address was satoshi.nakamoto@vistomail.com, and I remembered that one of the few known Nakamoto accounts had been with Vistomail. I tentatively opened the email.

It contained two lines of text, strewn with typos:

> satoshi is Dr Craig wright in australia and he is an asshole
>
> 200 million on bitrcoin shit and he lets his staff sasy nothing and treats us as shit and fires us if we cannot work like dogs

There were fifteen attachments.

At that moment, I had mostly tuned out Bitcoin news. The Mt. Gox implosion had dampened my interest. Nakamoto searchers had found only shadows. I was also feeling more paranoid than usual, having recently been approached while reporting an unrelated story by private investigators posing as sources. I'd bought a paper shredder and become even more wary of opening attachments from strangers.

I shrugged off the email as either a phishing attempt or a time-wasting, unfounded claim and archived it without trying to find out anything more about the man in Australia.

Bitcoin was just then at a fraught point in its maturation. It had crossed several thresholds in the past year. Microsoft and Dell had begun to accept payments in the cryptocurrency. Coinbase, the first regulated U.S. exchange, had launched. But internally, the Bitcoin community was divided over how the project should grow to handle more traffic. Scaling was the very problem people like Hal Finney and James Donald had warned about in 2009.

From the start, Bitcoin had harbored a paradox: it was never going to become the global, state-disrupting phenomenon its most fervent proponents wished for without going mainstream, but mass adoption was only going to happen, realistically, if it was regulated by governments and integrated in some way with traditional financial institutions. Libertarians and crypto-anarchists seemed unable to grasp that most people were never going to be libertarians and crypto-anarchists. There was no scenario where Bitcoin would be adopted without being co-opted.

This contradiction had now crystallized in a technical but bitter dispute, focused on how many transactions each block in the blockchain should be able to accommodate, and it threatened to tear apart a fragile ecosystem. Big Blockers like Gavin Andresen wanted to expand block size in order make Bitcoin a faster, more useful product. Small Blockers, who included many of the other core Bitcoin developers, thought larger blocks, which would require more powerful, expensive computers, would be less democratic, endangering Bitcoin's decentralization. Nick Szabo leaned Small Block, warning that a dramatic block-size expansion would be "reckless" and "a huge security risk." But because Bitcoin had no leader, arriving at any consensus over how to move forward was proving nearly impossible. Finally, Big Blocker and core developer Mike Hearn, fed up with the gridlock, had launched a spin-off* of Bitcoin called Bitcoin XT, incorporating Andresen-written code that would octuple block size and which further inflamed the controversy. At that point, someone with control over one of Nakamoto's email addresses (satoshi@vistomail.com) weighed in with a post to a listserv for bitcoin developers, calling Bitcoin XT "a very dangerous fork" and accusing Hearn and Andresen of "violating the 'original vision' they claim to honour . . . This present situation has been very disappointing to watch unfold." The most common response to this post was to assume that it wasn't from Nakamoto and that his email had been hacked.

Adding to the tensions, Bitcoin was no longer the only cryptocurrency people were talking about. A more flexible newcomer called Ethereum was generating excitement as a blockchain that went far beyond Bitcoin's capabilities, offering not just a currency but a platform that supported smart contracts and on which decentralized applications could be built.

The email about Craig Wright that I'd received, or ones like it, had also been sent to a number of other people who'd previously written about Satoshi Nakamoto, and some of them acted on the information. Gwern Branwen, the pseudonymous blogger who'd antagonized Nick Szabo by dismissing Bitcoin as a warmed-over rehash from the '90s, partnered with *Wired* writer Andy Greenberg, last seen at Hal Finney's house after *Newsweek*'s Dorian Nakamoto fiasco, to investigate the tip.

Greenberg and Branwen soon unearthed several Nakamoto-aligning factoids: Wright was a former subscriber to the cypherpunks list, a gold booster, a C++ programmer, a cybersecurity pro, a libertarian with a tax grievance against the government, an Australian, and a Japanophile.

---

* A "hard fork," in software vernacular.

They also found what appeared to be direct links between Wright and Nakamoto. On Wright's blog, a post from August 2008, months before the publication of the Bitcoin white paper, spoke of his forthcoming release of a "cryptocurrency paper." Another post, weeks after the white paper came out, asked readers contacting him to use a PGP key that the reporters discovered was linked to the email address satoshin@vistomail.com (nearly identical to the address Nakamoto had used when announcing the white paper to the Metzdowd cryptography list). And they uncovered a deleted page from Wright's blog, titled "Bitcoin" and dated January 10, 2009, that said, "The Beta of Bitcoin is live tomorrow. This is decentralized. . . . We try until it works." In fact, Bitcoin had gone live on January 9, but Greenberg and Branwen thought the timing made sense, given Wright's northeastern-Australian time zone. They found a later version of the same page, also deleted, in which the original text was gone, replaced by "Bitcoin—AKA bloody nosey you be. . . . It does always surprise me how at times the best place to hide [is] right in the open." And they found a publicly verified audit of one of Wright's companies showing that it appeared to own a large sum of bitcoin very few people would have been able to amass in Bitcoin's early years. Another deleted image from Wright's blog showed a letter of agreement for a company called SGI to build a supercomputer for Wright's company Cloudcroft. According to Wright's LinkedIn profile, he had received two PhDs.

In December, the *Wired* duo contacted Wright, "suggesting that we knew his secret and asking for a meeting." They then received an email from Tessier-Ashpool@AnonymousSpeech.com. Tessier-Ashpool was the name of a family in cyberpunk novelist William Gibson's *Sprawl* trilogy, AnonymousSpeech.com was one of the privacy-oriented email services Nakamoto had used, and *Wired* found that the IP address the email had come from was a Panama-based address owned by Vistomail, another of the email services Nakamoto had used. "You are digging," Tessier-Ashpool wrote back. "The question is how deep are you?"

Craig

Growing up in Brisbane, I would later learn, Craig Wright had been an awkward child, approaching peers with such overtures as "Would you like to play with my beetles?" He stayed in his room for hours, avoided sports, and became agitated in crowds.

His father was "weird and volatile," according to a family member, as well as physically and verbally abusive to his wife and three children. Craig's parents divorced when he was five, and Craig and his sisters were raised by their mother, who worked full-time and was an alcoholic.

For male role models, Craig had to look elsewhere. Most days after school, the Wright kids would walk to their maternal grandparents' house, where Craig would spend much of his time with Ronald Andrew Lynam, whom he called Pop, in the "hamshack" where Lynam did his amateur radio activities. Lynam's experiences in Asia during World War II were alive in the home. Oils he'd painted in the Philippines hung around the house, and in the hamshack he kept an old carton of occupation money, made by the Japanese for their presumed takeover of Australia. Pop spoke often of Japanese culture, and Craig developed an obsession. In his bedroom he had throwing stars and a genuine katana. Well into adolescence, he'd gone to local parks to swing the sword while wearing a black ninja costume that covered his face.

When Craig did connect with peers, it was through geeky interests like Dungeons & Dragons and Frank Herbert's Dune novels. Craig and his cousin Max, who was three months younger, bonded over their shared technical enthusiasms: they built circuit boards, noodled on Commodore 64 computers, played text-based adventure games, and tried to nuke each other's machines with distributed denial-of-service attacks. "We'd literally have code wars," Max said.

As a teenager, Craig dyed his hair orange and neglected his hygiene. His continuing ninja outings embarrassed his sister Danni and led other kids to call him a freak. At his private high school, which was run by Catholic friars, he was ostracized by classmates and bullied; on at least one occasion he lashed back, breaking another kid's nose.

He made up for his diminished present with visions of the future. He'd say he was going to be a chef, a wall paperer, a computer scientist. He claimed that he was in the Legion of Doom, a notorious hacker group. Danni would later say that he'd always talked about how he "would one day create something that would change the world!!!" An uncle, Donald Lynam, and his mother would both say that Craig had a tendency to make up details in his stories if he wasn't feeling sufficiently appreciated.

He was accepted into a nine-year officer training program in the Royal Australian Air Force but was discharged after less than a year. Donald Lynam would be left with the impression that it had to do with "his personality. . . . I think we all know that Craig is not known for his people skills." At twenty-six, Wright, by then making a career in cybersecurity, married a Canadian woman whom he'd met on the internet. She was eighteen years older than him and a year and a half younger than his mother.

Around the same time, Wright posted more than a dozen times to the cypherpunks list, sometimes correcting people's use of words and quoting from the *Oxford English Dictionary.* Among the topics that seemed to interest him was the idea of financial institutions offering services online. "While the average member of the public blindly trusts the banks to keep them safe, and until there is a user friendly means of encrypting data (that the US government supports)," he wrote, "I can see alot [*sic*] of room for fraud."

In another post, Wright responded to a libertarian thread of Tim May's: "Personally, I paid my way through uni . . . full fees. I took out a loan when I developed cancer." He added that although he was an engineer, "I have worked in a petrol station. So why and for what reason sould [*sic*] I have to pay several 10's of thousands each year to support others. I have never taken help from the government, I do not feel I should have to pay as well. And what am I paying for . . . to protect the status quo. I believe that there is more than enough help for ppl available. They just need to get off their butts and work."

He signed the message with one of the Japanese pseudonyms he sometimes used: "doshai."

"Do we really need your amateur political views?" responded another cypherpunk, a fellow Australian named Julian Assange.

Dave

In the early 2000s, Wright developed a friendship with an American named David Kleiman. By then, Wright was helping internet gambling companies like Lasseters Online Casino and Centrebet protect themselves. Kleiman was a computer forensics expert in South Florida who'd been paralyzed in a motorcycle accident in the 1990s. He wore an aircraft-grade aluminum flash drive around his neck, used his guns' serial numbers for passwords, and dated strippers.

After he and Wright met online, they bonded in part over a shared zeal for piling up credentials. For Kleiman, this meant professional certifications, and he appended so many of the multiletter abbreviations for them after his signature that friends called him Dave Mississippi. Wright, who had more than "200 vocational qualifications" and a growing number of advanced academic degrees, signed his emails "Dr. Craig Wright LLM GSE GSM GSC MMiT MNSA MinfoSec CISSP/ISSMP CISM CISA." They coauthored a paper entitled "Overwriting Hard Drive Data" and formed a partnership to seek contracts from the U.S. Department of Homeland Security.

Health problems weighed on Kleiman. Starting in early 2011, he spent much of the next two years hospitalized with infections, and in late March 2013, when he was forty-six, he checked himself out against medical advice. "I told the doctors," he said to a friend, "to go fuck themselves." The following month, Kleiman was found dead in his ranch house in Riviera Beach, an hour north of Miami. He was slouched in his wheelchair near his bed, a .45-caliber semiautomatic handgun with a magazine full of hollow-point bullets nearby. Police found what looked like a bullet hole in the mattress, open bottles of tequila and whiskey on the kitchen table, and wheelchair tracks and spatters of dried feces and blood throughout the house. Kleiman's body was in an advanced state of decomposition. A toxicology panel revealed cocaine metabolites in his blood. He was found to have died of coronary heart disease.

Wright heard the news from an email blast to Kleiman's friends and posted a tribute on YouTube. "Dave was a special man," he said, speaking haltingly and in a husky voice that occasionally broke. "Dave was someone who gave far, far more than he ever took . . . I'm proud to actually call Dave Kleiman my friend."

The following February, Wright wrote to Kleiman's father. "Hello Louis, Your son Dave and I are two of the three key people behind Bitcoin. . . . Please understand, I do not seek anything other than to give you information about your son. Know also that Dave was a key part of an invention that will revolutionise the world." He advised Louis to preserve Dave's computer systems and said he'd help him "recover what Dave owned."

Louis Kleiman was ninety-three, and his son Ira took over the correspondence. Ira was skeptical. He found it hard to believe that his brother could have had significant bitcoin holdings. When Dave died, friends were paying his cellphone bill, he'd stopped paying the mortgage on his home, and to stave off foreclosure he'd resorted to seeking credit from a high-interest, subprime lender.

"Dave may have been cash poor," Wright responded, "but he was not poor." Wright mentioned various offshore trusts that held millions of dollars' worth of bitcoin belonging to Dave and spoke of "several DHS research programs" the two men had been awarded through their company W&K. He wanted Ira to know that he was taking him into his confidence about the Satoshi Nakamoto pseudonym. "Nobody involved with this wants to ever (even after death) be known. The myth is more powerful than all of us combined. I want Dave's family to know, but please understand, he would not have wanted the world knowing."

Soon, Ira had changed his mind about Wright. He now remembered a Thanksgiving dinner in 2009 where Dave had talked to him about a "digital money" he was creating with a "wealthy foreign man." "I for one have to say I'm a believer," Ira told a friend of Dave's in an email, referring to Wright. "The evidence is overwhelming that he is legit. That or he's the most elaborate social engineering hacker ever. Seriously, I think he and Dave are a couple of geniuses. This stuff is just mind blowing."

Ira now hungered to know more about his brother's role in Bitcoin's birth. "Can I ask if Dave played a part in writing the original PDF under the asian alias?"

"I cannot say much right now," Wright responded, "but yes, Dave was involved with that PDF. He had the vistomail account. I had the gmx one."

By early March, Ira was both excited about the prospect of riches and afraid he might have blown his chance of getting them. After Dave's death, Ira had thrown out a bunch of his brother's papers and reformatted several of his hard drives. "I can't stop thinking that we may have 300,000 bitcoins, but simply don't know how to retrieve them," Ira told Wright. "It's certainly enough to change my family's life and my wife's family back in Thailand."

When Ira lavished praise on Wright, Wright insisted that "Satoshi was a team. . . . I am far from humble, but I will not take from Dave. I had an idea, but it would never have been executed without Dave. Dave was my sounding board, he fixed my errors."

A month later, Ira received an email from Andrew Miller, an investigator with the Australian Taxation Office, asking what he knew about Wright's legal actions against W&K, the Wright-Kleiman partnership. Miller sent him a pair of filings Wright had recently made in Australia, which bore Dave Kleiman's signature and transferred "all accountable value" to Wright.

Ira now became suspicious of Wright and bombarded him with questions. Wright had ready responses, and Ira was temporarily placated, but his frustration mounted. Wright had dangled the lure of a fortune due the Kleiman family, but there was always a reason why he couldn't get the money just yet. Ira began to consider filing a lawsuit. Then, in October 2015, Wright stopped responding to him.

A Treacherous Exercise

At 4:25 p.m. on December 8, 2015, *Wired* went live with its report: "Bitcoin's Creator Satoshi Nakamoto Is Probably This Unknown Australian Genius." Andy Greenberg and Gwern Branwen detailed their evidence and, with the Dorian Nakamoto fiasco fresh in memory, hedged, "Either Wright invented Bitcoin, or he's a brilliant hoaxer who very badly wants us to believe he did."

An hour and a half later, the tech site Gizmodo published its own exposé, with the twist that Wright hadn't worked alone: "This Australian Says He and His Dead Friend Invented Bitcoin." It quoted from what appeared to be a 2011 email to Wright from Dave Kleiman: "Craig, I think you're mad and this is risky, but I believe in what we are trying to do." The Gizmodo reporters sounded confident that Wright was Nakamoto, asserting that the emailed cache had been "corroborated in interviews," but they acknowledged that "writing about Satoshi Nakamoto . . . is a treacherous exercise." Both articles mentioned a trust, domiciled in the Seychelles, that supposedly held 1.1 million bitcoins and belonged to Wright and Kleiman.

In response to the *Wired* and Gizmodo bombshells, CSI Reddit crowdsourced reasons to be doubtful. A Bitcoin developer named Greg Maxwell showed that Wright's PGP key had likely been created using software that didn't exist at the time of its supposed creation. Motherboard's Sarah Jeong showed how a public directory of PGP keys hosted at MIT, which suggested that Wright's key had been created prior to 2008, could easily have been manipulated.

Even *Wired,* before publishing its article, had noticed discrepancies. "Most inexplicably of all," the magazine added almost as an afterthought, each of the three blog posts that were among the strongest evidence of Wright's involvement had been edited after the fact—including at least one of them after 2013—to add references to what seemed to be Bitcoin.

SGI, vendor of Wright's supposed supercomputer, told ZDNET that "Cloudcroft has never been an SGI customer and SGI has no relationship with Cloudcroft CEO Craig Steven Wright." Charles Sturt University, grantor of one of Wright's claimed PhDs, told *Forbes* that while Wright had earned three master's degrees from the university, it had never awarded him a doctorate. Bitcoiners noted that Wright's Man of Mystery self-presentation was antithetical to Nakamoto's low-drama personality and speculated whether Wright himself had sent the outing emails to reporters.

And just as the *Wired* and Gizmodo articles were appearing on the internet, federal police acting on behalf of the Australian Taxation Office, which had been auditing several of Wright's companies for years, executed raids on his home in the northern Sydney suburb of Gordon and his offices in nearby North Ryde and carted away trunks of material. Craig Wright, meanwhile, had already boarded a plane to Manila, and a few days later he flew to London.

Wired, three days after its original article, posted a second: "New Clues Suggest Craig Wright, Suspected Bitcoin Creator, May Be a Hoaxer." Gizmodo also backpedaled: "The Mystery of Craig Wright and Bitcoin Isn't Solved Yet."

Juola & Associates soon added Craig Wright to its batch of Nakamoto candidates and reran its stylometry tests. Hal Finney remained the closest match to Nakamoto.

I thought that this would be the last we'd hear of Craig Wright.

The Satoshi Checklist

In the summer of 2022, after my return from visiting J. K. Rowling-identifier Patrick Juola at his lab in Pittsburgh, I tacked, on a gray Homasote board leaning against my office wall, a spreadsheet of the hundred-plus candidates who'd ever been proposed as Satoshi Nakamoto. There were the usual suspects, most of them cypherpunks. There were more obscure names from adjacent fields like math, cryptography, and economics. Some of the people were programmers involved with the Bitcoin software project. Others were creators of newer cryptocurrencies. Many were just Famous Smart People: Bill Gates. Steve Jobs. John Nash, the mathematician portrayed in *A Beautiful Mind*. For each candidate, I listed arguments for and against. I was in the thick of what excited me about reporting, trying to learn something someone didn't want you to know. "A good puzzle, it's a fair thing," Ernö Rubik, of Cube renown, said once. "Nobody is lying, it's very clear, and the problem depends just on you." I wasn't sure the Nakamoto mystery qualified, but it was satisfying to be consumed by the project.

Above the spreadsheet, I taped a checklist, a column of criteria any plausible Nakamoto candidate would need to meet:

Software tools

Coding quirks

Age

Geography

Schedule

Use of English

Nationality

Prose style

Politics

Life circumstances (*How had Nakamoto found the time to launch Bitcoin? Why had he left the project when he did?*)

Résumé (*"I'm not a lawyer."*)

Emotional range (*humble, confident, testy, appreciative*)

Motivation to create Bitcoin

Rationale, and the foresight and skill, to create a bulletproof pseudonym (*Who would bother wiping a crime scene clean before it was a crime scene? Who was already that good at privacy in 2008?*)

Monkish capacity to renounce a fortune

The checklist assumed that Nakamoto, while epically tight-lipped, hadn't taken more elaborate steps to construct a fictional persona. But some Nakamoto-isms were more negotiable than others. C++ coding chops were something a person either had or didn't. But traces of Commonwealth English would be one of the easier things to fake, time stamps could be manipulated, and political orientation could be affected. While Nakamoto had in one instance used the libertarian phrasing "We can . . . gain a new territory of freedom," in another he'd referred to how Bitcoin would be "very attractive to the libertarian viewpoint," which sounded more detached.

On another wall, I assembled a collage.

Most stories I'd reported on came with built-in vividness or intimacy. In Guantanamo Bay, I could home in on the humble personal effects of a juvenile detainee: laceless running shoes, Mennen Speed

Stick. In a birthday-party clown's San Francisco apartment, I'd watched as he stood before a bathroom mirror in boxer shorts and applied rouge. In Poland, I'd spent a week with a railway worker—who'd awoken from a coma after fifteen years, having missed the end of Communism—and his devoted wife.

The intangibility of Bitcoin made it difficult to fix in your mind. Attempts to depict crypto often resorted to scrawled, *A Beautiful Mind*–style numbers floating toward the camera. In Miami, I'd strolled through a ten-thousand-square-foot expo hall, where a sign announced "the largest Bitcoin art gallery in history." It was hosting an exhibition titled *Bitcoin Renaissance*: "In 1494, the invention of double-entry accounting ushered in a new era of human prosperity and a golden age of artistic expression followed shortly after. Since 2008, the invention of Bitcoin has inaugurated the latest chapter of human flourishing."

This wasn't art you needed to furrow your brow to interpret. There were creative renderings of Bitcoin's ₿ symbol, public-key addresses, the white paper, popular slogans like "JUST HODL IT" (*hodling* was Bitcoinspeak for "holding," or buying bitcoin for the long term), Bitcoin celebrities like El Salvadoran president Nayib Bukele, and laser eyes, a popular meme for Bitcoiners to show their tribal allegiance. Someone had recast Vincent Van Gogh's *The Starry Night* with ₿s in place of stars. Someone had published an illustrated children's book: *Rhyming Bitcoin*. A lot of the images, in keeping with the tribal aggrievement of Bitcoiners, were combative: Jamie Dimon's face melting, a ₿ crossing swords with a $, a group of old white guys around a Monopoly board resting on the backs of multiracial slaves ("False Profits"), giant brass knuckles with a ₿ in the middle and the words "Fiat Facelifter," a leaderboard of "failed fiat currencies" (the Bolivar, the Papiermark) next to a leaderboard of "sound money alternatives" (bitcoin, gold, silver).

I'd been curious to see how Nakamoto, the faceless nonleader of Bitcoin's centerless utopia, would be visually translated. By now, the religious aspects of Bitcoin culture were barely latent. The white paper was scripture. The evangelizing Bitcoiners were the saved, everyone else the doomed. Satoshi, selfless hodler of an obscene fortune, was their noninterventionist God.

Graven images of him, such as a bobblehead doll sold on Amazon in 2016, had skewed generically Asian. In Miami, some artists had resorted to a faceless hooded figure, others to Guy Fawkes masks. Dorian Nakamoto's face was all over the place: in a pointillist painting, in place of a president on a dollar-esque "Bitcoin Banknote," on a Lucite-cased trading card. (Another of the cards featured Hal Finney.) A few years after *Newsweek*'s ill-begotten exposé, Dorian had started attending Bitcoin conferences, where he was embraced as a cult figure. The same community that had savagely denounced Leah Goodman for naming him as Satoshi Nakamoto now happily entertained the use of his image as a stand-in.

I understood why Bitcoin art was so literal. I shared the urge to make material the ethereal. The compulsion to hang pictures of Bitcoin paraphernalia felt akin to the impulse to substantiate Nakamoto by identifying him.

My office moodboard consisted of Vitamin D–deficient faces and strange-looking devices and puzzling actions. When I liked, I could swivel my chair and look at the images and be grounded for a moment. There were Casascius coins, metal tokens that were each embedded with a private key and bitcoin address and protected by a tamperproof hologram sticker. A mining rig. A hardware wallet. The Welsh landfill with the 8,000-bitcoin hard drive somewhere within. Men wearing Daft Punk helmets. Other men wearing face masks with digital avatars projected on them. A mountainous graph of Bitcoin's seismic price history.

The first time my wife saw all this—the spreadsheet, the checklist, the collage—she smiled. Really, it was a smirk.

"Are you going to add any string?" she asked.

As I reached out to sources past and hoped-for, I encountered a new resistance. Some of it was the internet polarization that had taken hold since the first time I wrote about Bitcoin. When I messaged Robert Hettinga, a voluble cypherpunk in Anguilla who'd long been keen on digital cash, he blocked me on Twitter and bragged to his 942 followers that ten years earlier "I'da given my left nut" to talk to a journalist, but now he'd go "full ranting UltraMAGA" on a writer for "libtard shit-shows."

More of the friction had to do with the taboo around Satoshi Nakamoto. There had always been the faction hostile to inquiry about his identity. *He has made a valuable contribution, so his wishes should be honored. What matters is not the person but the idea, the code.* As a legend accreted around Nakamoto, "the holy founder of this world-changing technology," in Gavin Andresen's words, simple questions about who he might be became triggering to Bitcoiners. And the Dorian Nakamoto outing curdled the whole enterprise. "Doxing," if you inhabited the Bitcoin bubble, now applied even to a newsworthy person's name. The editors of *Reason* ("Free Minds and Free Markets"), disgusted by the "unseemly ring of wide-eyed scribblers" who'd looked into Bitcoin's authorship, published an article headlined "Leave Satoshi Alone!" When I tried to talk to Peter McCormack, a Bitcoin-focused podcaster in England who on LinkedIn described himself as a "full time journalist," he sniffed: "I don't like stories which delve into the origins if they are looking who Satoshi might be, he chose to remain anonymous and I think that needs respecting."

The protective cordon seemed absurd to me. Nakamoto had plunked his gizmo in the public square. It was reasonable to inquire who'd put it there and why. I felt kinship with a Redditor who, reacting to the privacy cultists when Skye Grey came out with his Nick Szabo theory, wrote: "All the people saying they don't care who Satoshi is and never want to know: I admire the pride you take in having no curiosity, but I don't understand you at all. It's one of the last real mysteries left on the internet, and it's interesting as hell. Teach me your zen-like powers of apathy, I want to apply them to my love of cookies and cake."

When I spoke with Bill Dodd, a vandyked software manager in Mobile, Alabama, who'd applied machine learning to his own Nakamoto quest, he asked: "Where do you come down on the moral hazard of doxing a guy who clearly wants to be left alone?"

I glimpsed a scolding on the horizon, but Bill turned out to be a sweet guy with a very human mix of curiosity and empathy.

It would depend on who Nakamoto turned out to be, I said.

"Yeah, same," said Bill, who'd trained a neural network on the Metzdowd archive. "I started with just sort of wanting to know, and I didn't spend a ton of time. . . . I just kind of wanted to know, because it was formative." He'd initially been skeptical about Bitcoin, and "as a latecomer to it, I found it fascinating that ten years in, this mystery still persisted. And I think mystery is sometimes difficult to resist. I go back and forth too. On the one hand, you have something that has become such a large part of the zeitgeist that it almost feels like an incomplete story with the name not being known to people. And on the flip side, I wouldn't necessarily want the CNN vans showing up, when I'm in my fifties or sixties and I'm retired, at my retirement house in London or wherever. So I get it, I get both sides."

The sensitivity—as well as a certain amount of subject fatigue among Bitcoiners after years of botched Nakamoto outings—shaped how I approached people. Depending on who it was, I started sometimes to substitute the high-minded-sounding "Bitcoin's origins," when I first described the subject of my investigation, for the more potentially provocative "Satoshi's identity."

I thought about what circumstances might inhibit me from naming Nakamoto. Maybe the answer would be uninteresting. Would it matter to know that he was this person no one had ever heard of rather than that person no one had ever heard of? "I wish Satoshi were still around," Zooko Wilcox, a cypherpunk who'd worked at DigiCash, later started a more private cryptocurrency named Zcash, and was himself a Nakamoto candidate, wrote in 2017, "so we could see how ignorant and wrong and banal he is, just like the rest of us."

An Imperfect Human Being

Five months after Craig Wright was, and then wasn't, revealed to be Satoshi Nakamoto, on Monday, May 2, 2016, the Australian was back in my news feed. It now appeared that he was Nakamoto after all. This time the news came in an 8 a.m. blitz with scoops about Wright's claims from *The Economist* and the BBC, which announced: "Mr. Wright has provided technical proof to back up his claim using coins known to be owned by Bitcoin's creator. Prominent members of the Bitcoin community and its core development teams say they have confirmed his claims." One of these was Jon Matonis, a cofounder of the Bitcoin Foundation, a nonprofit formed to nurture Bitcoin's growth, who blogged about "How I Met Satoshi," told the BBC that he was "100 per cent convinced" that Wright was Nakamoto, and added that the invention of Bitcoin was "on the level of the Gutenberg printing press." But the person who gave Wright's claims the greatest credibility was Gavin Andresen, Bitcoin's former lead developer, who blogged, "I believe Craig Steven Wright is the person who invented Bitcoin": "We love to create heroes—but also seem to love hating them if they don't live up to some unattainable ideal. It would be better if Satoshi Nakamoto was the codename for an NSA project, or an artificial intelligence sent from the future to advance our primitive money. He is not, he is an imperfect human being just like the rest of us. I hope he manages to mostly ignore the storm that his announcement will create, and keep doing what he loves—learning and research and innovating."

Gavin also described how, a month earlier, he had been convinced.

Gavin's Favorite Number

In a hotel business suite one floor below a cobbled street in central London, a clutch of tense men in expensive suits hovered nervously. Gavin, bleary with jet lag, struggled to focus. Having caught a red-eye in Boston the night before, he'd slept poorly on the plane and, after arriving at the Covent Garden Hotel around 11 a.m., had managed to get just two hours of sleep before hearing a knock on the door. He had come to watch Craig Wright prove that he was Satoshi Nakamoto.

Gavin was an obvious choice to endorse Wright's claims. MIT's *Technology Review* had called him "the man who really built Bitcoin." He had made enough money from his early Bitcoin activity that he could retire if he wanted. He was now the chief scientist of the Bitcoin Foundation. And having had more direct interaction with Nakamoto than almost anyone, he was an ideal person to evaluate whether someone was or wasn't Bitcoin's inventor.

Gavin had taken some persuading even to get on a plane. He'd been contacted so many times by people claiming they were Nakamoto that he was jaded. But Jon Matonis had told Gavin that he should pay attention to Wright. And Gavin had emailed with Wright prior to coming here and found his voice to have a familiar ring. He sounded like the person Gavin had worked with for months, and he also impressed Gavin with his grasp of Bitcoin. Gavin became increasingly confident that Wright might be Nakamoto.

The beauty of public-key cryptography, though, was that Gavin didn't have to trust Wright. In theory, Satoshi Nakamoto would be able to provide cryptographic proof of his identity. The successful miner of any block automatically received a Bitcoin reward at a Bitcoin address presupplied by the miner, and since there were certain early blocks known to have been mined by Nakamoto, only he would be able to demonstrate possession of the private keys to those addresses (assuming the keys hadn't been stolen or given away). Wright had already performed this proof for Matonis, according to Matonis, and in the coming month he would also perform some version of it for the journalists taking part in the news rollout, but Gavin was by far his most important audience.

Before leaving for London, Gavin told Wright he wanted to see "some or all of the following": the phrases "so it goes" (a quote from Kurt Vonnegut, one of Gavin's favorite authors) and "April 7, 2016" (the date of the London meeting), each signed with Nakamoto's private PGP key; at least one message signed using a private key associated with a Bitcoin block mined by Nakamoto; and unpublished emails or private forum messages exchanged between Gavin and Nakamoto in 2010.

When Wright came into the hotel business suite, Gavin was struck by how well dressed he was. Wright was partial to fancy suits and watches. His hair was carefully styled. "He seemed like a person who was not poor, was not lower class," Gavin said later. Wright resolved some of Gavin's questions. Why had he disappeared in 2010? He was going through a divorce. Why had he made this or that design decision when creating Bitcoin?

Wright told Gavin the same thing that Gizmodo had reported: Satoshi Nakamoto wasn't just him. It also included Dave Kleiman and an unnamed third person who'd helped with the cryptography. As Wright spoke of Kleiman, he appeared to be on the verge of tears.

Then Wright flipped open his laptop and showed Gavin various Bitcoin addresses he said were his. Gavin asked Wright about the reported trust in the Seychelles and about what had happened to all the bitcoins he'd mined. Wright talked about his companies' fight for survival and about his supercomputer. Gavin was sleep-deprived and found it hard to follow everything Wright said.

Late in the afternoon, using software on his own laptop, Wright signed a message Gavin had proposed—"Gavin's favorite number is 11"—followed by "CSW," using a private key from a known Nakamoto-mined block.

"At that point," according to a later account, "it seemed to some of those in the room that Andresen's body language changed; he seemed slightly awed by the situation."

Then, from his own bag, Gavin pulled his personal laptop and a new, factory-sealed USB drive, which he began to unwrap. Wright had convinced him, Gavin said, but he wanted to be able to tell others that he had independently verified the signing on his own devices. He had informed Wright in advance that he'd be bringing these to their meeting, but Wright suddenly bristled. Hadn't he just signed a message to Gavin proving he was Satoshi? Wright stood and began pacing, clearly agitated. Finally, he sat down in a chair in a corner. "Maybe you and I could get to know each other better," he said. Wright didn't mean now. He meant: over some indeterminate period of time, he and Gavin could exchange more emails, and Wright could send him more messages signed with Nakamoto's keys.

Gavin was amenable to the suggestion, but Stefan Matthews and Robert MacGregor, the hovering, smartly dressed businessmen, spoke up. They represented a company called nCrypt, which was somehow connected with Wright. What was Wright doing? He'd already done the hard part. He only needed to repeat it on Gavin's laptop. "Look, Craig, you've just been alone for way too long," MacGregor would recall saying. "Gavin has dedicated a huge chunk of his life to what you invented. I think he has the right to see this. He is the friend you don't have: Stefan and I can't fill that role for you; Ramona [Wright's wife] can't. This is someone who really understands what you have been trying to do."

Wright phoned Ramona, who told him: "Do it."

Wright was still hesitant.

"So I'm listening to all this," Stefan Matthews would tell me later, "and I said, 'Hey guys, let's try to find a solution if we can.'"

Just before 6 p.m., MacGregor called his assistant and instructed her to bring a new, factory-sealed laptop to the hotel. She bought an IBM ThinkPad at Curry's, an electronics store at Oxford Circus, and hurried with it to Covent Garden. There were further delays as the new computer was unpacked and booted up. It then took some time for Wright to configure the machine, log onto the hotel Wi-Fi, and download a Bitcoin-wallet app called Electrum, which had a feature allowing anyone to demonstrate control of a private key by typing a message and digitally signing it.

The process ran longer than Gavin expected. His exhaustion was catching up with him.

In a box on the screen labeled "Message," Wright typed the same message he'd typed earlier: "Gavin's favorite number is 11." In a box labeled "Address," Wright entered the public Bitcoin address (42 characters) corresponding to the private key he'd used to sign the message on his own machine. In a box labeled "Signature," he typed the eighty-seven-character string of letters and numbers, unique to that specific message as signed by that specific private key, which the signing process on his machine had produced.

Finally, Wright pressed a button labeled "Verify."

It didn't verify. There was an excruciating pause until Gavin realized that Wright was leaving off "CSW," which had ended the earlier message, from the message signature he was trying to verify now. When Wright corrected this, it read: "Signature verified."

Wright stood, his eyes teary, and shook Gavin's hand. Gavin thanked him for his contribution to the world. Gavin was satisfied that he had met Satoshi Nakamoto. Wright had the same barbed personality he'd come to know working together on Bitcoin and had convincingly signed and verified a message using a known Nakamoto key.

The next morning, Wright, Matthews, and MacGregor joined Gavin for a full English breakfast at the hotel restaurant. Wright gave

Gavin a book about an eighteenth-century Japanese merchant and philosopher named Tominaga Nakamoto, who he said had inspired his pseudonym. Then Gavin returned to Massachusetts and waited, prepared to play his part in the grand unveiling of Wright one month later.

A Little Bit of Controversy for Fun

When Jean-Paul Sartre was awarded the Nobel Prize in Literature, he declined it in a letter to the Swedish Academy. "If I sign myself Jean-Paul Sartre," he explained in October 1964, "it is not the same thing as if I sign myself Jean-Paul Sartre, Nobel Prize-winner." He meant that his reputation should stand on its own, not piggyback on the prestige of an institution.

Half a century later, Craig Steven Wright cast his own situation in a comparable Existentialist vein. In a blog post to accompany his choreographed debut as Satoshi Nakamoto, he recounted Sartre's principled refusal of the Nobel and suggested that he, too, sought no validation from others. "If you put me up for an award"—no one had put him up for an award—"I will never accept the money that is associated with it. . . . If I sign Craig Wright, it is not the same as if I sign Craig Wright, Satoshi." He added cryptically, "Satoshi is dead. But this is only the beginning."

Finally, and in seeming contradiction of everything he'd just written, Wright offered a long explication of how cryptographic signing worked, followed by what purported to be a digitally signed copy of the Sartre quotation using the private key to a known Nakamoto-mined block, Block 9.

Within a few hours, everything started to fall apart.

Gavin Andresen, who was in New York City for the Consensus

2016 blockchain conference, had been expecting a brief, straightforward demonstration that Wright was Satoshi Nakamoto, a public signing of a message with one of Nakamoto's private keys. Instead, Wright had written "wacky" "gobbledygook" that was "incredibly technical and hard to follow."

Online, people who studied Wright's Sartre post discovered a bigger problem. A Redditor named JoukeH found, simply by copy-pasting Wright's supposed Nakamoto-signed Sartre quote into a Google search box, that the signature had been lifted from a 2009 transaction publicly available on the blockchain. "It would be like if I was trying to prove that I was George Washington," Bitcoin developer Peter Todd said, "and to do that provided a photocopy of the Constitution and said, 'Look, I have George Washington's signature.'"

Gavin was at the Times Square Marriott Marquis that morning to appear on a panel about the scaling controversy, which was still raging in Bitcoinland. But the topic quickly shifted to his endorsement of Wright and to criticism of Wright's blog post. Gavin explained why he was convinced that Wright was Nakamoto but cautioned the audience that he would "draw the line"—he made a blade of his hand and carved said line in the air—at revealing the content of his discussions with Wright, who wanted "privacy."

Vitalik Buterin, Ethereum's anti-Satoshi (founder, patron saint, and unofficial leader, with an unapologetically public persona), was sitting next to Gavin on the stage. "Just so there's a little bit of controversy for fun," Buterin said, before the moderator could ask another question, "I'll explain why I think he's probably not Satoshi." Wright could easily have provided *public* cryptographic proof if he had a Nakamoto-controlled private key, Buterin continued. "Signaling theory says if you have a good way of proving something and a noisy way of proving something, and you choose the noisy way, then that means chances are that's because you couldn't do the good way in the first place." As Buterin basked in laughter and applause, Gavin looked uncomfortable, a smile frozen on his face.

"I was not hacked," Gavin assured the crowd.

As the day went on, security expert Robert Graham provided a lengthy technical breakdown of "how Craig Wright's deception worked." Dan Kaminsky told his readers that "scammers always have more to say, but all that matters now is math." He also tweeted: "I understand that Satoshi is basically Moby Dick for Tech Reporters, but the identity of Bitcoin's absentee creator is not relevant." Even Electrum, maker of the wallet Wright had ostensibly downloaded onto the factory-fresh computer during the proof session for Gavin, released a statement saying that on the date in question no copies of the wallet had been downloaded from its site to a U.K. IP address. "Craig Wright really wants you to think he invented Bitcoin. Don't believe him," read one headline. Kaminsky's was: "The Cryptographically Provable Con Man."

Once again, a media outlet called on Juola & Associates for its stylometry expertise. This time, the caller was the *International Business Times,* incidentally owned by the same company as *Newsweek.* Juola's John Noecker deemed Wright an unlikely Nakamoto and said Hal Finney remained his top candidate.

Wright, meanwhile, was privately reassuring Gavin that he'd "f'd up" and "loaded the wrong post." He didn't explain why another post with a borrowed signature would even exist. Wright said he'd be putting up the correct one "shortly."

"Today, pretty please," Gavin replied the next day, when still no new post had appeared. "I'm starting to doubt myself and imagining clever ways you could have tricked me."

nCrypt's Stefan Matthews, trying to salvage what had become a farce, told Gavin that Wright would soon make several corrections to the Sartre post. Matthews gingerly asked whether Gavin would "entertain" sending a tiny sum of bitcoin to a Nakamoto address from Block 9; Wright would then send it back, proving he held the private key associated with the address. Wright was going to do the same with Jon Matonis and BBC reporter Rory Cellan-Jones. Gavin agreed and sent 0.11 BTC, worth $50 at the time.

The next day, there was a further delay. Wright's handlers revealed that Wright had apparently set up another trust, possibly in the Seychelles, possibly in Singapore, which he hadn't previously mentioned even to them, and which held the private keys, and that Wright, who had been unable to obtain them for various legal reasons, had faked them. Robert MacGregor said they now had "verbal consent" from the trustee to "move coin" and were just awaiting "written consent." Finally, on Wednesday, Wright seemed ready. "Extraordinary claims require extraordinary proof," his blog declared.

The BBC's Cellan-Jones and his crew set up a camera aimed at a computer screen that showed a green arrow pointing at the Nakamoto Block 9 address and the bitcoin Cellan-Jones had sent to it. As soon as Cellan-Jones received his bitcoin back from the address, the graphic would change, with a red arrow pointing to the new balance, and the BBC would get its TV moment.

Hours passed.

Stefan Matthews later described to me what had happened.

A Series of Screams

That morning, Stefan had gone to Wright's house to make sure Wright sent the coins, but when he got there, Ramona said: "We've got a problem. He doesn't want to do it."

Stefan then spoke with Wright directly. "He said, 'You know, I've always said I don't want to do this.'"

"I don't care what you've said, really, now," Stefan said. "I've got a situation I've got to manage. You've got a blog post that says you're going to do this. The whole fucking world thinks you're going to do this. It's almost like you're sitting at a poker table, and you're pot-committed."

Wright asked Ramona to make him a cup of tea, he and Stefan spoke for another minute, then Stefan started fiddling with his cellphone, and Wright got up and left the room. When Ramona returned, she asked where Craig was. Stefan said he'd assumed Craig was with her. Ramona left the room again.

"Then there's this fucking unbelievable scream," Stefan recalled. "It wasn't one scream. It was like a series of screams."

Ramona was at the top of the staircase, and "she was hysterical." Stefan hurried upstairs. "She pushed me into the bathroom, and the shower was running, and he was lying unconscious in the shower," most of his body outside it but his head and shoulders draped into it under the spray. Stefan pulled Wright out of the shower and a bathrobe off the back of the door. Wright had cuts on both sides of his neck, and Stefan wrapped the robe around it.

Gavin received an email from MacGregor: "All Stop. Craig has just tried to injure himself and is bleeding badly in the washroom. . . . Ambulance is on its way."

Rory Cellan-Jones received a similar message. At that point, he says, he was called into a high-level meeting at the BBC, which was taking the latest developments "very, very seriously," and was told by a senior executive to back off of the story: they had a "duty of care."

At Wright's home, a paramedic told Stefan to get away from the body. Another told him to turn off the shower and leave. In the next room, two police officers interviewed him. "Probably an hour later they take him out on a fuckin' stretcher," Stefan said. "The front street looked like a murder zone."

Despite the injury, Wright stayed in the hospital only one night. The next day he met a writer for coffee, and beforehand he emailed the writer a link to an article headlined "UK Law Enforcement Sources Hint at Impending Craig Wright Arrest." It suggested that Bitcoin's creator might be criminally liable for other people's Bitcoin-related crimes. Over coffee, Wright justified his recent actions by saying that if he'd gone through with the proof, he'd end up in jail, and "they destroy me and my family."

The link Wright had sent appeared to lead to SiliconANGLE, an industry news outlet, but Bitcoiners noticed that it was a copycat site, SilliconANGLE, with an extra "l." The site had only recently been registered. The article had appeared nowhere else. "I've never discussed it with Craig," Stefan said, when I asked him about it later.

The same day, Wright wrote privately to Gavin: "At no point did I lie to you nor deceive you, but it is better that I am a hoaxer." Better, he meant, that people see him that way than that he prove himself to be Satoshi Nakamoto. Publicly, he posted what sounded like a parting statement:

"I'm sorry. I believed I could do this. I believed that I could put the years of anonymity and hiding behind me. But, as the events of this week unfolded and I prepared to publish the proof of access to the earliest keys, I broke. I do not have the courage. I cannot. . . . I know now that I am not strong enough for this. I know that this weakness will cause great damage to those that have supported me, and particularly to Jon Matonis and Gavin Andresen. I can only hope that their honor and credibility are not irreparably tainted by my actions. They were not deceived, but I know that the world will never believe that now. I can only say I'm sorry.

And goodbye."

More of a Risk Than a Boon

At first, people had given Gavin the benefit of the doubt. Dan Kaminsky privately wrote to him, pointing to the obviously fraudulent signature in Wright's Sartre post and asking why Gavin would lend his good name to Wright's notion that "a public key operation could should or must remain private." The idea was nonsensical on its face: the entire premise of public key cryptography was that you could publicly demonstrate ownership of a public key (and by extension a bitcoin address formed from that public key) by using the matching private key to create a digital signature, without showing the private key to anyone.

"Yeah, what the heck?" Gavin wrote back. ". . . It was a mistake to agree to publish my post before I saw his—I assumed his post would simply be a signed message anybody could easily verify. And it was probably a mistake to even start to play the Find Satoshi game, but I DO feel grateful to Satoshi."

Emin Gün Sirer, a computer scientist at Cornell, wondered in an email to Gavin whether Wright might have used a particular kind of blockchain sleight of hand. It was "possible I was tricked," Gavin replied, but he ruled out the method suggested by Sirer, allowing instead that "a hijack of the wifi used to download Electrum is possible."

Soon, the Bitcoin community's tone toward Gavin became less

charitable. For true believers, who had more faith in code than people, there had been an uncomfortable and unnecessary degree of human trust and intuition woven through Wright's proof process. Robert MacGregor believed Wright was Nakamoto because Stefan Matthews had told him that Wright had showed him the white paper prior to Bitcoin's launch. Jon Matonis had asked Gavin to come to London as a favor to him, writing, "I've never asked you for anything before." Gavin had been convinced to come to London by an email that "sounded like" the Satoshi Nakamoto he'd corresponded with and by a couple of Wright's academic papers, which similarly "matched his academic, math-heavy voice." The media outlets taking part in Wright's official rollout had relied on Gavin's opinion because of his stature and reputation.

Some people began to question Gavin's motives. In the Bitcoin scaling wars, Gavin was aligned with the Big Blockers and Mike Hearn and, after Hearn's Bitcoin XT failed to catch on, had started pushing an alternative larger-block version called Bitcoin Classic. Some people thought Satoshi Nakamoto alone, were he to return, had the moral authority to resolve the ongoing block-size conflict. And Wright, who was claiming to be Nakamoto, happened to be on Gavin's side of the debate.

There was also a deeper, long-standing unease about Gavin's place in the Bitcoin world. He'd been the project's de facto leader, but wasn't Bitcoin supposed to be leaderless? Other developers had felt, as Gavin became the guy in a suit sipping oatmeal stout at the Beverly Hills Hotel after talking Bitcoin at the Milken Institute Global Conference, that his ego had run amok. They were disturbed when, at a block-size summit in London in 2015, he said: "I may just have to throw my weight around and say, 'This is the way it's going to be. And if you don't like it, find another project.'"

On the morning when Gavin endorsed Wright as Nakamoto, Bitcoin's core developers had temporarily revoked his access to the project's source code, citing the possibility that he'd been hacked. When he continued to stand by Wright, they made the change permanent. Some people felt the developers were being opportunistic, using a pretext to eliminate a foe with a rival vision for Bitcoin. But in the past Gavin had said that if Nakamoto ever came back, he'd happily return the project's alert key to him. So if Gavin truly believed Wright was Nakamoto, the core developers reasoned, then the project was at risk of being handed to someone who might be a con man. And if Gavin believed that Wright was Nakamoto, argued Bitcoin core developer Peter Todd, he was also "untrustworthy and/or incompetent."

Wladimir van der Laan, who'd succeeded Gavin as lead Bitcoin developer, later said: "He had become more of a risk to the project than a boon."

Scott and Stuart

Once I was back on the Nakamoto case in 2022, I'd developed a habit, every Sunday morning, of conducting a *Where's Waldo*–style search of *The New York Times* for a tiny classified ad printed in the newspaper's main section.

It had been published once a week, almost without fail, since October 1991, when a small, baffling announcement appeared in a corner of page 48 of the national edition, past the front-page coverage of Clarence Thomas's Supreme Court confirmation hearings and before the full-page ad for Michael Bolton's Time, Love & Tenderness Tour. It announced the debut of something called "TimeLink" and featured a nonsensical string of sixty-four numbers and letters, followed by "11:45 a.m. Oct 10 91." The ad had been placed by Stuart Haber and Scott Stornetta, who were both on my spreadsheet of Satoshi Nakamoto candidates (#10).

Three decades later, with the collapse of the classified-ads business, the ad was a lot lonelier. I imagined it was the longest-running classified in the paper. The ad looked like gibberish and felt like a sub rosa signal to a secret society, but it was a solution to a serious problem facing a world that was rapidly moving online in the early 1990s: How could you know that something on the internet was genuine?

Long before there were computers, the world had needed to deal with questions about documents: Exactly when was that old tycoon's will altered, reassigning his fortune from his children to his nurse? A regular person could send herself a sealed letter and later use the postmark to establish that the envelope's contents had existed on a certain date.

In the realms of science and invention, patents, fortunes, and reputations hinged on proving that you had an idea first. For centuries, scientists established priority with the help of cryptography. After Robert Hooke, a rival of Isaac Newton's, discovered his law of elasticity in 1660, he waited nearly twenty years to publish anything about it and did so as an anagram. This had the advantage of allowing him to conceal the discovery while he took advantage of it—the insight led to Hooke's creation of the hairspring, which was used in the first pocket watches—and also letting him assert credit for it later by revealing what the anagram stood for, a Latin phrase summing up the law.

Later, it became customary for scientists to keep bound laboratory notebooks that had numbered pages and followed a set of rules. A scientist would write in ink, fill each page (not leaving any large blank spaces, and not changing ink color within a page), initial and date each page in ink, and have the page also initialed and dated in ink by a witness, typically the head of the lab. In this way, if the scientist ever ended up in court over a discovery, she'd have a persuasive document to help make her case that something had happened exactly when she said it had happened.

It was just such a situation that first grabbed Scott Stornetta's attention. In 1989, when Scott, with a freshly minted PhD in physics from Stanford, was a young researcher at the Palo Alto Research Center, which at the time was Xerox Corporation's Silicon Valley think tank, he read about a case involving Thereza Imanishi-Kari, a pathology researcher at MIT. She had been accused of scientific misconduct over a paper on immunology she had coauthored and published in the journal *Cell*. Another researcher in her lab had accused her of fudging data. Because the research was federally funded, Congress got involved, and a forensic analysis of her notebooks by the Secret Service found that at least one-third of a crucial notebook presented evidence that was out of sequence with the dates it had been produced.

Imanishi-Kari was later fully exonerated, and the Secret Service analysis shown to have been flawed, but at the time her situation put a bug in Scott's mind. In an increasingly digital world, when there wouldn't be paper and ink to analyze, this kind of thing was only going to get worse and more common. It was easy to alter digital content and hard to detect the alteration. Online, there was no precise equivalent of a seal that would betray any attempt to tamper with it. When Scott moved across the country to work for Bellcore in New Jersey, he still had this problem on his mind. "I was convinced that without the integrity of the digital data itself, we'd come first to doubt history, and then doubt the ability to maintain the superstructure of our society. It really was an obsession."

There was another researcher at Bellcore, Stuart Haber, with whom Scott had hit it off while interviewing for the position, and who he thought might be interested in working on the problem with him. They weren't an obvious match. Scott was a Mormon and a libertarian with the impracticality of the theoretical physicist that he was by training. Stuart was a Queens-raised liberal who'd worked as a street juggler while in college at Harvard, as part of a three-person troupe at Great Adventure Amusement Park in New Jersey, where he wore full clown makeup, and as part of a two-man act in Paris. There he met his future wife, also an American juggler.

Eventually, Stuart got a PhD in computer science, just when public-key cryptography was dawning, and became enthralled by the math of secret codes. He'd been at Bellcore for around two years when Scott arrived. Scott had an inkling that cryptography might have a role in ensuring the integrity of digital records, and he sought Stuart out.

Their idea was to create the digital equivalent of a notary public, a way to stamp a document with proof of when it had been created and of its authenticity, and to do so without a trusted central authority. How could a user of the system be certain that the notary public wasn't susceptible to corruption or manipulation? After frowning at a screen for several weeks, Stuart was ready to give up. "I don't think there's a way to prove it," he told Scott, "but I'd like to get a publication out of it. Let's write a proof that you *can't* remove trust from the system."

One night soon after, Scott and his wife, Marcia, went out for dinner near their home in suburban New Jersey. As they waited for a table, an idea came to him. The reason trust couldn't be removed from the system, he and Stuart had realized, was that to do so would require the collusion of everyone in the world. Unless everyone in the world maintained a copy of a particular record, how could anyone without it know that it hadn't been changed? And that's how it hit him, in line at the Friendly's in Morristown: Yes! Exactly! Make everyone in the world collude! And so the attempt to prove that it couldn't be done had led to a way that it *could* be done. "It felt like turning a bag inside out," Scott said later. At the time, Scott turned to Marcia. "I think I have figured out something important," he said. "And I am the only one in the world who knows it."

The idea had two parts. One was technical, a cryptographic method of irreversibly linking documents together, making it impossible to tamper with one without changing every document that came after it in the chain. The other was social: have the document chain witnessed broadly, in order to create a shared collective reality immune to manipulation by individual parties. There was also a set of incentives. Everyone in the system would want to ensure its integrity because the integrity of their own documents depended on it.

The second idea proved unworkable at the time. Data storage was too expensive, and dial-up internet service too slow, to expect clients to maintain full copies of the records of everyone else in the network. But Scott and Stuart came up with a clever alternative. A colleague suggested they use Merkle trees, a cryptographic data structure that could take a set of documents, each having its own mathematical fingerprint, and boil them down to a single value that served as a kind of fingerprint of fingerprints. Every client who used the service would receive a copy of the sixty-four-character fingerprint representing the collection of documents time-stamped in the past week. They also created a second layer of protection. "We wanted to enable worldwide consensus on what those values were," Stuart says. Thus was born their weekly classified in the *Times*, featuring the latest fingerprint. At first Bellcore ran the service, but Scott and Stuart later set up their own company, Surety Technologies. Clients would come to include a pharmaceutical firm seeking to protect its intellectual property and a police department looking to document the chain of custody of its evidence. The newspaper ad was, as Scott put it, "an unassailable repository, widely witnessed." For $100 a week, it created a virtually uncrackable defense. Scott would call his contact at the paper every seven days and read out the numbers. The contact would read them back to him. "We had a routine down."

Stuart and Scott had invented the world's first blockchain. Though they weren't cypherpunks, they were sympathetic to the group's digital-privacy concerns, and Stuart sent an announcement of the time-stamping service to the cypherpunks list. Cypherpunks cofounder Tim May touted the importance of their work, and in the Bitcoin white paper three of the eight citations were to papers cowritten by Stuart and Scott. What Nakamoto had added, crucially, was the focus on currency and the mining incentive. Years later, Scott didn't think proof of work, which had always been controversial because of its inefficiency and energy-hogging, was a sustainable solution for Bitcoin. But "to me, Satoshi's work is a work of genuine genius over and above what Stuart and I did."

Although Scott had been paid in bitcoins more than once for consulting work, he had never bought the currency himself because he didn't want to be seen as speculating on its price. He also wanted to make a statement. Bitcoin was just an advertisement for something with much broader application: the blockchain. "What's the line in *Lord of the Rings*? 'The ring has a power of its own.' It will work its way into all the world's record-keepings and dealings. And right along with it will be money++. But we're still very much in the opening innings of the game." In their driveway, Scott and Marcia had blue and gray Teslas with license plates reading, respectively, BLCKCHN and BLKCHN2.

I asked Scott whether Satoshi Nakamoto might be a group. He didn't think so. "I feel like I've met any number of people that would have those general skills to pull that off. It just never struck me that a team was needed. When you read all the emails, he speaks with a casual spontaneous voice that doesn't have the sense of a committee or separate and distinct figures." Stuart wasn't so sure. "Designing a system, writing a pretty clearly written paper about it, and writing the code, those are three different things. That's a lot to ask for from one person."

Inevitably, Scott and Stuart were themselves on the list of possible Nakamotos. Before Bitcoin adopted the word *blockchain,* Nakamoto had used the term *timechain*. From the start, the *Times* classified ad called Stuart's and Scott's service TimeLink, and Surety's brochure featured an image of blocks chained together. And of all the cryptographic algorithms Nakamoto could have chosen for creating new Bitcoin addresses, he happened to use the same pair* that, I discovered, Surety had used. The whole idea of using a periodical to time-stamp Bitcoin's Genesis Block, in fact, was straight out of the Scott-and-Stuart playbook. The headline cemented Bitcoin's start date, establishing trust in Bitcoin's coin distribution fairness and fixed money supply by showing users that Satoshi couldn't have secretly mined earlier blocks before launch.

Scott, for one, would have had the time to pull it off. In 2007, the year before the Bitcoin white paper appeared, he had become a high school math teacher, giving him a schedule that would match tidily with Nakamoto's academic-ish schedule. And for the two years of his Mormon mission, in his early twenties, Scott had lived in Japan.

Scott's stock response, when asked whether he was Nakamoto, was to say, in Japanese, "No, I'm not Satoshi. And by the way, if I

* SHA-256 and RIPEMD-160

were, would I say that, here and now?" When Stuart was asked, as he had been numerous times, "I just say, 'No, it wasn't me.'"

"Stuart and I feel it's very important to be sort of like Switzerland on this issue," Scott told me. "We officially are neutral to anyone's claims for example about being Satoshi, and with respect to the various blockchain tribes."

That didn't stop Craig Wright from trying to rope them in, and they'd appeared with him on stage at a conference organized by CoinGeek, a Wright-aligned media outlet. They hadn't really dug into his story before agreeing to attend, and Marcia Stornetta was wary. At the conference, she says, "there were numerous attempts to get them to make a declaration" that Wright was Nakamoto. "As Scott mentioned, he and Stuart are agnostic when it comes to commenting on Satoshi pretenders."

"We actually got in some trouble, Scott and I," Stuart added. "There was going to be an article about something we were trying to do together soon after that conference. Then the CoinGeek guys released something showing us on stage with Craig. It became, 'You appeared with Craig Wright? What the—?' They walked away from it."

Scott and Stuart were simply too guileless, I thought, for either or both to be Nakamoto.

"Do You Have a Salad Spinner?"

Between late 2015 (when I received the Craig Wright–outing email, a bitcoin was worth around $375, and crypto was still something only your most eggheaded cousin had even heard of) and late 2021 (when Sahil Gupta flung his Elon Musk theory over the transom, a bitcoin was worth $52,000, and my immigrant Uber driver with young children spoke giddily of sinking his family's savings into some marginal NFT project), hobbyist detectives had continued to propose alternative Nakamotos.

In February 2021, a University of Pennsylvania graduate named Evan Hatch, who'd gotten into Bitcoin as a high schooler nine years earlier, proffered one of the more well-considered theories to date. Through a roommate who worked at Chainalysis, a firm that specialized in exploiting the blockchain's transparency to trace coin flows for investigators of hacks and money laundering, Evan had heard a rumor that Nakamoto might be a Belgian cryptographer. "I was like, 'That's weird,'" Evan told me. He decided to see if anyone matching that broad description synced up with Nakamoto in more specific ways, and "then found Len." Len was Len Sassaman, a ponytailed, vandyked, younger American cypherpunk. "I felt like there were these uncanny clues there," Evan recalled. "I kind of went deeper and deeper almost to disprove it to myself." Over the next several years, as he researched Sassaman, he became "more and more convinced I was right."

Sassaman had worked on his PhD in Belgium under David Chaum, which put him in one of Nakamoto's possible time zones, on an academic schedule, and adjacent to the Father of Digital Cash. He'd been a hacker and open-source programmer, had collaborated with Hal Finney on PGP, and was involved with financial cryptography. He also had an ideologue's conviction about pseudonymity. He signed his code "rabbi." He maintained the Mixmaster remailer, a more private successor to Hal Finney's generation of remailers. He coauthored a paper, "The Pynchon Gate," proposing an even more secure pseudonymous messaging system. He was well versed in peer-to-peer systems: Mixmaster ran on a P2P network, and he'd been roommates with Bram Cohen in San Francisco when Cohen was creating BitTorrent. Despite being American, Sassaman had a habit of using British English. And there was a sadly persuasive final way in which he matched to Nakamoto, accounting for both Nakamoto's sudden departure from the project and his otherworldly abstinence from his bitcoin fortune: in July 2011, three months after Nakamoto's final communication, Sassaman, who'd struggled with depression and other neurological issues since he was a teenager, hanged himself at age thirty-one. "WikiLeaks friend Len Sassaman has been permanently encrypted and anonymized," WikiLeaks tweeted. "Stay cool, Len, we continue with the fight."

Because of the fallout from *Newsweek*'s Dorian Nakamoto article, Evan hired a publicist to shop his story. "A ton of journalists were like, 'We don't want that, these stories have been bullshit, we don't want another,'" he recalls. "And maxis are touchy, they're committed to a religious version of this." The news site CoinDesk, he says, rejected his story because the Satoshi statement "I am not Dorian Nakamoto" had occurred three years after Sassaman's death. "My understanding was that was hacked," Evan says of the Nakamoto account that sent that message. (The available evidence suggests that the account wasn't hacked until September 2014, six months after the "I am not Dorian Nakamoto" declaration.) Evan ultimately self-published his theory on the blogging platform Medium, using his middle name, Leung, as a pen name. Though he'd written with great empathy for Sassaman's mental health struggles, he feared that Sassaman's family might take offense. Instead, he heard from Sassaman's widow, Meredith Patterson, and various friends, who found his treatment sensitive and the theory interesting. Patterson had no reason to think Len had been Nakamoto, she said, but she acknowledged that he'd left encrypted hard drives behind that she couldn't access. "He was such a secretive guy," she told Evan.

Sassaman's involvement would also align with a discovery by Jens Ducrée, a micro-fluid-dynamics professor at Dublin City University in Ireland who had become obsessed with the Nakamoto mystery and had zeroed in on the Bitcoin white paper's selection of citations. Jens explained to me that one of the eight, an obscure paper on time-stamping, hadn't appeared outside of the printed proceedings of the Dutch conference where it was presented, leading him to conclude that Nakamoto must almost certainly be connected in some way to the Benelux countries. Sassaman had, of course, lived in Belgium.

But I made less of the Belgian connection than Jens did. What were the chances that Nakamoto, as careful as he was, would leave such an obvious clue in plain sight? In any case, the printed proceedings of the conference were available at both the British Library in London and the National Science Library in Canada. An Estonian academic's online list of time-stamping resources had cited the paper, and an archived copy of Nick Szabo's old webpage included a link to the Estonian page.

I asked Evan about criticisms Sassaman had voiced about Bitcoin, including calling it "dumb."

"Len's a mischievous guy," Evan said. "He's a cosmic joker figure."

It was true that Sassaman was a hacker to the core. He and Meredith Patterson were both involved in the DIY biotech movement, and their courtship effectively began the day before Meredith was to give a demonstration at CodeCon of how to purify DNA using household items; she was short one centrifuge, and at a party that night Len went from person to person asking, "Do you have a salad spinner?" until he got a yes. When he proposed to Meredith in the middle of a later CodeCon, he improvised an engagement ring from a blue cable twist tie. He had a fascination with lock-picking, and Meredith told me that in his early twenties Len had worked for a company that did physical penetration testing of shops in malls. Len's job was to try to break in after hours, and whenever he succeeded, he'd leave a feather as his calling card.

But Meredith said that his criticism of Bitcoin was sincere. In high school in Pennsylvania, classmates had broken into his email, found love letters between him and a girlfriend, and "made his life miserable." The experience had sparked a lifelong obsession with privacy that led to his work in cryptography and computer security. He saw Bitcoin's traceability as a serious flaw. "'Cause everyone was championing it as some kind of victory for online anonymity," Meredith says. "He was like, 'No, it really isn't.'"

Other investigators were more dramatic in revealing their findings. "One candidate literally matches every single detail to Satoshi Nakamoto," Barely Sociable, an anonymous YouTuber who made slick videos combining spooky synthesizer soundtracks and found footage, said in a silky baritone. He then presented an in-depth case for Adam Back. Barely was a conspiracist. He argued that Gavin Andresen had never truly believed Craig Wright was Nakamoto and had been "in on" the truth about Back.

Many of Barely's arguments were familiar: Back was a cypherpunk; his Hashcash software played an essential role in Bitcoin; he had the technical chops; he was English. But Barely also highlighted a few overlooked details. Although Nakamoto's first email to Wei Dai referenced earlier correspondence with Back, Back had never released those emails. Barely suggested that Back's protestations that he was respecting netiquette by keeping private emails private were just "virtue signal[ing]." Barely thought the emails didn't exist. He also noted conspicuous lulls in Back's public activity: between 2005 and 2010, Back had stopped filing patents, and between 2007 and 2010, he'd gone dormant on the mailing lists he frequented. When Back resurfaced after that three-year hiatus, he was living in Malta, which Barely portentously described as "the location you move to if you're about to receive a large amount of money that you don't want to be taxed heavily on." In 2012, Back started updating Wikipedia articles about Bitcoin, even though he wouldn't get publicly involved with Bitcoin until April 2013.

Barely made a point of preempting attacks from Nakamoto worshippers. He called the idea that Nakamoto required privacy because people might come after his coins "complete bullshit," given all the other nonanonymous coin launchers who'd managed to stay both rich and safe. He removed his conspiracy goggles just long enough to label concerns that Nakamoto might be targeted by the government as still more "virtue signaling."

Back took to Twitter to respond. "I am not Satoshi," he began. He was just the latest suspect generated by superficial googling. Unlike Nick Szabo, whose terse responses tended to increase rather than dispel suspicion, Back elaborated on his denial: "Some factors & timing may look suspicious in hindsight; coincidence & facts are untidy." He confirmed all of Barely's Satoshi-aligning coincidences and added a few more that Barely hadn't mentioned. "still not Satoshi tho . . . the thing is the research is so much by non-programmers / non-comp-sci people that it's both more suspicious than they realize, but coincidentally wrong, and also wrong for conversational reasons that would take a bitcoin protocol expert to notice. eg questions Satoshi would know." Another ex-cypherpunk, Jon Callas, makes a more concise case: "The primary argument against Adam Back is he couldn't keep his mouth shut."

Anything Is a Legitimate Area of Investigation

Back was right. Liberal arts chumps like me, with little exposure to computer science, would notice that a particular candidate had, like Nakamoto, used a term such as *digital signatures* or programmed in C++, and see it as an *extremely meaningful* coincidence. Whereas, if we were in the relevant field or an adjacent one, we'd know how commonplace these things were and not give them undue weight. The supposed similarities didn't even have to be technical things. Nakamoto hounds often pointed to a candidate's use of two spaces after a period as a crucial detail, but I knew from my own experience that this was standard if you'd learned to type on a typewriter. The habit suggested Nakamoto might be a bit older, but not much else.

Skye Grey had made a similar point when he doubled down on his Nick Szabo theory with a follow-up post: "Occam's Razor: Who Is Most Likely to Be Satoshi Nakamoto?" "Occam's razor," I was starting to notice, was a go-to trope in Nakamotology. You could harness it in favor of just about any argument, which made it effectively meaningless. Something I heard almost as often was the medical-diagnostic injunction "When you hear hoofbeats, think horses, not zebras."

"Bitcoin is a very non-obvious idea, of the kind that takes years of crystallization, maybe an entire lifetime," Grey wrote. "An idea born of the cypherpunk mindset, developed over time by a person with a deep passion for economics of the most abstract kind and a mastery of unusual cryptography concepts. The recent suggestions in the press that every other person who has a scientific background could be the creator of Bitcoin only serve to show how little some 'journalists' understand about Bitcoin and its origins."

Looking back at the earliest Nakamotology efforts, I now saw them as case studies in this sort of long-distance pattern recognition. Things that seemed like a "crazy coincidence," as Reuters described the fact that Dorian Nakamoto's full name included "Satoshi," weren't that crazy. I'd gradually realized that when it came to the Nakamoto mystery, nobody, including me, really knew anything.

Clearly, I needed a deeper understanding of computer science. During Covid, instead of baking sourdough bread or growing scallions in my window box, I'd signed up for CS50, an introductory online comp sci course offered for free by Harvard University. Among its recent graduates was Rivers Cuomo, lead singer of Weezer and apparently something of a coding nut. Soon I was learning the grammar of the machine—loops and conditions and the logic of *and, or,* and *not.* Our teacher, David Malan, had cleverly structured the course to give quick payoffs. By week 2, we were writing a program that could look at any text and tell you what grade-level reading comprehension it required. By week 4, we were creating our own Instagram-style photo filters. One early assignment dealt with basic cryptography: we were tasked with writing a program, in C, that would use a Caesar cipher to scramble and unscramble a message.

I was a giddy tourist on an unfamiliar planet. I felt the adrenaline of watching my thoughts flow from brain to fingertips to keyboard to screen. I wasn't prepared for the speed, how instantaneously huge tasks could be accomplished. I glimpsed for the first time what programming was: turning the world into numbers, doing something to them, and turning them back. I wondered whether I'd shied away from coding because of its off-putting surface, how it butchered language, substituting weird punctuation, amputating words, cluttering itself with symbols. It was a language for speaking with aliens that happened to be machines. I'd mistaken its opacity for shallowness. What it concealed was depth, problem-solving, strategizing, thinking about thinking. Coding was finding a way to model some small slice of the world using only math and logic. To code was to will a hunk of metal and silicon to do your bidding. It made me think of Hal Finney: "The thing I always love is when there's an intellectual challenge that when you master it gives you practical abilities." A program offered its writer the productive satisfaction of a useful crossword puzzle.

I also experienced the head-splitting tedium of writing a program that didn't work and having no idea why and taking days to figure out that my only error, because of C's unforgiving syntax, was failing to put a semicolon at the end of a line. I made it to week 4 of CS50, at which point I was defeated by pointers, variables that refer to other variables. They were fine in theory but drove me insane when I tried to use them.

Now, in the summer of 2022, I decided to try again. That this seemed like the obvious thing to do was a sign, I knew on some level, of, if not some small derangement, then an extreme shrinking of the aperture through which I was looking at the world. But I could hardly hope to find my way in a strange land, I felt, without a conversational grasp of the native language. I also was still convinced there must be some way to automate the Nakamoto search at scale. Other people had done stylometry, but had they *really* done it? I wanted to download oceans of information from the internet and have my Mac sieve it for trace evidence. The computer people had numbers, but I had words. I'd hear things they hadn't, catch things they couldn't.

This time I learned Python, a higher-level language that was like a plane with half as many knobs and dials: you had less precise control, but there were fewer ways to go wrong. I read *Python for Kids* and *Python Crash Course*. I did interactive exercises on Codecademy and freeCodeCamp. I wrote a first program. Once a day, it would randomly chop up and remix the artist Jenny Holzer's Truisms, aphoristic sayings like "ABUSE OF POWER COMES AS NO SURPRISE" and "ANYTHING IS A LEGITIMATE AREA OF INVESTIGATION" (one of my faves), into a new hybrid and email it to me.

GUILT AND SELF-LACERATION CAN YIELD GOOD RESULTS.

YOU MUST BE INTIMATE WITH AUTHORITY FIGURES.

SALVATION IS INVARIABLY ATTRACTIVE.

My faith grew that the key to the ultimate digital mystery must itself be digital. To build the web scrapers I wanted to build—tools to trawl what remained of the early internet and slurp up terabytes of posts by cypherpunks and groups like them—I sought help. On Wyzant, a website that connects students with tutors, I found a Python tutor named Seth. He sent me a calendar link.

Then I made the mistake of trying to learn more about him. Wyzant omits last names, but by triangulating a few details in Seth's profile I found his Facebook page. Seth was a culture warrior. He had posted approvingly about Alex Jones. I wanted technical knowledge. Why did I care who I got it from? But I did. I found another tutor. Soon I was having regular video sessions with Christopher. I had no idea what his politics were. I had a new appreciation, though, for Bitcoiners' desire to separate their cherished technology from its human creator.

In fits and starts, I coded scrapers for each of the groups I wanted to target: cypherpunks, extropians, Rationalists, cryptographers, P2P people. Various self-assigned archivists had preserved, on their websites, the records of select mailing lists for select years. Wei Dai, for one, had a copy of the extropians list from 1996 to 2002. The first time I ran a scraper, it went for two hours, then crashed. I made a little fix and restarted it. The scraping of a single archive could take days. I suspected a more experienced coder could have built a much faster tool.

The jarring, abrasive sound conjured by *scrape* hardly conveys the serenity I felt each morning when I woke up and heard the white noise of my laptop's fan and saw that the program hadn't crashed while I slept. "How's your bitcoin mining going?" my wife asked the first few times she came across me babysitting my whirring computer in our living room. Then she started just asking me to move it to another room.

I felt an acquisitive rush. Soon I had gigantic spreadsheets with hundreds of thousands of rows, records of decades of conversations. Each row captured a single post: author, email, date, time, title, text, and a link to the page it had been retrieved from.

While waiting for my scrapings, I'd combed through the sixty thousand words Satoshi Nakamoto had left behind. He wrote in a plain style, rarely opining or showing personality. Whenever I found an exception, the slightest hint of individual style, I'd add it to a list of Nakamoto-isms, which eventually included more than two hundred words and phrases. *Wet blanket. Sweet. Clobbering.*

I wrote another program. The Satoshitizer could chew through the scraped archives, scanning for Nakamoto-isms and generating tables of statistics. I could instantly rank an archive using more than a dozen criteria. They included most prolific posters, users of Nakamoto-isms, users of Commonwealth English Nakamoto-isms, users of e-cash terminology, and discussers of Windows and other software tools employed by Nakamoto. I was looking for signal in the noise.

I soon felt validated in my approach. The machine was throwing off names I hadn't encountered or new insights about those I had. On Metzdowd, from 2001 to 2009, Robert Hettinga, blocker of writers for libtard shit-shows, had used the most Nakamoto-isms. When it came to average-Nakamoto-isms-per-post, the Satoshitizer coughed up the name Travis Hassloch, who'd employed Nakamoto-isms like *memoryless, hosed,* and *white paper.* He had worked at Visa. When I googled him, one of the first hits was a comment by someone named Dimitrios4615 on Ars Technica's blog: "The creator of bitcoin is Travis Hassloch."

Another revelation was how many native-born Americans had a habit of salting their prose with Britishisms. Guys from New Hampshire would reminisce about studying “maths” at “uni.” Hal Finney had used *bloody* and lots of *s* spellings in place of *z* spellings. Eliezer Yudkowsky, AI doomer-to-be, was egregious, throwing around *bloody* this and *loads of* that and *spot on*. What if Satoshi Nakamoto was just a bad speller or a pretentious Anglophile?

I started getting eye floaters from staring at lists of cryptographers’ names for too long. I’d see a Japanese cryptographer named Satoshi, then one nearby whose name ended in *oto*, and think I was onto something. I wasn’t sure precisely what I was looking for, what that one thing would be that pushed someone over the line, revealing him to be the creator of Bitcoin.

A significantly large number of people, in the hundreds if not thousands, had at least some expertise in the subjects in which Nakamoto had been expert. No wonder that civilians, encountering relevant expertise or even only vaguely related expertise in someone they knew, could be quick to think their friend or colleague might be Nakamoto.

I felt certain that this new track I was on was the right one.

DJ Sun Love

Nakamoto mania abhorred a vacuum. After Craig Wright's big fizzle in the spring of 2016, whenever the price of Bitcoin boomed, self-styled Satoshis would bloom like so many grand duchess Anastasias. Often they were selling something.

The wares of Prof. Dr. Jörg Molt, a forty-six-year-old German with shoulder-length hair and a past that featured deadbeat-dad accusations and a stint as a DJ named Sun Love, included Satoshi School courses, Bitcoin-branded sparkling wine, and a magnificently ill-conceived Bitcoin-based pension fund. Molt claimed he was Bitcoin's "cofounder." He was later arrested at the Frankfurt airport as he prepared to board a flight to Mexico, charged with bilking people out of several million dollars.

A Belgian named Jurgen Etienne Guido Debo called himself "Satoshi Nakamoto, the genuine one," despite writing in broken English and presenting backdated PGP keys as real ones.

An Australian named Phil "Scronty" Wilson published "Bitcoin Origins," a lengthy document in which he claimed to have cocreated Bitcoin with Wright and Kleiman. Alas, he had "obliterat[ed]" all relevant emails five years earlier.

A Hawaiian man filed for several Bitcoin-related trademarks and put up a website claiming: "I Ronald Keala Kua Maria also known as Satoshi Nakamoto inventor of Bitcoin and blockchain technology hereby affirm all my copyrights including an equity based electronic reserve currency peer-to-peer electronic cash system."

I received an email from another "Satoshi," vaguely soliciting my help as "a witness." This one had earlier published a book, *The Genesis Block: The Proof of Work,* by "Satoshi Nakamoto."

A website, nakamotofamilyfoundation.org, posted what purported to be a twenty-one-page excerpt from a forthcoming literary memoir by Bitcoin's founder titled *Duality,* but it contained odd ESL phrasings and misspellings and mischaracterized "Satoshi Nakamoto" as being, in Japan, as common as "John Smith." Bloomberg, amazingly, reprinted "Key Passages From Satoshi Nakamoto Excerpt on Bitcoin Beginnings."

Then there was Bilal Khalid, a Pakistani Brit who worked for England's National Health Service in London, was deeply interested in numerology, and had legally changed his name to James Caan for an elaborate set of reasons that included seeing the actor in *The Godfather* and realizing that "I am the Godfather of digital cash." Alas, the Godfather had lost his private keys "in a hard-drive accident" and his emails with Back, Finney, and Andresen to a "hack."

Several of these aspirant Nakamotos claimed to have been cypherpunks, a group that, like Woodstock, was turning out to be the party that many more people recalled attending than were actually there. And they held each other in contempt. Debo, the Belgian Satoshi, accused Craig Wright of impersonating him. Caan, the Pakistani-British Satoshi, mocked Wright's claim to have used scores of computers to mine bitcoin: "What a stupid thing to say!" And Wright sniffed that "Scronty" Wilson was a "Scam-toshi" and that the author of the purported Satoshi memoir excerpt "cannot get dates nor technical details correct."

One would-be Satoshi made it further than most. He first approached Tim Draper, a venture capitalist who'd savvily bought close to thirty thousand of Silk Road's seized bitcoins for $18 million at a U.S. Marshals auction in 2014. Tim told me he'd tried not to give much thought to the question of Nakamoto's identity; he liked the decentralized, leaderless nature of Bitcoin. But on the phone, the man, who spoke with an unspecified Asian American accent, was able to convince Tim that he was indeed Nakamoto. And he wanted, while remaining anonymous, to work through Tim to create Bitcoin 2.0. There were a few things he wanted to do differently this time around, he said.

"I was thinking: If this is Satoshi, that's pretty interesting," Tim recalled. They went through a process, "and then it got pretty hairy." Tim said they should discuss it with the SEC, and they did, with "Satoshi" dialing in for the call. But after Tim showed his lawyer all the documentation the man had given him, the lawyer found a discrepancy, "this minuscule difference," that was chronologically impossible. Tim called the man. "I said, 'You are in big trouble.'" The man threatened Tim and hung up. Tim changed his phone number and told the SEC the man was a fraud. "He must have been freaking out," Tim said later, picturing the man going through with the SEC call.

Tim never met or saw him. "I think that's the key," Tim told me. "You always want to make sure they show you their face."

None of the pretenders stood a chance, though, once Craig Wright reemerged.

Obviousness Fatigue

"I am sorry for last year," Wright wrote to Gavin Andresen in May 2017, apparently wanting to tie up a loose end, "but I cannot sign."

Six months earlier, Gavin, who found himself being asked if he still believed Wright to be Nakamoto, had blogged that "either he was or he wasn't. In either case, we should ignore him. I regret ever getting involved in the 'who was Satoshi' game, and am going to spend my time on more fun and productive pursuits."

By then, Gavin had withdrawn from working on Bitcoin. Because of his early involvement, and bitcoin's subsequent price rise, he considered himself to have been "well-compensated" for the work he'd done. Other than acknowledging that "personally" he "took a lot of heat and abuse" for endorsing Wright, he was, in his equable way, restrained in commenting on the core developers who'd taken over Bitcoin and banished him. Occasionally, one of his fellow early developers, such as Jeff Garzik, would defend him online against critics. But Gavin stopped talking to reporters. "Don't worry about me," he replied to Wright. "I'm enjoying semi-retirement. All the people I care about still love and respect me and don't care that you bamboozled me, and you did, just not in the way most people think." He added, with saintly forbearance, "If you ever need or want to talk, I'll be happy to listen."

Wright edged back into the limelight, first in a series of friendly interviews with CoinGeek, which was owned by nChain, the successor to nCrypt. Wright was now nChain's chief scientist. Jon Matonis, exactly a year after writing his "How I Met Satoshi" blog post, had taken a job with nChain as vice president of corporate strategy; in July, Matonis, booked to speak at a Bitcoin conference in Holland, ascended the stage, only to turn the mic over to "the legend from Sydney, Australia, Mr. Bitcoin Dundee, Craig Wright!" The audience clapped tentatively.

Wright gave a talk about "the future of Bitcoin," then took questions. The first was both skeptical and credulous, asking about the "fake proof" in Wright's Sartre blog post but then wondering, as if Wright was indeed Nakamoto, whether he intended to dump his hoard of bitcoins. "Quite frankly, none of your business," Wright said. "There is no fucking king, there is no glorious leader. . . . I am here to kill off Satoshi, not in the way that you want." He next spoke at a gaming conference, wearing sunglasses; he didn't take questions afterwards.

Wright grew bolder. When he spoke at a Zurich meetup in October and an attendee challenged his credentials, an assistant stepped from the wings pushing a wheelbarrow piled with Wright's framed certifications and academic degrees. His detractors grew bolder too. When Wright appeared onstage in Seoul in April 2018, Vitalik Buterin stood and asked: "Why is this fraud allowed to speak at this conference?"

By then, it had been revealed that the businessmen who had handheld Gavin in London, and the PR people who courted journalists for the Wright-is-Satoshi blitzkrieg, were part of a larger, murkier operation.

In the summer of 2015, Wright, under pressure from the Australian Taxation Office, which had recently concluded an audit finding that one of his companies owed $5.6 million, including a $1.9 million penalty, had gotten a lifeline. He'd told Stefan Matthews, for whom he'd done work when Matthews was an executive at Centrebet, that he'd invented Bitcoin. Through Matthews, a group of investors then formed nCrypt to make a deal with Wright: they paid $15 million to take on his debts and acquire the rights to his intellectual property. The plan to exploit the IP included an elaborate public introduction of Wright as Satoshi Nakamoto. nCrypt also retained a lauded Scottish novelist and journalist named Andrew O'Hagan as a ghostwriter to document the whole thing. Looming silently over it all was a man referred to in internal emails only as "c," who was Calvin Ayre, a Canadian online-gambling magnate.

Though Gavin had been aware of nCrypt's involvement, he seemed neither to have asked questions about the nature of its relationship with Wright nor to have thought through the implications of letting the company pay for his airfare and London hotel room, agreeing to sign an NDA, deferring to Wright's team on its media strategy, and coordinating his blog post with them.

Many of these facts were first exposed by O'Hagan, who had refused to sign nCrypt's NDA and later published an embarrassing account of the affair in the *London Review of Books*. O'Hagan was the writer Wright had met for coffee the day after his suicide attempt.

The journalists given the exclusive had known even less than Gavin, although in hindsight there were red flags. When Rory Cellan-Jones, the BBC's tech reporter, was first approached about Wright, he'd found the choice of publicity firm weird. It was known for doing music PR, working with clients like David Bowie and the Spice Girls. But this looked like a big scoop. "I was basically a competitive hack," Rory recalled," going: 'This could be a great story.'"

Wright had undergone three media-training sessions to prepare for the interviews, which didn't stop him from repeatedly telling an academic cryptographer accompanying one of the journalists to "fuck off" or from claiming that he'd never agreed that the BBC could film him, despite emails showing otherwise.

By the time Wright started appearing in public again in 2017, the gap between the original cypherpunk vision and the reality of what Bitcoin had become was impossible to ignore. Fees and other frictions had meant that Bitcoin didn't work for microtransactions and wasn't attractive for remittances—a cheap, low-hassle way for immigrants to send money home to their families. A growing blockchain-forensics industry was eroding the persistent myth of Bitcoin's privacy as a parade of hackers, embezzlers, and conmen were doxed and arrested. A new generation who'd never heard of the cypherpunks had grown up absorbing their values—witnessing Julian Assange's and Edward Snowden's revelations, becoming disillusioned about surveillance capitalism—but they tended to view Bitcoin mainly as a speculative investment instead of a useful technology. Even Bitcoin's vaunted decentralization seemed dubious. It was virtually impossible to use without relying on third-party exchanges like Mt. Gox, which had repeatedly violated users' trust. Mining was overwhelmingly concentrated in mining pools, and the biggest of these were located in China, the most autocratically centralized and privacy-invading country in the world.

And Bitcoinland was still having its civil war. The Small Blockers, whom Gavin and Wright opposed, had prevailed in dictating Bitcoin's future, agreeing only to a technical workaround that modestly increased block capacity. Wright and others were now pushing a big-block hard fork called Bitcoin Cash (BCH), in the hope that it would be accepted as the real Bitcoin.* Then Bitcoin Cash underwent its own schism, with Wright and nChain forking off in November 2018 to create an even-bigger-block blockchain. It was called BSV, short for Bitcoin Satoshi Vision.

Wright's claim to be Satoshi Nakamoto was now in service of

* A hard fork, in this context, means a new, separate blockchain, with its own set of miners running its own distinct software. When the new blockchain launches, it starts with a copy of the ledger from the blockchain it is forking away from. This means that all holders of the original blockchain's coins hold coins, free money, in the new blockchain as well. BTC owners became BCH owners too.

promoting a particular cryptocurrency, which alone embodied, he declared, the original plan of Bitcoin's inventor. nChain was aggressively building a patent portfolio based on this vision of a Bitcoin of unlimited scale. And Wright became increasingly provocative. "The code-is-law movement"—the push for algorithmic governance, the basis of smart contracts and blockchains like Bitcoin—was a "pernicious attack on freedom." The idea of private keys as proof of digital identity, which was the foundation of public-key cryptography, the cypherpunks, Bitcoin, and Satoshi Nakamoto himself, was "an idea that is miasmic through its virulent and noxious constitution. Being of mephitic nature reminiscent of toads wallowing in the pond they defecate in with its septic rankness, it pollutes the minds it touches." Wright badmouthed Bitcoin's software developers. He railed against the Australian Taxation Office. At a Transform Africa Summit in Rwanda, he told the crowd, "I've got more money than your country." He boasted about having a jet, a yacht, a Lamborghini, and a 1944 Patek Philippe.

Wright also became more confident in embracing the Nakamoto identity. In the spring of 2019, he filed to register the Bitcoin white paper with the U.S. Copyright Office. And he started filling in gaps in his biography with mythic, uncheckable tales. "In my early 20s I was treated for a late-stage cancer. . . . Facing death multiple times in youth changes a person." Why had he left the Bitcoin project in late 2010? He'd "started to go quiet" not just because his first marriage was ending but because he'd gone to Venezuela as part of "a 'Jawbreaker' team" battling sex trafficking; he was an "agent of influence" who'd been "shot twice" near the Colombian border. He fleshed out Bitcoin's origin story, too, speaking of a humble "shed in Bagnoo," an outbuilding on a ranch he owned in eastern Australia, four hundred kilometers from Sydney, in which Bitcoin had been born.

Bitcoin culture had always been fragile, and even after surviving the scaling wars and a 2017 boom in alternative cryptocurrencies it remained brittle. The network was only as strong as it was widespread, so any rival coins were "shitcoins," threats to Bitcoin's zero-sum supremacy. Hodling bitcoin was an article of faith, so Wright's attempt to make a business of Satoshi Nakamoto, the efforts to convince people to sell their bitcoins and buy BSV, and the insistence on taking their Lord's name in vain all enraged the One True Coin absolutists known as Bitcoin maximalists. There was also something deeper at stake. Bitcoin was an immutable record. It stood, to Bitcoiners, for Truth. They simply couldn't ignore Wright's endless prevarications.

As Wright grew more strident, so did Bitcoin Twitter. "Is Craig Wright a fraud?" a crypto-influencer named Dan Darkpill tweeted. More than a thousand people replied, more than a thousand liked Darkpill's tweet, and hundreds of people retweeted it. WikiLeaks called Wright a "serial fabricator" who'd been "repeatedly caught." Wright threatened to sue various people, further inciting the mob.

In March 2019, a Twitter user named Hodlonaut, whose avatar was a cat with laser eyes in an astronaut helmet, became one of the more persistent anti-Wright voices. Hodlonaut had recently gained thousands of followers, including Twitter's Jack Dorsey, after starting something called the Lightning Torch, a pass-the-bitcoin experiment to demonstrate how an app called Lightning could speed up the network. In a burst of tweets over ten days, Hodlonaut variously labeled Wright a "swindler," a "fraud," and "a very sad and pathetic scammer, clearly mentally ill. Everything about him induces deep cringe. I suffer from obviousness fatigue after still having to read posts arguing why he isn't satoshi." He exhorted his followers to join him in recognizing "#CraigWrightIsAFraud Week."

On March 29, Hodlonaut opened his DMs to find a letter from a lawyer representing Wright, demanding that Hodlonaut apologize on Twitter and affirm in open court that Wright was Satoshi Nakamoto. Hodlonaut had seven days to respond. His real name was Magnus Granath, and he lived in Norway. A lawyer there told him he should take the message seriously. Granath had little desire to get sued by a deep-pocketed adversary, but the insistence that he publicly agree that Craig Wright was Satoshi Nakamoto was something he knew he couldn't do.

Then Calvin Ayre, Wright's no-longer-so-secret backer, started tweeting at him.

"Magnus . . . I have a way out of your problem."

"Magnus last offer."

Granath wasn't sure how Ayre had learned his first name.

Because Wright lived in England, Granath spoke with a British lawyer, who advised him to delete the offending tweets. Granath did so. Some of the tweets had received no more than a dozen likes, and he figured that was the end of that.

But on April 11, Granath awoke to concerning news. Wright was offering $5,000 worth of BSV to anyone who could provide Hodlonaut's full name. CoinGeek reported that most of the offending Hodlonaut tweets had been posted from Oslo, and at least one from a bar there named Kasbah. CoinGeek also reprinted a photograph Hodlonaut had once posted, in which his back was to the camera but his tattooed arms were visible. CoinGeek informed its readers that Hodlonaut was scheduled to attend Baltic Honeybadger, an upcoming Bitcoin conference in Latvia, and urged them to be on the lookout for "individuals who seem unnaturally focused on keeping their sleeves rolled down."

Granath's life quickly became stressful. Someone claiming to be a detective from the local police station called the primary school where he taught and managed to get Granath's last name, phone number, and address. The next day, a private investigator phoned Granath and said he had paperwork for him to sign, confirming he was Hodlonaut. When Granath demurred, the man told him, "These aren't people you want to mess with." After consulting with his lawyers, who advised that delays would incur more legal costs and possibly annoy a judge, Granath called the investigator back and signed the papers.

Oslo was small, and now it felt different. BSV-ers started repeating his name as often as possible on Twitter, calling him everything from a "crypto troll" to "a childless alcoholic" who went around at Christmas begging for aquavit. Granath bought long-sleeved shirts to wear to the gym.

The Bitcoin world rallied around Hodlonaut. The right to pseudonymity exemplified by Satoshi Nakamoto was sacred and putting out a bounty on "an anon" an affront. Supporters changed their Twitter avatars to Hodlonaut's, an "I am Spartacus" gesture of solidarity that also made it harder to pinpoint which account was the real Hodlonaut's. #WeAreAllHodlonaut trended.

More people on Twitter started calling Wright a fraud, as well as, more poetically, "a cockwombling bunglecunt Faketoshi." Wright, in turn, demanded apologies from, sued, or threatened to sue half a dozen people, including Vitalik Buterin and Adam Back. Calvin Ayre tweeted a picture of himself and Wright, flanked by London barristers, captioned: "Craig and I polishing our muskets." Bitcoin podcaster Peter McCormack retweeted this, adding, "Craig Wright is not Satoshi! When do I get sued?" Wright sued him too. Binance and Kraken, two of the three largest cryptocurrency exchanges, delisted BSV, and Binance leader Changpeng Zhao retweeted, "An attack against one is an attack against all."

There had long been a small tribe of volunteer Wright investigators—one had obtained Wright's military records from the National Archives of Australia—but now they accelerated their efforts. DebunkingFaketoshi, whose real name was Jim and who worked at a hospital in Sydney, published an investigation of whether fiber-optic cable sufficient to launch Bitcoin had existed in Bagnoo, where Wright claimed Bitcoin was born. Arthur van Pelt, a technically savvy retiree in Amsterdam, wrote exhaustive chronicles of Wright's lies.

The lawsuit against McCormack was one of seven Wright would soon be involved in. He sued C0bra, the pseudonymous person who owned Bitcoin.org and hosted the white paper on it, for copyright infringement. He sued Roger Ver, a former ally who'd called him "a fraud" and "a liar," for libel. He sued the exchanges Coinbase and

Kraken for "misrepresenting" that BTC, rather than BSV, was the real Bitcoin. He sued sixteen Bitcoin developers to try to compel them to alter the Bitcoin software to enable him to retrieve private keys he claimed to have lost to 110,000 bitcoins he claimed to own. The Cryptocurrency Open Patent Alliance, started by Jack Dorsey, sued Wright, accusing him of forging the documents on which he'd based his Nakamoto claim. And before Wright sued Granath in London, Granath sued Wright in Norway, hoping to obtain "negative declaratory relief," a court finding that would preempt the U.K. case.

Wright was claiming to be the world's most elusive person, but he seemed increasingly set on demystifying himself.

Freedom of Information

In 2022, I came across another promising lead. In the spring of 2019, Rana Saoud, an assistant agent in charge in the Department of Homeland Security's division of Immigration and Customs Enforcement, had spoken at the OffshoreAlert Conference in Miami as part of a panel titled "Regulating Cryptocurrencies & ICOs: Security, Commodity, or Currency?" During the presentation, she recalled a colleague's investigation of Black Market Reloaded, one of the dark web bazaars that had succeeded Silk Road. "He is a really, really smart, forward-leaning agent. He goes, 'I want to go interview Satoshi Nakamoto.' . . . At the time, we're like, *Hey, it's a figment of someone's imagination, maybe it's true, maybe it's not true.* We thought, *Hey, if an agent wants to go talk to him, and we have some money, why don't we send him, let's find out how this works.* So, as it came to be, the agents flew out to California, and they realized that he wasn't alone in creating this, there were three other people, and they sat down and met with them and talked with them to find out how this actually works and find out what the reason for it was."

This anecdote had caused a brief stir on Reddit, then been forgotten. When I first listened to the audio of Saoud's remarks, I was skeptical. Why would anyone need to talk to Nakamoto to learn how Bitcoin worked? And the offhanded way she dropped the bombshell—*Yup, Satoshi is four people in California. Anyhoo*—indicated that she had no idea what a massive deal it would be if true: that it would be the first known physical encounter with Nakamoto, the first evidence that the government knew who he was, and the first confirmation that Nakamoto was not a single person but a group of them. It made me think she'd somehow misunderstood her colleague.

On the other hand, it wasn't impossible that Nakamoto was some people who wanted to remain anonymous to the internet hordes and the media but were ultimately law-abiding citizens who wouldn't try to evade federal criminal investigators. Perhaps these were even people dismayed by the black market association with their invention and eager to clear up the confusion.

I had so many questions. How had the agent contacted Nakamoto? What assurances had he given them? How long had Nakamoto talked to him? What had the agent learned? I called Agent Saoud. She said she needed to talk to the lawyers and "ethics people" at DHS. This turned into a wild goose chase, including a convoluted and ultimately fruitless series of Freedom of Information Act requests.

Eventually, I'd speak directly with the agent to whom Saoud had been referring. Ryan Landers had led the Black Market Reloaded investigation, which resulted in several arrests, including that of a man making international sales of ricin and other toxins. When I got Ryan on the phone, he told me they'd sought out Nakamoto because at the time they'd wanted to learn whether Bitcoin had any unknown exploits the investigators might use to trace illegal transactions. "We talked to his brother, his wife," Ryan said.

Wait, what? "So that sounds like Satoshi was an individual," I said, "and not four people."

Yes, Ryan confirmed.

There went the group theory, but wow, Ryan really did know who Nakamoto was.

"So, whose brother and wife was it that you talked to?" I asked, hoping Ryan wouldn't choose this moment to clam up.

"Dorian Nakamoto," he said.

Wait, what?

"It's our belief it's Dorian," he said.

This was unexpected. Had Leah Goodman been right all along, and the world had done her wrong? I asked Ryan to elaborate and waited to hear the new evidence that hadn't made it into the *Newsweek* story.

Dorian's estranged wife, a nurse in her sixties, had described him as being on the autism spectrum, obsessed with model trains, and "continually frustrated" by the banking and currency-exchange frictions of ordering model trains from England, Ryan recalled. "The story she told about Dorian, you could overlay his personality and motivations on the white paper," Ryan said.

And?

That was it. That was the evidence. It was no more convincing than Goodman's. Ryan later clarified: "I'm not sure I believed there was only one inventor, but I did suspect that Dorian Nakamoto was involved, and possibly authored the white paper."

He and a second agent also went to see Hal Finney. Fran Finney "was incredibly hospitable . . . and she did everything she could to attempt to help us," but Hal was beyond even using eye-gaze software by then and would die a few weeks later.

Negative Space

I was making little headway in my own investigation and beginning to despair.

With the most plausible Nakamoto candidates, even if you discounted their denials and allowed that Britishisms could be low-effort misdirection by non-Brits, you still needed to mute a fair amount of cognitive dissonance to conclude with any confidence that one of them was Nakamoto.

To give weight to Wei Dai as a candidate, for instance, you had to believe that someone who in 1998 had come up with a few interesting paragraphs about an imagined digital money, and who had then ditched the e-cash conversation for the next ten years and visibly refocused his interest toward AI safety, had suddenly sprung from the shadows with a fully working system.

With Wei or Adam Back, you needed to swallow the inconvenient fact of Nakamoto, an all-time OPSEC champ, naming his own work among just eight citations in the Bitcoin white paper.

The case for Len Sassaman presented the small glitch that he, a staunch cypherpunk, had criticized Bitcoin as an "overhyped" thing that "fails as a cypherpunk protocol" and "suffers from the worst of both worlds: no strong anonymity, yet no fraud reversal protection."

To believe that Nick Szabo was Nakamoto, you had to accept

that someone who wasn't primarily a coder had pulled off a masterstroke of coding, that someone who reveled in grand concepts informed by considerable erudition decided to devote two years of his life to technical gibberish like "win32's 16-bit wchar and 8-bit ansi dual-compile," and that someone who'd blogged for decades under his own name and took obvious pride in his ideas decided, upon producing his magnum opus, to forgo earthly pleasures and commit to life in a Benedictine monastery.

Hal Finney, in order to be Nakamoto, required that you fantasize an elaborate pantomime in which he created sock-puppet accounts to send emails to himself; in which, despite having access to hundreds of millions of dollars, he didn't spend any of it on life-extending healthcare or leave it to the family who would live on without him, or to the cause, ALS research, to which his wife Fran would soon devote herself; and in which he persisted in this ruse even though, as he'd told me, "I'd have little to lose by shedding anonymity."

And to conceive of Satoshi Nakamoto as a group, you had to imagine that a cabal in possession not only of the biggest secret in technology but also of the keys to a monstrously huge fortune, had defied incomprehensible odds and agreed: *Mum's the word*.

Every theory worth considering, in other words, had a critical flaw.

My brain rang with buzzwords and clichés.

Confirmation bias.

Occam's razor.

When you hear hoofbeats, think horses, not zebras.

I started seeing in my wife's eyes a look I had tried to keep out of my own eyes during my first foray into Bitcoinland. It was that look of frank uninterest common to anyone who'd ever been stuck at a party listening to a blockchain bore.

I found myself describing a family scheduling issue as "suboptimal."

"Do you really want to say that?" my wife asked.

"What's suboptimal?" my daughter asked.

"Nerd language," my wife said.

Maybe ChatGPT could help.

What are the best arguments for and against Travis Hassloch being Satoshi Nakamoto?

Make the case for Eliezer Yudkowsky being Satoshi Nakamoto.

What are the strongest unacknowledged influences on the Bitcoin white paper?

What was I looking for, exactly?

What are some creative ways a journalist could use GPT4 to help do his job?

What are the best first words to use in Wordle?

I refocused.

What demographic/age/geographic/etc. inferences can be drawn about a person who uses the word "hosed" to mean wrecked or screwed up?

You are going to interview a person you believe could be Satoshi Nakamoto, but you don't want to ask them directly. What would be some good questions to ask that might indirectly elicit confirmation that the person is likely Satoshi Nakamoto?

I asked dozens of questions.

Proof of laziness.

Keeping an open mind was getting annoying. If Satoshi could be anyone, where even to begin to look for him? Where to stop?

Over breakfast with my friend Chris Buck, I fretted about the prospect of an anticlimactic ending.

Maybe, Chris said, the story would be better without an answer.

I rolled my eyes.

"You know about negative space?" Chris asked. Chris was a photographer.

I vaguely recalled some college knowledge. The space around an object. Silences in music. Ellsworth Kelly. Hmm. Maybe Chris was onto something.

I perked up. Why had I thought I needed something as pedestrian as a *name*? What could we possibly learn from Nakamoto's biography? That he was some random professor who'd had a lucky brainstorm? No, what was most interesting about Nakamoto was his *absence*. He was defined by what we *didn't* know about him.

I walked home from breakfast feeling a buzz of excitement at the profound insight I'd achieved.

A few hours later, the buzz faded, replaced by a sinking feeling. Chris was hardly objective on this topic. He'd published an entire book consisting of portraits of celebrities where you couldn't see the celebrities. There'd be a nicely composed picture of a marble bathroom devoid of people, and on the opposite page an affidavit by a witness attesting to the presence of Robert De Niro, who was hiding somewhere in the frame. De Niro was one of fifty famous people Chris had convinced to do this. His portrait of Nas showed a fake tabletop Christmas tree in a sterile office. Sarah Silverman's picture was a catered buffet of deli platters. Chris had titled his book *Presence: The Invisible Portrait*.

I was a journalist, not a conceptual artist.

Craig Wright, on the other hand, was hard to look away from. It wasn't just the brazenness. It wasn't even that, in the absence of a known Satoshi, he was the next best thing. In some ways, he was better. He had a face. You could meet him. You could have feelings and opinions about him. He offered a respite from chasing ghosts on the internet.

Before Wright filed any of his lawsuits, he was the defendant in a case in Florida. In February 2018, Ira Kleiman had sued Wright, in federal court in Miami, on behalf of his brother Dave's estate. The complaint accused Wright of backdating a series of contracts and forging Dave Kleiman's signature on W&K partnership documents in order to steal "hundreds of thousands of bitcoins" and the intellectual property rights to "various blockchain technologies," collectively worth over $5 billion.

Although media suggested that the Miami trial would finally reveal the truth about Nakamoto—crypto press called it "Bitcoin's Trial of the Century," and even *The Wall Street Journal*'s headline was "Bitcoin Creator Satoshi Nakamoto Could Be Unmasked at Florida Trial"—the case didn't depend on proving whether Wright was or wasn't Nakamoto. Kleiman's lawyers argued only that Wright was a thief. "We are here today in this courtroom because that man, Craig Wright, chose to steal from his dead best friend and business partner," Kyle Roche told the jury in his opening statement.

Discovery had been a nightmare. Wright turned over more than two hundred thousand documents, 1.9 million pages, and Kleiman's lawyers questioned the authenticity of many of them. Roche obtained proof that the Department of Homeland Security had turned down all of W&K's research proposals. The creator of Bitmessage testified that on the date shown in a Bitmessage transcript produced by Wright, he hadn't yet released the app. Forensic experts testified that PDFs submitted by Wright as evidence contained fonts that didn't exist on the creation dates shown in the documents' metadata. When Kleiman lawyer Vel Freedman questioned Wright in an evidentiary hearing, Wright became so ruffled that he threw a piece of paper at Freedman, prompting the judge to threaten to have him arrested and adding to the pile of court-antagonizing behavior that would eventually lead Wright's own lawyers, seeking to mitigate the damage, to obtain and submit a psychiatric diagnosis finding Wright to have Asperger's.

Most damningly, after Wright testified under oath that he had no involvement with W&K, Kleiman's lawyers surprised him with Australian court documents showing how Wright had seized control of the partnership. "We destroyed him," Freedman recalled. Jamie Wilson, a former colleague of Wright's in Australia, testified about a sudden change in Wright's material circumstances and attitude, from a "low-key" developer who wore hoodies to one who was "I've got to be the man, I've got to be the CEO, new flash suits, ties, and it was just a massive change from where he was conservative to right out there." After Wright's lawyers suggested in a filing that "Dave intended to end his own life," Kleiman's countered that if Wright was allowed to testify to this, "Ira should be allowed to testify to the possibility that Wright had David murdered to steal his bitcoin fortune." A Miami jury found Wright liable for conversion and awarded damages of $100 million, to which the judge added another $43 million.

Wright was the opposite of negative space. He'd filled the Satoshi void with garish colors, an unending series of farfetched stories. Even when it came to his attempted suicide, I hadn't been able to shake the sense, as Stefan Matthews recounted the details, that he told the tale with an unseemly flair. And starting in interviews with the Australian Taxation Office, and continuing through his testimony in the Miami lawsuit, Wright repeatedly changed the explanation for why he couldn't provide a digital signature proving he held Nakamoto's keys. He told the ATO that the keys had been divided into slices and that a majority of them were held in an entity named the Tulip Trust, which he had created in the Seychelles, but which he was legally unable to touch, and the trustees of which he couldn't name. In a motion hearing, Bruce E. Reinhart, the magistrate judge in the case, told Wright's lawyers: "You realize it is facially incredible that in 2011 your client transferred potentially billions of dollars in bitcoin to someone and you can't tell me who that was. You understand that, right?"

Then Wright said that the key slices were scheduled to be delivered by "a bonded courier" six months later, and he had no way of contacting the courier. Later Wright said that the courier was a lawyer for the Tulip Trust named Denis Mayaka, but Judge Reinhart questioned whether he even existed. A month after the person Kleiman's lawyers derisively called "the bonded courier from the future" was scheduled to arrive, Wright announced that he'd discovered a ruinous hack of his home computer systems and their cloud backups, draining 1.1 million GBP worth of BSV, fifty white papers and associated paperwork for patent applications, and private keys controlling the 111,000 bitcoins supposedly held by the Tulip Trust, at that time worth nearly $2 billion. Wright later said that he'd found a wireless router called a pineapple in an inconspicuous area in his home in Surrey and that it didn't belong to him or anyone in his family. The hackers, he suggested, had either followed tradesmen into the house or broken in.

Another story Wright kept changing was the identities of the Second Man and the Third Man who made up the triune Satoshi Nakamoto he had long described. He told the ATO that the Third Man was David Rees, an English mathematician who'd done codebreaking work at Bletchley Park and whom Wright's grandfather had known. But Rees's daughters told the ATO that in 2008, when their father was ninety, he'd been "very frail, a little confused and suffered from some memory loss, his doctor regarded him as suffering from senile dementia," and they "considered it inconceivable that their father could have completed work of this nature without his family being aware."

Having earlier described Dave Kleiman as playing a key role, by the time the Miami trial began Wright would concede only that Kleiman had helped him spiff up the prose in the Bitcoin white paper: "If it had been a 60-page paper full of academic wankery, no one would read it." His past descriptions of Kleiman as Bitcoin's cocreator had merely been an act of kindness toward a dead friend. "I exaggerated Dave's role because I wanted him to be part of it and no one remember[ed] him."

In one of Vel Freedman's four depositions of Wright, the Second Man switched from Kleiman to Wright's uncle, Donald Lynam. And the Third Man, Wright now asserted, was "a former GCHQ MI6 operative who was killed by Russian agents, who was working on the tracking of basically money laundering funds, that I had helped and talked to before his death here in the U.K., named Gareth . . . Williams. . . . That is one name he used." Gareth Williams was a real ex-MI6 agent who'd been all over the news in 2011 when he was found dead in a padlocked duffel bag with the key inside and no evidence of another person's involvement. Escapologists had tried more than four hundred times to duplicate the scenario, without success. "But days after the inquest," *The Guardian* reported, "footage emerged of a retired army sergeant climbing into the bag and locking it from the inside." Freedman couldn't hide his disbelief: "So, Dr. Wright, were you a super spy for the government?"

In another of the four depositions, Wright refused to answer the Third Man question, saying that national security issues were at stake. But in a sealed court filing that was later unsealed, Wright gave a new name. It was redacted, but through an oversight a related footnote contained a link to the Wikipedia page of one Paul Calder Le Roux.

Le Roux scored decently on the Satoshi Checklist. He had coded Encryption for the Masses (E4M), an open-source cryptographic software package, was a South African–raised Australian, and had compelling reasons both to withdraw from the project and to keep his name off it: he was wanted in multiple countries on charges spanning arms dealing, money laundering, cocaine smuggling, blood diamonds trafficking, and murders for hire. After his arrest in 2012, Le Roux became a DEA informant and was sentenced to twenty-five years in prison—offering an explanation, if he was Nakamoto, for both Nakamoto's disappearance and his untouched coins.

Le Roux's biographer, Evan Ratliff, interviewed associates of Le Roux's who said he'd been talking about digital currency in the period preceding Bitcoin's release. Tantalizingly, Ratliff uncovered a fake Congolese diplomatic passport Le Roux had used that gave his name as Paul Solotshi Calder Le Roux. *Solotshi. Satoshi.* There was counterevidence, including dissimilar writing styles, but Le Roux joined the ever-growing list of plausible Nakamotos.

The Florida suit had been the biggest stage yet for Wright's one-man show, but it had little bearing on his Nakamoto claim. *Granath v. Wright,* which was coming to trial in the fall of 2022, would be the first case to address that question directly. The legal issue was whether, in calling Wright a fraud, Magnus Granath had acted reasonably. But the implications were more far-reaching. "The most important thing for me about this case," Wright debunker Arthur van Pelt told me before the trial, "is Craig Wright has to prove that he is Satoshi Nakamoto."

Eat Sleep Hodl Repeat

Courtroom 250 in the Oslo District Courthouse was a well-lit expanse of blond wood, glass dividers, and gentle lines populated by lawyers in formal black robes. On the wall behind Judge Helen Engebrigtsen's bench was a heraldic red shield with a crowned lion rampant in gold.

It was a Monday morning in September. Craig Wright, now fifty-one, swaggered in with his chest out, wearing a three-piece suit and a large pinky ring. He was shadowed by a tan, smiling, impeccably tailored bodyguard named Michel, who wore the gold trident of a Swedish amphibious special forces veteran. It was the first time I'd seen Wright in person. In the seven years since he'd come to public attention, he'd become grayer, softer-bodied, ruddier, jowlier. His mouth had settled in a frown.

Magnus Granath, a forty-five-year-old with sandy hair and a beard, wearing understated glasses, a gray sweater, and a blue anorak, took a seat on the opposite side of the room and from his messenger bag pulled a paperback book and a laptop covered with stickers.

It was a lopsided spectacle. Granath sat next to his two lawyers. Wright was flanked by nine, though they left an empty seat on either side of their client. The optics were off-message. Wright was claiming to be a victim of cyberbullying.

With the foreigners in the room wearing headphones for live translation from Norwegian, Judge Engebrigtsen started by saying that the point of this case wasn't to establish beyond a reasonable doubt whether Wright was Satoshi Nakamoto. But, she acknowledged, that question was central to whether or not Granath had defamed Wright.

Over the next few days, the trial settled into a rhythm. A team from CoinGeek sat in the press gallery on Wright's side of the courtroom, along with his wife, Ramona, and son Ben. A four-person team from *Bitcoin Magazine,* which was filming the trial, positioned themselves in the press gallery on Granath's side of the room, near his mother and girlfriend. Before the trial's start, Granath, knowing he was about to lose his anonymity and preferring to do so on his own terms, had given an interview to a Norwegian newspaper using his real name and allowed the paper to photograph him. But throughout the trial, *Bitcoin* would refer to Granath only as Hodlonaut and in video footage fuzz out his face. When the magazine's translator tweeted #WeAreAllHodlonaut, someone replied: "who needs objectivity." A Hodlonaut supporter named Norbert live-tweeted the trial, furiously typing on a laptop that bore the sticker "EAT SLEEP HODL REPEAT." I switched from side to side, worried that if I appeared aligned with a particular team, the other might stop talking to me.

Some of the case concerned the line between Twitter trash talk and actionable defamation. *Hadn't Wright given as good as he got?* Granath's lawyers argued, pointing to Wright tweets that labeled Julian Assange "a rapist" and said, "I look forward to seeing all soy boy beta asshats crushed." A foreigner stepping into the courtroom by accident would have seen lead Wright lawyer Halvor Manshaus, black-robed eminence of the Oslo bar, uttering a stream of incomprehensible Norwegian punctuated by "scamtard," "bitchboy," and "leet speakers." There ensued a conversation in which one of Granath's lawyers had to explain to the befuddled judge such terms as *cuck, Low T,* and *massive Tassy,* which we all learned was an Australian slur referring to the pubic-triangular shape of Tasmania. Wright's lawyers, for their part, had gone through Granath's roughly thirty-seven thousand tweets and found several disturbing ones, including "hard to verify how many Hitler killed, since questioning the sanctioned version of history is illegal in most of Europe," "The official story on 9/11 is as believable as CSW being Satoshi," and "Vaccine pushers are dangerous extremists. Enough."

At times, it seemed Bitcoin values were on trial. "It's difficult to hold someone accountable when they're anonymous," Manshaus argued. He invoked the Ring of Gyges, a story from Plato's *Republic* that Wright sometimes told about how people behave badly when they have the "cloak of anonymity."

Much of Granath's case reprised or built on evidence first introduced in Miami. On top of all the prior dings to Wright's credibility, Granath's team submitted a new, 227-page forensic report by KPMG finding that seventy-one documents submitted by Wright in this case appeared to have been manipulated, forged, or backdated.

Manshaus tried to overcome Wright's personality and credibility problems by linking them. It was Wright's *communication style* that had led five judges in four different courts to question his truthfulness. Wright deserved empathy, not scorn, Ami Klin, head of the Marcus Autism Center at Emory University, testified. When Granath's lead lawyer, Ørjan Salvesen Haukaas, cross-examined Klin, he asked whether symptoms of autism spectrum disorder and narcissistic personality disorder "might be similar."

"At a superficial level, you can make the case that those things look similar," Klin answered. "But at a clinical level, they absolutely are not similar."

Wright took a novel and decidedly un-cypherpunk position on how to prove identity. Besides Gavin Andresen and Jon Matonis, there were "80 to 100" people who knew "all about my history creating Bitcoin," he told the court. "My opinion is people are evidence. . . . Identity is not related to keys." A handful of Australian relatives and former colleagues testified on his behalf, though most had little to contribute regarding his Nakamoto claim.

Wright had also recently found some long-lost documents, including a roughly eighty-page handwritten draft of the white paper he said he'd begun in August 2007, and a new typed version, also from 2007, though a font that didn't exist prior to 2012 had somehow made its way into the latter document. And Wright told an entirely new story about why he couldn't access the Nakamoto private keys: back in 2016, after his suicide attempt, he had "stomped on the hard drive" and taken a hammer to a USB drive containing the key slices, so that he could never be forced to prove himself with cryptography, which would grant his enemies "the easy way out."

On Wednesday, the third day of the trial, more people were in the courtroom as Granath, wearing a blue oxford shirt beneath a thin v-neck sweater, took the stand and described his road to Bitcoin.

He had gotten his first computer when he was eight or nine, a Commodore 64, and had saved files to cassette tape. As a child, he noticed that year after year the price of the Krone-is ice cream cones he loved kept ticking upward. It was his first awareness of inflation, and he felt disillusioned.

He talked about his fascination with Bitcoin's fixed money supply and with the idea that if he held a token he owned a piece of that pie. He talked about the miracle of digital scarcity: unlike everything else online, Bitcoin was something that couldn't be copied.

Granath said he'd originally made his Twitter account pseudonymous so that if Bitcoin became very valuable he wouldn't be a target. Having earlier traded "altcoins, or shitcoins," he was by then already "what most would call a Bitcoin Maximalist," hodling bitcoin and disdaining all other cryptocurrencies. What made Bitcoin unique, he said, was that it didn't have a leader. Bitcoin's small block size meant anyone could run a network node. A more centralized cryptocurrency was merely "a database project, and can be edited by the people in control."

"You said an important point about Bitcoin for you was that it doesn't have any leader," Granath's lawyer Haukaas said, "but then we have this Satoshi Nakamoto character. Could you share your opinion of this person, or these persons?"

"I've personally never worshipped Satoshi," Granath said, but "I have an immense respect for whoever was behind Bitcoin and the name Satoshi Nakamoto. . . . I found the person, or persons, behind the name to seem like a humble and kind person, who seemed very dedicated to this project."

"Are you familiar with anyone else not being Craig Wright that has claimed to be Satoshi Nakamoto?"

"Eh, Craig Wright is probably the one who has most outspokenly claimed to be him. A lot of people are curious about this, and some have speculated on names. Like, a lot of people think Hal Finney had a part in it. Nick Szabo has been mentioned. I mean that it really doesn't have that much importance, and I haven't started digging into it. But there's absolutely others who have made the claim . . . I still get direct messages on Twitter, from some of the people claiming to be Satoshi. They have also sent me messages to 'help'"—he made air quotes—"in this case, but I don't reply nor believe in these."

When Granath first heard of Craig Wright, after the *Wired* and Gizmodo articles, he'd thought "it would be weird if a person or persons like Satoshi Nakamoto would be careless enough to be revealed in this way." He theorized that Wright had first claimed to be Nakamoto in order to get out of his tax jam in Australia and that later it became lucrative to be Nakamoto, once Wright launched a coin named Bitcoin Satoshi Vision.

"You can imagine how provoking it is, for people that, first of all, admire Satoshi and are against people being fooled," Granath testified. "Then you have somebody claiming they're Satoshi, and on top of this are going to sue everyone that says they're not Satoshi."

Granath had been heartened by how the Bitcoin community came together to support him. A nonprofit named OpenSats raised 15 million Norwegian krone, or $1.4 million, from more than 2,600 contributors, including some of the biggest companies in Bitcoin, to fund his legal defense. Even the detective who first contacted him on behalf of Wright's lawyers had later messaged him to say that he regretted taking the job and considered Wright a Nisse, a type of Nordic goblin. Granath sounded emotional as he talked about Bitcoiners having his back. He said that he felt like he was here representing them and Bitcoin.

After Granath finished his testimony, Judge Engebrigtsen asked whether he wanted to add anything about the incendiary tweets Manshaus had read. "I could but don't feel a strong need to," Granath said. Engebrigtsen said she just meant, since he hadn't had a chance to comment on them. "The tweet that I felt looked worst out of context," Granath said, referring to the one on "vaccine pushers," "I still stand behind all my opinions about . . . Remember, I don't have that many Norwegian followers." But he had friends in other countries who'd "been stripped of certain liberties if they refused to let themselves vaccinate. . . . I think maybe the tweet about extremists, that's when I saw [Canadian prime minister Justin] Trudeau talking to small kids, telling them to tell their parents they have to get the vaccine. I found that to be an untimely pushing of people to get vaccinated."

Wright wasn't doing press interviews during the trial, but after court adjourned the next day I had dinner with Kurt Wuckert, Jr., a CoinGeek correspondent and Wright's most able advocate. Kurt was limiting himself to one meal a day, so we were eating bowls of pork stew in the middle of the afternoon. Later, he'd go to an MMA studio to work out.

Kurt wasn't seeing the same trial I was. I thought Wright was getting destroyed, but Kurt had been live-streaming that Granath's body language looked anxious and, of the judge: "I think she got it." While Manshaus was "empathic," Granath's mouth "twitched" in amusement when his "cruel" tweets were read. Kurt thought Granath's lawyers looked worried. He was "pretty bullish, frankly," he told me. The momentum was "clearly on the side of Craig."

Kurt took Wright's outlandish excuses at face value. He'd gravitated toward Wright and BSV, he said, because Bitcoin's resistance to becoming a useful currency "drove me nuts." He felt that Wright talked about Bitcoin the way Nakamoto had. He was familiar with the arguments against Wright, "but I never expected the Satoshi story to be clean. He's an anonymous internet character from the dark web. Satoshi's a fundamentally dishonest character. He's an unreliable narrator. That's who Satoshi Nakamoto is. That's the point, right? So when people are like, 'Well, that doesn't make sense,' I don't know. I like literature. I like to read stories. I like grandiose nonsense and narratives and things. I always assumed Satoshi would be essentially disappointing, right? 'Cause the legend in your own head is always going to be great. It's like horror movies. Twenty, thirty years ago, when effects weren't nearly as good, you didn't show the monster until the last scene, but it was terrifying in your mind, because the story was good. And then you see the monster, and he's a rubber puppet, but it didn't matter, because you already scared yourself through the whole film. You'd fill in those blanks yourself. And it just was so much juicier with Satoshi. And when you meet Craig, it's like, 'Okay, he's this boisterous autistic Australian pain-in-the-ass guy, and that's okay. 'Cause what did we need him to be? We needed him to be what he was for this period of time, but it's okay if he's the rubber puppet at the end of the movie."

"Kurt is lying out of his ass about everything," Magnus Granath was saying. It was the next day, after court, and I was sitting with Magnus and his girlfriend, Katia, who was from Ukraine and went by Katoshi online. We were at a basement table in a cafe near the courthouse, and as Magnus ate an open-face shrimp sandwich, and Katia a slice of chocolate cake, we talked about *Citadel21*, a Bitcoin-culture 'zine they'd founded to highlight "grassroots voices."

The past few years had been stressful. Since the lawsuit began, Magnus had lost his father, and Katia hers. Then Russia invaded Ukraine, and Katia's mother came to live with them in Oslo. The lawsuit was taxing. During this trial, a five-person documentary crew with two cameras, employed by a PR company owned by Calvin Ayre, shadowed Magnus when he left the courthouse.

Magnus was the opposite of a crypto degenerate speculating on price swings. "*Bitcoin changes you,* a lot of people have said. Some have said, *It doesn't change you, it exposes your character.* I think the two are maybe equally true."

What about him?

"I don't think I've changed that much," Magnus said. "Bitcoin maybe made me even more determined to speak the truth. Some people call Bitcoin a cult. Some call it a religion. I think it's a fascinating perspective to ponder. Because it really is something special. For the first time in history, we have non-negotiable truth. Everyone agrees that the Bitcoin blockchain, it's shared all over, it's not up for discussion."

I thought about the low trust that permeated the Bitcoin world. The lifestyle of a true hodler now encompassed everything from deadlifting to eating liver to "sunning your balls," all so that you could "escape the matrix." The Citadel in the 'zine's title referred to a Bitcoin meme about an anarchic future when the Bitcoin faithful would cluster in hilltop fortresses, dependent only on themselves, while the rest of the world made do in the apocalyptic wastelands below.

Real-life Magnus was sincere and humble and able to laugh, and despite his conspiracy tweets, I found myself liking him. The tweets seemed mainly a defiant extension of the mistrust endemic among people skeptical of "fiat" and "trusted third parties" and "the official narrative" on pretty much any topic.

I asked about the book he kept opening during the trial. It was Marcus Aurelius's *Meditations,* Magnus said. He'd gotten into Stoicism after reading Tom Wolfe's novel *A Man in Full* twenty years earlier, long before it became the default philosophy for bone-broth bros. "I learned it was not a good idea for me to invest a lot of meaning or energy in stuff that's outside my control and instead just focus on the stuff that I can control. And obviously that comes into play in this trial." Before testifying, he'd told himself: *Don't complicate this, Magnus. Just go in there and tell the truth.* He'd made a point of not preparing, lest his answers sound canned. "If I was sitting there only thinking about the outcome, or only thinking about what will they say now, or what will they ask me on the stand, I'd probably be stressed out. And this is probably some of the most stressful stuff I've experienced: the doxing and the bounty and the preparation for the trial. I'm a father, I have a kid, I have a life outside of this, and this has taken up way too much time. But on the other hand, I guess I'm stubborn or principled, you can choose which. There was no way I could go to court and say that Craig Wright is Satoshi."

Magnus was particularly disappointed in Gavin Andresen, on whose original endorsement Wright continued to lean heavily. Since 2016, Gavin had modulated his position. Deposed in the Miami suit, he said it was news to him that Calvin Ayre was behind Wright. He called the decisive moment in the London hotel basement "the so-called proving ceremony." He said that it was clear Wright could be dishonest at times and that he'd been "bamboozled" by Wright's "gobbledygook."

But Gavin also seemed still to believe Wright was Nakamoto, explaining away Wright's behavior by wondering whether he had clinical "paranoia" and whether the reason Wright hadn't sent back Gavin's 0.11 BTC was that he didn't want to reveal that he'd improperly held on to private keys that were supposed to be locked in a trust.

When Wright lawyer Manshaus had asked Magnus about Gavin, Magnus said: "To be as concrete as possible, in my absolute total assessment of what happened to Andresen . . . he was tricked. . . . It's a painful, hard situation to face. . . . We see, in this case, how Matonis and Andresen are the evidence. So I'm wondering why they're not here to tell it themselves." In 2020, Magnus said, he'd asked Jon Matonis on Twitter if he still backed Wright, because it affected other people, since his backing was being used as evidence. Matonis blocked him. "Bitcoiners like the truth and want to verify," Magnus said. What they didn't like was "an appeal to authority."

Now, at the cafe, I wondered why Satoshi Nakamoto hadn't stepped forward to debunk Wright. "I would be disappointed," Magnus said. "I'm just so sure he won't. And I have no theory if he or they or she is even alive, but if so, I'd expect them not to do anything. Even if Satoshi came forward now, he wouldn't be able to control Bitcoin. Bitcoin is now a thing of its own. He could, of course. It wouldn't be good for the person or persons, and it wouldn't be good for the project either."

Couldn't Nakamoto at least publish the digitally signed message "I'm not Craig Wright"?

"It's not like I wouldn't think it was cool," Magnus said. "If suddenly I wake up tomorrow and, look, he's signed 'Free Hodlonaut' or something, of course that would be awesome, but I wouldn't want those persons to compromise themselves. I'm very aware of how small stake, small time, I and this thing is, compared to—I view Bitcoin as an enormous revolution with enormous implications for future human freedom. So, it's just very surrealistic to be involved in this stuff right now."

He hoped, after this was over, that he would again return to being a private citizen. "I think Hodlonaut will remain, but maybe I will prefer to have another account to be able to speak more freely. Let's see which direction the world keeps moving."

Judge Engebrigtsen wouldn't issue a ruling in the case for another month.

Alistair

I'd tried to stay open to possibilities and would idly follow little coincidences to see where they led. One day in late April of 2023, I found myself thinking about a word I'd seen in Nakamoto's writings: *hosed.*

Given Nakamoto's tendency to write in a style stripped of personality or anything that betrayed a milieu or sensibility, *hosed* stood out. I hadn't recently heard the word, in its sense of *screwed* or *wrecked,* and vaguely associated it with turn-of-the-1990s surfing or fraternity lingo. Online sources variously traced its origins to World War I military slang and to an early-'90s expression at the Massachusetts Institute of Technology about an education there being like "drinking water from a firehose."

I went back through my scraped archives and noted each time someone used the word. It wasn't as rare as I'd expected. Maybe two dozen cypherpunks had used it during the list's heyday. Fewer people on the extropians list had used it, though a handful stood out as having used it more than once, including Mark Grant, an elusive, self-described Oxford University graduate who'd written about digital cash for the 'zine *Extropy* and was a C++ coder with an interest in cryptography. Next, I looked at Metzdowd. In the three years leading up to October 31, 2008, when Satoshi Nakamoto first announced

Bitcoin there, the word had been used four times. Twice it was by the same person: James A. Donald.

Though Donald hadn't played much of a role in the public discussion of Bitcoin, he'd had a cameo in its early history, as the first person on the list to respond to Nakamoto. The response had been a technical criticism, related to Bitcoin's scaling potential, and after a few exchanges with Nakamoto he'd dropped out of the conversation.

So many Nakamoto suspects had been proposed over the years. If a person had the slightest, most tenuous overlap with Bitcoin or digital money or sometimes just a neighboring topic, someone at some point had thrown that person's name into the ring. In May 2014, one Phinnaeus Gage had kicked off a thread on BitcoinTalk: "Definitive Proof That Satoshi Nakamoto is James A. Donald." He included time stamps of Donald's initial response to Nakamoto, and Nakamoto's response to Donald, and claimed that it had taken Nakamoto just forty-two seconds to digest Donald's response, compose a fleshed-out reply, and send it. "I can only imagine Satoshi jumping into his DeLorean E-MC2 and heading on down to Milliways after accomplishing such a feat," Gage, evidently a comedic science-fiction buff, added with a football-spiking flourish that alluded to both *Back to the Future* and *The Hitchhiker's Guide to the Galaxy*.

The only problem with the theory was that Gage had taken the time stamps from a mirrored archive of the original posts. The time stamps on the Metzdowd list, where the emails first appeared, seemed to indicate that Nakamoto had not, in fact, responded so quickly. He had responded nearly two hours later. Gage, after sheepishly acknowledging his error, added the word "Debunked" to his thread's title.

In more rigorous Nakamoto-suspect roundups, Donald hadn't rated a mention. He was in none of the lineups stylometrists had made public. There'd been no particular reason to focus on him. He was one of many cypherpunks, and one of many who'd been interested in digital money. And though he'd been a regular contributor to Metzdowd and other lists, he had a slippery internet presence.

Websites variously declared that he was Canadian, that he had died, and that "James A. Donald" wasn't his real name.

Donald was on my Suspects spreadsheet, too, like a lot of other people, for flimsy reasons—he was a cypherpunk and libertarian who'd coded in C++. He was nowhere near the top of the list, notching in at #42, between someone named Ashish Gulhati, whom I couldn't remember when I'd added him to the list or why, and an "Unnamed Candidate" a British sleuth had described in vague terms.

Now, intrigued by the "hosed" coincidence, I went back and looked at the lists of rare words the Satoshitizer had compiled when analyzing the scraped archives. These were the Nakamoto-isms that appeared least often in a particular archive. If an unusual word used by Nakamoto was also an unusual word on a list he might have frequented under his true name, I'd figured, it could tie his pseudonym to a real person. I wanted to see whether Donald had used any other rare Nakamoto-isms.

He had. Donald showed up as the only person on any of the two decades' worth of lists I'd scraped who had ever used the word *fencible*—in the sense of stolen goods "able to be fenced." This was a word Nakamoto had used once, in the expression *non-fencible.* And it appeared in a post by Donald on the cypherpunks list in October of 1998.

My brain started pinging.

The verb *fence* was common-enough slang, but the adjective *fencible* was an oddity. A Google search turned up hardly any instances on the Internet. When I queried the archives of the daily *New York Times,* which went back to 1857 and included more than thirteen million articles, *fencible,* in the sense I was interested in, hadn't appeared once (it appeared in a different sense, as a noun referring to a pre-twentieth-century defensive military regiment). I next tried the sites linguists use to assess a word's rarity: *fencible* wasn't in the Corpus of Contemporary American English, which contained more than one billion words, or the Corpus of Global Web-Based English, which had nearly two billion. In News on the Web, a 17.6-billion-word corpus, it appeared once, on a New Zealand news site in 2017, in a quote about retail theft.

Unlike, say, *trusted third party* or *zero-knowledge proofs,* which to outsiders can look like smoking guns but are unexceptional when you zoom in on conversations among digital-cash or crypto experts, *fencible* and *hosed* weren't words unique to cryptography or even to computer science. They were more revealing of someone's voice.

I began looking more closely at Donald. He'd been an active poster on several lists Nakamoto would plausibly have been on: cypherpunks, extropians, Metzdowd, P2P hackers, coderpunks. In his posts, he almost never revealed personal details, but a few were strewn here and there. He was Australian but had lived in Silicon Valley for many years, which was consistent with Nakamoto's posting times. Like Nakamoto, he sometimes used American spellings and other times used Commonwealth spellings and words.

Ideologically, Donald had been one of the most hardcore cypherpunks, fusing a libertarianism so extreme that it was really anarcho-capitalism with a fervent conviction in the world-changing power of cryptography. "So guys, that is the plan," he told cypherpunks in 1996. "We destroy the state through higher mathematics. We do this by replacing the current institutional mechanisms of corporations with cryptographic mechanisms. This will give more people the opportunity to evade and resist taxes."

He had a particular interest in digital money. "Eventually people will bypass the banks, directly transferring funds to each other," he wrote in 1995. "This will reduce the bank fees to zero. The banks will gradually lose control of the indecently lucrative funds transfer business." In 1998, he wrote, "That is the big remaining battle. Net money. Net money that is reasonably liquid, that many people acquire, that many people spend, money that is readily convertible to worthwhile goods and services." Around the same time that Nakamoto registered Bitcoin.org, I recalled, he also registered the domain Netcoin .com. On Metzdowd, between 2006 and 2009, Donald employed more of the e-cash vocabulary Nakamoto used than any other poster.

Next, I turned to Donald's programming style. In the late 1990s on the cypherpunks list, he'd promoted a piece of communications encryption software called Crypto Kong, intended to improve on PGP. He'd written it in C++, the same language Nakamoto used for Bitcoin. Using the Wayback Machine, I found an archived copy of the source code. Crypto Kong bore other similarities to Bitcoin. Like Nakamoto, Donald had coded the software for Windows and, more esoterically, used Hungarian notation. Like Nakamoto, Donald used sweeping lines of slashes to separate sections of code. Like Bitcoin, Crypto Kong used elliptic curve cryptography to generate private-public key pairs.

From an online database, I gleaned more information about Donald. Early Bitcoin developers had surmised that Nakamoto was a bit older, based on his coding style; Donald was born in 1952, so was now around seventy. He was stringently private, and well practiced at controlling his public footprint. Though in one sense he was all over the internet, having published tens of thousands of words on his own and other blogs, he was effectively invisible. He wasn't on Twitter or Facebook or LinkedIn, at least under his own name. His $2.8 million Palo Alto house was blurred on Google Street View, as was his $400,000 Austin house. This was an option you could exercise only by submitting a formal request to Google (or perhaps by working at Google, as one of Donald's two sons had). There were no easily found photographs of him. Like Nakamoto, Donald used a privacy-focused email provider, Switzerland-based Proton Mail, and his email prefix was a jumble of seemingly meaningless consonants and one vowel. He had a blog titled *Jim's Blog,* untethered from his last name. He had spent, he'd told the blog's readers, "a lot of time off the grid."

Click-click-click. The tumblers were falling into place.

Maybe Donald had been overlooked as a candidate because his response to Nakamoto had been critical. And you couldn't just google him; he was so well obscured that you quickly hit a wall on readily available information about him. Unless you had a reason to dig deeper, it was natural to set him aside and move on to more intuitive Nakamoto suspects.

I now began to think that the more salient fact about Donald's response to Nakamoto than its content was that it had been first. I pictured Nakamoto in 2008: he'd just launched his work of genius into the world and . . . *crickets*. So he decided to nudge things along by lobbing a criticism at himself. It might have been sincere. "Not only should you disagree with others," Nick Szabo had written, "but you should disagree with yourself . . . [Q]uantum thought, as I call it . . . demands that we simultaneously consider often mutually contradictory possibilities." Doing so had the added benefit of obscuring any role Donald might have played.

Donald required fewer qualifications than Hal Finney or Nick Szabo. He wouldn't have had to pretend to be an inconsistent user of Commonwealth English. And if you were prepared to believe that Hal Finney sent himself private emails from an alter ego, it was even easier to believe that Donald interacted with himself through a sock puppet on a public forum. Unlike Hal or Nick, Donald had never denied that he was Nakamoto—or even been asked the question, as far as I knew. On his blog, he'd made the observation that Bitcoin "is a prototype that is prematurely being used as the final system."

Jim's Blog revealed a few more clues. In the run-up to October 31, 2008, Donald had been focused on the financial crisis. His post on October 11, titled "The Cause of the Crisis," began: "The bailout will fail." What had been the London *Times* headline embedded in Bitcoin's Genesis Block? "Chancellor on Brink of Second Bailout." The following month, Donald blogged about "the degeneration of Britain."

The blog also yielded an answer to the question of why Nakamoto had "moved on to other things" when he did. Donald's wife had died in April of 2016 after "a long and terrible illness." If he was Nakamoto, couldn't that explain his departure from the project? He was a husband incapacitated by responsibility and grief?

Above all, *Jim's Blog* offered a compelling answer to one of the most confounding questions about Nakamoto: Why had he chosen, and then stuck with, a pseudonym?

I'd always wondered whether the mystery of Satoshi Nakamoto might turn out to be more compelling than its resolution. Guessing who Deep Throat was had been a decades-long Washington parlor game that animated the history of Watergate, but the revelation that he was Mark Felt had been underwhelming. The legend took up space in our imaginations. The person not so much.

"Satoshi's identity doesn't matter," Ray Dillinger, who along with Hal Finney had done code review for Nakamoto before Bitcoin's launch, had recently asserted. "The protocol is what it is. If it's a third-world dictator, a homeless guy living under a bridge in Belize, a Bedouin working from a cell phone as she traverses Bir Tawil on a camel, or a pushcart vendor in Nairobi, the protocol is exactly the same as it would be if it were a cryptanalyst working for the NSA or someone at a 'troll farm' drawing a salary from the GRU, or a well-known Security researcher or Cypherpunk. 'Satoshi' doesn't exist outside that protocol. Satoshi is just a hat somebody wore while they were developing it. And it doesn't matter who was wearing the hat."

I agreed, to a point. Either Nakamoto was someone whom lots of people already assumed to be Nakamoto—a Nick or a Hal—and confirmation wouldn't add much to the picture, or he was someone no one had heard of. In that case, learning his name, and that he was a bright graduate student who physically lived in wherever-ville but effectively lived on his computer and who'd had a fluky insight, would feel academic. What would knowing his True Name tell us?

Though "Jim" rarely mentioned any details that betrayed his identity or location, there were exceptions here and there in his posts and in his replies to comments. Before he was a libertarian or crypto-anarchist, he'd been a radical leftist. At age fifteen, he'd joined the Spartacists, a faction of Trotskyites, but "I became disillusioned with the sparts, and disillusioned by participatory democracy—and none too keen on representative democracy either." At seventeen, he joined two other radical groups, the anarcho-socialists and the Maoists, "mostly because these were the two groups most hated by the trots." Eventually he concluded that freedom lay in property rights, and he became an anarcho-capitalist. He'd named his Crypto Kong encryption software after Hong Kong, as a symbol of resistance to "oppression by the state." He clearly enjoyed being an *ist* of one kind or another.

He showed up elsewhere online as the author of two academic papers published in the 1970s, and I spoke with people who'd known him when he was a graduate student in the School of Physics at the University of Sydney.

Bob Hewitt, who was on the department faculty, interviewed Donald as part of the application process. Donald had come from Melbourne, and Bob recalled him as "bohemian"; asked whether he'd arranged for a place to stay in Sydney, Donald, who at the time was known as Sandy, said he wasn't worried, he'd sleep under a bridge. He was "quite pleasant," Bob said, "a friendly kind of guy, just strange."

One time, Donald observed that with petrol bombs, which student radicals of the era favored, you had to shake up the ingredients to get an emulsion before throwing them. He came up with the idea that if you substituted a solvent for one of the ingredients, you could skip the shaking step. Donald stored bottles of the liquid in the physics department and recruited another student to help test them. Bob was waiting for a ride home one day, he recalled, when "I heard a little bang. He told me the next day, when I asked if it was him, 'It's okay, we only got a conflagration rather than a detonation.'"

Another time, Bob invited Donald and other students in the department to his home for lunch. After everyone left, "I started getting calls from the other students he'd offered a lift to. They said, 'We got home safely,'" but it had been "a pretty hair-raising ride. They got to a point where the route was blocked by a raised mound to indicate you weren't supposed to cross it. He drove over it."

One of Donald's papers delved into parapsychology. Brian Martin, a fellow grad student who cowrote the paper, "Time-Symmetric Thermodynamics and Causality Violation," told me that the idea, that precognition could be mathematically explained, had been Donald's. Brian later described Donald as "one of those rare individuals who actually fits partially the stereotype of the brilliant, but incomprehensible scientist. . . . [H]e casually skipped over stages of argument which were so obvious to him that he did not realize others might need to struggle to understand each little step."

Donald never completed the PhD program. Every student was supposed to give a colloquium, Bob Hewitt remembered. "They were supposed to be fifty minutes. His lasted ten, and there were hardly any questions. No one understood what he was saying. We couldn't say he was brilliant, but he was certainly incomprehensible when he tried to explain his paper." Donald ended up dropping out after his dissertation, "Assumptions of the Singularity Theorems and the Rejuvenation of Universes," was rejected, unfairly, thought Bob, who felt Donald had been pushed by his adviser to publish too soon.

Instead of going into academia, Donald started writing software for Apple computers, including "Sandy's Word Processor" and a fast-disk operating system, then moved to the U.S. and programmed videogames for Epyx. Later, he worked at database companies including Informix. Nakamoto had once written knowingly about database lingo in an email to Hal Finney: "To the rest of the world, 'log' means delete-at-will, but to database people it means delete-and-lose-everything-in-your-other-files." Nakamoto had once written, of Bitcoin's Wikipedia page: "I hope it doesn't get deleted. If it does it'll be hard to overcome the presumption. Institutional momentum is to stick with the last decision." Nakamoto later edited this remark to add, "or at least I assume so, that's how it usually works, but maybe Wiki is different." Donald had been a Wikipedia contributor.

Poring over *Jim's Blog*, I saw that Donald had an authoritative understanding of Bitcoin and its vulnerabilities without being a blind cheerleader; he clearly took a long, historical view of it as a stepping-stone toward a particular future he wanted. He claimed, responding to a reader's comment: "I know who Nakamoto was and what his political and social goals were." But that wasn't the most interesting thing I found.

I had never shared the presumption, prevalent in the Bitcoin world, that Satoshi Nakamoto must be a benign figure. I'd always felt that the Bitcoiners who elevated Nakamoto to semidivine status were indulging in wishful projection: That he was selfless. That he was humble. That he had come from the future to exalt humanity. Hal Finney had made for a particularly appealing Satoshi Nakamoto because he lived up to that image.

Donald did not. On his blog, subtitled "Liberty in an Unfree World," Donald espoused his latest *ism*: an internet ideology called neoreaction that had beguiled certain people in Silicon Valley. Neoreactionaries took a dark view of the world. They believed that society had been hijacked by what they called the Cathedral—academic and media and bureaucratic elites. They disdained efforts to achieve social justice. The best way forward, they argued, was to jettison democracy and restore a monarchy. Donald's particular flavor of neoreaction also incorporated an overtly Christian element and a generous dose of paranoia; he attributed the covid pandemic to a Jesuit conspiracy.

Along with his baroque politics, Donald produced a regular feed of beyond-the-pale language and opinions that were racist, homophobic, and misogynist. He was so abrasive that, in the 1990s, the extropians listserv had kicked him out. In 2014, *Slate Star Codex,* an influential Silicon Valley blog with a history of tolerating discussion of taboo subjects like IQ science, had banned him. But in the safe space of his blog, hosted on a relatively uncensorable domain in Laos, he advocated "whipping a woman on the buttocks or upper back" to keep her in line, argued that "very few rape accusations are true," and asserted that "the problem is not adult male sexuality towards young girls. The problem is young girls, often alarmingly young girls, sexuality toward adult males." Donald had a substantial following in the red-pilled, alt-right blogosphere. Some of his posts got more than one thousand comments.

If Donald was Nakamoto, wasn't it obvious why he'd chosen a pseudonym when launching Bitcoin? He was so toxic that any association with him would have strangled his brainchild in the crib. He wanted his work of genius to be taken on its own terms rather than dismissed because it was his. If Donald was Nakamoto, his current fascist politics bore little resemblance to the antiauthoritarian cypherpunk values esteemed by Bitcoiners. He had hidden not because Bitcoin could be a risk to him but because he could be a risk to Bitcoin.

Bitcoin already had enough reputational challenges. Each of cryptocurrency's boom-and-bust cycles had featured the same mix of promise and excitement and excesses and scams. Each boom was bigger than the last, and so was each bust. In the most recent run-up, a bitcoin had topped a new high of $69,000, and in the most recent collapse, the cryptocurrency exchange FTX had joined the leaderboard of history's biggest financial frauds. Bitcoiners could justly complain that the scams were unrelated to Bitcoin itself; they were examples, in fact, of the problem of trusted third parties that Bitcoin used decentralization to solve. But Bitcoin, with its values of pseudonymity and the bypassing of governments and banks, wasn't entirely off the hook.

I wondered whether there were crypto people who knew or suspected that Donald was Nakamoto. What were the chances that I alone had stumbled on this dark truth? If Nakamoto was a harmless private citizen like Dorian Nakamoto, "Satoshi deserves his privacy" was at least a reasonable position to take. If Nakamoto was a dissident living under an autocratic regime, I'd want to protect his secret too. But if Nakamoto was Donald? It would undermine the narrative of Bitcoin's inventor as a crypto Christ who'd passed up fame and treasure for the sake of a higher good, or as a shy genius before whom the world should genuflect. Was it possible that some of the Satoshi-deserves-his-privacy people, recognizing that it would be a PR calamity for Bitcoin to have been invented by a foul-mouthed bigot and child rape apologist, were really just safeguarding the reputation of their religion and the value of their investments? In June 2020, after someone tweeted, "let's not elevate him to sainthood just yet" about a Bitcoin YouTube influencer, Nakamoto usual suspect Adam Back had replied: "Maybe we should get mentally prepared to disown Satoshi. Nuke the nym from orbit, just to be safe."

Donald wasn't the only Nakamoto candidate who could cause blowback. Nick Szabo, in recent years, had become an intemperate figure on Twitter, retweeting Tucker Carlson and raging about election fraud and Black Lives Matter. Eventually he'd left Twitter and started posting on Gab, an alt-right Twitter alternative where Donald, as "Jim," also posted. "The decline of Nick Szabo," Ethereum's Vitalik Buterin had written, "has been truly sad to watch. We even named our 10^6 subunit after him . . . [tearful emoji]."

Tim May, after the cypherpunks' heyday, had lived alone with his cat—Nietzsche—and a large gun collection in the foothills of the Santa Cruz Mountains, becoming increasingly unhinged. His last years intermingled racial hatred (thirty-five million Black, Jewish, and Hispanic Americans, he wrote, using uglier words, "need a trip up the chimneys"), conspiracy theories about the CIA, and online reviews of local taquerias, until he drank himself to death. In hindsight, it was unsurprising that some of the people yearning to build a utopia with math and cheat death with science should, defeated by the earthbound constraints of the human condition, wind up deeply alienated.

Bitcoiners talked a lot about it not mattering who Satoshi Nakamoto was. And if they didn't know who he was, that might be true. But they actually needed him not to be terrible. Bitcoin was still insecure about its place in the world. That was why its fans were always going on about hodling and shitcoins. Bitcoin couldn't afford a Bad Satoshi. If Donald was Nakamoto, good luck recruiting more women, kids, black people, gay people, and risk-averse corporations, not to mention literally anyone uncomfortable with using a product made by a hate-mongering pedophilia booster. And if you believed Bitcoin was a bridge to a better future, and were already concerned about the brand damage inflicted by the hordes of scammers, you might reasonably fret that the disclosure of a vile creator could indelibly taint the technology and set back human progress.

It was a strange feeling, walking around in sole possession of one of the world's biggest secrets. I imagined the glory that awaited my reportorial coup. I felt the euphoria that Davis, Penenberg, Goodman, Greenberg, Branwen, and other Satoshi sleuths before me must have felt.

I found further coincidences. The British chancellor referred to in the Genesis Block ("Chancellor on brink of second bailout for banks") was Alistair Darling. The A. in James A. Donald stood for Alistair. What were the chances? Surely this had been an Easter egg. Donald owned several pieces of property in Hawaii. On June 19, 2008, two months before Adam Back received the first email from Satoshi Nakamoto, the *Honolulu Star-Advertiser* had run an obituary for "Satoshi Nakamoto," a veteran of World War II who'd died at eighty-four. Could Donald have lifted the name when casting about for a pseudonym to use?

I started looking over my shoulder. I dusted off the paper shredder I'd bought years earlier while working on a different paranoia-inducing story. I switched on my phone's private-relay setting, masking its IP address. In public places, I became mindful of who could see my laptop screen. When I referred to Donald in my notes, I used only his initials. Nick Szabo, after being out of touch for months, emailed me shortly after I contacted someone else, and I found myself wondering whether the events were connected.

I wrote to Donald asking for an interview. Several days later, to my surprise, I heard back from him. "Email discussion would be convenient," Jim wrote, but he might be able to talk over phone or video, he'd have to let me know in a few days.

Why would one communication method be easier than another? I couldn't think of a reason why that would be an issue unless Jim was somewhere with unreliable high-speed internet. In 2009, Nakamoto had written, "Unfortunately, I can't receive incoming connections from where I am, which has made things more difficult." Was Jim writing from an internet cafe in the town closest to his off-the-grid home in Hawaii? Or did he not want to give away his time zone?

Two months later, Jim still hadn't made himself available for a live conversation. By then, I'd decided to visit him, and I'd started figuring out what I'd need to do first. I suspected he was either in Hawaii or back in Australia, where his late wife was buried. I'd need to verify where he was and possibly take the precautions my former-news-producer sister was advising.

There was only one thing that gave me pause about Jim as Nakamoto. Nakamoto, in his communications, displayed a recognizable range of emotion. He could be appreciative ("Many thanks"), compassionate ("poor thing"), humble ("my apologies"), and modest ("I'm better with code than with words"), none of which seemed Jim-like. I scrolled through years of Jim's writings, squinting for a trace of empathy or gratitude or enthusiasm, hoping to see an exclamation point, or an apology, or a thank-you, or a moment of sympathy or fellowship. Instead, I saw only flatness.

I couldn't help noticing that the more confident I became that Jim was Nakamoto, and the more supporting evidence I found, the less I wanted to acknowledge counterevidence, or even to look for it. I was anxious that I was one step away from learning something that disproved my hypothesis. And so, before getting on a plane to see him, I knew that there was one more thing I needed to do first.

Meh

Ben Laurie was at home on his farm in Wales, sitting in an airy office with fieldstone walls and exposed beams. He wore a beige fleece over a bright blue T-shirt, and his sixty-ish-year-old face was framed by oval rimless glasses and a quiff of white hair. He had a hoop earring and was speaking through a headset.

I thanked him for taking the time to talk about Bitcoin.

"No problem," Ben said. "Always an amusing topic." He had a ready, toothy smile.

Ben was a principal engineer at Google, focused on security, but he was best known as a pioneer of the open-source software movement. Among other things, he'd cofounded the Apache Software Foundation, a nonprofit to support open-source projects.

He had also been one of Bitcoin's most consistent critics in the technical community. But I first wanted to ask him about Lucre, his own digital cash system, which he'd proposed in 1999 and continued updating for the next decade.

Ben had been on the cypherpunks list and taken part in the late 1990s debates about micropayments and Hashcash. "The only contender for anonymized money was Chaum's scheme," Ben recalled, "but it was patented, so I was just noodling about it." He realized there was a way to do something similar using a different "cryptographic primitive" conceived by one of his cryptography mentors,

David Wagner. "Lucre was an anonymized digital currency that you might be able to do micropayments in," he said.

For a few seconds, Ben's face froze on my screen. "My internet is down," he said, when the screen unfroze. "Has been for the last thirty-six hours. I'm tethered to my phone, so it's a bit flaky." Ben lived "in the middle of nowhere," he said.

I asked what had kept Lucre from catching on. "I did it more as an academic exercise," Ben said. "I made some stupid mistakes, which my cryptography mentors helped me fix. It was to show you could do that. I didn't particularly want to start pushing a currency." He hadn't followed other efforts to create digital money, he said. "I don't think I even saw RPOW. And I didn't see Bitcoin either. I mean, I must have been on the mailing list, but I guess I wasn't reading it. My mail has always been a disaster. I don't try very hard to stay on top of it."

Even before Bitcoin arrived, Ben had been a vocal critic of proof of work, which had originally been intended as a way to deal with spam and later became a core component of Bitcoin. He and a computer scientist at Cambridge named Richard Clayton had concluded that it "was non-viable because the costs to genuine users were too high. It's a nice idea, but it doesn't work in practice."

In 2011, Ben tweeted "Bitcoin. Meh." On his blog, he wrote, "A friend of mine alerted me to a sudden wave of excitement about Bitcoin. I have to ask: why? What has changed in the last 10 years to make this work when it didn't in, say, 1999, when many other related systems (including one of my own) were causing similar excitement?" The post, and a follow-up, drew mainly negative comments. Jon Matonis wrote that what had changed was that peer-to-peer systems now worked more robustly, adding, "I'm really surprised that a friend had to 'alert' you to bitcoin!" Zooko Wilcox wrote that he, too, was surprised to be hearing this sentiment from Ben, and suggested that Ben hadn't taken the time to properly understand Bitcoin before posting.

Later, Ben elaborated on his critique of Bitcoin. He thought proof of work was an environmental travesty and Bitcoin a Ponzi scheme. He argued that a decentralized currency would always be impossible because any network that didn't have at least 50 percent of all existing computing power could always be overwhelmed by a greater concentration of computers. Satoshi Nakamoto had warned about the danger of a so-called 51 percent attack, but Nakamoto believed Bitcoin's incentives made it more attractive for such an attacker to mint coins than to devalue the currency. Ben didn't assume an attacker could have only a financial motive.

Was there any part of Bitcoin that Ben admired? I asked.

Ben looked up. "Hmmm." He laughed again and stroked his chin. "I don't think there is. I think it's quite badly designed, and . . ."

He stroked his chin again, looking up to one side.

"Well, I guess I admire it in the sense that it somehow captured people's imaginations and got them to start actually using it, but only slightly, because they used it for entirely the wrong things, and it's horribly inefficient and wasteful."

He allowed that "the underlying blockchain technology, as in the idea of verifiable ledgers, I'm a huge fan of, because they're incredibly useful." He just didn't think you could "make a working system that is decentralized."

And the blockchain hadn't been invented by Nakamoto, as Nakamoto acknowledged in the white paper.

"Yeah," Ben said, "I didn't read the white paper for a very long time."

"Have you spent any time wondering who Satoshi Nakamoto might be?"

"Oh, yeah. I mean, I don't have any insights at all. I think it's really interesting that they effectively disappeared, given how much money they had. And I can only come up with two explanations for that. One is that they're dead. And the other is that they lost their private keys and they're just too fucking embarrassed to admit it."

He belly-laughed and grinned.

How about Len Sassaman?

He wrinkled his nose skeptically. "I knew Len pretty well. . . . And Len was not the kind of guy to be modest about things. I really don't think that he could possibly have done it and not told us." He laughed.

What about Hal Finney?

"In some ways, he's my favorite. He has the useful distinction of being dead. But Satoshi had been silent for some time before he died. But Hal's health was declining. I mean, none of them seem plausible, especially Hal, because he was very ill. A lot of money would have been helpful." Unless he lost the keys.

"Well, here's one for you," I said to Ben, after we'd finished talking about all the reasons he thought Bitcoin was stupid, and about his own take on the Nakamoto mystery. "Have you heard of code stylometry?"

He took a moment to answer, looking up and to the left.

"Yes," he said.

Brian

Before I flew to Australia to doorstep James Donald, I'd decided that I needed real evidence. I felt no qualms about revealing Donald as Nakamoto. It might be the nicest thing anyone could say about him. But given the time, expense, and effort needed to go to him, his self-branding as a "scary" person with guns, and my reservations about the apparent emotional mismatch between him and Nakamoto, I wanted to know that I was acting on more than a circumstantial hunch.

Lex Fridman, the podcaster who periodically played the Nakamoto guessing game with guests, did so again in June 2021 when he interviewed Charles Hoskinson, a cofounder of Ethereum who had gone on to create the cryptocurrency Cardano.

"Is it possible that you are, in fact, Satoshi Nakamoto?"

"No," Hoskinson said, adding that he thought Adam Back was "the Occam's razor candidate. . . . He's the right place, right time, right age, right skill set." The code and cryptography, he thought, weren't up to Hal Finney's skill level and sophistication. "But I mean, if you really care . . . there's a lovely paper written by the U.S. Army" about "code stylometry," a machine-learning technique "to actually kind of develop a fingerprint for the way that people write code."

For the 2015 paper, which was titled "De-anonymizing Programmers via Code Stylometry" and based on research funded in part by the army, a group of American computer scientists reported the results of a study of C and C++ code samples. From a pool of 1,600 programmers, the researchers had gathered nine files authored by each, assembling a total of 14,400 files. When they anonymized the files and tried to match them to their authors, they achieved a remarkably high accuracy rate of 94 percent.

Like most technologies, code stylometry could be used for good or ill. An Iranian programmer had been sentenced to death after the tool linked harmless photo-sharing software he'd written with software used by porn sites. But the technique also offered a way to catch authors of malware.

The army-funded researchers had focused on features that were "not trivial to obfuscate," such as the depth to which code was nested: a subroutine within a subroutine within a subroutine, say, instead of just a subroutine within a subroutine. And the paper had come out seven years after Bitcoin's launch.

I'd held off on pursuing this approach until I had a better idea of which candidates to apply it to. Now I reached out to Rachel Greenstadt, a coauthor on the 2015 paper, who currently led the Privacy Security and Automation Lab at NYU's Center for Cybersecurity. She put me in touch with one of her PhD students, Brian Timmerman. On Zoom, Brian appeared to be sitting in front of a window with a panoramic view of nighttime Manhattan, but it was 11 a.m., and he was somewhere rural near the Canadian border. The best results, he confirmed, came from comparing programs written in the same language.

I scrounged around for code to send Brian. C and C++ were close enough, and I was able to find samples, often buried in the Wayback Machine, for several of the main candidates. These included James Donald, Hal Finney, Adam Back, Wei Dai, Len Sassaman, and Paul Le Roux. I also included samples for Bram Cohen and Zooko Wilcox, who'd worked on Mojo Nation,* an early P2P system with its own digital currency; Mark Grant, who'd written about digital cash for *Extropy*; Pr0duct Cypher, the pseudonymous cypherpunk who'd come up with a digital cash system called Magic Money; Ben Laurie, author of Lucre; plus a wildcard Canadian ex-PGP programmer named Colin Plumb.

Two weeks later, around lunchtime on a weekday in mid-August, Brian emailed me his results. I was nervous and hesitated to open the attached file. Depending on what Brian had found, it would significantly guide my remaining reporting. Though I wasn't exactly eager to travel thirty hours and show up unannounced at the home of a crazy white supremacist with his own arsenal, I hoped Donald was a match. It would be international news. It would be a surprise ending.

I opened the PDF Brian had sent. It had the straightforward title "Test Report: Results of Code Stylometry Application." My eyes skipped to the "High Level Overview" section: "The models suggest Laurie-lucre as the author of main.cpp." The authorship of the other core Bitcoin file, node.cpp, was a three-way tie between Laurie (40 percent), Cohen-Wilcox of Mojo Nation (30 percent), and Hal Finney (30 percent).

Could this be right? Laurie was #69 on my Nakamoto Suspects spreadsheet, between an Irish trio of computer scientists known as the Crypto Mano Group and Richard Clayton, Laurie's coauthor on the paper debunking proof of work. Laurie had been lacerating about Bitcoin as far back as 2011, and about proof of work as early as 2004. Though he'd been on the cypherpunks list, he'd never espoused libertarian views, as far as I knew, and—

---

* When I first provided the Mojo Nation files to Brian Timmerman, I labeled them as having been written by Jim McCoy, a cypherpunk who with Doug Barnes had cofounded Mojo Nation and who was friendly with Nick Szabo, but Jim later informed me that the C coding on the project had been done by Bram Cohen, Zooko Wilcox, and Greg Smith. As for Jim: "I'm a Python guy!"

I caught myself. Here I was, looking for reasons to discount the results because they weren't the results I wanted. Laurie, I feared, would make for a less interesting Satoshi Nakamoto.

Brian said the classification models he'd used had a 77.2 percent accuracy rate. And the results came with all sorts of other qualifiers. Factors having nothing to do with individual style, such as the purpose of the code, could skew the outcome.

I asked Brian to rerun the test, excluding Laurie. This time, Cohen-Wilcox was the closest match for main.cpp, while for the second file, node.cpp, Finney matched 70 percent of the time, and Cohen-Wilcox matched 30 percent of the time.

I asked Brian to run one more test, this time looking only at the hardest-to-obfuscate and most-domain-independent features, also known as "the abstract syntax tree." This time, 100 percent of the models assigned both main.cpp and node.cpp to Laurie.

I still couldn't conclude that Laurie was Nakamoto, any more than someone else, running the same experiment without Laurie and getting Finney or Cohen-Wilcox as the closest match, could conclude that either of them was Nakamoto. What the tests did suggest, though, was that James Donald *wasn't* Nakamoto, or at least wasn't Bitcoin's primary coder. And faced with this knowledge, I had to admit there were a handful of inconvenient contradictions I'd ignored.

Jim's code looked similar to Nakamoto's in certain ways but different in others. Some of Nakamoto's diction, like *adult site,* seemed uncharacteristically delicate given Jim's habitual bluntness. And Jim had eventually answered some of my questions over email. Why had he and others on Metzdowd been so muted in their initial reception of Bitcoin? "People are dumb," Jim replied. "Only the smarties realized how much this mattered. Also, we thought that there was considerable personal danger, so people did stuff out of sight. As it turned out, the danger was less than thought, because the government did not understand the threat. Still does not." Would Satoshi Nakamoto have even bothered responding to me? Then again, after my next email, in which I presented the case for Jim being Nakamoto, he never replied.

I dug into Ben Laurie as a more serious candidate. His father, Peter, was a freelance journalist who'd been early to the computer beat, but before that, in 1970, he'd written a cult book, *Beneath the City Streets: The Secret Plans to Defend the State,* illuminating Britain's underground network of civil nuclear-war defenses, a web of secret tunnels connecting a hidden subterranean world of human shelters, food depots, and safehouses for senior officials. In 1998, Ben, his brother Adam, and Dominic Hawken, a sometime session keyboardist for Boy George, saw an ad in the *Daily Telegraph*. The Ministry of Defense was putting one of its Cold War–era nuclear bunkers up for sale. Ben and his partners bought the facility and started a secure-internet-hosting business called the Bunker. The underground, sixty-thousand-square-foot, three-floor building beneath an eighteen-acre property in Kent was all the marketing they needed. Above ground, the property had CCTV and guard dogs and barbed wire. Nearly a hundred feet below ground, it had thirteen-foot-thick concrete walls, nine-ton blast doors, electromagnetic-pulse shielding, and three generator systems, including underground diesel tanks to keep the facility running for three months without grid electricity. I thought about Peter Laurie's book, *Beneath the City Streets.* What was Bitcoin but an underground network that could survive a nuclear war?

I half-heartedly connected more dots. Ben had published a revision of his Lucre white paper on October 30, 2008, one day before Nakamoto published the Bitcoin white paper. Ben was deeply involved in open-source programming. He had coded Lucre in C++, using Hungarian notation. He had a math background and had overseen the development of an open-source cryptography library, later used by Bitcoin, called OpenSSL. Back in 2006, Ben's email signature had been a quote from former Coca-Cola CEO Robert Woodruff: "There is no limit to what a man can do or how far he can go if he doesn't mind who gets the credit." Before that, Ben's sig was a quote from Indira Gandhi: "My grandfather once told me that there are two kinds of people: those who work and those who take the credit. He told me to try to be in the first group; there was less competition there." Nakamoto had seemed more pragmatist than libertarian, and that described Ben as well. The first person Nakamoto was known to have contacted was Adam Back, whose Hashcash Ben had studied when writing his critique of proof of work, and whom Ben knew from British computer security circles. Two months after Bitcoin's launch, Ben blogged about a new Visa security program he thought would put customers at risk: "Not content with destroying the world's economies, the banking industry is also bent on ruining us individually, it seems."

The cousin of long-distance pattern recognition was its near-sighted opposite: Almost any candidate, if you looked closely enough, would start to cough up data points that confirmed the person as a plausible Nakamoto. Or was it possible that Ben's criticism of Bitcoin had been, as I'd thought James Donald's might be, a misdirection?

Bacula

After Ben said, "Yes," he'd heard of code stylometry, I explained that I'd sent twelve code samples to someone with expertise in it.

"And you," I said, "were the closest match."

"Nice!" Ben said, rocking backward, clapping his hands together, and laughing. "Well, I wish it was me, because I'd have a much fancier house." He laughed again.

"I'm actually quite good at keeping backups," he said, waving his hand in the air and gesturing around his office. "I do in fact do daily backups of all of my computers here." He meant that he wasn't someone likely to have lost his keys. He used backup software called Bacula. "It comes in the night and sucks the essence from the machine," he said, and laughed again.

If someone was Satoshi Nakamoto, I said, "it would be a pretty good cover to become one of Bitcoin's best-known critics."

"It would, wouldn't it," Ben said, laughing again and taking a sip from a tall can.

I said I wanted to go over the parallels between him and Nakamoto that supported the theory that they were the same person.

"I like it," Ben said. "Carry on. You're not the first to suggest it is me, obviously, but . . ."

I then mentioned a theory a computer science professor named

Andrew Miller, at the University of Illinois, had offhandedly described online in 2014 while acknowledging he had no evidence to support it: Bitcoin was Wei Dai's idea; Nick Szabo had written the white paper; and "Ben Laurie wrote the code, but hates the idea."

"Nice," Ben said, "but I didn't. Anyway, yeah."

Now I was ready to hit him with what I thought was quite a keen insight I'd had. In early 2009, Nakamoto had written, "I can't receive incoming connections." That sounded to me a lot like Ben's impregnable bunker. What did he have to say to that? "Absolutely not," Ben said. "We had redundant fiber into that place. That was the whole point. It was a secure hosting service."

Okay, well, what about his email signature about not needing credit? "Yeah, I love this theory. No one's pulled that one on me before. And actually the code stylometry, that's an interesting angle."

There was the Genesis Block quote from the print edition of the London *Times* too. There were Nakamoto's British spellings. "I'm a bit purist about it," Ben said, not prone to mixing in American spellings.

I suggested that publishing a new version of his Lucre white paper the day before Nakamoto published the Bitcoin white paper could have been a clever sleight of hand: *The guy posting digital-money A couldn't possibly be the guy posting digital-money B one day later.* Ben laughed and nodded. "Interesting," he said. "I'm loving this conspiracy theory."

I opened the throttle: he was a coder; he used cryptography; there were the code parallels—C++, open source, Hungarian notation.

"I've never actually looked at the code," Ben said. "Did he use Hungarian in the code? Interesting. I used to use Hungarian pretty religiously. . . . I stopped using Windows a long time ago now, because I absolutely fucking hated programming for it."

"I've got a few more for you."

"Go on, go on," he said, clasping hands. "I'm loving it, carry on."

Ben had been on the relevant lists. Cypherpunks. Metzdowd. Coderpunks. P2P. He'd studied proof of work and understood it deeply, even if he didn't like it. He was a computer security expert, and Bitcoin's code had been praised for its security.

"I have to look at the code now actually," Ben said. "Do you have a copy of the original code? The reason I ask is I have an unusual style for C++ that I don't strictly use anymore, because I've kind of gone with the flow of what other people do." He had a habit, he explained, of vertically lining up the opening and closing curly braces used to set off a block of instructions with the block itself. "Which is pretty unusual."

He was on the advisory board of WikiLeaks, I continued, and it was WikiLeaks' interest in accepting Bitcoin that had seemed to spook Nakamoto. Ben also had worked on PGP applications.

He nodded, noncommittally.

"If nothing else, interesting," I said.

"Yeah, it's super interesting, I love it. I mean, people have suggested before there was evidence that it might be me. The intermittent Britishness . . . I can't even remember whether the stylometry for papers showed anything interesting with regards to my writing and his writing. But I'd not heard the Hungarian angle before, that's fun. And other coincidences."

"By the way," he continued. "If I was going to use a newspaper, I actually never read *The Times*. *The Guardian* is my paper . . . I read *The Guardian* because I do the *Guardian* cryptic crosswords . . . My wife and I both do crosswords. And my parents got it. I started doing cryptic crosswords when I was at school. *The Times* includes too many literary references for my liking."

Did he think Nakamoto was a group or an individual?

"I don't have any view on it, to be honest. It's particularly tricky, because I never interacted with Satoshi, which maybe is more evidence that it's me, right?" He laughed. "Though I guess if I was covering for myself I should have interacted with him." He helixed his finger in the air, as if working through the convolutions. "Pretty poor cover."

He continued to muse about the group question. "Maybe actually that would explain the English-American thing, but I mean, if it was a group, it was a group with high trust. Because it's very difficult to operate as a group and be timely about stuff, and that kind of thing, unless you give everyone a license to do their thing. There definitely was a lot of trust in the cypherpunk community amongst some of the people. Possible."

"You're planning to write about this, I presume," Ben said.

I only had theories, I said. Some were more interesting than others.

"I definitely like your evidence," he said. "It's fun."

I offered to send him a copy of the early Bitcoin code.

"It would be a fantastic coincidence if he used my indent style," Ben said. "It was unique as far as I know. I never saw anybody else do it." He laughed. "I might be hoisting myself with my own petard here."

In general, he said, he was "pretty cynical" about cryptocurrency. "The whole idea of unregulated finance, history shows it's a really fucking stupid idea." Bitcoin had become "a great way to separate suckers from their money. . . . And you don't need the price to go up . . . you just need it to wiggle. Volatility is good."

Had he speculated on Bitcoin?

He looked down. "Nope."

Why not take advantage of that volatility?

He continued looking down and sighed. "Because . . . because I have morals. I'm not prepared to make money by burning the planet."

I thanked him for his time.

"I'll be interested to see what you write," Ben said. "Like I say, I find it amusing, the whole thing, though irritating too. Because it's stupid. Because people are sinking all this money in, and have this weird belief that it's worth something, in this thing that clearly isn't worth anything. In the same sense that tulips weren't worth anything when tulips did their thing."

"But . . . all money is a social construction, right? I mean, nothing is worth anything until we decide it's worth something, right?"

Ben screwed up his face. "I don't think that's 100 percent true. I think that's actually quite a lazy view of money, because if you look at conventional currencies—what do they call them in Bitcoin world? Sovereign currencies . . ."

"Fiat?"

"Fiat," he said. "In what sense is Bitcoin not fiat? The fiat coming from the people rather than from the dictators, you know."

"Well, legal tender is enforced by government mandate," I said stiffly.

"But that's what gives it value," Ben said. ". . . Anyway, fiat currency is effectively backed by the GDP of the country that makes it. And that is an actual, valuable asset, unlike burning electricity. The thing I always say about Bitcoin is that what I'm going to do is I'm going to take a $100 bill and I'm going to burn it and I'm going to put the smoke in a bottle, and you're supposed to believe that that bottle is now worth $110, which is such obvious bullshit that I don't know why anyone buys it." He laughed. "And another thing people always quote at me is, 'What about the gold standard?' And I'm like, 'The gold standard that we abandoned in the 1970s, that we decided was a stupid idea and we don't do anymore?'"

After we disconnected, I thought that if Ben was Nakamoto, and he'd just been confronted by a journalist presenting evidence that the jig was up, he'd done a masterful job of maintaining his sense of humor and lightness about it. He'd make a likable Satoshi. Maybe, as Andrew Miller suggested, he'd coded something he hated.

During the conversation, I hadn't known off the top of my head whether the original Bitcoin code vertically lined up its opening and closing curly braces in the same way Ben's did. When I looked now, I saw that it did not.

I remembered how the conversation with Ben had begun. His screen had frozen, and he'd said we were connected through his tethered phone. There were internet problems where he lived. "I actually have fiber to the property," he said, but it had taken years to get it. Wales was supposed to install superfast broadband in the countryside, but year after year it hadn't happened. Eventually, Ben and his wife had organized a petition to get a community grant to cover the installation in their area. "It was a nightmare. It was kind of hilarious, because I would say at least 50 percent of the people around here that we talked to were like, 'I came here to get away from the internet, I don't want fiber.' It was like, 'Ugh, you do realize that this is essential. . . . Your house will be worth nothing if you don't have internet.'"

He laughed.

I thought again of what Satoshi Nakamoto had written to Hal Finney in January of 2009: "Unfortunately, I can't receive incoming connections from where I am, which has made things more difficult."

But Ben later said that he'd only moved to Wales around 2011.

I Support the Current Thing

A couple of weeks after the *Granath v. Wright* trial, my request to interview Craig Wright was granted. The Norwegian court had ruled against him, with Judge Engebrigtsen writing that "the court believes that Granath had sufficient factual grounds to claim that Craig Wright is not Satoshi Nakamoto in March 2019." Wright had filed an appeal, and his publicist Eileen Brown told me he wouldn't discuss anything having to do with the case.

At this point, I really just wanted to more directly experience Craig's Craigness. We were on Zoom. He was sitting in his home office in Surrey, wearing an open-necked button-down shirt, surrounded by computers named after cyberpunk novels like *Wintermute* and *Snowcrash*, a rack of katanas to one side. I asked about the three framed photographs of Muhammad Ali hanging on a wall. "He came from very little," Craig said. "Built up a brand around himself. Worked incredibly hard to get where he wanted to go. I mean, people say it's just boxing, but there's a lot more to boxing than just boxing."

I could also see whiteboards dense with scribbles behind him. "I'm just completing my MA in English literature," Craig said. "I've completed my MA in medieval history and Latin at Birmingham. My philosophy dissertation on the philosophy of time has just been granted. It's from Birkbeck." He was also currently working on a PhD in forensic psychology and a master's in therapeutic psychology, he said. He was writing a paper about "some of the types of people who run Ponzis . . . usually in the Dark Triad-type areas," and another about "social media and the formation of tribal groups."

A man derided as #faketoshi, who was a Twitter warrior, was studying fraud and internet polarization? Craig raised his eyebrows and smiled. "Yes, that's part of why I did it. My way of understanding is generally doing formal classes."

When I mentioned Nick Szabo—Bitcoin demigod, pioneer of smart contracts, a leading Nakamoto candidate—Craig was casually dismissive. "Without saying anything too bad, he's rather clueless. That's about the best I could say." In what regard? "In every regard. There's a reason his proposed system never got off the ground. He doesn't know how to code it. He didn't understand that it had all been done before. People who try and promote Bitcoin as the first decentralized cryptocurrency—I've written a few papers demonstrating that there were at least thirty, in the twenty-year period before Bitcoin, proof of work, distributed, peer-to-peer, digital-cash systems, or cryptocurrencies."

I'd read hundreds of pages of Craig's sworn testimony and spent ten days observing him in a courtroom, and this was exactly the kind of thing he'd say. It was a bold claim that was virtually impossible to fact-check in real time. I hadn't heard it before. Had I not read widely enough? Or was he stretching the definition of cryptocurrency and inflating the number, and if pressed he would come up with a handful of never-implemented systems that he'd argue, with still further uncheckable claims, were in fact cryptocurrencies even if they weren't called such? It was easy to see how people who didn't devote themselves to studying this stuff, which was nearly everyone, could start to believe Craig was a genius. Was this why, after everything that had happened, he still had disciples?

"I have been too angry for too long as I cared for external validation," Craig tweeted soon after our conversation. "That ends." He announced that he'd be holding a series of workshops starting in January. If conferences were going to disinvite him (as he claimed), or not invite him in the first place (as other evidence suggested), then he would host his own. If general audiences were going to jeer him or question his claims, then he would speak to friendly crowds. The first of the workshops was to take place in London and would focus on topics like privacy, anonymity, and identity.

The day it began was chilly and overcast. The workshop was in a small brick building on a posh side street in Marylebone, the address divulged to us by email only the day before, lest anti-Craig trolls disrupt the event. We were told we might be asked at the door for identification.

We took our seats in burgundy-upholstered metal chairs in a carpeted, high-ceilinged room on the second floor that had dark wainscoting and a balcony from which a video team would shoot the workshop. I was one of about three dozen people, mainly younger men, who'd come to learn from Craig. A number of them worked at nChain, and Craig's son Ben, who was studying computer science and cryptography at university, sat in the front row. Another three hundred people were live streaming the event, Eileen the publicist told me.

Craig was peacocking, that day, in a slate-gray pinstripe three-piece suit, a dark red shirt with French cuffs, a black-and-red patterned tie, and scarlet socks. Though he was a pariah outside the BSV bubble, before the curated crowd he paced the dais waving a Sharpie and holding forth, engaging his listeners in a Socratic dialogue and occasionally pausing to jot something on a whiteboard. At one point, he held up a bound volume he'd found in the glassed-in shelves at the back of the room and apparently flipped through. "The book here is lying. *The Complete Works of Shakespeare,*" he said with a smirk. "They don't have '*Timon of Athens.*'"

Someone laughed politely.

Along with his insistence that private keys didn't prove identity, Craig seemed to have dropped even the pretense of holding beliefs, or having a personality, consistent with the Satoshi Nakamoto of Bitcoin's early years. Instead, anonymity was "better for the bad guys." Libertarians were "just criminals." Decentralization was juvenile: "Welcome to real life."

He gyrated between stodgily defending the rule of law, boasting about his speeding tickets, and implying that he'd walked around an airport with a "near-field scanner" and virtually peered into strangers' passports. "Welcome to the life of an ex-hacker." He made bitter jokes about being audited. He put himself in the courageous company of "Reverend King," Nelson Mandela, and Gandhi.

The second day, when we broke for lunch, Craig's local bodyguard, a tall man with a Russian priest's beard and a watchful, unsmiling demeanor, brought me to a side room, where Craig was waiting.

I kept expecting it to happen, but at no point had either Craig or Eileen asked whether I believed that Craig was Satoshi Nakamoto, or even said anything suggesting they assumed I did. They didn't seem to care whether I believed it. While Craig's claims drove the Bitcoin faithful crazy, and BSV was a marginal cryptocurrency, Craig and nChain continued to amass patents. A layperson who didn't follow the story closely could easily get the impression from how often Craig was in the news that he was indeed Nakamoto.

Nearly everything he said to me he'd said in many interviews before. I kept my pen moving mainly out of politeness. But I was curious how he reconciled his Establishment views with his earlier libertarian attitude. "There's libertarians and there's libertarians," he said. "If some guy wants to dress up in a gimp suit and have fun with other guys in gimp suits, then go for it. I don't really care."

Eileen gave him a look.

"What? Some of my best friends are gay. I take the piss out of straight people, too, so don't worry."

"The minute you said 'gimp suit,'" Eileen said, "I just went to the furries. Furries, they just scritch each other, and you don't know what sex you're scritching. It just blows my mind."

"Well, generally you do," Craig said, "because, well, I don't know if someone told you this, but men don't have the same two holes as women."

"Yeah, but they're wrapped up in a furry suit, so initially you have no idea, if they're not talking."

"Mmm, yeah, I think I would," Craig said, and proceeded to explain just how.

I marveled that anyone could continue to believe Craig was Nakamoto. But among the workshop attendees, Craig's Satoshi-ness was simply assumed. It lurked on the fringes of the conversation, occasionally alluded to.

BSV people were different from Bitcoin people. At Bitcoin events, you might see someone wearing a helmet or a face mask, and a panelist might go by a pseudonym like Wiz, Coinicarus, or OhGodAGirl. Here, everyone showed their faces and used their real names.

During a break, I chatted with Philipp Schnell, a tall, German BSVer with a mischievous smile, whom I'd seen battling Bitcoiners on Twitter. "I do it a bit for fun and sport," he said with a grin. When he'd first dabbled in crypto, buying various coins during the 2018 boom, he was working for an augmented-reality company in Scotland. Like many people, he found crypto perplexing at first. "I never understood, like, where does the value come from? You know, everyone's like, 'future of finance,' with a wishy-washy kind of explanation. It was nothing concrete. And I think at the time, nothing really worked. Transaction fees were very expensive." He drifted away from crypto for a time, and when he drifted back, the insularity of Bitcoin "just bugged me. Like, where's the usefulness?"

Meanwhile, there was this intriguing mystery about Satoshi Nakamoto, and there was a guy who said he was Nakamoto but whom lots of people called a scammer. When Philipp read up on Craig, he became more interested. "He spoke about it in a completely different way from everyone." Where others saw grandiosity, Philipp saw a "grand vision." Where others heard gobbledygook, Philipp heard a "deep" and "native" understanding of Bitcoin. Then he looked at

BSV, which claimed it would eventually be able to handle 1.1 million transactions per second, compared with Bitcoin's paltry maximum of seven. "It blows everything else out of the water," Philipp said.

The claimed technical superiority of BSV was a recurring theme among workshop participants. They took a sensible view of cryptocurrency. *Of course* it should do practical things like make micropayments possible. This view was a lot closer to regular people's needs and interests, I thought, than the views held by crypto-zealots. Most people wanted privacy but were willing to trade some of it for convenience. Most people wanted money with less friction but were happy to outsource their personal security. The loudest Bitcoiners had enabled Craig and BSV, I was convinced, by ceding a reasonable attitude toward blockchain utility. While they evangelized about decentralization and self-sovereignty, Craig spoke of real-world commercial uses of the technology.

I thought I'd encounter people at the workshop who didn't buy Craig's claims that he was Nakamoto and simply thought BSV was a better product. But the people I spoke with all believed him to be Satoshi. "The more I looked at it, it just becomes incredibly likely to me that he seems like if he's not the sole creator, he was the architect or something," Philipp said.

Within ten minutes of meeting Craig, Eileen told me, "I knew." She'd worked at Microsoft for a number of years and gotten a lot of experience "managing Aspies," she said, and Craig was "an autistic savant." The controversy around Craig was part of what convinced her he must be Nakamoto.

I spoke with Richard Waddy, an older man with a gray ponytail who was wearing jeans, a MAKE ORWELL FICTION AGAIN baseball hat with reading glasses perched on the brim, and an I SUPPORT THE CURRENT THING T-shirt mocking sheeple who believe *the official narrative*. Richard had come down from Dorset for the workshop. He felt empathy for Craig, he said, because of all the abuse he got online. Craig followers and Bitcoin maximalists weren't so different, I thought. If Bitcoiners were Scientologists, BSVers were a niche splinter group of Scientology apostates. Both groups saw consensus as an orthodoxy to reject.

For the first time, I entertained the question: Was there a chance that Craig actually was Nakamoto? What a twist that would be. The best argument in his favor that I'd heard was: *Why hasn't Satoshi debunked him?* How could Craig move so blithely through the world claiming to be Nakamoto if he knew there was someone else out there who could step forward at any moment and cryptographically show him up? One theory suggested to me was that Paul Le Roux, the imprisoned multihyphenate lawbreaker, was Nakamoto, and he and Craig had made a devil's deal, where Craig would front as Nakamoto in return for who-knows-what. Alternatively, I thought, if Craig was himself Nakamoto, and if repeatedly being caught in lies and fabrications was an intentional obfuscatory tactic, he'd played an ingenious long game: his credibility was so frayed that even if he was Nakamoto, no one could reasonably believe it at this point.

His Excellency

I still didn't understand how Craig had managed to secure and maintain the backing of Calvin Ayre, who had taken over his debts and bankrolled his life and lawsuits. BSV and Craig were propped up almost entirely by this one man. Even Gavin Andresen, who'd emerged from a London hotel business suite in 2016 believing he'd met Nakamoto, had by now responded to the pressure campaign to disavow Craig, appending a headnote to his original Craig-is-Satoshi blog post: "I don't believe in rewriting history, so I'm going to leave this post up. But in the seven years since I wrote it, a lot has happened, and I now know it was a mistake to trust Craig Wright as much as I did . . ." Ayre was seemingly a shrewd entrepreneur. How, after all the contrary evidence and preposterous excuses, could he still believe Craig?

On a drizzly spring day a month after the workshop, I entered a building on London's Golden Square and found Ayre waiting in a first-floor conference room. These were the offices of Lightning Sharks, the branding and PR firm he owned that had sent the documentary crew to chase Magnus Granath around Oslo with cameras and a boom mic.

Calvin wore black leather shoes with visible stitching around the soles, black jeans, a black T-shirt, and a cashmere sports coat in a mustard-and-brown checked pattern. At sixty-one, he looked youthful. He wore his hair in a buzz cut that culminated at his brow in a gelled quiff; this had only recently replaced a slicked-back mohawk he'd cribbed from a movie about bootleggers.

Calvin was wholly self-created, the son of a pig farmer in Saskatchewan who'd been convicted of marijuana smuggling. Calvin himself had gotten into trouble with the British Columbia Securities Commission for various stock violations early in his career, then made a fortune in internet gambling. In 2006, he appeared on the cover of *Forbes*'s "Billionaires" issue. For a time, he presented himself to the world as Goldfinger, as photographed by *Maxim*. Presiding from Costa Rica and later from an Antiguan compound over his Bodog online-betting empire, he flaunted a lifestyle accessorized with yachts, a bulletproof Hummer, his own submarine of sorts (it could only go down ninety feet), and often mostly Asian women in bikinis. Bodog put on a pay-per-view Lingerie Bowl, scheduled during the Super Bowl halftime show, featuring models in garters and helmets tackling each other. Calvin used the words *billionaire playboy* in his own publicity materials. Like Richard Branson, one of his inspirations, Calvin made his lifestyle and his company's brand inextricable from each other. Even after being indicted in Maryland on money-laundering and other charges, he hadn't shied away from the roguish aura that came with technically being a fugitive.

Eventually, he pled guilty to a single misdemeanor count that kept him out of jail, and these days he seemed more interested in rehabilitating his image. The day before our meeting, one of his publicists sent me two documents making the case that the Maryland indictment had violated international law and suggesting that Calvin had been railroaded by the U.S. government. Now at Lightning Sharks, waiting for me on the table in front of my seat was a creamy, expensive-looking business card announcing "His Excellency Calvin Ayre. Special Economic Envoy. Government of Antigua and Barbuda. With Responsibility for Economic & Business Development."

His Excellency shook my hand without smiling. He had a cold, he said. He'd flown in from Antigua by private jet a week earlier.

nChain was in London, and Calvin came here often. Beyond the glass wall separating the conference room from a reception area were two attractive young Asian women who Calvin said were his nurses who traveled with him. He also had a doctor on staff. Tomorrow he would leave for Bangkok, where he had a house and was going for a wellness treatment. He spent a lot of his time on wellness these days, he said. "Stem-cell stuff, exosomes, everything that's ready for prime time." Despite the shared interest in longevity, Calvin didn't strike me as someone who would have fit in particularly well among the extropians.

We were sitting at a long blond-wood table with glass bottles of mineral water and a dish of nuts with a pair of miniature tongs to pick them up. Before we began the interview, Calvin had a question for me: "Are you being paid by anybody to do this?" I mentioned my publisher, though I was pretty sure that wasn't what he meant.

"They're the only people you're involved with?" he asked.

"Yes."

He mulled this for a moment, then seemed to accept it. He mentioned a book about Craig by two foreign journalists that had been scheduled for publication a few years earlier, only to be cancelled a week before its release date. Calvin said it had been "catch-and-kill . . . never to be seen again." He seemed to believe the book would have vindicated Craig's claims and that anti-Craig forces had somehow gotten it scrapped.

"Is it possible," I wondered, "that they were worried about getting sued for defamation?"

"By who?" Calvin said.

"By you and Craig?"

Craig hadn't sued that many people, Calvin insisted, and he hadn't had a problem with the book coming out.

Calvin had kept a low profile in 2015 and 2016, he said, because of his legal problems in Maryland, which he only resolved in 2017. He said he believed it was Ira Kleiman who had doxed Craig, because in order to sue him Kleiman needed Craig to be publicly identified as Nakamoto.

Craig and BSV were pariahs, Calvin acknowledged. Craig, on the rare occasions he managed to book a speaking slot at a conference, would often find himself disinvited without explanation, Calvin claimed. And anyone from outside the BSV bubble who agreed to speak at its upcoming conference was "trolled remorselessly," Calvin said. "We've lost five already. It just never stops."

Calvin didn't think the resistance was spontaneous. "This is all about powerful people scared of Craig's ideas," he said. "Very powerful people," he added darkly. "We're talking the whole Silicon Valley model. We're talking about the U.S. payments model. And we're talking about the entirety of crypto."

I wondered whether Calvin and Craig had bonded over a shared sense of persecution. What incentive would venture capitalists have, I asked, to marginalize a technology if they thought they could make money from it?

"That is a very good question," Calvin said. "I ask myself all the time: Why do they do it? We do know how disruptive this is to their traditional model. The whole Google-Facebook model where people are the product: that gets disrupted entirely by this tech. But why they don't break ranks is mystifying to me."

Calvin was remarkably sanguine about Craig's legal prospects. He had repeatedly predicted victory in Norway, only to see Craig lose. Now that the case was on appeal, Calvin's optimism was undimmed. "The young female judge that presided over that case didn't get the law in Norway correct," Calvin said. "I think Craig is going to win in a landslide."

He implied that the fix had been in for Hodlonaut. "I think more evidence is going to come out in the second trial, about how conflicted he is, and how commercial the attacks on Craig are." What? "I personally believe there was corruption in that case." Magnus Granath was "associated with one of the richest people in Norway." He seemed to be referring to Kjell Inge Røkke, a Norwegian oil billionaire, at whose company Seetee Magnus had worked a few years earlier helping manage Bitcoin investments. Calvin felt that the speed with which Magnus had moved to preempt Craig legally, and the fact that he'd "gloated on the internet before about how Craig was going to lose. It just feels like a guy that knew he'd won already."

I was curious about the period when the lawsuits began. "Starting in early 2019," I said, "a few months after BSV launched—"

"BSV did not launch," Calvin interrupted. "BSV is the original Bitcoin, on the original exchange. It goes right back to 2009." What he meant—and this belief was universal in BSV World—was that, although a bitcoin was now worth $30,000 and a unit of BSV only $36, BSV wasn't a fork of Bitcoin. Bitcoin was the fork. It had just stolen the name.

What I really wanted to know was why he continued to stand by Craig. "Does it ever bother you when judges question Craig's credibility?"

"Craig is a hard guy to like when he's angry," Calvin said, "and his enemies know that and are constantly trying to push his buttons." nChain's job, Calvin said, was to present "the warmer, nicer side of Craig," which came out when Craig was giving academic lectures, and "he's actually quite a jovial fun guy at a party."

I mentioned Craig's Asperger's diagnosis.

"I was just with him," Calvin said. "He was talking all over the place about shit nobody fucking understands. I just stop listening to him sometimes when he does that."

I asked about a private proof session Calvin had said he witnessed around the time of Gavin Andresen's proof session. "It was actually right here in this room," Calvin said. "Some other tech people were getting shown it. I knew it was a historic thing. I wanted to be able to say I saw one myself, so I just tagged along. The tech people qualified to know what they saw were impressed. I know that. But I'm not that guy who can tell you what I saw. I saw people that looked like they were happy they got what they came for."

Bitcoin was trust-minimized. Calvin was trust-maximized. He trusted that Craig was Nakamoto because Craig had told him he was Nakamoto and because Calvin trusted Stefan Matthews, who'd told him that Craig had shown him an early version of the white paper,* and because some technical people "looked happy" after a private proof session.

Did Calvin ever think Craig might be a liability for BSV? "No, absolutely not. The guy is brilliant, and his ideas are predominantly right about everything. And people that ask that question usually have been tricked by the nonsense that's out there into a fictional version of Craig."

"I'm not talking about *Craig,*" I tried, "but about his *public image,* which is, he has an extremely radioactive reputation."

"They've spent hundreds of millions of dollars to create the *fiction* that Craig has a radioactive reputation," Calvin replied, "and that's the one you're feeding off of with your questioning right now. But that's not the real Craig, and our job is to let people see the real Craig." He seemed agitated. "And the real Craig is the massive advantage that we've got that they don't have, because his vision is the one that's going to win." He was glaring at me.

It seemed reasonable to ask my next question.

"Has Craig been net-profitable to you?"

Now Calvin stared at me. Then he looked at Gary, his PR guy. Maybe Calvin was seeking a nod of approval before answering? No, the look was more like, "Who are you wasting my time with?" or "Gary, you should start looking for a new job."

Calvin then fixed me with an expression that suggested I'd asked the stupidest or most offensive question imaginable.

"What are you talking about *profits* for?"

It took me a moment to process what he was asking.

"You're a . . . businessman?" I ventured. "Businessmen care about . . . profits?"

---

* This "early version," which Matthews hadn't kept, was less of a case-clincher than it sounded. A judge in London would later call Matthews's claim to have received it "a barefaced lie."

"This isn't about *profits,*" said the offshore-gambling tycoon as if I'd accused him of sex trafficking. "This is *legacy,* my friend."

Calvin talked about Bitcoin having "multiple death vectors" but allowed that it would "languish on" because of its momentum. "Vitalik knows Craig's Satoshi as well," Calvin said, referring to Ethereum cofounder Vitalik Buterin. "But he's terrified by other people finding out."

This seemed ludicrous to me. "What makes you say that," I asked, "given that Vitalik has publicly stated several times that he doesn't think Craig is?"

Again Calvin looked at me like I had a cognitive deficit.

"Well that's what tells he *does,*" he said with a dismissive laugh. "How does that fucking know-nothing kid know that Craig's not Satoshi? How's that even possible that he can say that? What is that based on?"

Calvin had his own media organ, his own facts.

"I know Calvin's been quite pointed," Gary chimed in, "but the media, unfortunately, at the moment, they've almost drunk the Kool-Aid a little bit."

Eight months later, Calvin would fire Craig from nChain. And nChain's own recently departed CEO, now calling Craig #faketoshi, would leak an email Calvin had written to Craig.

"As I sit here I am on a beach in southern Spain," it began. "I have a good life. I have every intention of keeping it this way. Right now the only negative in my life is your litigation disaster. . . . I will accept your explanation that you did not actually threaten me." Calvin proceeded to write that if Craig wouldn't cryptographically prove his ownership of the Nakamoto coins, he would lose the upcoming Cryptocurrency Open Patent Alliance case. Calvin also said he would no longer fund the lawsuits. "So either you are a moron for intentionally losing this case, or you are a moron for actually not having the keys. . . . Either way, I am not following you over the cliff."

In March 2024, the COPA trial in London would conclude, with Justice James Mellor ruling from the bench, in the most definitive declaration by a court yet, that the evidence was "overwhelming" that Craig was "not the author of the Bitcoin White Paper . . . not the person who adopted or operated under the pseudonym Satoshi Nakamoto in the period 2008 to 2011 . . . not the person who created the Bitcoin System," and "not the author of the initial versions of the Bitcoin software."

"W," Jack Dorsey crowed, on the platform he used to run.

"I know he is Satoshi . . . ," Calvin Ayre continued to insist, "but that is moot . . . look Craig's invention will go on. this is only a problem for Craig and I feel for him."

A day later, Calvin wrote, "Goodbye everyone," saying he was handing over his Twitter account to a team involved with BSV, as he was going to "take off on an adventure I've been planning for the last year."

Soon after, Craig dropped his actions against Magnus Granath—both the appeal in Norway and the suit in London. "I'm extremely happy," Magnus told me afterwards. "We will still move to claim costs, of course, but there is no longer any litigation against me."

Finally, the COPA judge in London ordered Craig to post a humiliating statement on his website: "DR. CRAIG STEVEN WRIGHT IS NOT SATOSHI NAKAMOTO . . . The Court found that Dr Wright 'lied to the Court extensively and repeatedly.'" The judge also referred the case to the Crown Prosecution Service to consider whether to criminally prosecute Craig for "his wholescale perjury and forgery of documents," and/or arrest him, and/or extradite him. By that point, Craig's whereabouts were unknown.

Florian

In the fall of 2023, I asked Florian Cafiero if he would take a run at the Nakamoto problem. Florian was himself a man with a double identity. In one life, he was an operatic tenor who performed Puccini and Wagner before large audiences in Europe. In another, which took most of his time these days, he was a lecturer in Artificial Intelligence for the Humanities and Social Sciences at Paris Sciences et Lettres University. His work included applying AI to author attribution questions, and with his colleague Jean-Baptiste Camps, an associate professor in computational philology, he had used stylometry to clarify who'd written disputed plays by Molière. What had led me to Florian and Jean-Baptiste, though, was their feat of identifying who was behind the Q of QAnon. They had showed convincingly that Q was two people and precisely when one of them took over from the other.

I sent Florian an archive of all posts made to the Metzdowd list in the four years and ten months leading up to Nakamoto's appearance there. I also sent several years' worth of cypherpunks and extropians archives, as well as longer writing samples for many of the leading Nakamoto candidates.

In both the Molière and QAnon cases, the results had immediately and starkly shown who the authors were. But the Nakamoto case proved more challenging. Over a span of two months, as Florian tried various approaches, he got a confusing mix of results. For the white paper, the most consistent matches were Hal Finney and Bram Cohen. For the Metzdowd posts, the most consistent match was Ray Dillinger, who'd been one of the first list members to engage with Nakamoto in 2008. But in both cases, the match wasn't so close that Florian had confidence that any of them was Nakamoto. There were some candidates whom it was possible to rule out because they never matched to Nakamoto in any of the tests: these included Nick Szabo, Len Sassaman, and Ben Laurie. It seemed equally or more likely that the person behind Nakamoto's writings was someone else entirely who wasn't in the sample set. If there was anything definitive that Florian's tests revealed, it was that all of Nakamoto's writings, from the white paper to the forum posts to the private emails, consistently clustered together, seeming to indicate they'd been written by one person.

One morning some months later, I awoke to a series of messages from Florian on Signal. "3rd day straight on Nakamoto," the first read. We hadn't communicated in several weeks. Clearly, Florian had developed his own obsession with the puzzle. He and Jean-Baptiste had recently been focusing on the possibility of "collaborative authorship," Florian wrote. They thought this was a more plausible explanation for Nakamoto's success at eluding linguistic detection than the idea that he might have significantly altered his writing style, given the tools available in Bitcoin's early years, when ChatGPT was still more than a decade away. Florian thought the collaboration could have worked in one of two ways: either two or more people had taken frequent turns writing, or members of the group rewrote each other before posting anything.

Then Florian asked me about a candidate I'd dismissed some time ago, a frequent Metzdowd poster named Travis Hassloch. Hassloch was a name that had popped up in my amateur Satoshitizer results as sharing some unusual vocabulary with Nakamoto, and that had led, when I'd googled it plus "Bitcoin," to the comment, on an Ars Technica blog post: "The creator of bitcoin is Travis Hassloch."

With no context, no apparent way to contact the writer of the comment (Dimitrios4615), and no obvious pointers linking Hassloch to Nakamoto or even Bitcoin, I hadn't spent much more time on him as a candidate. Florian, too, had discarded him, because in his earlier efforts, using my amateurishly processed samples, Hassloch hadn't been a close match. But since then, Florian and Jean-Baptiste had cleaned the text themselves, removing static like math equations and email addresses that could bury a text's signal. And now Hassloch was looking a lot more interesting. "It's the first time I am so thrilled about a lead on this case," Florian wrote. "Not sure at all for now, but he's the first one to actually be classified as 'likely Nakamoto' by our AI and not 'close to Nakamoto.'"

The next week, Florian and Jean-Baptiste spent another full day on the problem. They'd narrowed the group they were looking at to twenty-six, including all the usual suspects. They took the sixty-ish thousand words of Nakamoto text and sliced it into two-thousand-word tranches, then ran their model to see who, if anyone, the model would assign to each tranche. Most of them matched either to Hassloch or Ray Dillinger, more often than not to Hassloch. For the first time, Florian said, the collaborative pair of Hassloch and Dillinger being Nakamoto was statistically at least as likely as the possibility that the person or group behind Nakamoto simply wasn't in the set of texts being analyzed. And now, while nearly all of the Nakamoto texts still clustered together, there was one exception: the white paper appeared to have been authored by someone else.

Coincidentally, Craig Wright's COPA trial was at that moment taking place in London. As part of the proceedings Adam Back had finally made public his early email exchange with Nakamoto, and Martti Malmi, Nakamoto's first collaborator on the open-source Bitcoin project, had released 120 pages of private emails with Nakamoto, including twenty thousand words of Nakamoto-written text. Protectors of the Myth, hoping to preempt a new burst of Nakamoto-seeking, were unambiguous about the low character of anyone who'd dare make use of the email dump to speculate on Nakamoto's identity: it would be "absolutely disgusting," "immoral," and "so fiat." Any such speculator was "a massive asshole."

I read the new texts, noting a few colloquialisms that hadn't appeared in the old texts, such as *heck, darn, dang, pwn, professorial,* and *retarded.* Then I sent the texts to Florian and Jean-Baptiste, they reran their model, and they got the same results as before: Hassloch-Dillinger, but primarily Hassloch. On the one hand, Hassloch seemed unlikely: Wouldn't Satoshi Nakamoto, under his real name, have demonstrated a pronounced interest in digital money before he went ahead and decided to create one? On the other hand, if Nakamoto had come from that pool of outspoken digital-cash buffs, why could none of them be definitively pegged as Nakamoto? This suggested the possibility that, unlikely as it might seem, Nakamoto could *only* be some person or combination of them who appeared unlikely. I was reminded of something Jon Callas, the security researcher, had told me: "It's a Sherlock Holmes thing. If you go and you look at all the places where the obvious suspects are, and you can disprove them, you have to go look at the people who are not your obvious suspects."

There were some broad ways Hassloch did match Nakamoto. He was a staunch believer in the open-source movement. He was a regular on the Metzdowd cryptography list, had a bachelor's in computer science, and had spent much of his career in the areas of cryptography and cybersecurity for financial services companies. He was also a self-described "privacy fanatic" who'd used multiple pseudonyms including "Solinym" and "Shugenja," the latter a Japanese-named spellcaster in Dungeons & Dragons. He attended Burning Man and, to the extent that he was political, seemed squarely leftish, though he'd previously been a libertarian. His beef seemed more with banks than with governments, which matched my sense of Nakamoto's priorities. A few years earlier, when Hassloch was working for the no-fee, no-minimum-balance, banking app Chime, he'd written: "Nothing banks do hurts me more than when they know a person can't pay a transaction, let them go negative, and then charge them $35 NSF fee. That's worse than taking everything they have. It's punishing the poor and making them your debt slave." He started working for PayPal in 2007, then left that job in October 2008, the same month Nakamoto published the white paper. Hassloch didn't start another job until February 2009, suggesting he had time to devote himself to a project during the four months when Nakamoto was finishing the Bitcoin code and launching it into the world.

I was soon on the phone with Ray Dillinger. His voice was hoarse, which he attributed to how rarely he had conversations like this. "I guess I'm out of practice," said Ray, who'd grown up in Kansas with a mother who was a schoolteacher and a father who managed a grain elevator. Over the years, Ray had repeatedly denied being Nakamoto. He had even had to deal with a stalking incident. In 2020, after the pandemic began, a man parked across the street from his house in Silicon Valley for three weeks. A couple of times when Ray was out shopping, his wife saw the man get out of his car and walk around the house. "She was pretty freaked out about it," Ray recalled. During that three-week period, whenever the car was parked out front, Ray noticed that his cellphone had two extra bars on it. "Which makes me believe he had a StingRay in that car"—a device that simulates a cellphone tower—and was hoping to intercept communications with Nakamoto. "But if they had, the joke would have been on them, because nothing from Satoshi was on that phone, or on my previous phone."

Ray said he'd long ago destroyed his private correspondence with Hal and Nakamoto. "Once Bitcoin started becoming a thing, I started feeling like one day a subpoena might arrive, so I got rid of pretty much everything I had from Satoshi and Hal about it with the exception of one that had code I reviewed." He'd taken an eight-pound sledgehammer to his hard-drive, and he thought Nakamoto was likely to have done something similar. "His OPSEC was flawless. He's like me, I think, in that he would delete those emails, he would not leave evidence." This struck me as interesting. Adam Back, Martti Malmi, Hal Finney, and Wei Dai, among others, hadn't felt a need to destroy their emails with Nakamoto.

In the past, Ray had called Nakamoto's true identity a "non-topic" and "goddamn trivia" and those who tried to discover it "idiot[s]" and "hysterical children." But on our call, he was willing to discuss

Nakamoto's general profile. Ray thought the wildcard, outsider-artist Nakamoto theory was unlikely. "I don't think someone who hadn't been on the cypherpunks and crypto list would be as familiar with everything as he was." Despite the non-cutting-edge cryptography Nakamoto used, Ray believed he was a seasoned cryptographer. "A lot of cryptographers, including me, tend not to trust new crypto primitives or protocols until they've been out for several years and stood fast through many attacks and reviews and the best people in the business looking at them for any kind of vulnerability." He also thought Nakamoto's inclusion of the British newspaper headline in the Genesis Block had been "weird," because he didn't think Nakamoto was British. "I can't really say why not. It was just a feeling. There were a few Britishisms" in Nakamoto's language, "but there are a few in my language, too, just because I read a few books."

I questioned whether legal exposure could really be a concern for Nakamoto, fifteen years after Bitcoin's launch. Thousands of other blockchains had launched without their creators being arrested. "Satoshi may have been in an unusually vulnerable position," Ray suggested. "A reason I think of Hal as a possibility is because he'd been in trouble before, so may not have wanted to get in trouble again." Ray meant when Hal Finney was working on PGP in the 1990s and, disregarding the laws classifying it as a weapon, sent the software "over the wires to basically anyone who wanted it, no matter what country." As a result, Ray said, Hal "was in some serious Dutch with American security agencies" and was "on the no-fly list for a while." (Fran Finney doesn't recall Hal being on such a list.) This wasn't the only time in our conversation that Ray mentioned Hal as a possible Nakamoto. He'd known Hal through the lists for twenty years, and he saw Hal as more stridently ideological than I had. "I think in 2008, he got really, really angry at financial institutions and wanted to get rid of them. . . . He was one of the bandleaders who put Bitcoin up as a way to get back at banks or take your autonomy back from banks." Ray thought it was possible that Nakamoto had thrown out his keys, then died. And Hal, as Ray noted, "is sort of dead."

Then Ray contradicted himself, saying he thought it more likely than not that Nakamoto was still alive, because Nakamoto didn't seem like someone who'd lose his keys, and if he'd died, they'd have gone to his heirs, who'd be less likely to resist the temptation to spend Nakamoto's fortune.

Years earlier, Ray had written programs that would alert him to any movement of those coins on the blockchain. "The coins move, Satoshi's dead, it means someone inherited his keys, and I wanted to know about that, because I guess I sort of valued him and wanted to keep track of him. He was the real deal. He was someone who had the good of the world at heart."

When I told Ray that stylometry had shown him, Ray Dillinger, to be one of the two people on the Metzdowd list whose writing matched most closely to Nakamoto's, he said, "I don't really have a response to that. I still get one or two people a year who think I'm Satoshi."

I returned my attention to Travis Hassloch. Dimitrios4615, the Ars Technica commenter who without any explanation had in 2018 identified Hassloch as Bitcoin's creator, turned out to have made the same assertion elsewhere using his full name, Dimitrios Tsoulogiannis. A LinkedIn page described him as "Pope of the Church of Satoshi" and gave his location as Las Vegas. It wasn't at all clear what his connection might be to Travis Hassloch. Soon we were talking on the phone.

Dimitrios now lived in Florida, but in 2018, he told me, he was an ex–blackjack dealer who'd just opened a bricks-and-mortar Bitcoin exchange in Vegas with a bitcoin ATM. Two days after it opened, a man named Thomas Stowe came in, offering to help. "I didn't know much," Dimitrios said. "He didn't know much more. He stayed with me at the office for two or three months. He was playing poker, mining, doing the Bitcoin thing."

Stowe "had some crazy stories," Dimitrios said. One was that someone he knew named Travis Hassloch "was involved in some way" in creating Bitcoin. Dimitrios told me it might even have been

Stowe who put up the social media posts, using Dimitrios's accounts. Dimitrios's own theory was that Bitcoin had been created by the government of "a major power," such as the United States, China, or Russia.

I couldn't talk to Stowe, because he'd died in 2022 when he was just forty-one, but Dimitrios had said Stowe came from Texas, where I knew Hassloch came from too. I wrote to Hassloch at several addresses and didn't hear back. After several days, I again wrote to him, this time letting him know that his name had come up as a possible Nakamoto, and he wrote back. "I'm afraid that was a rumor started by a friend of mine who was . . . a bit of a raconteur. . . . I suspect he wanted to impress someone he was working with doing bitcoin ATMs in Las Vegas. It hasn't helped me in my personal life. If I had invented bitcoin or even been an early participant, this would be the least of my worries; I'd own an island or country somewhere and have a military to defend my assets, and not still be a wage slave." Travis added that he was "allergic to exposure" and had "strong ethical concerns about/against being involved with cryptocurrency" and pointed me toward an essay on the topic that he'd published anonymously.

The essay was a wide-ranging overview of Bitcoin, written in 2017 as if by someone trying to work out his own thoughts on the topic. There was nothing about it that suggested it was written by an insider, much less by Bitcoin's inventor.

I wrote back to Travis explaining that what had led me to contact him were the stylometry results finding him to be a match to most of the Nakamoto texts. After some back-and-forth, I laid out in full the theory that he was Nakamoto, including the striking coincidence that perhaps the only person on earth publicly and definitively named by a friend as Nakamoto also happened to be the main person from Metzdowd whom stylometry classified as likely to be Nakamoto.

After a few days, he wrote back:

"It's not me."

Numero Uno

There remained the most compelling Nakamoto candidate I hadn't been able to exclude. Many months earlier, I'd stumbled on another crumb. It was an internet echo of an echo, a passing mention of a Facebook post by someone named Will Price, who'd worked with Hal Finney and had told his Facebook friends that he believed Hal to be Satoshi Nakamoto. A screenshot captured the first few lines of the post, which had quickly been deleted.

Hal had remained a usual suspect in Nakamoto speculations. He was much more practiced at tactical secrecy than Nick Szabo, having written code for PGP, steganography, and remailers. The early stylometry assessments by Juola & Associates, admittedly of a limited field of candidates, had found Hal the closest match to Nakamoto. And there were ways in which the facts of Hal's life and death synced with Nakamoto's profile. Hal had made his first post to BitcoinTalk in November of 2010, only a month before Nakamoto made his last post there. Hal's declining health would explain the timing of Nakamoto's departure from the project. Hal's death could explain the untouched coins and the immaculate maintenance of the pseudonym in the years that followed.

His commitment to the ideal of decentralization had run deep. After his death, former colleagues began to talk more about the nature of his role with PGP, which had made the first popularly available public-key encryption software. A lingering issue with public-key cryptography was how to ensure that a public key belonged to the person you thought it belonged to. When Phil Zimmermann released the second version of the software in 1992, it featured a "web of trust," where people would cryptographically sign the keys of people they knew. It did away with the need for a central authority that mapped keys to real-world identities. You could judge a key's trustworthiness by the number and quality of connections you had to it. A main activity at the monthly cypherpunks meetings was a nerd key party where everyone signed one another's PGP keys. Hal had been largely responsible for implementing and coding the web of trust.

There was another argument for Nakamoto being someone who'd worked on PGP. Emin Gün Sirer, who cofounded the Avalanche blockchain, studied Bitcoin's source code and concluded that Nakamoto was self-taught and probably a single person, but above all that Nakamoto had gone "out of his way to think adversarially." Nakamoto had been so paranoid about the possibility that intelligence agencies had back doors into the most widely used cryptographic algorithms that he'd taken the step of using two of them, from different sources (one American, one European), to generate new Bitcoin addresses—essentially, using a double-scrambler. "This is not something that a normal person would do," Sirer argued. "It has to have been somebody who spent a lot of time worrying about what state actors are capable of. It has to have been somebody who has experience writing code for adversarial use cases, so that really narrows down who Satoshi could be." Someone who'd worked on PGP, according to Sirer, was exactly the kind of person he was thinking of. "So Hal makes a very, very good Satoshi candidate in my book."

I thought Sirer might be on to something. "I inculcated a pervasive attitude in all the people who worked on PGP that we're up against major governments," Phil Zimmermann told me. One of the reasons Hal's role in the web of trust became known only years after he built it was that during the years when Phil was under threat of prosecution, Phil made a point of never mentioning Hal to investigators. He did this, with Hal's agreement, in order to protect him. "I was feeling guilty about not mentioning his name more often," Phil recalled. "He deserved credit." But the anonymity aligned with both Hal's modesty and his comfort with working in secret.

Despite all this, I'd been skeptical of Hal as a candidate ever since he gave me what seemed like a sincere denial in 2011. He'd even produced documentation in 2014, when he provided *Forbes* with copies of his private email exchanges with Nakamoto. Bitcoin had an elegance that Hal's RPOW lacked. Hal released RPOW under his own name, so why would he not do the same with Bitcoin? "I don't mean to sound like a socialist, I don't care if wealth is concentrated," which Nakamoto once wrote, seemed uncharacteristically callous for Hal. So when I dutifully got in touch with Will Price, ex-Hal colleague and deleter of the Facebook post asserting Hal was Nakamoto, I wasn't hopeful.

Will was born into a prominent Hollywood family. His father Frank was a legendary studio head who at different times ran both Columbia Pictures and Universal Studios. Frank had been born poor and had become a voracious reader, and when Will, one of four boys, was growing up in Beverly Hills, history and Greek and Latin and literature were revered in the Price home. Will ended up majoring in classics in college, and he loved it.

His real obsession, though, was computers. Starting when he was fourteen, using a cell modem he rigged up in his dorm room at Phillips Academy, in Andover, Massachusetts, he earned hundreds of dollars selling a piece of software he'd written that let people post messages on an early-internet bulletin board service. In his early twenties, wanting to encrypt the files on his hard drive, he taught himself cryptography and wrote and released a piece of software called CryptDisk.

This brought him to the attention of Phil Zimmermann, who just then was busy worrying about being prosecuted by the government and overseeing a small circle of volunteers working to expand PGP. While Hal was working on PGP 2.0, Phil wanted Will to code PGP

Phone, software to enable encrypted calls over the internet. Will was speaking with Phil on January 11, 1996, when Phil put him on hold to take another call. When Phil clicked back over, he said: "Will, they're dropping the investigation. It's over."

After that, PGP entered a new phase, incorporating as a company and seeking venture capital. Will and Hal were Phil's first two hires. Twelve months into its new for-profit life, Will says, PGP had $7 million in funding and was spending it profligately. For a trade show in Manhattan, the company splashed out $2 million, serving PGP-branded sushi, putting on a PGP-branded laser light show, and adorning its booth with three Roman pillars, each carved with a word: "Privacy. Security. Anonymity." That CEO soon left.

Will was Hal's direct boss for many years, and it was for this reason, he told me, that he was almost certain that Hal was Nakamoto. Will had watched firsthand as Hal worked in Phil's shadow. He had seen how comfortable Hal was with not receiving public credit. Hal also, as the full-time employee of a corporation, had reason to fear it could make a claim on anything he created. "I guarantee you," Will said, "somewhere in those contracts, there's something that says, *If you write code, we own it*." By 2008, Will and Hal and others who'd started out as idealists with Phil were "so done with" PGP's post-Phil corporate ownership, which was doing work for Barclays Bank and, they suspected, the CIA.

Will also knew Hal's programming style intimately. "I spent twenty years reading Hal's code," Will said. "No one looked at Hal's code more than I did." Will felt that the bolted-together nature of the original Bitcoin source code was typical of Hal. Though Hal was best known as a C coder, he'd used both C and C++ at PGP. And Will agreed with Sirer about Nakamoto's use of two different cryptographic algorithms. "These things are our bread and butter," Will said. "Some of this is a bit of witchcraft . . . If you want to last for hundreds of years, you have to assume an algorithm will break."

"My job from 1996 to 2009," he continued, "was hiring, finding, and managing crazy cryptographers, of which Hal was by far numero uno, in terms of ability and knowledge." Where most cryptographers were good at this or that aspect, Hal was "one-size-fits-all. He could easily hold his own with Diffie and Hellman at a lunch table . . . Meanwhile, he could write code for us, and he could turn it into productizable code . . . My job was knowing all these people, and the reality is, the number of people capable of doing Bitcoin would fit at a small dinner table in those years."

What most convinced Will, however, was that he knew Hal's schedule. He knew what Hal was working on and when. "We'd spent years developing a latent dislike for the company, so it wasn't like, 'Let's make the company rich.' For many years"—including, Will said, the period immediately preceding Bitcoin's appearance—"I assigned him almost nothing. So he had years of work fully paid in order to do this. He was a senior fellow, above reproach, with a bunch of free time. . . . No one's ever been in as cushy a position to do exactly this." In August 2009, Hal announced to his PGP colleagues that he had ALS. There was a ceremony at the time, but he would only officially retire from the company in early 2011, which also coincided with Nakamoto's withdrawal from the Bitcoin project.

How, then, did Will explain the anomalies: the posting hours, the double spaces, the Anglicisms? These were trivial, in Will's view. "With a pseudonym, you establish rules: *This guy wakes up at 10, uses double spaces, lives in England*. That's the whole idea. You create the character, create multiple email addresses for that person. Whatever you need to do. Hal's not a dummy. He knows you have to create all these things for it."

But what about the email from Nakamoto to Hal, where Nakamoto wrote, "That means a lot coming from you, Hal"? Would Hal really write that to himself? "I'd reverse that sentence," Will said. "Isn't that what you'd do? Don't you want evidence that you've communicated, that you were a recipient? There has to be email evidence. People really underestimate Hal if they think these things are [difficult]. If you're going to have a believable pseudonym, you have to make it real." Will found it laughable when people talked about

Hal's "computer," as if he had only one. "'We have seen the computer, the computer had these transactions on it, and so now we have proof he didn't do this.' And the reality is, of course, the guy had at least *six* computers."

Other questions, like how Hal could die and not leave a fortune, Will could only speculate about. Maybe he lost the keys. Maybe he hid the keys. Will said he'd deleted his Facebook post at the request of Hal's family, but he now felt that the naming of Hal as Nakamoto was overdue. "It saddens me the story isn't out there," he said. ". . . I totally disagree with these morons—'Isn't it better if we never know?' No, he's been dead eight years. I feel like he should get the credit . . . There are people offended at the idea of exposing Satoshi . . . I was never on that bandwagon. To me, Hal created it."

There was also, I knew, a possible explanation, other than that Hal simply wasn't Nakamoto, for his late-in-life denials and the release of the private emails. There had been a series of events that would have made him highly motivated to double down on pseudonymity, perhaps not even coming clean to his own family, and made the Finney family understandably concerned about Hal being identified as Nakamoto.

As if anticipating would-be malefactors, in his goodbye-Bitcoiners post in March 2013 Hal wrote, "My bitcoins are stored in our safe deposit box . . ." Public speculation around Hal as Nakamoto had already prompted threats, and someone calling himself Bitcoin Troll told the Finneys that he'd release personal information about the family online if they didn't pay a ransom of one thousand bitcoins. It was more than the Finneys had, and ALS was an expensive disease, with many treatments uncovered by insurance. The Finneys needed their money to keep Hal comfortable, not to pay off extortionists.

On the morning of May 29, 2014, not long after the Dorian Nakamoto low-speed chase and the *Forbes* article in which Hal again denied being Satoshi, a call came into the employee phone line at the Santa Barbara Sheriff's Department. A man on the other end said he'd murdered his wife and child. Now, he said, he was going to kill himself and burn his house down. He gave his address. It was Hal Finney's home.

Santa Barbara police were already on edge. Days earlier, a man named Elliot Rodger had terrorized UC Santa Barbara, going on a stabbing and shooting rampage that killed six people and injured fourteen others. Now the police were quick to mobilize. Several local schools went into lockdown mode. The Finneys' next-door neighbors were evacuated, and other residents of the block were instructed to shelter in place. When the phone rang in the Finney home, a ranch house on a dead-end street, Hal was in the middle of being washed by Fran and a nurse in a roll-in shower. Fran took a moment to answer the phone. The caller was a 911 operator, whose first questions were "Are you okay?" and "Is anyone being attacked in your house?" The operator continued: "I need to let you know that you are about to have a SWAT team come to your home, and they're going to ask you to leave."

Fran Finney looked out her door. The house was surrounded by police in tactical gear holding assault rifles. A helicopter hovered overhead. The police yelled at Fran to put down her phone and come outside. Jason Finney and Hal's nurse then brought Hal out; because he'd been mid-shower, he was off of life support. For the next half hour, while police conducted a thorough search of the house and backyard, he had to wait on the lawn, shivering. He couldn't swallow, and the whole time Fran was wracked with worry that he'd choke on his saliva. "I was just panicking that he was going to need suction or something," she later told *Wired*. "He didn't have anything with him except his ventilator."

Police found nothing. The phone number of the caller was nonlocal. This had been a swatting, a dangerously viral hoax at the time. It wasn't even the only one the Finneys experienced during that period, but it did the most damage. It also became clear that the swatter was Bitcoin Troll, who'd been harassing the Finneys for nearly a year.

And he wasn't done. In the two months after the swatting, he called the Finney home nine times, threatening to assault family members and publish their personal information. He was never caught.

Fran Finney largely stopped speaking publicly about Hal, and years later she was still angry. Not only had the incident harmed Hal's health and shortened his life, but "it took away some of the peace that he could have had for the last few months of his life. This was taking up a lot of his emotional energy."

Now Fran spent her time on ALS work. In 2021, she started an annual half-marathon, the Running Bitcoin Challenge, to raise money towards a cure for the disease that killed her husband.

I thought it entirely possible that Will Price, like some crazed treasure hunter in the Rockies or an irresponsible parent who'd quit his benefits-paying journalism job to look for an anonymous and probably unfindable inventor, was in the grip of apophenia. But then I spoke with Jon Callas, the computer security expert who'd been chief scientist at PGP and held senior positions at Apple and the Electronic Frontier Foundation. Jon had a soup-strainer mustache and an absurdist sense of humor; he once gave a nearly three-and-a-half-minute speech that consisted entirely of him repeating the word *blockchain* more than two hundred times.

"In retrospect," Jon said, "there are conversations I had with Hal in which I essentially didn't know I was opting out of working on Bitcoin." Hal would talk a lot about proof of work, for instance. "I was very negative about proof of work. I remember Hal saying, 'You're absolutely right, but I don't see another way to do this.' Many of us who knew Hal say: *Who else could Satoshi be?*"

Jon thought that Hal's overlap with Dorian Nakamoto in Temple City couldn't have been mere coincidence. Not that he believed *Newsweek*'s Nakamoto had anything to do with the invention of Bitcoin. He just thought it likely that when Hal was trying to settle on a pseudonym, he'd been inspired by that name. Maybe he was flipping through a local phonebook. Maybe, a third ex-PGP colleague named Gene Hoffman suggested, he knew it from one of his runs.

When Jon last visited Hal at his home in Santa Barbara, Hal was already in a wheelchair. He showed off a flat-screen TV and cashmere socks, known in the house as "the Bitcoin socks," which he'd bought for his family using bitcoin. "I flat out asked Hal, and he said 'no' in a way that I couldn't tell if it was a wink-wink nudge-nudge." Jon also asked Fran and Jason, "and they both denied it." Phil Zimmermann, Hal's longtime mentor and boss, also visited and asked Hal whether he was Nakamoto. "And he said 'No.' I mean, he flat-out said 'No.' And I asked his wife. And she said 'No,' also." Jon was among those who believed that Nakamoto lost his private keys. Maybe he started mining on Monday, and lost the keys on Thursday. Was he going to start over and undo half a week's work?

But Jon didn't think the solution to the Nakamoto mystery was as simple as Satoshi = Hal. There was a public record of Hal running a ten-mile race in Santa Barbara on the morning of April 18, 2009, at a time when Satoshi Nakamoto was sending an email to another Bitcoin developer. "You have to explain a photograph of Superman and Clark Kent taken together," Jon said. There was also the fact that C, and not C++, was Hal's primary language. "So you have to say, this guy wrote in C his whole life, but his magnum opus is not that."

"I find it very interesting that the more people look for who Satoshi was, what they keep finding is 'Here's this little anomaly that, if you believe Hal and Satoshi are the same person, you have to explain,' and not the other way, that you keep finding evidence arguing it *is* him."

"Are you familiar with Antony Flew, the philosopher?" Jon asked. He went on to describe Flew's "Parable of the Invisible Gardener." "You come to this meadow in the middle of the woods, and it's beautiful, and it looks like a garden, and you ask, 'Oh, who takes care of this garden?' And someone says, 'Well, this gardener who comes in, but no one has ever seen the gardener,' and you do things like say, 'Why don't we put bells on the bushes to try and see who the gardener is?'" And when the bells don't ring, someone says, *Well, the gardener must be invisible.* "And then there are more and more cascading excuses, and his expression was 'death by a thousand qualifications.' You can say, 'Well, maybe Hal was off on a marathon, so he got Jason to do it.' But now, all of a sudden, you're complicating your theory, being cute. *It's not just Hal who was Satoshi, but Hal in conjunction with Jason.* It stops making sense after a while."

The upshot was that Jon didn't believe Hal had worked alone.

I'd been certain for quite some time that Nakamoto wasn't a group. Apparently, Jon needed some knowledge dropped on him. "What was it Ben Franklin said? 'Two can keep a secret if one of them is dead.'"

I waited patiently for the grateful flicker in Jon's eyes as the lightbulb switched on in his endearingly naive brain.

"*Three* can keep a secret if *two* of them are dead," Jon corrected me. It was an expression he used frequently in his talks. He was, after all, a *leading security engineer.*

"Well, in this case one of the people *is* dead," Jon said. "I believe there were two people. I believe it was Hal and someone else. Maybe even a third person. I've seen everybody's ideas about who Satoshi could be. I think there are fingerprints all over the place to say there are people who worked together."

I wondered aloud whether Hal might have partnered with Len Sassaman. After speaking with Evan Hatch, who'd first advanced the Sassaman theory, I'd spoken with Bram Cohen, who'd lived with Sassaman in San Francisco and written the "Pynchon Gate" paper with him and one other person. Bram said he didn't think it was out of the question that Sassaman had been Nakamoto. Sassaman had always been very into pseudonymity, Bram said as a giant cat treadwheel spun slowly behind him. "I have a vague memory, mostly because Len told me about it and I wasn't paying close attention, that there was a nym called Pr0duct Cypher which pseudonymously posted to cypherpunks and then disappeared. The implication with that one seemed be that it was Hal or Len or some combination of the two." Sassaman had pushed Bram to release BitTorrent anonymously "to validate that this was a reasonable thing to do," Bram said, adding that he'd ignored this advice because "I don't want to live that way."

"I don't think Len had the tech skills to come up with it," Bram continued, "but almost everything about the writings of Satoshi are consistent with it being Len. Particularly the public posts. This fake British thing. Europe. His MO. The cypherpunks list was dying off at the time. It seems quite plausible to me that Hal and Len were joining forces. They were both big on this concept of internet money. Len had talked excitedly about this."

But Jon Callas, who'd worked with Sassaman at PGP, was skeptical that he'd been part of any Nakamoto partnership. Sassaman was "more of a QA person than a coder," Jon said, meaning someone who tests code rather than writes it. And like Ben Laurie, Jon didn't think Sassaman would have been capable of keeping such a secret. "Len was a very close friend of mine as well. I don't think he would have been involved."

Jon thought the best place to look for a coconspirator of Hal's would be among the extropians, the group to which Hal, Wei Dai, and Nick Szabo had all belonged. "Those are extraordinarily smart people, self-educated polymaths. And somebody there who was medium-good at cryptography and asked the right, oblique questions, would be good candidates to work on it with Hal."

I thought about the intermittent British spellings. The shifts in tone from ideological ("a new territory of freedom") to detached ("the libertarian viewpoint"). The presence of both the Donaldism *fencible* and evidence of a more balanced personality ("poor thing"). A collective creator would make sense of several inconsistencies.

Occam's Razor

Soon after my conversations with Will and Jon, I had lunch with my friend Andrew and mentioned my epiphany.

"It's not a group," he said quickly.

Clearly he had no idea what he was talking about, but I humored him. "Why are you so sure?"

"Occam's razor," he said. "Two people can't keep a secret."

"*Three* people," I said smugly. "Yes, I was always inclined toward that view myself, but—" Here I regurgitated some of Jon Callas's points, like how a group would explain why for every plausible individual candidate there were anomalies. I strained to think of successful conspiracies. There weren't many.

"The NSA keeps secrets every day," I said.

In fact, I went on, even before the three California cryptographers invented asymmetric cryptography in the '70s, a trio in England independently achieved the same breakthrough. But unlike the Americans, the three Brits worked for GCHQ, the U.K.'s signals-intelligence agency, and their achievement remained publicly unknown until it was finally declassified in 1997, after twenty-five years.

Andrew indulged me for a moment, mentioning COINTELPRO. In 1971, a group of eight activists calling themselves the Citizens' Commission to Investigate the FBI had picked one lock and crowbarred another to break into a field office near Philadelphia. They'd driven away with suitcases full of documents and mailed them to newspapers, exposing the FBI's domestic surveillance and harassment of dissident political groups, a program code-named COINTELPRO. The FBI investigated the burglary until 1976, when the statute of limitations expired. The perpetrators had vowed to remain silent about what they'd done, and they never again met as a group. Only forty-three years after the burglary did five of the eight reveal their involvement.

So yes, it did happen very rarely.

I could tell Andrew was still skeptical.

But after years of thinking it unlikely that Nakamoto was a group, I now thought the opposite.

Valley Boy

I dug more deeply into Hal Finney's history and found an early-'90s email exchange between Tim May and other cypherpunks. May had become curious after someone named Tiia Roth-Biester posted to the list. He'd never heard of her, and the cypherpunks skewed so male that the arrival of a woman was notable. As May read a post in which Roth-Biester presciently talked about how technologies such as digital cash would allow people to live as untaxable nomads, he was struck that she sounded very much like Duncan Frissell, an attorney active on the list. Indeed, Frissell had written it.

This experience prompted May to muse that, beyond a gut recognition of someone's style, "Imagine what can be done with word and phrase frequency analysis, with examination of punctuation styles, and so on. . . . Someday this may be important." Other cypherpunks suggested that unconscious traits would betray writers. "Take this pretentious word 'nym,' for instance, that some of the cypherpunks are so fond of," a Scotsman named Graham Toal wrote, noting that in the past month only four nonanonymous people on the list had used the word. Any quirk—consistently misspelling a word, using the Oxford comma, using "DigiCash" instead of "digital cash"—could be a tell. Someone else mentioned how frequency analysis had shed light on the authorship of the disputed fraction of *The Federalist Papers*.

May believed that the CIA and NSA almost certainly had powerful tools to do such analyses, and he asked whether any cypherpunks wanted to help build a "nymalizer" to perform authorship attributions on the list. Instead, these being cypherpunks, the discussion shifted toward countermeasures to thwart close-reading adversaries. May suggested that deliberately imitating another person's style could be effective. Someone else thought that machine-translating a message from English to a foreign language and back might help. A third person imagined software that would filter a message and "randomly modify spacing, indentations, punctuation styles, spelling, replace words with random synonyms, reorder words in phrases, etc."

Hal Finney, who'd been one of the four nonanonymous posters who'd used the word *nym* in the past month, noted that there were already software filters available, including ones called "jive" and "valspeak," which could alter a writer's voice to sound like a Valley Girl. "These are pretty amusin'," Hal wrote. "Perhaps a variation on these filters, fer shure . . . like, ya know, this messages [sic] has been processed by thuh valspeak filter."

Maybe, as Will Price had suggested, nontechnical people like me underestimated the length to which a cypherpunk would go to conceal his identity because we overestimated the difficulty of doing so. Maybe we should see contradictions and anomalies and untidy facts not as disqualifiers but as prerequisites.

I was finding that Hal lined up with Nakamoto in other ways. In 2005, when he'd demonstrated RPOW at a conference, he'd combined it with BitTorrent, fusing two of Bitcoin's central technologies: proof of work and P2P networking. Around the same time, he wrote that "one project I'm hoping to work on" was "a P2P gambling game (like poker or something)" using RPOW; the original Bitcoin software included code for a poker game, which was dropped from later versions. Hal was a licensed pilot who'd flown within California many times. Nakamoto's leaked IP address was from the area around Van Nuys. Was it possible Hal had stopped at the Van Nuys Airport on one of his trips and logged in from there?

I also learned more about Temple City's geography. Hal and Dorian Nakamoto had lived a two-mile drive from each other, but I found out that Hal's sister Kathy, who was ten years older than him and had helped to raise him, lived considerably closer to Dorian: *three and a half blocks* as the crow flies. What were the chances? *Maybe Hal knew Dorian Nakamoto's name from one of his runs,* Gene Hoffman had said.

Hal's own description of his involvement with Bitcoin now struck me as implausible. There was almost no one better able to instantly grasp Bitcoin's technological breakthrough, or more interested in what Bitcoin was trying to achieve, than Hal. Yet by his own account he had briefly been involved in early 2009, then ignored it for two years. "The next I heard of Bitcoin was late 2010," he wrote in his March 2013 reminiscence titled "Bitcoin and Me," "when I was surprised to find that it was not only still going, bitcoins actually had monetary value." The final sentence read: "I'm comfortable with my legacy."

After that, he posted only a few more times to BitcoinTalk. In a thread started by someone else and titled "Another *Potential* Identifying Piece of Evidence on Satoshi," Hal quoted loosely from the new *Man of Steel* movie: "Lois Lane: How do you find someone who has spent a lifetime covering his tracks? For some, he was a guardian angel. For others, a ghost, who never quite fit in. What's the S stand for?" Years after his death, Walter Bright, who'd lived in the dorm room next to Hal's at CalTech, would remark, "Being Satoshi is just the kind of elaborate prank Hal would have loved."

If Hal was Nakamoto, it would provide an alternative explanation for facts that had led so many people to suspect Nick Szabo. Nakamoto's quote that Bitcoin "supports a tremendous variety of possible transaction types that I designed years ago," including "escrow transactions, bonded contracts, third party arbitration, multiparty signatures," had seemed to point toward Nick. But in the 1990s, I found, Hal had talked specifically, while reading up on potential legal bases for digital money, about promissory notes and negotiable instruments. Maybe the initials SN, rather than being an Easter egg left by Szabo, had been an Easter egg left by Hal in *tribute* to Nick. Nick had never credited Hal as Nakamoto, but he also had never said, "It's not Hal Finney." He had never even said, publicly anyway, that he didn't know who Nakamoto was. Perhaps his silence was cypherpunk omertà, or maybe it was a mark of respect for his friend's wishes. Maybe Nick's defenses of Bitcoin had been on behalf of his stricken pal, about whom Nick wrote, on his death, "we will miss you Hal Finney."

Maybe everyone had made this too complicated.

Occam's razor.

If you hear hoofbeats, think horses, not zebras.

If Hal was indeed Nakamoto, it would be the best possible outcome for Bitcoin enthusiasts. It would justify the sanctification of Satoshi. It would support the belief that he had acted from a benevolent selflessness—that Bitcoin was his gift to the world. James Donald was the Satoshi people feared. Hal Finney was the Satoshi they wanted.

I wanted Hal to be Nakamoto too. The idea that a good man had created a great thing offered a pleasing thrum of moral congruence that true stories rarely do. And serious people who'd known Hal well and worked closely with him believed he was Nakamoto. In most situations, that would carry a lot of weight. Maybe I'd even call it a day, mission accomplished. I felt the gravitational pull toward a finite ending.

But Will Price and Jon Callas, though closer to Hal than many, weren't immune to the risk of overweighting their intuitions. And even they didn't think Hal had done it alone, leaving open the question of whom he'd worked with.

Vincent Adultman

There was no paternity test for Bitcoin. There was no treasure chest to confirm that you'd read the clues right. There was no way to prove who Nakamoto was unless he came forward and demonstrated that he had the relevant private keys, or at least nonforged contemporaneous documents supporting his story. The closest anyone else could theoretically get would be if Nakamoto had made a misstep or confided in someone. But as years passed, the trail, if there was one, grew ever fainter. Maybe Nakamoto had made it impossible even for him to prove who he was, by throwing out his machines, his private keys, and his passwords to email accounts and never telling anyone his secret.

Ben Laurie had argued that unless the Bitcoin network represented at least 50 percent of the world's total computing power, it would always be vulnerable to an attack by a larger network. With Nakamoto, unless you had a writing sample from every English-language writer alive in 2008 and a coding sample from every C or C++ coder, you could never be certain that someone whom stylometry had pegged as the closest match was actually him.

Even if the Nakamoto writings could all or nearly all be ascribed to one person, others might have conceived and designed and coded Bitcoin, and I still thought a group Nakamoto would explain a lot, including the use by Nakamoto of three email accounts and the remarkable security of the original Bitcoin code, which was a tall order for a lone coder.

I mulled combinations. Thinking horses, not zebras, it seemed crushingly obvious that Nick Szabo was involved in some way—that even if he wasn't Nakamoto, he at least knew more than he'd let on. Maybe he'd been in the background, and someone else handled the coding and community interactions. As for Hal Finney, while he hadn't been the closest hit with either text stylometry or code stylometry, he was close enough that neither had ruled him out.

I considered different teams. Nick Szabo and Hal Finney. Nick Szabo, Hal Finney, Ray Dillinger, and Travis Hassloch. Three of the four, plus Ben Laurie or Bram Cohen or Zooko Wilcox or James Donald. Gwern Branwen had speculated about Elaine Ou, a younger blockchain programmer, sometime Bloomberg opinion columnist, experienced C++ coder, and wife of Nick Szabo. She was from LA. In February 2009, she'd tweeted: "Working on something fantastic."

There was a thematic harmony to the idea of Nakamoto as a group. Bitcoin was decentralized. So was its creator. *"Recall Nero's wish that Rome had a single throat that he could cut. If we provide them with such a throat, it will be cut."* A distributed mask let any single member deny, truthfully, that he was Satoshi.

I pictured Nakamoto as Vincent Adultman, the *BoJack Horseman* character who is three boys in a trench coat posing as a grown-up. Perhaps the members of Nakamoto took turns. When Nakamoto wrote, "I'm not a lawyer" and "I'm better with code than with words," Nick Szabo was off-duty. When Nakamoto wrote "non-fencible," James Donald was at the wheel.

My understanding of Nakamoto was decentralized, too, a cloud of influences and possibilities. Maybe he was one of the people already suspected. Maybe he was several of them. Or maybe we were all drunks beneath a streetlight, and Nakamoto was in the bushes, unseen. He was a zebra after all. He was a she. He was a team at the NSA.

If Nakamoto was still alive, I wondered what he thought about his offspring. Even as Bitcoin had become extremely valuable and almost mainstream, you couldn't look at it in 2024 and say it had fulfilled its creator's vision. It still wasn't a working cash system. It was still arguably very centralized, with four mining pools controlling more than 75 percent of the network, and just two controlling more than 53 percent. Its originally vaunted privacy had proven to be much exaggerated. It had never escaped its reliance on third-party exchanges as on-ramps from the fiat-money system, a shocking number of those exchanges had proved untrustworthy, and these chokepoints were increasingly susceptible to regulation. Bitcoin still struggled to scale.

The gulf between Bitcoin's origins and its use mainly as an asset for speculation or wealth storage had turned off people who might otherwise be expected to have liked it. "I'd say Satoshi is at the very least face-palming over this, if not ranting, 'That's not what we built this for,'" Jon Callas said. Leslie Lamport, who founded the theory of distributed computing, the basis for both the internet and multiprocessor computers, and was one of the first to define the network-coordination problem Bitcoin tried to solve, told me, "I see very little real use for it, other than creating a cryptocurrency for criminals." Cypherpunk hero Phil Zimmermann, whose laptop now bore a harrumphing sticker ("CRYPTO MEANS CRYPTOGRAPHY"), called Bitcoin "an embarrassment" and "a ghetto of criminality and fraud." Mike Hearn, the early core developer who'd been frustrated by resistance to scaling, had sold his coins, quit the project, and declared it "an experiment" that had "failed." Ray Dillinger, likewise, had deemed Bitcoin "a failure" and "a disaster" and sold all his coins. "I've been really kind of disgusted with what happened with blockchain speculation," he told me. "I have this old-fashioned idea that business should leave both the vendor and the customer better off, and when you do speculation, which is basically what Bitcoin did, you always have for every winner an equal and opposite loser." As for Nakamoto, Ray said, "I think Satoshi would be disturbed by what has happened. He envisioned what I'd call respectable uses of Bitcoin even after it was out of the realm of normal people." Ray meant that Nakamoto had always expected Bitcoin to evolve from something individuals interacted with to background infrastructure for a new financial system that would be built atop it. "He didn't think people would be ripping people off with the hype. So yeah, him leaving might have been him throwing up his hands and saying, 'No more.'" Even Tim May had written, before his death, "I think Satoshi would barf," though in May's case the gripe was about how lawfully compliant the cryptocurrency industry had become.

But for all the outright frauds and fake utopians and Wall Street suits parroting cypherpunk lingo, some of the most far-seeing cypherpunks—and Nakamoto candidates—were able to look beyond the crime and froth and politics and garishness of crypto. Bitcoin had done its job. It had been a necessary experiment, a proof of concept that, by knocking down conceptual and technical barriers previously seen as insurmountable, had opened up new vistas of possibility and invention. These more sanguine types were keeping their eyes on a future they still saw as inevitable.

Zooko Wilcox, from his days as a nineteen-year-old college dropout turned junior coder at DigiCash in the mid-1990s, had been focused on the importance of preserving privacy. When Bitcoin appeared, he admired what it was trying to do, and he would come to "worship" Nakamoto, but "I immediately understood that its lack of privacy was a fatal flaw and would ultimately kill it." He had also watched as Bitcoin became "ossified." After other computer scientists in 2013 figured out a way to use a cutting-edge, privacy-first form of cryptography called zero-knowledge proofs to create a better Bitcoin, Zooko devoted himself to building a cryptocurrency called Zcash using the new method.

James Donald, for his part, maintained a balanced, high-altitude view, lamenting Bitcoin's lack of anonymity and relative centralization but praising its speed and convenience for "money laundries" and seeing promise in recent software innovations that enhanced privacy and enabled faster transactions on the network. Nick Szabo had briefly become a proponent of Ethereum, only to later denounce it as "a shitcoin" that had "devolved into a centralized cult." He seemed to disdain the normie-lization of crypto, writing, "Multitudes and charlatans have entered the cryptocurrency and smart contract spaces who not only lack cypherpunk values, but hate cypherpunk values, including the values such as trust minimization that give cryptocurrencies like Bitcoin their market values." That hadn't stopped him, though, from adding Bitcoin-maxi laser eyes to his Twitter avatar. And Adam Back, whose avatar also featured laser eyes, was all-in on the original cryptocurrency, happily embracing the hodler meme, calling Bitcoin "digital gold for the next millennia," celebrating every price rise, simultaneously extolling cypherpunk values and news stories about institutional adoption, and running one of the largest private companies in the industry.

I still had only theories, some of which were more interesting than others. There were so many reasons to think Hal Finney had been Nakamoto, and to want that. But every time I was tempted to embrace this satisfyingly simple answer, the inconsistencies nagged at me. The fact of both textual stylometry and code stylometry finding other people (Hassloch, Dillinger, Laurie) to be closer matches. The natural-sounding email exchanges between Hal and Nakamoto, both in public and in private. It was a gap I couldn't skip past. If Hal was Nakamoto, he had found a way to create an unbridgeable chasm between suspicion and proof.

A loose thread dangled. Some of the cypherpunks most preoccupied with digital cash, including Finney and Szabo, had never said they didn't know who Nakamoto was, but neither had they said that they did know. There was one exception. "I know who Nakamoto was," James Donald had written, in a comment on a comment on a post on *Jim's Blog,* "and what his political and social goals were." This made James the only original cypherpunk who'd ever publicly said anything so definitive about Nakamoto's identity. Maybe, true to his online persona, he was being a blowhard, and when he said he knew, he really just meant that he had a preferred candidate. But he was someone who actually *could* know, which would make him the only person on record who credibly possessed this knowledge. It was my last solid lead, or what looked like it, and I decided I should go to see him after all.

Looking through real estate assessment records for James's various U.S. properties, I'd found that for a couple of years in the 2000s, a house he owned in Austin was registered to James at a street address on the northeastern coast of Australia. In more recent assessments, the U.S. properties were registered to James in the same Australian town, though now only a PO box was given. Clearly, James owned or had owned a house there. But he'd spent most of his career in California, and I was unsure how the Australian property fit into his constellation of residences. Did he live there all year? Part of the year? Was it mainly a correspondence address? Did the PO box mean he no longer lived at the street address?

I knew his wife had died in 2016, and using the Find a Grave site, I found a photograph, from the Australian town's cemetery, of a plaque memorializing her. So James likely had been living there at least until then. Five years later, he'd posted a small photo on his blog of what appeared to be the view from his deck: In the foreground was a small glass and a jug of what he described as homemade moonshine. In the distance was a gleaming blue sea, the horizon disrupted by a couple of small islands. I compared this view with other ocean-view images taken from the same town, and they seemed to match. So he was there at least until 2021. But a lot could have happened over the next three years. I wasn't going halfway around the world without confirmation that he was still there. I'd already started looking at flights, and none was easy. One of the faster ones had three stops and went through Fiji.

I searched online for private investigators in Queensland and found one, Daniel Quinn, who lived within a reasonable drive of the seaside town where I suspected James lived. I sent Daniel the house address and a twenty-year-old photo of James I'd found on an abandoned college blog of one of his sons.

A few days later, Daniel sent me a report from his first hours of surveillance. "The yard is in a very unkempt state with very long grass and overgrown shrubbery and trees, he's definitely not a plant lover." He attached a photo of James's house and the patchy, asphalt, private driveway it shared with two other homes. There was a lonely palm tree near the curb, and up the hill a bungalow on stilts, set amid the overgrowth, with a deck looking out at the Coral Sea.

Daniel didn't see James that day, but one Saturday morning several weeks later, I awoke to a message: Daniel had managed to get a photo of a man standing in the house's doorway. He was a clear, twenty-years-older match to the man in the photo I'd sent. Same dense beard, though now it was white. Similar large metal-rim glasses. Same fleshy nose. Three days later, I was on a plane to Australia.

There was a screen door and no doorbell, so I knocked on James's doorframe. I'd left my car at the base of the hill and was out of breath from climbing the banked driveway, veering at some banana trees onto the gravel drive to James's house. My mouth was dry from nerves. I was mostly convinced that James wasn't himself Nakamoto, but I didn't rule out that he could have been part of Nakamoto, and he was the one person I knew of who might have the answer I was seeking.

But I'd begun to think more about how James would see my visit. A lot of people might view a reporter on the doorstep as intrusive and annoying, but no more so than a Jehovah's Witness or an uninvited real estate appraiser. James, though, had gone out of his way to be unfindable. He lived at the end of a private driveway up a steep hill. This was his secret sanctuary.

I'd arrived in town a day earlier, after flying to San Francisco, then Melbourne, then Brisbane, then a small city in Queensland, where I'd rented a car and driven forty minutes to the coast. But before I left the United States, I'd written once more to James, who'd stopped responding to me the previous fall after I asked about the parallels between him and Nakamoto. Now I mentioned I was going to be in Australia, and asked if we could meet. I wanted at least to give him a heads-up that I knew what continent he was on, and I wanted to try a more polite approach.

He hadn't responded, so now I was trying a rude one. Crossing his porch toward the front door, I could see James through a plate glass window, sitting at a computer in the living room and wearing headphones. His latest blog post, put up just a few hours earlier, was a rambling screed about how Georgians (as in the country of Georgia) don't want "their Churches destroyed or turned into shrines of Gaia and gay sex, their old and beautiful buildings bulldozed and replaced by demonic postmodern eyesores." Western NGOs were working to see "Georgia faggotized and thrown into the meat grinder against Russia."

The porch held a few houseplants and offered a panoramic view of the Pacific. After a minute, I tried knocking directly on the front door. A moment later, James opened it and stepped outside.

He was leaner than I expected and wore black long johns and a red-camouflage long-sleeved shirt.

I started talking. I'd sent him an email and—

"Oh, I'm rather sporadic at reading my emails," James said, and he hadn't received mine. I reminded him of our exchange the prior year and of the book I was writing.

"Ah, right," James said.

I said something about how I'd have been remiss if I didn't make every effort to speak with him.

"Okay," James said, "well, the short of it is, that I can't even tell you what I don't tell you." His tone was pleasant, bemused.

I pointed out that he was the only cypherpunk who'd publicly insisted that he knew who Nakamoto was and what his social and political goals were. Could he elaborate?

"No, sorry."

"Okay. . . . Do you really know? Or do you sort of think you have a strong idea of who it might be?"

"I have a very good idea of who it might be, but I don't actually, uh, no."

"Do you think it was Hal Finney?"

"I can't answer that."

"Is that just because you're respecting his privacy?"

"I'm not allowed to tell anyone anything, and I'm not allowed to tell people what I've already told 'em."

Could I buy him a beer while I was in town?

"Ah," James said. "In wine there is truth. And I'm obligated not to tell people the truth."

"Lunch?" I offered, "so there'll be no truth-prising liquor."

James laughed. "Look," he said, "I have a tendency to talk too much, and I have a big tendency to talk too much after a few drinks, so I'm sorry."

I tried to keep the conversation going—giving him my contact information, and another book I'd written, which I thought he might enjoy—but his answers became monosyllabic. I had the sense that after initially being caught off guard, he was now computing how and why a nosy stranger had appeared on his porch.

"Well, I can understand why you'd live here," I said, gesturing at his stunning view.

"Yeah," James said, looking down.

I thanked him and made my way back down the hill.

I'd learned to code, inflicted my overheating laptop and obsessive preoccupation on my forbearing family, recruited a machine-learning expert and a stylometry specialist and a private investigator, and made a thirty-seven-hour journey for a three-minute encounter. I was pretty sure no one had spent as much time as I had in trying to solve this. I'd been careful not to fix on a single candidate or theory without solid evidence, but I was starting to feel a kinship with Sahil Gupta, who couldn't be persuaded that Nakamoto was anyone other than Elon Musk. At some point, I needed to stop.

HBO would soon add to the pile of Nakamoto guesses with a documentary called *Money Electric* that named Peter Todd, the former Bitcoin core developer, as Bitcoin's creator. Todd was a relatively unusual suspect, and the filmmaker, Cullen Hoback, had assembled a handful of intriguing coincidences, including an early Todd post on the Bitcoin forum, the timing and content of which, Hoback argued, suggested it had been an accidental log-in by Nakamoto using Todd's account. I thought it was an interesting theory. I wasn't convinced it was right, but it seemed at least plausible. Todd denied it, but I knew that wasn't meaningful.

The Bitcoin community was generally disapproving for the usual tsk-tsk-ing reasons—the documentary put a target on Todd's back, and it was better for Bitcoin if Nakamoto remained unknown. Bitcoiners were also roundly skeptical that Hoback was right, and some of their specific criticisms, even if merely intuitive, seemed worth taking seriously: Amir Taaki, the former Bitcoin core developer, reiterated all the reasons Nakamoto's code seemed to point to an older author. Jens Ducrée, the Dublin-based Nakamoto scholar, recalled in a new update to his now-eight-hundred-page opus on the Satoshi question that Nakamoto had discussed "transaction types that I designed years ago," including "bonded contracts" and "multi-party arbitration," which hardly sounded like the words of a twenty-three-year-old art student in Toronto, which Todd had been at the time. Adam Back questioned whether Satoshi Nakamoto, OPSEC master and committed anon, would be interviewed multiple times on camera for a documentary. "I don't think Satoshi is going to be identified at this point . . . ," Back told me in an email. "[O]ne can equally construct arguments for and against any earlier contributor or electronic cash researcher."

I was particularly struck that while Hoback described himself as "very, very confident" that he'd found Nakamoto, he hadn't tried to corroborate his claim using stylometry. Asked why not by the *New*

Yorker's Gideon Lewis-Kraus, Hoback "said that he was happy to leave such details as an exercise for the public."

I hastily gathered more than twenty thousand words of Todd-written prose from various Internet sources and sent them to Florian Cafiero, the stylometry expert. As I'd assembled the text, I noticed that Todd, unlike Nakamoto, made a lot of typos. I also sent several programs Todd had written in C and C++ pre-Bitcoin—some from his public Github page, others sent to me by Peter at my request—to Brian Timmerman, the machine-learning expert.

Brian responded that most of the programs were too slight and boilerplate to provide much signal, but he noted that artifacts in the code pointed to them having been created in the Linux operating system, using the Vim code editor. This matched what I knew of Peter's history of programming primarily for Linux and differed from the tools Nakamoto had used when creating Bitcoin: the Windows operating system and the VS Code editor. In fact, Nakamoto, when seeking to create a Linux version of his program, had sought and apparently needed help from other developers. I also saw that Peter, unlike Nakamoto, hadn't used Hungarian notation in his code.

There was one program Peter sent me, for a videogame called Corporate Raiders that he'd written in 1999, that was substantial enough for Brian to do code stylometry on. When Brian ran his classification models on the set of candidates he'd assessed earlier, with Peter now included, Ben Laurie remained the closest match for the two main Bitcoin files (main.cpp, node.cpp). Peter was the closest match only for a Bitcoin file called node.h. I asked Brian to distill the significance of his findings. "I would say these tests are indeterminate and don't point strongly to anyone in the candidate pool," he replied. As for Peter specifically, "even within this context of no strong claims, the results don't really point his way."

Florian and Jean-Baptiste Camps, after a busy weekend re-running their models with Peter included, found no indication that he was the author of any of Nakamoto's writings. "I don't think it's Todd," Florian concluded.

I thought Hoback had made a worthy contribution to the canon of Nakamoto theories, but he was probably wrong. In presenting a highly debatable claim with such self-assurance, he'd become the latest Nakamoto hunter to parade heedlessly into the who-is-Satoshi tarpit. "It's ironic," Peter Todd told CoinDesk, "that a director who is also known for a documentary on QAnon has resorted to QAnon-style coincidence-based conspiracy thinking here, too."

There were people who thought an answer was inevitable. Zooko Wilcox, who in 2013 had written that "Satoshi will be, or already has been, de-anonymized by stylometry, and there is nothing they or anyone can do to prevent that," hewed to this belief more than a decade later. "I still think I'm right," he told me. "I think, yeah, AIs will be able to tell us any day now," unless whoever was behind Nakamoto never published anything else on the internet. But I was convinced that we might never know, beyond a reasonable doubt, who Nakamoto was. Memories fade. People die. Time was the enemy of a solution. Even as I'd probably ruled out some possibilities, I couldn't say I was closer to the answer. He or she or they might well be in these pages. But unless I *knew* who Nakamoto was, he still might be someone I'd never heard of. The last great unsolved mystery might remain so.

I felt some relief in accepting this. I remained dazzled by the achievement of Nakamoto's invention, but almost equally by the perfection of his vanishing. And as I played through each scenario in my head, none, and none I could think of, beat the mystery itself. Maybe something that had begun for quotidian reasons had assumed a mystique it didn't deserve. "Watergate moved history," Bob Woodward once wrote about Mark Felt's role as Deep Throat, "and there is certainly a tendency—on my part and of many others—to associate epic outcome with an epic motive. Perhaps that is an unnecessary stretch."

Or maybe Bitcoin had sprung from a motive more epic than I had even imagined.

A New Life Form

After doing his seminal work in cryptography, Ralph Merkle, who keeps a list of pessimistic predictions that turned out to be wrong, started looking for other interesting problems to solve. This led him to life extension. "I was thinking about it one day," he told me. "I said, *I understand this growing up and stuff, but getting old is a drag, and this dying business—Is there an alternative? Maybe not dying?* It's not that I'm deeply opposed to dying, but is there something better that one might do?"

At first, he was put off by cryonics. "I thought it was a fairly bad idea," he recalled, given everything involved in cooling and warming the massively complex molecular machine that is a person in a minimally destructive way. But it seemed like a problem worthy of his attention. "I started thinking about what is life and death," he said. He did this for the next "six or twelve" months and emerged from his period of reflection with a new conception of the problem. There was clinical death, and there was "information-theoretic" death. Clinical death was shutting off a computer. Information-theoretic death was dissolving the computer in acid. If you thought about people as information, a matrix of molecules, rather than as bags of blood and bones, then cryonics became a method of preserving information. If someone was cremated, there'd be no helping them. But if they'd merely experienced clinical death, you could worry less about all the ways the molecular machinery might fall apart or be impossible to reassemble, and focus instead on whether the information that made up one's self was recoverable. Merkle saw the information recovery process as just another type of cryptanalysis, decoding the ciphertext of a damaged but intact cryopreserved body to find the plaintext of the original person. "Once I reached that conclusion, it was transparently obvious that not only was cryonics a reasonable contender, but a very reasonable contender." Merkle was at the time a researcher at Xerox PARC, and he wrote a paper on how electron microscopy could recover information from the brain, which convinced him it was feasible. He was further convinced by the book *Engines of Creation,* by K. Eric Drexler, which laid out how, in theory, nanotechnology could repair cells using tiny cell-repair machines called assemblers. Merkle became an active board member of Alcor.

On an April afternoon, I drove through the nondescript desert flatness of North Scottsdale, Arizona. Construction had shut down roads, requiring rerouting. My destination, when it came into view, was so bland it might have housed a dentist's office or publisher's fulfillment service. It was a low, blocky building faced with light-gray stucco and sparsely landscaped with regional flora. There were a few cars in the parking lot, and video-camera balls dangled from the building walls. An inconspicuous sign in blue letters read: ALCOR.

The world's most active cryonics organization had moved here from California in 1994. There'd been trouble with the Riverside coroner and health department, which hadn't fully shared the cryonics dream. Arizona offered geological and meteorological calm. No earthquakes or typhoons disturbed the Sonoran desert. The state's don't-tread-on-me politics were also congenial to the project.

In this place, my ignorance of Satoshi Nakamoto's identity seemed like a trivial concession to the unknowable. Didn't we all manage to live with much grander metaphysical questions our entire lives without succumbing to existential catatonia? Yet here was a temple built by and for a group of people who, faced with the greatest mystery of all, were confident they had an answer to it.

When I entered the building, a single administrative employee was in sight. The large lobby included a display of old issues of *Cryonics* magazine. One featured the story of a past Alcor executive whose "First Life Cycle" lasted from 1941, when he was born, until 1991, when he was cryopreserved.

A few moments later, a man rode up on his motorcycle and strode into the building, wearing a bicep-hugging black T-shirt around a weightlifter's torso, black athleisure pants, and black sneakers. At fifty-eight, there was still some strawberry blond in his receding hair. He had fair skin and a bit of stubble. "Max More," he said, extending a fist for a bump.

As Max O'Connor, growing up in Bristol, England, he had been an insatiable reader of science fiction. His earliest doodles were of rockets and flying boots. When he was five, he watched the Apollo landings on TV. By his teen years, he was reading libertarians like Murray Rothbard and David Friedman and the books of Robert Anton Wilson, who wrote about things like AI and brain-augmenting drugs. It was through Wilson, who'd had his daughter Luna's brain cryopreserved after she was murdered at age fifteen, that Max learned that cryonics was a real thing. When he was seventeen, he started taking the train to London once a month for meetings of a life extension group, and as an undergraduate at Oxford he founded England's first cryonics organization and a magazine called *Biostasis*. After getting six weeks' training at Alcor in California, he returned to his dorm room at St. Anne's College toting a box of cryopreservative drugs and a heart-lung pump.

Max couldn't wait to move to California, which seemed the center of so many of the things he was interested in. When he went for a PhD in philosophy, he did it at UCLA. The same year, Drexler's nanotechnology book came out. Suddenly, cryonics had a road map. "'Cause before, it was kind of a mystery," Max said. "How the heck can you solve it, you know, repair trillions of cells?" In 1986, when he was twenty-two, Max signed up to become Alcor Member #68. Cryonics just made sense to him, and he wanted to be an example to others. Like most members, he afforded the service by buying life insurance and naming Alcor as the beneficiary.

It was also then that he legally changed his name to Max More and invented his own philosophy, extropianism. With Tom Bell, aka Tom Morrow, he cofounded the extropians group and launched the 'zine *Extropy: Vaccine for Future Shock*. Max met his future wife, who'd been born Nancie Clark and would become Natasha Vita-More, at a party in 1992 at the home of Timothy Leary, who was interested in cryonics at the time. "He changed his mind," Max said ruefully. "He was surrounded by people who believed in reincarnation and that kind of stuff. I think he also had some not-so-good experiences with a couple of the not-very-social-minded cryonicists, maybe . . . He dropped it and ended up having his ashes sent into space, I think. It's too bad, 'cause he was kind of an early influence, in a way. He had the SMI^{2}LE formula, which I always thought was kind of a proto-extropian thing: Space Migration, Intelligence Increase, Life Extension."

Max had been CEO of Alcor until two years before my visit, and he was still an ambassador for the organization and the cause. In the lobby, we looked at photographs of cryopreserved Alcor members. One was a woman from China. "Very difficult to get people out of there," Max said, "so I don't think we'll be doing that again." The youngest member was a two-year-old girl with brain cancer, the child of doctors, who'd been flown in from Thailand after several surgeries failed. FM-2030, an Iranian American transhumanist who'd been born Fereidoun M. Esfandiary in 1930, had died of pancreatic cancer, or been "de-animated," at age sixty-nine. "A friend of mine," Max said. "He didn't quite make it to 2030, but hopefully he'll be back." There were also pictures of Lyekka, a cat, and Nutmeg, a German shepherd. Alcor had preserved some ninety pets so far. Max's first dog, a fifteen-year-old goldendoodle, was among them. "I didn't really like dogs until we got Oscar, but my wife insisted. And he was such a great dog that we had to cryopreserve him."

At the moment, around 1,700 people were signed up for Alcor's service. It cost $220,000 for full-body and $80,000 for neuro. DJ Steve Aoki has said he's a member, and Peter Thiel has been reported to be a member. A number of Max's old extropian friends were members too. Max said that atheist computer people represented the largest contingent. "The hacker mentality basically sees a very difficult, complex problem and thinks: *Well, you just break it down to components and you can solve it.*" But Alcor had religious members as well. "I guess there's less motivation if you think you're going to heaven, whatever that's supposed to be—I never really got a clear answer on that—but I don't see an incompatibility, because to me it's just an extension of emergency medicine, right?" First you try diet and exercise, then conventional medicine and pharmaceuticals, then critical medical care; "if you're really screwed . . . you might go through a clinical trial; and at the very end, if that doesn't work, you've got cryonics."

A milestone for the field was the publication in 1964 of *The Prospect of Immortality,* by Robert C.W. Ettinger, now considered the Father of Cryonics. "An unfortunate title," Max said, ". . . because we don't like the word 'immortality.'" Stories about Alcor often used the word, but it overpromised. Who knew if the universe would last forever? And a person could be all paid up in his Alcor membership but be murdered or die in a car crash—in a way that left his brain irretrievably damaged—or be killed by "asteroids landing on your head."

The myth of immortality was saddled with dark literary baggage. There was "an awful story by Karel Čapek," Max said, referring to a play called *The Makropulos Affair,* with a character who's unable to die. The Greek goddess Eos asked Zeus to grant eternal life to her husband, Tithonus, but failed to specify that he remain young, so Tithonus lived on, withering away. *Zardoz,* a 1974 John Boorman film—"It's pretty bad, actually"—featured the Eternals, a "society of stagnant immortals" who'd thought up a god, the titular Zardoz, to control a group of savages called the Brutals. Sean Connery played a Brutal named Zed, and "They're all begging the savage to kill them, 'cause they're so bored of life."

We came to a room separated from us by a wall of floor-to-ceiling banker's glass. Beyond it were two neat ranks of Dewar flasks containing Alcor's 234 preserved members. A scissor lift stood ready for the next pod that needed to be lowered into one. A couple of technicians were at work replacing a leg on one of the giant tanks. Some Dewars were squat, others taller. A standard Dewar could accommodate four whole-body patients. There was a new model, a Super Dewar that Max called Bigfoot, that could accommodate twelve whole-body patients and had a tapered top that slowed boil-off of the liquid nitrogen. Each had been trucked in from an East Coast manufacturer and cost around $25,000 for a standard and $100,000 for a Super. "The neuro patients are in a separate one," Max said. "We get like ten times as many neuro patients in the same Dewar." Max and his wife, like around half of Alcor's members, were signed up for neuro. "Everything else is replaceable," Max said, "so I'd rather focus on the bit that matters."

Inside of the steel chambers in front of us were the head and body of Ted Williams, the baseball player; Marvin Minsky, considered the father of AI; and Hal Finney, who might or might not have invented Bitcoin. I asked which Dewar Hal was in. Max said he didn't know off the top of his head. "We don't generally identify them," he said, "for security reasons."

So many of the extropians' visions had come to pass. On the internet, memes ruled the day. Elon Musk was, among other things, the standard-bearer for a push to colonize the stars. Musk's Neuralink was pioneering a brain-computer interface, and not entirely unserious people were debating whether humanity's best chance of survival lay in volunteering to be pets of Artificial General Intelligence. The techno-libertarian dream of Exit burned eternal: seasteading had now given way to "network states"—internet-enabled intentional societies—and pilot projects such as Próspera (Honduras), Praxis (the Mediterranean), and Cabin (a "distributed," blockchain-coordinated "city" of far-flung cabins in woodsy places) aimed to take them 3D.

"That is kind of pleasing," Max allowed of recent history's extropian drift, but he was disappointed by the progress made in conquering death. "I'm not very optimistic that we'll fix aging in my lifetime. I was, thirty years ago. I thought that was very likely. But we just didn't get the funding. So it's going to take a long time. It's not like we have an Apollo project that could probably make a big difference. So I don't think I'm going to make it, even if I live another forty years. So I think I'll need to be cryopreserved, which kinda sucks. I don't want to be in there. But it's better than the alternative, is my view."

Cryonics and cryptocurrency were symbiotic. Future-minded people were attracted to both: Roger Ver, the early Bitcoiner known as Bitcoin Jesus (and later sued by Craig Wright), had signed up with Alcor when he was twenty. Vitalik Buterin had donated crypto to life extension organizations, and in 2018 an investor named Brad Armstrong made the largest gift yet to Alcor, $5 million worth of a currency called Stellar, to set up a Hal Finney Cryonics Research Fund.

There was a more profound connection as well. In the early 1990s, an extropian named Mark Plus coined the term *aeonomics* to describe "the study of the economic problems of immortal existence." The idea of radically extending life span required the rethinking of many things, not least of them how additional years on earth might affect your 401(k) plan. Cryonics added the twist of how to ensure that the money you had when you de-animated was still available when you reanimated. If extropians were going to freeze themselves, they'd need a way to send money into the future, ready to be claimed upon awakening. In this way, digital cash would be a boon to cryonics.

Ralph Merkle once took a stab at describing why technical people were so smitten with Bitcoin, calling it "the first example of a new form of life." It lived on the internet, it paid people to keep it alive, and no one could change it or corrupt it or stop it. Anyone could run its software. Anyone could see what it did and how it worked. "If nuclear war destroyed half of our planet, it would continue to live, uncorrupted," Merkle wrote. "It would continue to offer its services. It would continue to pay people to keep it alive."

Andreas Antonopoulos, author of the book *Mastering Bitcoin*, had likened it to "a sewer rat." Nick Szabo and Elaine Ou, in recent years, had been working on inoculating Bitcoin against even the death of the internet. Ou had been inspired in 2016, when China was threatening to ban cryptocurrencies, and she and Szabo began to experiment with extending the Bitcoin network using ham radio.

The blockchain was everlasting. After Len Sassaman died, friends embedded in a Bitcoin transaction an ASCII portrait of his bearded face along with the inscription "LEN 'rabbi' SASSAMA 1980–2011 Len was our friend. A brilliant mind, a kind soul, and a devious schemer." The transaction became part of Block 138725, which meant that it would live in the blockchain as long as the blockchain existed, with copies of it on every computer that made up the network.

As a utopian project, Bitcoin had, like all utopian projects, never stood a chance. The magic and wildness were fading. But as a new asset class, it had proved resilient. Its price was rising once again, reaching a new all-time high above $73,000 in March 2024. Fidelity now advised retail clients to allocate a small portion of their investment portfolios to cryptocurrency. And blockchain technology felt inevitable, the creative space it opened up still exciting.

Satoshi Nakamoto was something that whoever was behind the pseudonym could never be. It was a name and an idea and, without a body or a history to drag it down, it would live forever.

Sources

An invention designed to eliminate trust, praised for the self-effacement of its creator, and based on computer science can be forbidding territory for a journalist interested in telling a human story. I am grateful to a legion of cypherpunks, extropians, cryptographers, computer scientists, peer-to-peer networkers, coderpunks, monetary enthusiasts, stylometrists, Bitcoiners, Nakamotologists, would-be Nakamotos, would-be-Nakamoto debunkers, and others whose paths have intersected with the mystery of cryptocurrency's birth, for gamely answering a civilian's questions over the past thirteen years. They are:

Al (Payment Coin (Pod)), Kimon Andreou, Gavin Andresen, Calvin Ayre, James Bachini, Doug Barnes, Michel Bauwens, Tom Bell, Stefan Brands, Sameer Parekh Brenn, Jon Callas, Rory Cellan-Jones, Jeremy Clark, Bram Cohen, Matthew Cromer, Wei Dai, DebunkingFaketoshi, Ray Dillinger, James A. Donald, Tim Draper, Dr. Funkenstein, Jens Ducrée, Hal Finney, Eric Watt Forste, Vel Freedman, Zeming Gao, Jeff Garzik, George Gleason, Magnus Granath, Jack Grieve, Sahil Gupta, Stuart Haber, G. W. Habraken, Laszlo Hanyecz, Richard Harvey, Travis Hassloch, Evan Hatch, Mike Hearn, Bob Hewitt, Gene Hoffman, Douglas Jackson, Tom Jennings, Patrick Juola, Dan Kaminsky, Mark Karpelès, Ethan D. Kirschner, Ken Kittlitz, Dave Krieger, Leslie Lamport, Ryan Landers, Ben Laurie, Brian Martin, Jon Matonis, Stefan Matthews, Jim McCoy, David McFadzean, Ralph Merkle,

Max More, Ryan Nakashima, Meredith Patterson, Will Price, Vikram Rihal, Kyle Roche, David Rolfe, Marius Schilder, Philipp Schnell, Tim Starr, Scott Stornetta, Mark Suppes, Nick Szabo, Amir Taaki, Theymos, Stefan Thomas, Bill Todd, Dustin Trammell, Dimitrios Tsoulogiannis, Arthur van Pelt, Richard Waddy, Bruce Wagner, Steve Wang, Or Weinberger, Todd A. White, Will Whitehouse, Zooko Wilcox, Craig Wright, Kurt Wuckert Jr., and Phil Zimmermann.

All quotes and thoughts not otherwise attributed in the text or in these notes come from my interviews with those involved.

Several digital archives were invaluable in reconstructing the early activities of key groups and members:

For records of the cypherpunks' email list, I relied most frequently on the archives at cypherpunks.venona.com, https://marc.info, and https://cryptoanarchy.wiki.

Repositories of the extropians' email list are scattered. A rare collection of the group's digests from 1992 to 1994 is at https://diyhpl.us/~bryan/irc/extropians/raided-mailing-list-archives/archives/. Wei Dai hosts a mirror of the list covering 1996–2002 at extropians.weidai.com. Posts from 2003 onward can be found at lists.extropy.org/pipermail/extropy-chat/.

Archives of the 'zine *Extropy* are at https://hpluspedia.org/wiki/Extropy_Magazines and fennetic.net/irc/extropy/.

The Internet Archive and its Wayback Machine were indispensable for excavating vanished swaths of digital history.

NakamotoInstitute.org hosts an unrivaled collection of texts relevant to Bitcoin, including the complete writings of Satoshi Nakamoto. The Bitcoin Forum at bitcointalk.org is an essential resource for anyone seeking to understand Bitcoin's past.

I benefited immensely from the prior work of other journalists, interviewers, and researchers who have covered parts of this story. In particular, I am indebted to articles, books, and podcasts by John Biggs, Gwern Branwen, Thomas Brewster, Adrian Chen, Andy Cush, Dustin Dreifuerst, Tim Ferriss, Lex Fridman, Andy Greenberg, Adrianne Jeffries, Steven Levy, Cheyenne Ligon, Jameson Lopp, Giana

Magnoli, Max Marty, Peter McCormack, Robert McMillan, Andrew O'Hagan, Arthur van Pelt, Nathaniel Popper, Jamie Redman, Ed Regis, Bailey Reutzel, Pete Rizzo, Kai Sedgwick, Charlie Shrem, Tom Simonite, Paul Vigna, Daniel Walters, Nicole Weinstock, and Rob Wile.

In these notes, I use the following abbreviations:

CP: cypherpunks list

EX: extropians list

CR: The Cryptography and Cryptography Policy Mailing List (https://www.metzdowd.com/mailman/listinfo/cryptography)

BF: Bitcoin Forum (https://bitcointalk.org)

UN: Usenet (https://usenetarchives.com)

KW: Case of IRA KLEIMAN, as the Personal Representative of the Estate of David Kleiman, Plaintiff, v. CRAIG WRIGHT, Defendant. Case 9:18-cv-80176-BB, United States District Court, Southern District of Florida, February 14, 2018 (https://www.courtlistener.com/docket/6309656/kleiman-v-wright/)

WM: Wayback Machine (https://wayback-api.archive.org)

It's Him

1 ***Wired*'s first feature article about Bitcoin:** Benjamin Wallace, "The Rise and Fall of Bitcoin," *Wired,* December 2011.

1 **you could see Kanye West:** Jacqueline Lindenberg and Adam S. Levy, "Kanye West Steps Out for a Solo Outing in Beverly Hills," *Daily Mail Online,* October 17, 2022.

1 **adherents had unveiled the first statue of Nakamoto:** Will Feuer, "Statue of Anonymous Bitcoin Creator Satoshi Nakamoto Unveiled in Hungary," *New York Post,* September 17, 2021.

1 **In the Vanuatu archipelago:** Prianka Srinivasan, "Satoshi Island Project Aims to Turn a Remote Pacific Island into a City Built on Cryptocurrency," ABC News Australia, October 10, 2022.

2 **A trio of libertarians bought a decommissioned cruise ship:** Sophie Elmhirst, "The Disastrous Voyage of Satoshi," *The Guardian,* September 7, 2021.

2 **More than one fellow technologist lobbied:** Sead Fadilpaši⊠, "MIT Research Scientist Says Satoshi Nakamoto Should Win a Nobel Memorial Prize," CryptoNews, October 23, 2023.

2 **Elon Musk and Peter Thiel, among others, speculated:** Lex Fridman, "#252—Elon Musk: SpaceX, Mars, Tesla Autopilot, Self-Driving, Robotics, and AI," *Lex Fridman Podcast,* December 28, 2021; Nathan Crooks, "Peter Thiel Tells Crowd Where He'd Look for Elusive Bitcoin Founder Satoshi," Bloomberg News, October 21, 2021.

2 **We'd learned who Bob Woodward's secret source was:** John D. O'Connor, "I'm the Guy They Called Deep Throat," *Vanity Fair,* July 2005.

2 **We finally knew the proof of Fermat's Last Theorem:** Gina Kolata, "At Last, Shout of 'Eureka!' In Age-Old Math Mystery," *The New York Times,* June 24, 1993.

2 **likely copped his bagels at Zabar's:** Nancy Jo Sales, "Tracking Down Thomas Pynchon," *New York Magazine,* June 27, 2008.

2 **"mission impossible":** "Where in the World Is Bitcoin's Mysterious Creator, Satoshi Nakamoto?," *60 Minutes Overtime,* May 17, 2019.

A Straight-Up Legend

4 **"I'm the SpaceX Intern":** Sahil Gupta, "I'm the SpaceX Intern Who Speculated Satoshi Is Elon Musk. There Is More to the Story," Medium, December 22, 2021.

4 **Musk was "probably" Nakamoto:** Sahil Gupta, "Elon Musk Probably Invented Bitcoin," HackerNoon, November 22, 2017.

5 **This one contained a link to a page on GitHub:** sahil5d, "Hints That Elon Musk Is Satoshi Nakamoto," GitHub, n.d., accessed June 27, 2024.

6 **"a straight up legend":** Sahil Gupta, Patrick Lauppe, and Shreyas Ravishankar, "Fedcoin: A Blockchain-Backed Central Bank Cryptocurrency," (senior thesis, Yale Law School, May 10, 2017).

7 **Bloomberg News covered it:** Nour Al Ali and Chris Kingdon, "Musk: I Am Not Bitcoin's Satoshi Nakamoto," Bloomberg News, November 28, 2017.

7 **"Not true.":** @elonmusk, Twitter, November 27, 2017.

7 **on a panel at Davos:** "Can Digital Currencies Strengthen Trust in a Chaotic World?," Davos World Economic Forum panel, January 23, 2019.

7 **inadvertently betrayed an IP address:** BountyHunter, *Who Is Satoshi Nakamoto?* (blog), chapter 6, "California," February 20, 2016.

8 **worst year of his life:** Scott Pelley, "Fast Cars and Rocket Ships," *60 Minutes,* March 30, 2014.

8 **system he called a hyperloop:** Elon Musk, "Hyperloop Alpha," Tesla website, August 12, 2013.

Pretend Internet Money

10 **"untraceable digital currency":** Adrian Chen, "The Underground Website Where You Can Buy Any Drug Imaginable," Gawker, June 1, 2011.

11 **a detailed breakdown of how Bitcoin worked:** "Bits and Bob," *The Economist,* June 13, 2011.

11 **world-changing potential:** Ben Popper, "Fred Wilson Says USV Is Paying 25-50% More to Enter Deals," *The New York Observer,* May 23, 2011.

12 **Nakamoto had posted a short write-up:** Satoshi Nakamoto, "Bitcoin P2P e-cash paper," CR, October 31, 2008.

12 **an obscure, moderated email list about cryptography:** https://www.metzdowd.com/mailman/listinfo/cryptography.

12 **largest bankruptcy in U.S. history:** Josh Zumbrun, "Stop Equating the Latest Bank Failures to the 2008 Crisis," *The Wall Street Journal,* May 12, 2023.

12 **to bail out AIG:** Matthew Karnitschnig et al., "U.S. to Take Over AIG in $85 Billion Bailout," *The Wall Street Journal,* September 16, 2008.

12 **"Thanks for bringing up that point":** Satoshi Nakamoto, "Bitcoin P2P e-cash paper," CR, November 3, 2008.

12 **"I appreciate your questions":** Satoshi Nakamoto, "Bitcoin P2P e-cash paper," CR, November 8, 2008.

13 **Nakamoto released an alpha version:** Satoshi Nakamoto, "Bitcoin v0.1 released," CR, January 8, 2009.

13 **127 people downloaded the Bitcoin software:** Stefan Thomas, interview.

14 **"electronic currency and cryptography":** Dustin Trammell, email to Satoshi Nakamoto, incorporated in Satoshi Nakamoto, email to Dustin Trammell, January 13, 2009.

14 **"We definitely have similar interests!":** Satoshi Nakamoto, email to Dustin Trammell, January 13, 2009.

15 **"I love the idea":** Satoshi Nakamoto, "Re: [p2p-research] Bitcoin open source implementation of P2P," p2p-research list, February 13, 2009.

15 **projected to hit around the year 2140:** Stephen Katte, "The Last Bitcoin: What Will Happen Once All BTC Are Mined?," Cointelegraph, July 21, 2023.

15 **fish who don't know they're in water:** David Foster Wallace, "This Is Water," commencement speech at Kenyon College, May 21, 2005.

16 **priced a single bitcoin:** William J. Luther, "The Rise of Bitcoin," American Institute for Economic Research, May 6, 2021.

16 **1984 Fleetwood Southwind RV:** Jeff Garzik, "Bitcoin's Wild Decade: An Early Developer Reflects," *Breaker Magazine,* October 29, 2018.

16 **Rare-coin enthusiasts:** Benjamin Wallace, "The Rise and Fall of Bitcoin," *Wired,* November 2011.

16 **more than 60 percent of the population:** Mexico: "Mexicans Lack Access to Credit," *The Economist,* December 10, 2020; Philippines: Chrisee Dela Paz, "Majority of Filipinos Still Have No Bank Account—World Bank," Rappler, May 6, 2018; Africa: "Percent People with Bank Accounts," TheGlobalEconomy.com database, 2021.

17 **extremely volatile:** "The Bitcoin Flash Crash to $0.01 in June 2011," *BitMEX Blog,* July 19, 2018.

17 **stolen by hackers:** Jeff Wilser, "The Legacy of Mt. Gox—Why Bitcoin's Greatest Hack Still Matters," CoinDesk, May 4, 2023.

18 **$473 million:** hacked coins' value on November 6, 2021.

18 **20 percent of all outstanding bitcoins:** Nathaniel Popper, "Lost Passwords Lock Millionaires Out of Their Bitcoin Fortunes," *The New York Times,* January 12, 2021.

18 **father of two:** gavinandresen, "I'm Gavin Andresen, Chief Scientist at the Bitcoin Foundation. Ask me anything!," Reddit, r/Bitcoin, October 21, 2014.

18 **"My wife can tell you":** Gavin Andresen, continued videotaped deposition, February 27, 2020, KW.

18 **He rode a unicycle.:** gavinandresen, "I'm Gavin Andresen."

18 **Gavin left a salaried position:** Gavin Andresen, deposition, February 26, 2020, KW.

18 **spent the next six months in Queensland:** Gavin Andresen, *Cassowary Tales* (blog).

18 **a tech-blog post:** Neil McAllister, "Open Source Innovation on the Cutting Edge," InfoWorld, May 24, 2010.

18 **he sat on the legislative body:** gavinandresen, "I'm Gavin Andresen."

18 **took an active interest in local school politics:** See the letter supporting passage of funding for Amherst, Massachusetts, schools that he signed: "Dear Town Meeting Members," May 21, 2008.

18 **volunteered to help:** Gavin Andresen, "CMS Made Simple: Very Nice!," *GavinTech* (blog), March 3, 2008.

19 **selling alpaca socks for bitcoin:** Ariella Brown, "Alpacas: The Unofficial Mascot of Bitcoin?," CoinDesk, September 10, 2021.

19 **10,000 bitcoins for two large pizzas:** Galen Moore, "10 Years After Laszlo Hanyecz Bought Pizza with 10K Bitcoin, He Has No Regrets," CoinDesk, May 22, 2020.

20 **"pretend Internet money":** Tom Simonite, "The Man Who Really Built Bitcoin," *MIT Technology Review*, August 15, 2014.

20 **"enlightened self-interest":** Simonite, "Man Who Really Built Bitcoin."

20 **could become a major world currency:** Andresen, deposition, February 26, 2020, KW.

20 **First, Nakamoto gave Gavin direct access:** Andresen, deposition, February 26, 2020, KW.

20 **control of both the code repository:** Andresen, deposition, February 26, 2020, KW.

20 **and the project's "alert key":** Gavin Andresen, "Eleven Years Ago Today . . . ," *Gavin Andresen* (blog), April 26, 2022.

20 **a team of five other volunteer coders:** Gavin Andresen, interview.

21 **PayPal and Visa froze WikiLeaks' accounts:** Jonathan Haynes, "PayPal Freezes WikiLeaks Account," *The Guardian*, December 4, 2010; "Visa Suspends Payments to WikiLeaks," AP, December 7, 2010.

21 **"Bring it on":** RHorning, "Wikileaks contact info?," BF, December 4, 2010.

21 **"Don't 'bring it on.'":** Satoshi Nakamoto, "Wikileaks contact info?," BF, December 5, 2010.

21 **an article in *PC magazine:*** Keir Thomas, "Could the Wikileaks Scandal Lead to New Virtual Currency?," *PCWorld*, December 10, 2010.

21 **"kicked the hornet's nest":** Satoshi Nakamoto, "PC World Article on Bitcoin," BF, December 11, 2010.

21 **"a mysterious shadowy figure":** Satoshi Nakamoto, email to Gavin Andresen, April 26, 2011, in Andresen, "Eleven Years Ago Today."

21 **he'd agreed to give a talk on Bitcoin:** Gavin Andresen, email to Satoshi Nakamoto, April 26, 2011, in Andresen, "Eleven Years Ago Today."

21 **"emails to at least one other programmer":** Satoshi Nakamoto, emails to Mike Hearn, April 20–23, 2011.

Shiny Pony

22 **the second place Nakamoto had announced his white paper:** Satoshi Nakamoto, "Bitcoin open source implementation of P2P currency," P2P Foundation Forum, February 11, 2009.

22 **a headline from the London *Times*:** "Chancellor on Brink of Second Bailout for Banks," *The Times* (London), January 3, 2009.

22 **he had done so through a masking service:** Hunter Walker and Rob Wile, "What Did This Swiss Software Developer Have to Do with the Launch of Bitcoin?," Business Insider, April 1, 2014.

23 **hiding his IP address by using TOR:** theymos, "Satoshi might be mentally deranged," BF, April 17, 2013.

23 **"one programming geek talking to another programming geek":** Gavin Andresen, deposition, February 26, 2020, KW.

23 **authorial styles:** Andresen, deposition, February 26, 2020, KW.

23 **slightly dated:** Andresen, deposition, February 26, 2020, KW.

23 **Nakamoto used Hungarian notation:** Mike Hearn, August 31, 2017, comment on sillysaurus3, "I've spent a lot of time reviewing the original Bitcoin codebase," Hacker News, August 30, 2017.

23 **top 10 percent of programmers:** Andresen, deposition, February 26, 2020, KW.

23 **lived in a squat in London:** Joshi Herrmann, "Silicon Roundabout's Not for Him: Meet Super-hacker, Master Coder and Bitcoin Boy Amir Taaki in His Hackney Squat," *The Standard* (UK), January 29, 2014.

23 **activist for 3D-printed guns:** Andy Greenberg, "Waiting for Dark: Inside Two Anarchists' Quest for Untraceable Money," *Wired,* July 11, 2014.

23 **front lines of Syria's civil war:** Andy Greenberg, "How an Anarchist Bitcoin Coder Found Himself Fighting ISIS in Syria," *Wired,* March 29, 2017.

24 **a small group or even just one person:** Andresen, deposition, February 26, 2020, KW.

24 **"a Satoshi":** R2D221, "How did 'satoshi' become the name of the base unit?," BF, January 9, 2014.

24 **The same month, someone noticed:** kiba, "Is Satoshi Alive?," BF, January 12, 2011.

24 **"along the lines of Nicolas Bourbaki":** alowm, comment, January 14, 2011, on kiba, "Is Satoshi Alive?"

25 **a useful glamor:** ribuck, comment, February 28, 2011, on kiba, "Is Satoshi Alive?"

25 **"the guy just wants some privacy":** ShadowOfHarbringer, comment, February 28, 2011, on kiba, "Is Satoshi Alive?"

25 **people couldn't help throwing names around:** wobber, "Who Is Satoshi Nakamoto?," BF, April 30, 2011.

25 **"a tricky bug":** mizerydearia, comment, January 13, 2011, on kiba, "Is Satoshi Alive?"

25 **might be Gavin Andresen:** bitcoinBull, comment, April 24, 2011, on kiba, "Is Satoshi Alive?"

25 **an Australia connection:** Andresen, deposition, February 26, 2020, KW.
25 **"central intelligence":** Mellisa Tolentino, "Did the NSA 'Create' Satoshi Nakamoto?," SiliconANGLE, August 12, 2014.
26 **The U.S. Naval Research Laboratory had birthed The Onion Router:** Keren Elazari, "How to Use Tor," *Wired*, May 2015.
26 **The FBI would later secretly create:** Jon Brodkin, "FBI Sold Phones to Organized Crime and Read 127 Million 'Encrypted' Messages," Ars Technica, June 8, 2021.
26 **three researchers in the Cryptology Division:** Laurie Law, Susan Sabett, and Jerry Solinas, "How to Make a Mint: The Cryptography of Anonymous Electronic Cash," white paper, National Security Agency Office of Information Security Research and Technology, Cryptology Division, June 18, 1996.
26 **a portmanteau of big tech-company names:** ShadowOfHarbringer, "Re: Is Satoshi Alive? Thread," BF, February 27, 2011.
26 **Redditors pooled their deciphering skills:** mavensbot, "If you rearrange the letters in Satoshi Nakamoto you get . . . ," Reddit, r/Bitcoin, October 20, 2013.
26 **"Satoshi could be *anybody*":** Gwern Branwen, "Bitcoin Is Worse Is Better," gwern.net website, May 27, 2011.
26 **graphing the time stamps:** Stefan Thomas, "Satoshi's Posting Times," BF, August 17, 2011.
27 **he discovered a technical glitch:** Kim Zetter, "Kaminsky on How He Discovered DNS Flaw and More," *Wired*, July 22, 2008.
28 **had written Hashcash:** Adam Back, "[ANNOUNCE] hash cash postage implementation," CP, March 28, 1997.
28 **who had written to him in August of 2008:** Pete Rizzo, "Read Adam Back's Complete Emails with Bitcoin Creator Satoshi Nakamoto," *Bitcoin Magazine*, February 23, 2024.
28 **driving a Volkswagen van:** Steven Levy, "E-Money (That's What I Want)," *Wired*, December 1994.
28 **sitting in a hot tub:** Adriana Hamacher, "How David Chaum Went from Inventing Digital Cash to Pioneering Digital Privacy," *Decrypt*, April 8, 2022.
28 **"I don't tell that to people.":** Levy, "E-Money."
29 **"mathematicians with guns":** Tim Starr, interview.

Mathematicians with Guns

30 **twenty revolutionaries gathered in a living room:** Details of the first cypherpunk meeting are from Steven Levy, *Crypto: Secrecy and Privacy in the New Code War* (New York: Penguin, 2002), 209–11; Andy Greenberg, *This Machine Kills Secrets: Julian Assange, the Cypherpunks, and Their Fight to Empower Whistleblowers* (New York: Plume, 2013), 79–81; and Timothy C. May, email to Seth Morris, "GAMES: The 'Crypto Anarchy Game,'" CP, February 23, 1994.
30 **Tim May, a friend of Hughes:** Details of his bio are from Jim Epstein, "Tim May, Father of 'Crypto Anarchy,' Is Dead at 66," *Reason*, December 16, 2018; and Nathaniel Popper, "Timothy C. May, Early Advocate of Internet Privacy, Dies at 66," *The New York Times*, December 21, 2018.
30 **the inspirations that swirled in his brain:** Timothy C. May, "The

Cyphernomicon: Cypherpunks FAQ and More," Nakamoto Institute, September 10, 1994.

30 **May became convinced:** Timothy C. May, "Libertaria in Cyberspace," EX, September 1, 1992.

31 **For more than two thousand years:** An excellent overview of the history of cryptography can be found in Simon Singh, *The Code Book: The Evolution of Secrecy from Mary, Queen of Scots, to Quantum Cryptography* (New York: Doubleday Anchor, 2000).

31 **a remarkable discovery:** Martin E. Hellman, "An Overview of Public Key Cryptography," *IEEE Communications Society Magazine,* May 2002.

31 **"A specter is haunting the modern world":** Tim May, "The Crypto Anarchist Manifesto," in Peter Ludlow, *Crypto Anarchy, Cyberstates, and Pirate Utopias* (Cambridge, MA: MIT Press, 2001), 61–63.

32 **which May called "Libertaria in Cyberspace":** May, "Libertaria in Cyberspace."

32 **the same class as Tomahawk cruise missiles:** 58 FR 39287, Code of Federal Regulations, Part 121—The United States Munitions List, July 22, 1993.

32 **pursuing possible legal action against him:** Peter H. Lewis, "Software Author Focus of U.S. Inquiry," *The New York Times,* April 10, 1995.

32 **John Gilmore:** Dennis Roddy, "Grounded: Millionaire John Gilmore Stays Close to Home While Making a Point About Privacy," *Pittsburgh Post-Gazette,* February 26, 2005.

32 **Jude Milhon:** Levy, *Crypto,* 211.

32 **"Cypherpunks write code":** Eric Hughes, "A Cypherpunk's Manifesto," in Ludlow, *Crypto Anarchy,* 81–83.

33 **a prince of Liechtenstein:** Gene Hoffman, interview.

33 **Another came to meetings in full leathers:** Hoffman, interview.

33 **"the mathematical consequence of paranoid assumptions":** Levy, *Crypto,* 206.

34 **"code is speech":** Alison Dame-Boyle, "EFF at 25: Remembering the Case That Established Code as Speech," Electronic Frontier Foundation, April 16, 2015.

34 **T-shirt printed with an export-banned encryption formula:** "Munition T-shirt," CypherSpace, accessed June 28, 2024.

34 **tattoos of the outlaw algorithms:** Adam Back, "BIO-MUNITION: GIFs of perl-RSA tattoo," CP, December 12, 1995.

34 **When a grand jury was considering indicting:** Adam C. Bonin, "First and Fifth Amendment Challenges to Cryptography Regulation," *University of Chicago Legal Forum,* no. 1, article 15 (1996).

34 **"Big Brother Inside":** Levy, *Crypto,* 252; "'Big Brother Inside' sticker Origins," IHTFP Hack Gallery, 1994.

34 **a cypherpunk named Doug Barnes:** Sabine Schmidt, "Interview: Neal Stephenson über 'Corvus,'" Goldmann Verlag website.

35 **anonymous information market:** May, "Cyphernomicon."

35 **"Assassination Politics":** James Bell, "Assassination Politics," *Cryptome,* April 3, 1997.

35 **Bell later spent years in federal prison:** Declan McCullagh, "Crypto-Convict Won't Recant," *Wired,* April 14, 2000.

35 **stalking and harassing IRS agents:** Thomas C. Greene, "Cypherpunk Bell Gets Ten Years," *The Register,* August 28, 2001.

35 **"the Cypherpunks Gun Club is going shooting":** Phil Zimmermann, interview.

35 **he announced that it would explicitly exclude topics:** Cory Doctorow, "CodeCon Is a P2P Event," *Boing Boing,* January 18, 2002.

36 **Eric Hughes worked at DigiCash for a time:** "Who Holds the Keys?," transcript of panel discussion, Electronic Frontier Foundation, March 30, 1992.

36 **Chaum convinced Mark Twain Bank:** Tom Steinert-Threlkeld, "The Buck Starts Here," *Wired,* August 1, 1996.

36 **"Recall Nero's wish":** James A. Donald, "Bitcoin P2P e-cash paper," CR, November 18, 2008.

37 **gathering at a beer garden:** Lucky Green, "Blind Signature Patent Expiration Party this Saturday," CP, July 13, 2005.

37 **cypherpunks tried to launch an offshore data haven:** Simson Garfinkel, "Welcome to Sealand. Now Bugger Off," *Wired,* July 1, 2000.

37 **the most successful of these, e-gold:** Kim Zetter, "Bullion and Bandits: The Improbable Rise and Fall of E-Gold," *Wired,* June 9, 2009.

37 **"terminal grumps":** James Donald, "Return of the death of cypherpunks," CP, October 1, 2003, forwarded by R.A. Hettinga, CR, October 2, 2003.

37 **"We have a long way to go":** James Donald, "Return of the death of cypherpunks."

Wei

38 **Dai still maintained it:** Wei Dai, email to author.

38 **B-money, as he called it, combined several ideas:** Wei Dai, bmoney.

38 **He'd graduated from the University of Washington:** Morgen E. Peck, "Bitcoin: The Cryptoanarchists' Answer to Cash," *IEEE Spectrum,* May 30, 2012.

39 **"refining the art of human rationality":** Roko, "What Is Rationality?," *LessWrong* (blog), April 1, 2010.

Boom Boom

40 **"security through obscurity":** Tim Ferriss, "The Quiet Master of Cryptocurrency—Nick Szabo (#244)," *The Tim Ferriss Show* (podcast), June 4, 2017.

40 **"libertarian realpolitik":** Nick Szabo, "ANARCHY," EX, November 20, 1993.

40 **he wrote a pamphlet:** Nick Szabo, "How to protect your electronic privacy—consumer pamphlet," CP, April 27, 1993.

40 **went on a Portland-area TV forum:** Nick Szabo, "Wiretapping chip: vid clips & sound bites," CP, April 18, 1993.

40 **he offered $200:** Nick Szabo, "Re: Big Brother Inside," CP, July 28, 1993.

40 **"'encrypting' one's image":** Nick Szabo, "Re: Spooking of neural nets," CP, August 12, 1993.

40 **Szabo had grown up in Washington State:** Nathaniel Popper, *Digital Gold: Bitcoin and the Inside Story of the Misfits and Millionaires Trying to Reinvent Money* (New York: Harper, 2015), 341.

40 **inherited a contempt for socialism:** @NickSzabo4, Twitter, August 17 and 18, 2019; February 6 and June 6, 2020.

40 **his father, Julius:** @NickSzabo4, Twitter, August 17 and 18, 2019; February 6 and June 6, 2020.

41 **became a plant scientist:** Julius Gyula Szabo, "Freezing Injury to Apple Seedling Roots at Selected Temperatures and Times of Year" (MS thesis, University of Vermont, 1966); Joan Elder, "Second Cup of Coffee," *Nevada State Journal* (Reno), June 19, 1964.

41 **Nick's mother, Mary:** @NickSzabo4, Twitter, August 28, 2018.

41 **favorite science fiction novel:** Nick Szabo, "re: favorite sf," REC.ARTS .SF-LOVERS, UN, April 19, 1991.

41 **a decade before Wei:** Szabo graduated in 1989, per "New York Times: UW CSE Alum Nick Szabo = Satoshi Nakamoto?," *Allen School News,* May 15, 2015; Dai attended in the late 1990s, per Wei Dai, "Have Epistemic Conditions Always Been This Bad?," *LessWrong* (blog), January 24, 2020.

41 **an internship at the Jet Propulsion Laboratory:** @NickSzabo4, Twitter, June 24, 2015.

41 **The experience changed his life.:** Nick Szabo, "solar sails," SCI.SPACE, UN, February 18, 1991.

41 **"sacraments of the astronaut cult":** Nick Szabo, "Soviet Energia: Available for Commercial Use?," SCI.SPACE, UN, April 3, 1993.

41 **"overhead slide artists":** Nick Szabo, "Re: Mars Observer Update," SCI .ASTRO, UN, August 26, 1993.

41 **the more than one hundred women he'd asked out:** Nick Szabo, "He's tearing you apart, ooh everyday," SOC.SINGLES, UN, January 9, 1991.

41 **"over half" of the times:** Nick Szabo, "Re: desperation," SOC.SINGLES, UN, January 8, 1991.

41 **"Dust in the Wind":** Nick Szabo, "A Song for You," SCI.MED, UN, February 16, 1993.

41 **he'd been bullied until he started punching back:** @NickSzabo4, Twitter, January 5, 2020.

41 **"Thanks for the memories, Gramps":** Nick Szabo, "Mars or bust!," SCI .SPACE, UN, June 13, 1991.

41 **"I assumed you were halfway intelligent":** Nick Szabo, "_This_ is a Flame," SCI.SPACE, UN, February 25, 1991.

41 **"Here's a reform proposal":** Nick Szabo, "NASA bureaucrat whines about salary again," SCI.SPACE, UN, September 21, 1993.

42 **suggested he needed lithium:** Fred J. McCall, "Re: Your $15 billion/year back in your face," SCI.SPACE, UN, June 9, 1993.

42 **"desperately lonely":** Douglas Creel, "Fred's Operatic Death," SCI.SPACE, UN, June 17, 1991.

42 **"Did someone . . . molest you as a child?":** Dennis Wingo, "Re: plans, and absence thereof," SCI.SPACE, UN, March 23, 1993.

42 **Szabo had moved from Oregon:** Nick Szabo, "Species Monopoly," EX, April 7, 1993; Nick Szabo, "Future History (was Singularity)," EX, January 15, 1994.

42 **in order to be near:** Timothy C. May, "JW Weatherman Interviews Cypherpunk Legend Timothy C May—Author of the Cyphernomicon," *Under the Microscope* (podcast), June 9, 2018.

42 **online interactions at least as stimulating:** Nick Szabo, "Can backwaters like Louisiana make it in the coming era?," EX, September 9, 1993.
42 **"a spectacular bursting fireball":** Nick Szabo, "Meteors," EX, August 13, 1993.
42 **Two days after that:** Nick Szabo, "Cypherpunk trends & visions," CP, August 15, 1993.
42 **Romana Machado:** John Whalen, "Freeze Head, Save Ass," *MetroActive CyberScape,* 1995; Sandy Sandfort, "Security Through Obscurity," *Wired,* March 1, 1994.
42 **"Future Rapture":** Nick Szabo, "Vinge's Technological Singularity," EX, December 21, 1993.
42 **"nom de humor":** Tim May, "'Pretty Good Paranoia' and 'Dining Detweilers Net,'" CP, November 28, 1993.
42 **The extropian T-shirt:** Ed Regis, "Meet the Extropians," *Wired,* October 1994.
42 **!Boom!Boom:** e.g., Nick Szabo, "META: Is an armed society a polite society?," EX, March 17, 1993.
42 **!Boom!Boom von Past Primeval:** e.g., Nick Szabo, "the extropian panopticon," EX, January 2, 1994.
43 **he liked to lie in bed:** Nick Szabo, "Dream screen," EX, March 15, 1993.
43 **He joined the Life Extension Foundation:** Nick Szabo, "DIET: The May Equation," EX, June 14, 1993.
43 **went on a weight loss plan:** Nick Szabo, "DIET: Weight Loss Plans," EX, June 20, 1993.
44 **a mental-clarity nootropic:** Szabo, "Dream screen."
44 **a proponent of Pascal's Wager:** Nick Szabo, "Political Rapture: Detweiling the Poor & other Entertainments," EX, December 23, 1993.
44 **He took an interest in nanotech:** Nick Szabo, "Diamond nanotechnology (fwd)," EX, November 23, 1993.
44 **and in definitions of death:** Nick Szabo, "BASICS: Death," EX, September 26, 1993.
44 **"If I got an orgasm on payday":** Nick Szabo, "PHIL/UPLOAD/STORY," EX, March 6, 1993.
44 **billed the Extropaganza:** Geoff Dale, "Party with the Extropians! at Nexus-Lite!," CP, February 26, 1994.
44 **Machado would walk around a party:** Regis, "Meet the Extropians."
44 **The extropian playlist:** Max More, "EDITORIAL: Suggestions Wanted," *Extropy,* no. 6 (Summer 1990); Dave Krieger, interview.
45 **"nice" and "mild-mannered":** Ken Kittlitz, interview.
45 **considered himself a "communitarian":** Nick Szabo, "PHIL: GS + Objectivism (+ Extropianism) = ?," EX, April 30, 1993.
45 **"making freedom for myself in an unfree world":** Nick Szabo, "Extropian priorities," EX, April 11, 1993.
45 **cryptography-enabled "smart contracts":** Nick Szabo, "Smart Contracts," 1994, WM.
45 **It was on lib-tech:** Peter McCormack, "#163—Nick Szabo: Cypherpunks, Money, and Bitcoin," *What Bitcoin Did* (podcast), November 1, 2019.
45 **"trust independent digital money":** Nick Szabo, "Bit Gold: Towards Trust-Independent Digital Money," Nick Szabo's Papers and Concise Tutorials, WM.

46 **reposting a 2005 bit gold blog post:** Nick Szabo, "Bit Gold," *Unenumerated* (blog), December 27, 2008.
46 **The first time Szabo acknowledged Bitcoin:** Nick Szabo, "Liar-Resistant Government," *Unenumerated* (blog), May 7, 2009.
46 **"an implementation of the bit gold idea":** Nick Szabo, "Tech Roundup 01/22/11," *Unenumerated* (blog), January 22, 2011.
46 **Szabo came to Bitcoin's defense:** Nick Szabo, "Bitcoin, What Took Ye So Long?," *Unenumerated* (blog), May 28, 2011.

An Evening of Pseudonymous Socializing

49 **Gavin Andresen had traveled:** Nathaniel Popper, *Digital Gold: Bitcoin and the Inside Story of the Misfits and Millionaires Trying to Reinvent Money* (New York: HarperCollins, 2015), 103.
49 **who'd originally created Mt. Gox:** Jed McCaleb, "2014 Jed McCaleb MtGox Interview," interview by Gwern Branwen, gwern.net, February 16–18, 2014.

Mr. Rogers

51 **Finney once posted an ad:** David Rolfe, interview.
51 **working in the nascent videogame industry:** Scott Stilphen, "Hal Finney Interview," Atari Compendium, 2006.
52 **Finney had always liked puzzles.:** Fran Finney, interview by Dustin Dreifuerst, "Episode 73: Fran Finney," *Did You Know* (podcast), February 20, 2020.
52 **jotted his own secret codes:** Nicole Weinstock, "Alcor Patient Profile: Hal Finney," *Cryonics,* 2nd Quarter 2019.
52 **"a deliciously scary thrill":** Hal Finney, "HUMOR: UFO's From Future?," EX, April 1, 1993.
52 **"Why was I born here and now":** Hal Finney, "PRESS: Space colonies," EX, May 28, 1993.
52 **Back in California:** Weinstock, "Alcor Patient Profile."
52 **someone who could crack a textbook for the first time:** Weinstock, "Alcor Patient Profile."
52 **"take us all out to Tommy's":** Walter Bright, comment on Hal Finney, "Dying Outside," *LessWrong* (blog), October 4, 2009.
52 **named their children and pets:** Weinstock, "Alcor Patient Profile."
52 **name of their Rhodesian ridgeback:** Nathaniel Popper, *Digital Gold: Bitcoin and the Inside Story of the Misfits and Millionaires Trying to Reinvent Money* (New York: HarperCollins, 2015), 3–4.
52 **avoided alcohol:** Fran Finney, interview by Dreifuerst, "Episode 73."
52 **a more extreme step:** Weinstock, "Alcor Patient Profile."
53 **a more expensive, full-body package:** "Hal Finney Becomes Alcor's 128th Patient," Alcor website, December 16, 2014.
53 **"He did not believe in God":** Weinstock, "Alcor Patient Profile."
53 **"It just blew me away":** Hal Finney, "Why remailers . . . ," CP, November 15, 1992.
53 **"the mystery and the paradox":** Hal Finney, "Bitcoin and Me (Hal Finney)," BF, March 19, 2013.
53 **"The thing I always love":** "Hal Finney Last Words," Finney home video on Alfre Mancera channel, YouTube, retrieved March 19, 2024.

53 **"untraceable identities":** Hal Finney, "Re: Virtual City (tm) Network FAQ 1.0 (fwd)," CP, October 8, 1993.
53 **As he'd read the novella:** Finney, "Why remailers . . ."
54 **Secret Squirrel:** Hal Finney, "Mr. Squirrel?," CP, October 10, 1992.
54 **"It seemed so obvious to me.":** Finney, "Why remailers . . ."
54 **spent his evenings as a volunteer in the trenches:** Fran Finney, interview by Dreifuerst, "Episode 73."
55 **cryptography could have helped abolitionists:** Hal Finney, "Game items . . . ," CP, October 14, 1992.
55 **"real benefits to all members of society":** Hal Finney, "Re: more ideas on anonymity," CP, February 26, 1993.
55 **"published anonymously":** Hal Finney, "Re: The Utility of Privacy," CP, November 17, 1996.
55 **He had himself used multiple pseudonyms:** Hal Finney, "A favor re Detweiler," CP, October 25, 1993.
55 **"For me, cryptoanarchy is a way to oppose":** Hal Finney, "Re: more ideas on anonymity," CP, February 26, 1993.
55 **"worst disaster that could occur":** Hal Finney, "Re: Virtual City (tm) Network FAQ 1.0 (fwd)," CP, October 8, 1993.
55 **"It's sickening":** Hal Finney, "Re: Catch-22," CP, July 28, 1994.
55 **raided at the behest of the Church of Scientology:** Peter H. Lewis, "Behind an Internet Message Service's Close," *The New York Times,* September 6, 1996.
56 **one of the first encrypted, anonymous remailers:** Andy Greenberg, "Bitcoin's Earliest Adopter Is Cryonically Freezing His Body to See the Future," *Wired,* August 28, 2014.
56 **posted a challenge to fellow cypherpunks:** Steven Levy, "Wisecrackers," *Wired,* March 1, 1996.
56 **thirty-two hours:** Richard Clayton, "Brute Force Attacks on Cryptographic Keys," University of Cambridge, last modified October 29, 2001.
56 **practical reasons for his interest:** Hal Finney, "Re: Voice/Fax Checks," CP, July 22, 1994; Hal Finney, "Re: Physical to digital cash, and back again," CP, August 19, 1993.
56 **a more ideological one:** Hal Finney, "Re: The American money capture," CP, May 1, 1994.
56 **history of private banknotes:** Hal Finney, "Re: e$: Cypherpunks Sell Concepts," CP, August 6, 1994.
56 **workarounds to Chaum's patents:** Hal Finney, "Re: Electronic Banking," CP, November 30, 1992.
56 **"choke point":** Hal Finney, "Re: Re: re: re: digital cash," CP, March 16, 1994.
56 **"an educational game":** Hal Finney, "Re: Electronic Banking," CP, November 30, 1992.
57 **Finney bandied about possible names:** Hal Finney, "Anonymous Address problems, etc.," CP, December 7, 1992.
57 **he proposed "CRASH":** Hal Finney, "Name for crypto cash," CP, December 6, 1993.
57 **"the wrong direction":** Hal Finney, "Chaum on the wrong foot?," CP, August 23, 1993.
57 **quick to take Chaum's e-cash product:** Hal Finney, "ecash speed," CP, November 8, 1995.

57 **"Wow! Hot stuff!":** Hal Finney, "Re: Magic Money Digicash System," CP, February 4, 1994.

57 **might have a security flaw:** Hal Finney, "Attack on Magic Money and Chaum cash," CP, February 6, 1994.

57 **"startlingly beautiful":** Hal Finney, "The Joy of Digicash," CP, March 16, 1994.

57 **he released his own implementation:** Hal Finney, "RPOW—Reusable Proofs of Work," CP, August 15, 2004.

58 **Finney was the first person:** Hal Finney, "Bitcoin P2P e-cash paper," CR, November 7, 2008.

58 **He gave Nakamoto feedback on the source code:** Finney, "Bitcoin and Me."

58 **the second node in the network:** Finney, "Bitcoin and Me."

58 **"Running Bitcoin":** @halfin, Twitter, January 10, 2009.

58 **his weight had gone from 170 to around 250:** Fran Finney, interview by Dreifuerst, "Episode 73."

58 **Eventually he'd get down to 160.:** Fran Finney, interview by Dreifuerst, "Episode 73."

Always Look on the Bright Side

The specifics of Finney's advancing symptoms, and his perspective on them, come from Hal Finney, "Dying Outside" (and in comments), *LessWrong* (blog), October 4, 2009; Giana Magnoli, "Hal and Fran Finney Finish Strong in Santa Barbara Marathon," *Noozhawk,* December 7, 2009; Giana Magnoli, "Hal and Fran Finney Are Running for a Cause," *Noozhawk,* November 29, 2009; Giana Magnoli, "After a Year of ALS, Reality Begins to Hit Home for Hal and Fran Finney," *Noozhawk,* October 17, 2010; Nicole Weinstock, "Alcor Patient Profile: Hal Finney," *Cryonics,* 2nd Quarter 2019; and Fran Finney, interview by Dustin Dreifuerst, "Episode 73: Fran Finney," *Did You Know* (podcast), February 20, 2020.

59 **"No one can talk and run at the same time.":** Fran Finney, interview by Dreifuerst, "Episode 73."

59 **"I didn't want to be right.":** Fran Finney, interview by Dreifuerst, "Episode 73."

59 **he stopped on the Sunset Strip:** Weinstock, "Alcor Patient Profile."

59 **he and Fran had gone on a bike ride:** Weinstock, "Alcor Patient Profile"; Fran Finney, interview by Dreifuerst, "Episode 73."

59 **"It is annoying and worrisome":** Finney, "Dying Outside" (and in comments).

60 **Fran ran the tracking chip:** Magnoli, "Hal and Fran Finney Finish Strong"; Magnoli, "Hal and Fran Finney Are Running."

60 **an expert on the slopes:** Weinstock, "Alcor Patient Profile."

60 **he skied for the last time:** Magnoli, "After a Year of ALS."

60 **Phil Zimmermann likened it:** Phil Zimmermann, interview by Dustin Dreifuerst, "Episode 34: The Legend Phil Zimmermann," *Did You Know* (podcast), May 5, 2019.

60 **"Well, I have more time to read now.":** Phil Zimmermann, interview by Dreifuerst, "Episode 34."

60 **"Maybe people here will understand.":** Finney, "Dying Outside" (and in comments).

61 **nothing a lift chair and a nearby pole couldn't fix:** Fran Finney, interview by Dreifuerst, "Episode 73."

61 **"He was gleeful about doing this":** Fran Finney, interview by Dreifuerst, "Episode 73."

The Pin, Not the Bubble

63 **twenty-six thousand people:** @davidfbailey, Twitter, June 17, 2022.

63 **Blockstream, a $3 billion blockchain-infrastructure company:** Joanna Ossinger, "Bitcoin Infrastructure Firm Blockstream Valued at $3.2 Billion in New Deal," Bloomberg News, August 24, 2021.

64 **On a 2012 episode of *The Good Wife*:** *The Good Wife,* season 3, episode 13, "Bitcoin for Dummies," aired January 15, 2012.

64 **On *The Simpsons*:** *The Simpsons,* season 25, episode 7, "Yellow Subterfuge," aired December 8, 2013.

64 **850,000 bitcoins went missing:** Chris O'Brien, "Mt. Gox Files for Bankruptcy as 850,000 Bitcoins Go Missing," *Los Angeles Times,* February 28, 2014.

64 **cleared of theft but eventually:** Larry Cermak, "Mt. Gox CEO Mark Karpeles Found Guilty on Only 1 Count, Given a Suspended Sentence," The Block, March 14, 2019.

64 **"driving a revolution":** Richard Branson, interview, *Squawk Box,* CNBC, November 22, 2013.

64 **"exciting," "better than currency":** Bill Gates, interview, *Street Smart,* Bloomberg TV, October 2, 2014.

64 **"techno tour de force":** "Munger/Buffett Disagree on Corporate Tax Rates," video, Fox Business, February 3, 2017.

64 **"We're quite confident":** Brian Fung, "Marc Andreessen: In 20 Years, We'll Talk About Bitcoin Like We Talk About the Internet Today," *The Washington Post,* May 21, 2014.

65 **to the chagrin of cryptographers:** Phil Zimmermann, interview by Dustin Dreifuerst, "Episode 34: The Legend Phil Zimmermann," *Did You Know* (podcast), May 5, 2019.

65 **more than sixteen thousand different cryptocurrencies:** CoinMarketCap data, reported in Jordan Major, "Number of Cryptocurrencies Surpasses 16,000 This Year, Adding over 8,000 in 2021," Crypto News, December 31, 2021.

65 **recently passed $3 trillion in value:** Joanna Ossinger, "Crypto World Hits $3 Trillion Market Cap as Ether, Bitcoin Gain," Bloomberg News, November 8, 2021.

65 **Eighty-six percent of Americans had heard of crypto.:** "16% of Americans Say They Have Ever Invested in, Traded or Used Cryptocurrency," Pew Research Center, November 11, 2021.

65 **more than $5 billion worth of bitcoin:** Arnold Kirimi, "MicroStrategy CEO Won't Sell $5B BTC Stash Despite Crypto Winter," Cointelegraph, January 20, 2022.

67 **A man in Wales:** Chris Morris, "The Welshman Who Accidentally Threw Out 8,000 Bitcoin in 2013 Is Mounting an $11 Million Campaign to Get It Back," *Fortune,* August 1, 2022.

67 **robbers wearing balaclavas:** Melanie Kramer, "Dutch Bitcoin Trader Suffers Brutal Torture with a 'Heavy Drill' in Violent Robbery," Yahoo!Finance,

February 25, 2019; "Violent Robbery of Bitcoin Trader Included Water Boarding and a Power Drill," *NL Times,* February 2, 2020.

69 **"rat poison":** Tae Kim, "Warren Buffett Says Bitcoin Is 'Probably Rat Poison Squared,'" CNBC, May 5, 2018.

69 **dissing Bitcoin as "worthless":** Paul R. La Monica, "Jamie Dimon Bashes Bitcoin Again, Calling It 'Worthless,'" CNN Business, October 12, 2021.

69 **dumped a large bitcoin position:** Tabby Kinder and Richard Waters, "Peter Thiel's Fund Wound Down 8-Year Bitcoin Bet Before Market Crash," *Financial Times,* January 18, 2023.

69 **ninth most valuable asset in the world:** Companies Market Cap, on April 3, 2022, WM.

70 **some clever analysis:** Sergio Demian Lerner, "The Well Deserved Fortune of Satoshi Nakamoto, Bitcoin Creator, Visionary and Genius," Bitslog, April 17, 2013.

70 **instant market value of $86 billion:** "Coinbase Valued at $86 Billion in 'Landmark Moment' for Crypto," *The New York Times,* April 14, 2021.

70 **one of the risk factors listed in the prospectus:** Form S-1, Coinbase Global, Inc., February 25, 2021.

70 **Thiel himself had speculated:** Nathan Crooks, "Peter Thiel Tells Crowd Where He'd Look for Elusive Bitcoin Founder Satoshi," Bloomberg News, October 21, 2021.

71 **cost him more than $100,000:** Non-Party Andrew O'Hagan's Motion for Order Compelling Plaintiffs to Pay Fees and Costs Related to Document and Deposition Discovery in England and Incorporated Memorandum of Law, November 5, 2021, KW.

71 **"death threats":** Cale Guthrie Weissman and Carmel DeAmicis, "Newsweek EIC Tells Pando 'We've Hired Security to Protect Our Reporter. Social Media Head: 'We Won!,'" *PandoDaily,* March 8, 2014, WM.

71 **A site called Bitcoin Obituaries:** https://99bitcoins.com

71 **"Please do not try to approach me":** Will Stephenson, "Cryptonomicon," *Harper's,* March 2022.

71 **"pioneers of the years BB":** Title of Szabo's talk at Bitcoin 2022.

Satoshi Studies

72 **showed up at Crypto:** Joshua Davis, "The Crypto-Currency," *The New Yorker,* October 3, 2011.

73 **"I could never allow myself":** James O'Shea, "The Secret Irishman Likely Behind Bitcoin, the Internet Currency Code," IrishCentral, October 4, 2011.

73 **previously exposed the journalistic frauds:** Michael Noer, "Read the Original Forbes Takedown of Stephen Glass," *Forbes,* November 12, 2014.

73 **came upon a striking similarity:** Adam L. Penenberg, "The Bitcoin Crypto-Currency Mystery Reopened," *Fast Company,* October 11, 2011.

74 **a newly created blog:** Skye Grey, "Satoshi Nakamoto Is (Probably) Nick Szabo," *LikeInAMirror* (blog), December 1, 2013; Skye Grey, "Occam's Razor: Who Is Most Likely to Be Satoshi Nakamoto," *LikeInAMirror* (blog), March 11, 2014.

75 **a throwaway line:** Nick Szabo, "Liar-Resistant Government," *Unenumerated* (blog), May 7, 2009.

75 **"Anybody want to help me code one up?":** Nick Szabo, comment on "Bit Gold Markets," *Unenumerated* (blog), December 27, 2008 (originally posted April 2008).

75 **"simple curiosity":** John Biggs, "Who Is the Real Satoshi Nakamoto?," *TechCrunch,* December 5, 2013.

76 **zeroed in on the combination of expertises:** Dominic Frisby, *Bitcoin: The Future of Money?* (London: unbound, 2015).

77 **confronted Nick at an industry gathering:** Nathaniel Popper, "Decoding the Enigma of Satoshi Nakamoto and the Birth of Bitcoin," *The New York Times,* May 15, 2015.

77 ***The New York Times* named Nick:** Popper, "Decoding the Enigma."

77 **"research in digital contracts and digital currency":** "Graduación UFM y doctorado a Nick Szabo," Universidad Francisco Marroquín, May 9, 2017.

77 **"the quiet master of cryptocurrency":** Tim Ferriss, "The Quiet Master of Cryptocurrency—Nick Szabo (#244)," *The Tim Ferriss Show* (podcast), June 4, 2017.

Anonymous

79 **English professor named Donald Foster:** Donald Foster, "Primary Culprit," *New York,* February 26, 1996.

79 **"For God's sake, definitely":** Mary B. W. Tabor, "Author, Subject of Article, Denies He Wrote 'Colors,'" *The New York Times,* February 21, 1996.

79 **sixty-second outgoing voice message:** Tabor, "Author."

79 **denied it on CBS News:** Howard Kurtz, "Author's Lie Costs Joe Klein His CBS Job," *The Washington Post,* July 25, 1996.

79 **denied it to his own colleagues:** Howard Kurtz, "Klein Apologizes to Newsweek Colleagues," *The Washington Post,* July 24, 1996.

79 **Eventually, Klein admitted:** Caryn James, "Anonymous Shows His Colors," *The New York Times,* July 21, 1996.

79 **Felt testified before a grand jury:** Bob Woodward, *The Secret Man: The Story of Watergate's Deep Throat* (New York: Simon and Schuster, 2005), 131–32.

80 **"a composite":** Dennis Farney, "If You Drink Scotch, Smoke and Read, Maybe You're 'Deep Throat,'" *The Wall Street Journal,* June 25, 1974.

80 **"I never leaked information":** Mark W. Felt, *The FBI Pyramid: From the Inside* (New York: G. P. Putnam, 1979), 226.

80 **"No, it's not me. I would have done better.":** Woodward, *Secret Man,* 158–59.

80 **Eventually Felt admitted:** John D. O'Connor, "I'm the Guy They Called Deep Throat," *Vanity Fair,* October 17, 2006.

80 **"only solidified my sad understanding":** Woodward, *Secret Man,* 213.

80 **Woodward knew whereof he spoke:** Woodward, *Secret Man*, 218, 149–50.

80 **"I deny being Satoshi.":** Max Marty and Daniel Walters, "Ralph Merkle—On Nanotech and Manipulating the Microcosmos," *Cryonics Underground* (podcast), February 8, 2022.

A Spectacular Display of Hindsight

81 **"In my limited experience":** Nick Szabo, "Re: on anonymity, identity, reputation, and spoofing," CP, October 18, 1993.

81 **"Bitcoin is an implementation":** Satoshi Nakamoto, "Re: They want to delete the Wikipedia article," BF, July 20, 2010.

82 **"bitgold coins":** James A. Donald, "Bitcoin P2P e-cash paper," CR, November 18, 2008.

82 **"I found that there is a sourceforge project":** Hal Finney, "Re: Bitcoin P2P e-cash paper," CR, November 13, 2008.

82 **Gwern Branwen argued:** Gwern Branwen, "Bitcoin Is Worse Is Better," gwern.net, May 27, 2011.

82 **"a spectacular display of hindsight":** Nick Szabo, "Bitcoin, What Took Ye So Long?," *Unenumerated* (blog), May 28, 2011.

82 **"pathetic corporate norms":** @NickSzabo4, Twitter, January 5, 2020.

82 **clearly saw himself as the father of crypto:** Nick Szabo, "The Many Traditions of Non-governmental Money (Part i)," *Unenumerated* (blog), March 23, 2018.

83 **"If you don't believe me":** Satoshi Nakamoto, "Re: Scalability and transaction rate," BF, July 29, 2010.

83 **"If you don't get it":** Nick Szabo, "Re: Invasion of Employee Privacy: you can expose unethical practices," ALT.PRIVACY, UN, September 19, 1993.

83 **"The design supports a tremendous variety":** Satoshi Nakamoto, "Re: Transactions and Scripts . . . ," BF, June 17, 2010.

83 **"I'm particularly interested in the art of writing contracts":** Nick Szabo, "Contract law & operating in many jurisdictions," MISC.LEGAL .COMPUTING, UN, May 8, 1994.

83 **a hardheaded rigor:** Nick Szabo, "Hello Kitty People," *Unenumerated*, October 2, 2008.

83 **"First we start meeting people's needs":** Nick Szabo, "Re: Powersats," SCI .SPACE, UN, February 18, 1992.

83 **"a welfare case":** Nick Szabo, "Manned vs unmanned space exploration," SCI.SPACE, UN, February 10, 1989.

83 **he'd put his own money on the line:** Nick Szabo, "Use of Soyuz/ELV Combos for SSF," TALK.POLITICS.SPACE, UN, January 23, 1992.

83 **he'd take offense:** Nick Szabo, "Fred's Operatic Death," SCI.SPACE, UN, June 17, 1991.

83 **terraform Venus:** Nick Szabo, "Re: Is NASA really planning to Terraform Mars," SCI.SPACE, UN, September 9, 1992.

83 **"Reality does not wreck dreams":** Nick Szabo, "NSS and Space Settlement," SCI.SPACE, UN, October 2, 1989.

83 **a penetrating study of money's origins:** Nick Szabo, "Shelling Out—The Origins of Money," 2002, WM.

84 **"remarkably free of politicians' faces":** Nick Szabo, "Bank notes from the free banking era," *Unenumerated* (blog), August 8, 2008.

84 **"software architecture and engineering":** Nick Szabo, "Consulting Services," *Unenumerated* (blog), April 2, 2008.

84 **"extensive hacking skills":** Nick Szabo, "Extropian priorities," EX, April 11, 1993.

84 **no fewer than six C/C++ books:** Nick Szabo, "Books on my desk," EX, May 15, 1993.

84 **"I knit some mean code.":** Nick Szabo, "Culture: My Extropian Name," EX, March 14, 1993.

84 **studied Japanese:** Nick Szabo, "funny message," SCI.LANG.JAPAN, UN, January 10, 1991.

84 **fascinated by Japanese culture:** Nick Szabo, "Re: Scientific value of Apollo (was Re: Motives)," SCI.SPACE, UN, December 16, 1989.

Sniffing Bronze

85 **An eccentric art dealer in Santa Fe:** Benjamin Wallace, "The Great 21st Century Treasure Hunt," *New York,* November 9, 2020.

85 **pre-Columbian artifacts:** "Fenn's Treasure Auction: Item Pricing and Total Sales," Fenn's Treasure website.

87 **Fenn had said the purpose of his treasure hunt:** e.g., Clayton Sandell, "Mysterious decade-long treasure hunt finally turns up gold," ABC News, June 8, 2020.

88 **an interview with Musk:** Lex Fridman, "#252—Elon Musk: SpaceX, Mars, Tesla Autopilot, Self-Driving, Robotics, and AI," *Lex Fridman Podcast,* December 28, 2021.

Slow, Not Furious

90 **a feature story in *Newsweek*:** Leah McGrath Goodman, "The Face Behind Bitcoin," *Newsweek,* March 6, 2014.

90 **Its newest owner, IBT Media, had decided:** Puneet Pal Singh, "Newsweek magazine relaunches print edition," BBC.com, March 7, 2014.

92 **rewritten two-thirds of Nakamoto's original code:** Tom Simonite, "The Man Who Really Built Bitcoin," *MIT Technology Review,* August 15, 2014.

92 **"regret talking to Leah":** @gavinandresen, Twitter, March 6, 2014.

92 **"Okay, no questions right now":** "Satoshi Nakamoto: is this bitcoin's founder? – video," *The Guardian,* March 6, 2014.

93 **live-tweeted the action:** @JoeBelBruno, Twitter, March 6, 2014.

94 **Ryan's AP story:** Ryan Nakashima, "AP Exclusive: Man denies he's Bitcoin founder," AP News, March 6, 2014.

94 **With CNN still broadcasting images of Dorian:** "Is This the Founder of Bitcoin?," CNN, March 7, 2014.

95 **"I am not Dorian Nakamoto.":** Satoshi Nakamoto, reply to "Bitcoin open source implementation of P2P currency," p2pfoundation.ning.com, March 7, 2014.

95 **Juola & Associates:** Matthew Herper, "Linguistic Analysis Says Newsweek Named The Wrong Man As Bitcoin's Creator," *Forbes,* March 12, 2014.

95 **King again came out on top:** Herper, "Linguistic Analysis."

95 **"NOT enough data":** @truth_eater, Twitter, March 10, 2014.

95 **Patrick Juola:** Herper, "Linguistic Analysis."

95 **"high editorial and ethical standards":** "Newsweek's Statement on the Bitcoin Story," *Newsweek,* March 7, 2014.

95 **sending a car to check on Dorian:** Tami Abdollah, "LA Sheriff Backs Newsweek Quotes of Nakamoto Visit," AP, March 7, 2014.

95 **"colossal arrogance":** Joe Mullin, "The Colossal Arrogance of Newsweek's Bitcoin 'Scoop,'" Ars Technica, March 20, 2014.

95 **"half-baked theory":** Felix Salmon, "The Satoshi Paradox," *Columbia Journalism Review,* March 7, 2014.

95 ***Newsweek* had also published the forged "Hitler Diaries":** Michael Hiltzik, "The Nakamoto Affair and Newsweek's 'High Editorial Standards,'" *Los Angeles Times,* March 8, 2014.

96 **"Is there anyone left on planet earth":** Marc Andreessen, annotation of Goodman's *Newsweek* article, News Genius, March 6, 2014.

96 **"four million people":** Balaji Srinivasan, annotation of Goodman's *Newsweek* article, News Genius, March 6, 2014.

96 **a lawyer for Dorian issued a strongly worded statement:** Chris O'Brien, "Dorian S. Nakamoto Hires Lawyer to 'Clear His Name' of Bitcoin Claim," *Los Angeles Times,* March 17, 2014.

96 **"NEWSWEEK'S ARTICLE HURT MY FAMILY.":** Joe Mullin, "Dorian Nakamoto, fingered as Bitcoin's creator, wants to sue Newsweek," Ars Technica, October 14, 2014.

96 **forty-eight bitcoins from two thousand donors:** Kai Sedgwick, "'Fake Satoshi' Dorian Nakamoto Is Probably $273,000 Richer After Selling His Bitcoins," Bitcoin.com, December 19, 2017.

97 **"it has lots of buttery taste":** Dorian S. Nakamoto, "royal danish butter cookies tastes great," customer review, Amazon.com, February 2, 2011; referenced by J32926, "Dorian S. Nakamoto either isn't the bitcoin founder, or he is massively trolling the Internet with his Amazon.com reviews," Reddit, r/Bitcoin, March 6, 2014.

Hungarian Brainstorming

98 **b-money was first proposed on his own private lib-tech list:** Peter McCormack, "#163—Nick Szabo: Cypherpunks, Money, and Bitcoin," *What Bitcoin Did* (podcast), November 1, 2019.

98 **original blog post dates were still visible in the URLs:** Skye Grey, "Satoshi Nakamoto is (probably) Nick Szabo," *LikeInAMirror* (blog), December 1, 2013.

99 **"reruns season":** Nick Szabo, "Reruns," *Unenumerated* (blog), August 20, 2008.

99 **"Anybody want to help me code one up?":** Nick Szabo, comment on "Bit gold markets," *Unenumerated* (blog), April 2008.

99 **a year and a half to write the software:** Satoshi Nakamoto, "Bitcoin P2P e-cash paper," CR, November 17, 2008.

99 **focused on the complicated pricing:** Szabo, comment on "Bit gold markets."

99 **"I am not a lawyer":** Satoshi Nakamoto, email to Mike Hearn, April 27, 2009.

99 **"I'm better with code than with words":** Satoshi Nakamoto, "Bitcoin P2P e-cash paper," CR, November 14, 2008.

99 **he acted as if he'd never heard of Wei Dai's b-money:** Satoshi Nakamoto, email to Adam Back, August 21, 2008.

99 **"expands on your ideas into a complete working system":** Satoshi Nakamoto, email to Wei Dai, August 22, 2008.

99 **smart drugs, genetic engineering, the corporation of the future:** Nick Szabo, "Recommendations of Technical SF," REC.ARTS.SF-LOVERS, UN, January 13, 1991.

100 **"spectacularly large list of projects":** Nick Szabo, "Re: costly colonies," TALK.POLITICS.SPACE, UN, January 12, 1992.

100 **Play-Doh Fun Factory–designed structure:** Nick Szabo, "Self-Reproduction, Complexity, and the Food Chain," EX, June 24, 1993.

100 **N-Cat (Nick's Catalog):** Nick Szabo, "Introducing N-CAT!," EX, September 30, 1993.

100 **methodology for pricing memes:** Nick Szabo, "PHIL: GS + Objectivism (+ Extropianism) = ?," EX, April 30, 1993.

100 **Hungarian Brainstorming:** Nick Szabo, "Meta-Brainstorm," EX, June 1, 1993.

100 **"comet materials processing":** Nick Szabo, "Looking for chemical engineers, etc.," EX, June 5, 1993.

100 **"microrobot" cute enough:** Nick Szabo, "Cute but working microrobot," COMP.ROBOTICS, UN, December 14, 1994.

100 **"Operation Desert Blossom":** Nick Szabo, "Desert Blossom: A Proposal for Post-War Iraq," ALT.DESERT.SHIELD, UN, January 22, 1991.

100 **a piece of speculative fiction:** Nick Szabo, "LIT: Comedy of Reputations," EX, June 19, 1993.

100 **"Distributing Authorities and Verifying Their Claims":** Nick Szabo, 1997, Nick Szabo's Essays and Concise Tutorials, WM.

100 **"The Mental Accounting Barrier to Micropayments":** Nick Szabo, 1996, Nick Szabo's Essays and Concise Tutorials, WM.

100 **a history of commercial institutions:** Nick Szabo, "New Writing—The Birth of Insurance," *Unenumerated* (blog), October 23, 2005.

100 **a new programming language:** Nick Szabo, "Short Takes" (and comment), *Unenumerated* (blog), December 10, 2011.

100 **a conclave of Bitcoin brains:** Bitcoin and Cryptocurrency Research Conference, Department of Computer Science, Princeton University, March 27, 2014.

"My Father Is an Honest Guy"

102 **"Even if it's NOT him":** Rob Wile, "Bitcoin Community Goes into a Rage over Newsweek Story," Business Insider, March 6, 2014.

102 **a rumor circulated at a Bitcoin conference:** Andy Greenberg, "Nakamoto's Neighbor: My Hunt for Bitcoin's Creator Led to a Paralyzed Crypto Genius," *Forbes,* March 25, 2014.

102 **Hal Finney had lived:** in early 1990s; "General Population by City, Los Angeles County, 1960-2000 U.S. Census," LA Almanac.

102 **Robin Hanson speculated:** Robin Hanson, "Conspiracy Theory, Up Close & Personal," *Overcoming Bias* (blog), March 26, 2014.

102 **a variant theory:** Greenberg, "Nakamoto's Neighbor."

103 **Bitcoiners donated twenty-five bitcoins:** Andy Greenberg, "Bitcoin's Earliest Adopter Is Cryonically Freezing His Body to See the Future," *Wired,* August 28, 2014.

103 **flew by chartered air ambulance:** "Hal Finney Becomes Alcor's 128th Patient," Alcor website, December 16, 2014; and Fran Finney, email.

103 **Paradise Valley Hospital:** Nathaniel Popper, "Hal Finney, Cryptographer and Bitcoin Pioneer, Dies at 58," *The New York Times,* August 30, 2014.

104 **member A-1436's arrival:** "Hal Finney Becomes Alcor's 128th Patient."

104 **his mind wasn't as quick as it once was:** Nicole Weinstock, "Alcor Patient Profile: Hal Finney," *Cryonics,* 2nd Quarter 2019.

104 **family said their goodbyes:** "Hal Finney Becomes Alcor's 128th Patient."
104 **thirty-eight hours later:** "Hal Finney Becomes Alcor's 128th Patient."
104 **"to maintain viability of the tissue":** Max More, interview.
104 **Fran was in the room:** Max More, "Hal Finney being cryopreserved now," EX, August 28, 2014.
104 **"Hal Finney is being cryopreserved now":** More, "Hal Finney being cryopreserved now."
104 **Hal's body temperature:** "Hal Finney Becomes Alcor's 128th Patient."
105 **"Hal, I know I speak for many":** More, "Hal Finney being cryopreserved now."
105 **took comfort from the knowledge:** Greenberg, "Bitcoin's Earliest Adopter."
105 **"to be able to see what the world turned into":** Weinstock, "Alcor Patient Profile."
105 **Some Bitcoiners took to calling one ten-millionth of a coin a Finney.:** coinguycanada, "Honoring Hal Finney," BF, August 30, 2014.

Bag of Words

106 **a professor of computational linguistics:** Sascha Carroll, "What's in a Name: Linguistic Study Identifies Nick Szabo as the Real Satoshi Nakamoto," Cointelegraph, April 17, 2014.
106 **Juola & Associates, which had originally named Neal King:** Matthew Herper, "Linguistic Analysis Says Newsweek Named The Wrong Man As Bitcoin's Creator," *Forbes,* March 12, 2014.
106 **and later Hal Finney:** Andy Greenberg, "Nakamoto's Neighbor: My Hunt for Bitcoin's Creator Led to a Paralyzed Crypto Genius," *Forbes,* March 25, 2014.
106 **told Dominic Frisby:** Dominic Frisby, *Bitcoin: The Future of Money?* (London: unbound, 2015), 99.
106 **Georgetown University computer science student:** Michael Chon, "Stylometric Analysis: Satoshi Nakamoto," Medium, December 26, 2017.
106 **Another pair of scholars:** Varun Ramesh and Jean-Luc Watson, "Shakespeare and Satoshi—De-anonymizing Writing Using BiLSTMs with Attention," unpublished paper, Stanford University, December 31, 2018.
107 **"human stylome":** Hans van Halteren et al., "New Machine Learning Methods Demonstrate the Existence of a Human Stylome," *Journal of Quantitative Linguistics* 12, no. 1 (2005): 65–77.
107 **the Caesar cipher [footnote]:** Simon Singh, *The Code Book: The Evolution of Secrecy from Mary, Queen of Scots, to Quantum Cryptography* (New York: Doubleday Anchor, 2000), 9–11, 17–19.
107 **The pioneering scholars:** Frederick Mosteller and David L. Wallace, *Inference and Disputed Authorship: The Federalist* (Reading, MA: Addison-Wesley, 1964).
107 **"bag of words":** Jacob Murel, PhD, and Eda Kavlakoglu, "What is bag of words?," IBM website, January 19, 2024.
108 **The *Times* reporter's evidence was circumstantial:** Richard Brooks, "Whodunnit? JK Rowling's Secret Life as Wizard Crime Writer," *The Times* (London), July 14, 2013.
108 **Could Patrick help settle the matter?:** Patrick Juola, "How a Computer Program Helped Show J. K. Rowling Wrote A Cuckoo's Calling," *Scientific*

American, August 20, 2013; Alexi Mostrous, "JK Rowling Unmasked as Author of Bestselling Crime Novel," *The Times* (London), July 15, 2013; Patrick Juola, "The Rowling Case: A Proposed Standard Analytic Protocol for Authorship Questions," *Digital Scholarship in the Humanities* 30, suppl. 1 (December 2015).

110 **H. R. Haldeman, citing his own confidential source:** Bob Woodward, *The Secret Man: The Story of Watergate's Deep Throat* (New York: Simon and Schuster, 2005), 85.

110 **A federal prosecutor became aware:** Woodward, *Secret Man*, 4, 131–32.

110 **Felt told a girlfriend:** Woodward, *Secret Man*, 194–95.

110 **Woodward told:** Woodward, *Secret Man*, 4.

110 **"because it was a big part of my past":** Woodward, *Secret Man*, 191.

110 **Nora Ephron believed:** Woodward, *Secret Man*, 191.

110 **apparently shared the news with their son Jacob:** Woodward, *Secret Man*, 158–59.

110 **The person who'd tipped off the British newspaper:** Allan Kozinn, "Lawyer Is Fined for Revealing Rowling as Author of Detective Novel," *The New York Times*, January 2, 2014.

111 **"Trusted Third Parties Are Security Holes":** Nick Szabo, 2001, Nick Szabo's Papers and Concise Tutorials, WM.

111 **sounded alarmingly like her husband's hermit brother:** "Unabomber Ted Kaczynski's Brother, Sister-in-Law Recall Turning Him In to FBI," ABC News, February 10, 2016.

111 **"grossly insufficient":** Rob Wile, "PROFESSOR: There Is a Big, Gaping Flaw in New Satoshi Study," Business Insider, April 17, 2014.

"How Deep Are You?"

115 **Microsoft and Dell had begun:** Aaron Smith, "Microsoft Begins Accepting Bitcoin," CNN, December 11, 2014; Laura Pevehouse, "We're Now Accepting Bitcoin on Dell.com," Dell Technologies, July 18, 2014.

115 **the first regulated U.S. exchange:** Davey Alba, "Coinbase Opens First Licensed Bitcoin Exchange in the US," *Wired*, January 26, 2015.

115 **Scaling was the very problem:** Hal Finney, "Re: Bitcoin Bank," BF, December 30, 2010; James Donald, "Bitcoin P2P e-cash paper," CR, November 2, 2008.

115 **"reckless" and "a huge security risk":** @NickSzabo4, Twitter, August 16, 2015.

115 **Mike Hearn, fed up with the gridlock:** Mike Hearn, "The resolution of the Bitcoin experiment," *Plan99.net* (blog), January 14, 2016.

116 **"a very dangerous fork":** "Bitcoin XT Fork," bitcoin-dev listserv, August 15, 2015.

116 **The most common response to this post:** Rudd-X, "'Satoshi' broke his silence on the controversy about block size (plus authenticity analysis of the email)," Reddit, r/Bitcoin, August 17, 2015.

116 **sent to a number of other people:** @nathanielpopper, Twitter, December 8, 2015; @truth_eater, Twitter, December 9, 2015.

116 **Greenberg and Branwen:** Andy Greenberg and Gwern Branwen, "Is Bitcoin's Creator This Unknown Australian Genius? Probably Not (Updated)," *Wired*, December 8, 2015.

Craig

118 **"Would you like to play with my beetles?":** Legal Case Evaluation: Autism Diagnostic Interview, Revised (ADI-R), May 18, 2020, KW.
118 **"weird and volatile":** Legal Case Evaluation, KW.
118 **an alcoholic:** Legal Case Evaluation, KW.
118 **Most days after school:** Danielle DeMorgan, "Is he Satoshi or is he my Brother?," *danni*-d, August 13, 2018, WM.
118 **"hamshack":** Donald Joseph Lynam, deposition, April 2, 2020, KW.
118 **old carton of occupation money:** Lynam, deposition, KW.
118 **throwing stars and a genuine katana:** Lynam, deposition, KW.
118 **black ninja costume:** DeMorgan, "Is he Satoshi"; Legal Case Evaluation, KW.
119 **"We'd literally have code wars":** Max Lynam, trial testimony, *Granath v. Wright*, Oslo District Court, September 16, 2022.
119 **dyed his hair orange and neglected his hygiene:** Legal Case Evaluation, KW.
119 **His continuing ninja outings embarrassed his sister:** Legal Case Evaluation, KW.
119 **and led other kids to call him a freak:** Transcript of Trial Day 1, November 1, 2021, KW.
119 **he lashed back:** Legal Case Evaluation, KW.
119 **visions of the future:** DeMorgan, "Is he Satoshi."
119 **claimed that he was in the Legion of Doom:** Plaintiff's Response in Opposition to Defendant's Motion to Exclude Improper Character Evidence at Trial, October 6, 2021, KW.
119 **a tendency to make up details:** Legal Case Evaluation, KW; Andrew O'Hagan, "The Satoshi Affair," *London Review of Books,* June 30, 2016.
119 **discharged after less than a year:** Jameson Lopp, "OP ED: How Many Wrongs Make a Wright," *Bitcoin Magazine,* April 18, 2019.
119 **"Craig is not known for his people skills":** Lynam, deposition, KW.
119 **eighteen years older than him:** Legal Case Evaluation, KW.
119 **"While the average member of the public":** Craig Wright, "Banking over the Net," CP, September 19, 1996.
120 **"Personally, I paid my way through uni":** Craig Wright, "Re: Risk v. Charity," CP, September 17, 1996.
120 **"Do we really need":** Julian Assange, "Re: Risk v. Charity," CP, September 18, 1996.

Dave

121 **Lasseters Online Casino and Centrebet:** Approved Judgment, COPA v Wright, High Court of Justice, Business and Property Courts of England and Wales, Intellectual Property List, May 20, 2024.
121 **motorcycle accident:** D. Stewart MacIntyre, Jr., MD, expert report, December 13, 2019, Attachment 14 to Plaintiffs' Omnibus Daubert Motion to Strike Defense Experts, May 18, 2020, KW.
121 **aircraft-grade aluminum flash drive:** Patrick Paige, deposition, December 10, 2019, KW.
121 **around his neck:** Dr. Craig Wright's Motion to Continue Mediation or Permit Attendance By Videoconference, June 5, 2019, KW.

121 **guns' serial numbers:** Paige, deposition, KW.
121 **dated strippers:** Kimon Andreou, deposition, December 3, 2019, KW.
121 **friends called him Dave Mississippi:** Andreou, deposition, KW.
121 **"200 vocational qualifications":** Craig Wright, interview by Greg Mahoney, Australian Taxation Office, August 11, 2014, Attachment 5 to Plaintiffs' Motion for Partial Summary Judgment on Defendant's Affirmative Defenses, May 18, 2020, KW.
121 **signed his emails:** e.g., Craig Wright, email to Ira Kleiman, February 14, 2014, Attachment 54 to Joint Notice of Filing Admitted Exhibits, December 16, 2021, KW.
121 **coauthored a paper:** Craig Wright, Dave Kleiman, and Shyaan Sundhar R.S., "Overwriting Hard Drive Data: The Great Wiping Controversy," paper presented at the Fourth International Conference on Information Systems Security, December 16–20, 2008, Hyderabad.
121 **formed a partnership:** Amended Complaint, May 14, 2018, KW.
121 **hospitalized with infections:** Andreou, deposition, KW.
121 **"I told the doctors":** Andy Cush, "The Strange Life and Death of Dave Kleiman, a Computer Genius Linked to Bitcoin's Origins," Gizmodo, December 9, 2015.
121 **Kleiman was found dead:** Investigative Report, Palm Beach County Medical Examiner's Office, Case #130467, Doug Jenkins, April 27, 2013.
122 **toxicology panel:** Autopsy report, Office of the District Medical Examiner, Palm Beach County, Case # 13-0467, June 10, 2013, Attachment 19 to Plaintiffs' Omnibus Motion in Limine, May 18, 2020, KW.
122 **email blast to Kleiman's friends:** Carter Conrad, email to Wright et al., April 29, 2013, Attachment 9 to Joint Notice of Filing Admitted Exhibits, December 16, 2021, KW.
122 **"Dave was a special man":** "Dave Kleiman—RIP (1967–2013)," Craig Wright channel, YouTube, April 29, 2013, WM.
122 **"Hello Louis":** Craig Wright, email to Louis Kleiman, February 11, 2014, Attachment 20 to Complaint and Jury Demand, February 14, 2018, KW.
122 **Ira was skeptical.:** Ira Kleiman, email to Craig Wright, February 16, 2014, Attachment 55 to Joint Notice of Filing Admitted Exhibits, December 16, 2021, KW.
122 **friends were paying his cellphone bill:** Paige, deposition, KW.
122 **he'd stopped paying the mortgage on his home:** William R. Nicholson, expert report, December 13, 2019, KW.
122 **high-interest, subprime lender:** Nicholson, expert report.
122 **"Dave may have been cash poor":** Craig Wright, email to Ira Kleiman, February 15, 2014, quoted in Transcript of Trial Day 3, December 20, 2021, KW.
122 **"several DHS research programs":** Craig Wright, email to Ira Kleiman, February 15, 2014, Attachment 5 to Complaint, February 14, 2018, KW.
123 **"The myth is more powerful than all of us combined.":** Craig Wright, email to Ira Kleiman, February 16, 2014, quoted in Transcript of Trial Day 5, December 20, 2021, KW.
123 **now remembered a Thanksgiving dinner:** Ira Kleiman, email to Angie Ojea, April 24, 2016, Attachment 93 to Joint Notice of Filing Admitted Exhibits, December 16, 2021, KW.
123 **"The evidence is overwhelming that he is legit.":** Ira Kleiman, email to

Patrick Paige, February 15, 2014, Attachment 1 to Dr. Wright's Statement of Material Facts in Support of Motion for Summary Judgment, May 8, 2020, KW.

123 **"Can I ask if Dave played a part":** Ira Kleiman, email to Craig Wright, February 15, 2014, Attachment 54 to Joint Notice of Filing Admitted Exhibits, December 16, 2021, KW.

123 **"I cannot say much right now":** Craig Wright, email to Ira Kleiman, February 14, 2014, Attachment 54 to Joint Notice of Filing Admitted Exhibits, December 16, 2021, KW.

123 **reformatted several of his hard drives:** Ira Kleiman, deposition, January 10, 2020, filed with court on May 8, 2020, KW.

123 **"I can't stop thinking":** Ira Kleiman, email to Craig Wright, March 7, 2014, Attachment 17 to Plaintiffs' Opposing Statement of Material Facts, June 1, 2020, KW.

123 **"Satoshi was a team":** Craig Wright, email to Ira Kleiman, March 7, 2014, Attachment 17 to Plaintiffs' Opposing Statement of Material Facts, June 1, 2020, KW.

123 **an email from Andrew Miller:** Andrew Miller, email to Ira Kleiman, April 15, 2014, Attachment 10 to Supplemental Joint Notice of Filing Admitted Exhibits, December 17, 2021, KW.

123 **pair of filings Wright had recently made:** *Craig Steven Wright v. W & K Info Defense Research LLC,* Statements of Claim, NSW Supreme Court, July 25, 2013, and August 12, 2013, Attachment 10 to Supplemental Joint Notice of Filing Admitted Exhibits, December 17, 2021, KW.

123 **"all accountable value":** Ira Kleiman, email to Craig Wright, April 23, 2014, Attachment 21 to Complaint and Jury Demand, February 14, 2018, KW.

124 **Ira now became suspicious:** Ira Kleiman, email to Craig Wright, April 23, 2014, Attachment 21 to Complaint and Jury Demand, February 14, 2018, KW.

124 **Wright had ready responses:** Craig Wright, email to Ira Kleiman, April 23, 2014, Attachment 21 to Complaint and Jury Demand, February 14, 2018, KW.

124 **Ira was temporarily placated:** Ira Kleiman, emails to Craig Wright, April 23, 2014, Attachment 21 to Complaint and Jury Demand, February 14, 2018, KW.

124 **his frustration mounted:** Ira Kleiman, email to Craig Wright, June 22, 2015, Attachment 31 to Plaintiffs' Opposing Statement of Material Facts, June 1, 2020, KW.

124 **Ira began to consider filing a lawsuit.:** Ira Kleiman, email to Angie Ojea, April 24, 2016, Attachment 93 to Joint Notice of Filing Admitted Exhibits, December 16, 2021, KW.

124 **Wright stopped responding:** Complaint and Jury Demand, February 14, 2018, KW.

A Treacherous Exercise

125 ***Wired* went live with its report:** Andy Greenberg and Gwern Branwen, "Bitcoin's Creator Satoshi Nakamoto Is Probably This Unknown Australian Genius," *Wired,* December 8, 2015, WM.

125 **An hour and a half later, the tech site Gizmodo published:** Sam Biddle and Andy Cush, "This Australian Says He and His Dead Friend Invented Bitcoin," Gizmodo, May 2, 2016.

125 **A Bitcoin developer named Greg Maxwell:** nullc, "Blockchain Scale Tests by (alleged) Satoshi! 340 GB blocks, 568k transactions," Reddit, r/Bitcoin, December 8, 2015.

125 **Motherboard's Sarah Jeong:** Sarah Jeong, "Satoshi's PGP Keys Are Probably Backdated and Point to a Hoax," *Vice,* December 9, 2015, WM.

126 **"Cloudcroft has never been an SGI customer":** Aimee Chanthavadong, "SGI Denies Links with Alleged Bitcoin Founder Craig Wright," ZDNET, December 10, 2015.

126 **Charles Sturt University:** Thomas Brewster, "Time to Call a Hoax? Inconsistencies on 'Probable' Bitcoin Creator's PhD and Supercomputers Revealed," *Forbes,* December 11, 2015.

126 **raids on his home:** Elle Hunt and Paul Farrell, "Reported 'Bitcoin' Founder Craig Wright's Home Raided by Australian Police," *The Guardian,* December 8, 2015.

126 **a plane to Manila:** Stefan Matthews, interview.

126 **posted a second:** Andy Greenberg, "New Clues Suggest Craig Wright, Suspected Bitcoin Creator, May Be a Hoaxer," *Wired,* December 11, 2015.

126 **Gizmodo also backpedaled:** Andy Cush, "The Mystery of Craig Wright and Bitcoin Isn't Solved Yet," Gizmodo, December 11, 2015.

126 **Juola & Associates soon added:** David Gilbert, "Craig Wright Is Not Bitcoin Creator Satoshi Nakamoto, According to New Text Analysis," *International Business Times,* January 22, 2016.

The Satoshi Checklist

127 **"A good puzzle, it's a fair thing":** John Tierney, "The Perplexing Life of Erno Rubik," *Discover,* March 1986.

128 **"gain a new territory of freedom":** Satoshi Nakamoto, "Bitcoin P2P e-cash paper," CR, November 6, 2008.

128 **"very attractive to the libertarian viewpoint":** Satoshi Nakamoto, "Bitcoin P2P e-cash paper," CR, November 14, 2008.

129 **"In 1494, the invention of double-entry accounting":** https://b.tc/conference/2022/bitcoin-art-gallery.

130 **a bobblehead doll:** Satoshi Nakamoto Bitcoin Bobble Head.

130 **started attending Bitcoin conferences:** Kai Sedgwick, "How Dorian Nakamoto Became Satoshi Nakamoto," Bitcoin.com News, December 18, 2017.

131 **"I'da given my left nut":** @hettinga, Twitter, October 10, 2022.

131 **"the holy founder":** Gavin Andresen, deposition, February 26, 2020, KW.

131 **"unseemly ring of wide-eyed scribblers":** Andrea O'Sullivan, "Leave Satoshi Alone!," Reason, December 15, 2015.

131 **"Teach me your zen-like powers of apathy":** bn2b, comment on "Satoshi Nakamoto is (probably) Nick Szabo," Reddit, r/Bitcoin, 2014.

132 **"I wish Satoshi were still around":** @zooko, Twitter, June 14, 2017.

An Imperfect Human Being

133 **scoops about Wright's claims:** "Craig Wright Reveals Himself as Satoshi Nakamoto," *The Economist,* May 2, 2016.

133 **"Mr. Wright has provided technical proof":** "Creator of Bitcoin Digital Cash Reveals Identity," BBC News, May 2, 2016, WM.

133 **"How I Met Satoshi":** Jon Matonis, "How I Met Satoshi," Medium, May 2, 2016.

133 **"100 per cent convinced":** Andrew O'Hagan, "The Satoshi Affair," *London Review of Books,* June 30, 2016.

133 **"I believe Craig Steven Wright is the person":** "Satoshi," *Gavin Andresen* (blog), May 2, 2016.

Gavin's Favorite Number

My account of Gavin Andresen's proof session draws largely from a two-day deposition of Andresen, conducted in Hadley, MA, on February 26 and 27, 2020, as part of discovery in *Kleiman v. Wright*; from emails between participants; from my interview with Stefan Matthews; from my own experiments with the Electrum wallet; and from Andrew O'Hagan's "The Satoshi Affair," *London Review of Books,* June 30, 2016, an essential source of contemporaneous details.

135 **he could retire if he wanted:** Tom Simonite, "The Man Who Really Built Bitcoin," *MIT Technology Review,* August 15, 2014.

135 **he was jaded:** Gavin Andresen, deposition, February 26, 2020, KW.

135 **Jon Matonis had told Gavin:** Andresen, deposition, February 26, 2020, KW.

135 **a familiar ring:** Andresen, deposition, February 26, 2020, KW.

136 **Wright had already performed this proof:** Jon Matonis, "How I Met Satoshi," Medium, May 2, 2016.

136 **Before leaving for London:** Gavin Andresen, email to Craig Wright, April 6, 2016, Attachment 81 to Joint Notice of Filing Admitted Exhibits, December 16, 2021, KW.

136 **"He seemed like a person who was not poor":** Gavin Andresen, continued deposition, February 27, 2020, KW.

137 **"Andresen's body language changed":** O'Hagan, "Satoshi Affair."

137 **"Maybe you and I could get to know each other better":** O'Hagan, "Satoshi Affair."

137 **"you've just been alone for way too long":** O'Hagan, "Satoshi Affair."

137 **Wright phoned Ramona:** O'Hagan, "Satoshi Affair."

138 **IBM ThinkPad:** Judgment, *COPA v. Wright.*

138 **It then took some time:** Andresen, deposition, February 26, 2020, KW.

138 **his eyes teary:** Andresen, deposition, February 26, 2020, KW.

A Little Bit of Controversy for Fun

140 **"If I sign myself Jean-Paul Sartre":** "Sartre on the Nobel Prize" (translated by Richard Howard), *The New York Review of Books,* December 17, 1964.

140 **he recounted Sartre's principled refusal:** Craig Wright, "Jean-Paul Sartre, Signing and Significance," *Dr. Craig Wright* (blog), May 2, 2016.

141 **"incredibly technical and hard to follow":** Gavin Andresen, deposition, February 26, 2020, KW.

141 **the signature had been lifted:** JoukeH, "Creator of Bitcoin reveals identity," Reddit, r/Bitcoin, May 2, 2016.

141 **"like if I was trying to prove that I was George Washington":** Jordan Pearson and Lorenzo Franceschi-Bicchierai, "Craig Wright's New Evidence That He Is Satoshi Nakamoto Is Worthless," *Vice,* May 2, 2016, WM.

141 **Gavin explained why he was convinced:** "Gavin vs Vitalik," Jim channel, YouTube, May 2, 2016.

142 **"how Craig Wright's deception worked":** Robert Graham, "Satoshi: That's Not How Any of This Works," *Errata Security* (blog), May 2, 2016; Robert Graham, "Satoshi: How Craig Wright's Deception Worked," *Errata Security* (blog), May 3, 2016.

142 **"scammers always have more to say":** Dan Kaminsky, "The Cryptographically Provable Con Man," *Dan Kaminsky's Blog* (blog), May 3, 2016.

142 **Even Electrum:** @ElectrumWallet, Twitter, May 3, 2016.

142 **"Craig Wright really wants you to think":** Timothy B. Lee, "Craig Wright Really Wants You to Think He Invented Bitcoin. Don't Believe Him," *Vox,* May 2, 2016.

142 **"The Cryptographically Provable Con Man":** Kaminsky, "Cryptographically Provable Con Man."

142 **Once again, a media outlet:** David Gilbert, "Craig Wright Is Not Bitcoin Creator Satoshi Nakamoto, According to New Text Analysis," *International Business Times,* January 22, 2016.

142 **reassuring Gavin that he'd "f'd up":** Andresen, deposition, February 26, 2020, KW.

142 **"Today, pretty please":** Andresen, deposition, February 26, 2020, KW.

142 **soon make several corrections:** Andresen, deposition, February 26, 2020, KW.

143 **"verbal consent":** Andrew O'Hagan, "The Satoshi Affair," *London Review of Books,* June 30, 2016.

143 **"Extraordinary claims":** Craig Wright, "Extraordinary Claims Require Extraordinary Proof," *Dr. Craig Wright* (blog), May 3, 2016, WM.

Series of Screams

145 **"All stop. Craig has just tried to injure himself":** Gavin Andresen, deposition, February 26, 2020, KW.

145 **taking the latest developments "very, very seriously":** Rory Cellan-Jones, interview.

145 **Wright stayed in the hospital only one night:** Stefan Matthews, interview.

145 **he met a writer for coffee:** The writer was Andrew O'Hagan; O'Hagan, "The Satoshi Affair," *London Review of Books,* June 30, 2016.

145 **"UK Law Enforcement Sources Hint":** "Craig Wright faces criminal charges and serious jail time in UK after claiming to be Bitcoin's founder Satoshi Nakamoto," SiliconANGLE.com, May 3, 2016, WM.

145 **"they destroy me and my family":** O'Hagan, "Satoshi Affair."

145 **site had only recently been registered:** StealthyExcellent, "Response to 'Fragmentation of Truth: A story about Craig Wright's Sartre post,'" Reddit, r/bsv, December 18, 2023.

145 **"At no point did I lie to you":** Andresen, deposition, February 26, 2020, KW.

146 **"I'm sorry. I believed I could do this.":** Craig Wright, "I'm Sorry," *Dr. Craig Wright* (blog), May 5, 2016, WM.

More of a Risk Than a Boon

147 **Kaminsky privately wrote to him:** Dan Kaminsky, "The Cryptographically Provable Con Man," *Dan Kaminsky's Blog* (blog), May 3, 2016.

147 **"Yeah, what the heck?":** Kaminsky, "Cryptographically Provable Con Man."

147 **Emin Gün Sirer:** Emin Gün Sirer, "Logical Fallacies in the Hunt for Satoshi," *Hacking, Distributed* (blog), May 4, 2016.

147 **"possible I was tricked":** Sirer, "Logical Fallacies."

148 **Robert MacGregor believed:** Andrew O'Hagan, "The Satoshi Affair," *London Review of Books,* June 30, 2016.

148 **"I've never asked you for anything before.":** Jon Matonis, email to Gavin Andresen, March 14, 2016, quoted in Gavin Andresen, deposition, February 26, 2020, KW.

148 **"sounded like":** Andy Greenberg, "How Craig Wright Privately 'Proved' He Created Bitcoin," *Wired,* May 2, 2016.

148 **"matched his academic, math-heavy voice":** O'Hagan, "Satoshi Affair."

148 **the Bitcoin scaling wars:** these events are exhaustively recounted in Jonathan Bier, *The Blocksize War: The Battle for Control Over Bitcoin's Protocol Rules* (independently published, 2021).

148 **Some people thought Satoshi Nakamoto alone:** miragecash, "Satoshi Nakamoto PLEASE resolve this debate? 1MB blockstream vs 8MB Gavin Blocks," BF, August 30, 2015.

148 **the guy in a suit sipping oatmeal stout:** Tom Simonite, "The Man Who Really Built Bitcoin," *MIT Technology Review,* August 15, 2014.

148 **his ego had run amok:** Bailey Reutzel, "Where Is Gavin Andresen? The Quiet Exile of Bitcoin's Former Face," CoinDesk, May 19, 2017.

148 **"I may just have to throw my weight around":** Reutzel, "Where Is Gavin Andresen?"

148 **core developers had temporarily revoked his access:** @peterktodd, Twitter, May 2, 2016.

148 **they made the change permanent:** Wladimir J. van der Laan, "Dazed and confused, but trying to continue," *Laanwj's blog* (blog), May 6, 2016.

149 **Some people felt the developers:** supermari0, comment on "Gavin's commit access 'unlikely to be restored,'" Reddit, r/Bitcoin, May 3, 2016.

149 **he'd happily return the project's alert key to him:** van der Laan, "Dazed and confused."

149 **"untrustworthy and/or incompetent":** @peterktodd, Twitter, May 2, 2016.

149 **"He had become":** Reutzel, "Where Is Gavin Andresen?"

Scott and Stuart

151 **waited nearly twenty years:** Henry Petroski, *Invention by Design* (Cambridge, MA: Harvard University Press, 1996), 10-11.

151 **customary for scientists to keep bound laboratory notebooks:** "Lab notebooks – handwriting at the core of science," British Library (Science blog), January 23, 2019.

151 **She had been accused of scientific misconduct:** Warren E. Leary, "Lab Notes Are False, Secret Service Says," *The New York Times,* May 15, 1990.

152 **Imanishi-Kari was later fully exonerated:** "Imanishi-Kari case ends, but debate on scientific conduct continues," MIT News, July 24, 1996.

154 **Stuart sent an announcement:** Stuart Haber, "Surety Technologies announces: Digital Notary System is on-line," CP, January 19, 1995.

154 **Tim May touted the importance of their work:** Timothy C. May, "Cyphernomicon: Cypherpunks FAQ and More," Nakamoto Institute, September 10, 1994.

155 **the term *timechain*:** Cryddit (Ray Dillinger), "Bitcoin source from November 2008," BF, December 23, 2013.

155 **the same pair:** "Why Use AbsoluteProof From Surety?," Surety.com.

155 **Nakamoto's academic-ish schedule:** In Search of Satoshi, "The Time Zones of Satoshi Nakamoto," Medium, February 13, 2018.

156 **they'd appeared with him onstage:** Nidhi Arora, "Blockchain technology will boom like Internet: Scott Stornetta talks to CoinGeek backstage," CoinGeek, November 11, 2021.

"Do You Have a Salad Spinner?"

157 **one of the more well-considered theories to date:** Evan Hatch, "Len Sassaman and Satoshi," Medium, February 21, 2021.

158 **worked on his PhD:** Len Sassaman website.

158 **"The Pynchon Gate":** Len Sassaman, Bram Cohen, and Nick Mathewson, "The Pynchon Gate: A Secure Method of Pseudonymous Email Retrieval," WPES '05: Proceedings of the 2005 ACM workshop on Privacy in the electronic society, November 2005.

158 **He maintained the Mixmaster remailer:** Mixmaster, mixmaster.sourceforge .net.

158 **hanged himself at age thirty-one:** Adrianne Jeffries, "Cracking suicide: hackers try to engineer a cure for depression," The Verge, August 14, 2013.

158 **"permanently encrypted":** @wikileaks, Twitter, July 5, 2011.

158 **The available evidence suggests:** Robert McMillan, "Someone's Threatening to Expose Bitcoin Founder Satoshi Nakamoto," *Wired*, September 8, 2014; theymos, "satoshin@gmx.com is compromised," BF, September 8, 2014.

159 **Evan ultimately self-published his theory:** "New Theory Claims Cryptographer Len Sassaman Is Bitcoin Creator Satoshi Nakamoto," The Daily Hodl, March 7, 2021.

159 **a discovery by Jens Ducrée:** Jens Ducrée, *Satoshi Nakamoto and the Origins of Bitcoin: The Greatest Mystery in the Entire History of Science and Technology*, published by Ducrée, June 17, 2023.

159 **the printed proceedings of the conference were available:** Canadian National Science Library; British Library.

159 **An Estonian academic's online list of time-stamping resources:** Helger Lipmaa, "Digital Time-Stamping," Laboratory for Theoretical Computer Science, Helsinki University of Technology, February 7, 2005, WM.

159 **an archived copy of Nick Szabo's old webpage:** Nick Szabo, "Nick Szabo's Essays, Papers, and Concise Tutorials," 2004, WM.

160 **"One candidate literally matches every single detail":** Barely Sociable, "Bitcoin—Unmasking Satoshi Nakamoto," YouTube, May 11, 2020.

161 **"I am not Satoshi":** @adam3us, Twitter, May 11, 2020.

Anything Is a Legitimate Area of Investigation

162 **a follow-up post:** Skye Grey, "Occam's Razor: Who Is Most Likely," *LikeInAMirror* (blog), March 11, 2014.

163 **a "crazy coincidence":** Felix Salmon, "The Satoshi Paradox," Reuters, March 25, 2014, WM.

163 **something of a coding nut:** Brian Heater, "Rockstar Programmer: Rivers Cuomo Finds Meaning in Coding," TechCrunch, November 25, 2020.

166 **the sixty thousand words Satoshi Nakamoto had left behind:** This would later be augmented by Martti Malmi's release of his emails with Nakamoto, which added another twenty thousand words or so to Nakamoto's publicly accessible texts.

166 **"The creator of bitcoin is Travis Hassloch":** Dimitrios4615, comment on "Man who claims he created bitcoin committed perjury, lawsuit says," Ars OpenForum, May 15, 2018.

DJ Sun Love

168 **deadbeat-dad accusations:** Michael Lavere, "German DJ Faces Backlash After Claiming to Be Satoshi Nakamoto," CryptoGlobe, November 4, 2019.

168 **Bitcoin's "cofounder":** Graham Smith, "Satoshi 'Nakamolto' Emerges with Great Hair and Questionable Claims," Bitcoin.com, November 3, 2019.

168 **later arrested:** Jamie Redman, "Self-Proclaimed Bitcoin Inventor Jörg Molt Arrested for Alleged Crypto Pension Fraud," Bitcoin.com, July 14, 2021.

168 **as he prepared to board a flight to Mexico:** Nicolás Antiporovich, "Autoproclomado creador de bitcoin es arrestado por presunto fraude," CryptoNoticias, July 16, 2021.

168 **"Satoshi Nakamoto, the genuine one":** Jurgen Etienne Guido Debo, "I am, the genuine 'Satoshi Nakamoto,'" website "Satoshi Nakamoto," 2019.

168 **presenting backdated PGP keys as real ones:** Jamie Redman, "Another Self-Proclaimed Satoshi Appears in the High Profile Bitcoin Lawsuit," Bitcoin .com News, July 24, 2019.

168 **"Bitcoin Origins":** Jamie Redman, "New Satoshi Challenger Tells All—But Is He Legit?," Bitcoin.com, September 2, 2018.

168 **Alas, he had "obliterat[ed]":** Phil "Scronty" Wilson, "Bitcoin Origins," https://vu.hn.

168 **"I Ronald Keala Kua Maria":** "Bitcoin Cash Copyright Notice."

169 **nakamotofamilyfoundation.org:** The site is inactive but is archived at Nakamoto Family Foundation, WM.

169 **Bloomberg, amazingly, reprinted:** "Key Passages from Satoshi Nakamoto Excerpt on Bitcoin Beginnings," Bloomberg News, June 30, 2018.

169 **deeply interested in numerology:** As told to Ivy McLemore, "My Reveal," August 18, 2019.

169 **"I am the Godfather of digital cash":** Sean Keach, "COIN ARTIST: Bitcoin Founder Mystery Deepens as 'British NHS Worker' Claims to Have Invented It—but 'Lost Hard Drive Containing GBP8.1BILLION Early Coins,'" *The Sun* (UK), August 21, 2019.

169 **"a hard-drive accident":** "Satoshi Nakamoto the Creator of Bitcoin," YouTube, October 31, 2019.

169 **to a "hack":** Samuel Town, "Pakistani man claims to be real Bitcoin creator," ACS Information Age, August 27, 2019.

169 **accused Craig Wright of impersonating him:** Jamie Redman, "Another Self-Proclaimed Satoshi Appears in the High Profile Bitcoin Lawsuit," Bitcoin .com, July 24, 2019.

169 **"What a stupid thing to say!":** Ivy McLemore, *Finding Satoshi: The Real Story Behind Mysterious Bitcoin Creator Satoshi Nakamoto* (Kemah, TX: Ivy McLemore and Associates, 2022), 168.

169 **was a "Scam-toshi":** Redman, "New Satoshi Challenger Tells All."

169 **"cannot get dates nor technical details correct":** Stan Schroeder, "'Satoshi Nakamoto' Says He's Writing a Book, but Is It Really Him?," Mashable, July 2, 2018.

169 **close to thirty thousand of Silk Road's seized bitcoins:** Gertrude Chavez-Dreyfuss, "Venture capitalist Draper wins U.S. bitcoin auction," Reuters, July 2, 2014.

Obviousness Fatigue

171 **"I am sorry for last year":** Craig Wright, email to Gavin Andresen, May 3, 2017, Attachment 89 to Joint Notice of Filing Admitted Exhibits, December 16, 2021, KW.

171 **"either he was or he wasn't":** Gavin Andresen, "Either/or: ignore!," *Gavin Andresen* (blog), November 16, 2016.

171 **"well-compensated" for the work:** Gavin Andresen, deposition, continued, February 27, 2020, KW.

171 **"took a lot of heat and abuse":** Gavin Andresen, deposition, February 26, 2020, KW.

171 **"Don't worry about me":** Gavin Andresen, email to Craig Wright, May 3, 2017, Attachment 89 to Joint Notice of Filing Admitted Exhibits, December 16, 2021, KW.

171 **"I'll be happy to listen":** Andresen, deposition, February 26, 2020, KW.

171 **series of friendly interviews with CoinGeek:** Eli Afram, "Craig Wright Interview Part 1 – An Introduction," CoinGeek, June 12, 2017; Afram, "Craig Wright Interview Part 2 – Project Work," CoinGeek, June 15, 2017; Afram, "Craig Wright Interview Part 3 – Academic Record Truths," CoinGeek, June 21, 2017.

172 **exactly a year after:** "nChain Appoints Vice President of Corporate Strategy," Hedgeweek, May 2, 2017.

172 **"Mr. Bitcoin Dundee":** Future of Bitcoin Conference, Arnhem, Netherlands, June 30, 2017.

172 **He next spoke at a gaming conference:** iGaming Super Show, Amsterdam, Netherlands, July 13, 2017.

172 **an assistant stepped from the wings:** Bitcoin Association Switzerland meetup, Zurich, November 30, 2017.

172 **"Why is this fraud allowed to speak":** Deconomy conference, Seoul, South Korea, April 3, 2018.

172 **By then, it had been revealed:** Andrew O'Hagan, "The Satoshi Affair," *London Review of Books*, June 30, 2016; Stuart McGurk, "Bitcoin: inside the £8bn swindle," British GQ, September 13, 2016.

172 **which had recently concluded an audit:** Australian Taxation Office, letter to Andrew Sommer, June 22, 2015, Attachment 6 to Plaintiffs' Response in Opposition to Defendant's Omnibus Motion in Limine, June 1, 2020, KW.

173 **they paid $15 million:** O'Hagan, "Satoshi Affair."

173 **also retained a lauded Scottish novelist:** O'Hagan, "Satoshi Affair."

173 **a man referred to in internal emails only as "c":** E.g., emails between Craig Wright and Calvin Ayre, June 2015, Attachment 58 to Joint Notice of Filing Admitted Exhibits, December 16, 2021, KW.

173 **he seemed neither to have asked questions:** Gavin Andresen, deposition, February 26, 2020.

173 **Wright had undergone three media-training sessions:** Nick Caley, email to Craig Wright et al., Attachment 4 to Plaintiffs' Opposing Statement of Material Facts, June 1, 2020, KW; and, e.g., Attachment 13 to Plaintiffs' Opposing Statement of Material Facts, June 1, 2020, KW.

173 **"fuck off":** Stuart McGurk, "Bitcoin: Inside the £8bn Swindle," British GQ, September 13, 2016.

173 **emails showing otherwise:** @ruskin147, Twitter, July 3, 2022.

174 **Bitcoinland was still having its civil war:** See, e.g., Jonathan Bier, *The Blocksize War: The Battle for Control Over Bitcoin's Protocol Rules* (independently published, 2021).

175 **"code-is-law movement" . . . "a pernicious attack on freedom":** Craig Wright, "Proof," Medium, March 13, 2019.

175 **"an idea that is miasmic":** Wright, "Proof."

175 **"I've got more money than your country":** Transform Africa summit, Kigali, Rwanda, May 9, 2018.

175 **He boasted about having:** Brendan Sullivan, "Craig Wright goes 'full billionaire mode' and doesn't care what you think," Modern Consensus, November 4, 2018; and Onose Enaholo, "Did Craig Wright Lie About His Yacht?," CoinJournal, January 26, 2023.

175 **"a late-stage cancer":** Craig Wright, "The Fury," Medium, December 10, 2018.

175 **"agent of influence":** Craig Wright, "The Story of Bitcoin, Continued," Medium, February 9, 2019.

175 **"shed in Bagnoo":** Craig Wright, "Two Steps Forward, One Step Back," *Dr. Craig Wright* (blog), April 6, 2019.

176 **"Is Craig Wright a fraud?":** @DanDarkPill, Twitter, March 17, 2019, WM.

176 **"serial fabricator":** @WikiLeaks, Twitter, December 12, 2019.

176 **"repeatedly caught":** @WikiLeaks, Twitter, December 12, 2019.

176 **the Lightning Torch:** Colin Harper, "Lightning Torch's Bitcoin Payment Is Running a Worldwide Marathon," *Bitcoin Magazine,* February 5, 2019.

176 **"a very sad and pathetic scammer":** This and other Hodlonaut tweets are recorded in Judge Helen Engebrigtsen's verdict in *Granath v. Wright,* Oslo District Court, October 20, 2022.

177 **"Magnus . . . I have a way out of your problem.":** @calvinayre, Twitter, April 12, 2019.

177 **"Magnus last offer.":** @calvinayre, Twitter, May 2, 2019.

177 **Wright was offering $5,000:** Bill Beatty, "Dr. Craig S. Wright Targets Crypto Troll Hodlonaut for Defamatory Internet Posts," CoinGeek, April 11, 2019, WM.

178 **from a "crypto troll" to "a childless alcoholic":** Testimony of Magnus Granath, *Granath v. Wright,* Oslo District Court, September 14, 2022.
178 **"a cockwombling, bunglecunt Faketoshi":** BTCShadow, "Faketoshi," UrbanDictionary.com, April 13, 2019.
178 **"Craig and I polishing our muskets.":** @calvinayre, Twitter, April 10, 2019.
178 **"Craig Wright is not Satoshi! When do I get sued?":** @petermccormack, Twitter, April 10, 2019, recorded in Judgment, *Wright v. McCormack,* High Court of Justice (U.K.), Queen's Bench Division, Media and Communications List, August 1, 2022.
178 **Changpeng Zhao retweeted:** @cz_binance, Twitter, April 12, 2019.
178 **one had obtained Wright's military records:** Jameson Lopp, "OP ED: How Many Wrongs Make a Wright," *Bitcoin Magazine,* April 18, 2019.
178 **DebunkingFaketoshi:** @jimmy007forsure, Twitter, June 25, 2019.
178 **exhaustive chronicles of Wright's lies:** See the articles at MyLegacyKit, Medium.
178 **He sued C0bra:** Approved Judgment, *Wright v. C0bra,* High Court of Justice, Business and Property Courts of England and Wales, Intellectual Property List, June 28, 2021, WM.
178 **"a fraud" and "a liar":** Helen Partz, "Craig Wright Files Another Libel Suit Against Roger Ver After 2019 Fail," Cointelegraph, August 31, 2020.
179 **"misrepresenting" that BTC:** "Bitcoin Creator Launches IP Claims Against Digital Currency Exchanges," Ontier, press release, May 3, 2022.
179 **He sued sixteen Bitcoin developers:** Particulars of Claim, *Tulip Trading Limited v. Bitcoin Association for BSV, et al.,* High Court of Justice, Business and Property Courts of England and Wales, Business List, April 29, 2021.
179 **The Cryptocurrency Open Patent Alliance . . . sued Wright:** Particulars of Claim, *Crypto Open Patent Alliance v. Craig Steven Wright,* High Court of Justice, Business and Property Courts of England and Wales, Chancery Division, Intellectual Property List, April 12, 2021.

Freedom of Information

180 **"a really, really smart, forward-leaning agent":** "Regulating Cryptocurrencies & ICOs: Security, Commodity, or Currency?," OffshoreAlert channel, YouTube, May 24, 2019.
181 **a man making international sales of ricin and other toxins:** "Florida man who produced and sold deadly ricin gets prison," AP News, February 18, 2015.

Negative Space

183 **an "overhyped" thing:** @lensassaman, Twitter, March 22, 2011.
183 **"fails as a cypherpunk protocol":** @lensassaman, Twitter, June 5, 2011.
183 **"suffers from the worst of both worlds":** @lensassaman, Twitter, June 15, 2011.
184 **"win-32's 16-bit wchar":** Satoshi Nakamoto, "Re: A few suggestions," BF, December 14, 2009.
186 **Chris had titled:** Chris Buck, *Presence: The Invisible Portrait* (Heidelberg: Kehrer Verlag, 2012).

186 **"hundreds of thousands of bitcoins":** Complaint and Jury Demand, February 14, 2018, KW.

187 **"Bitcoin's Trial of the Century":** Cheyenne Ligon, "Kleiman v Wright: Bitcoin's Trial of the Century Kicks Off in Miami," CoinDesk, November 1, 2021.

187 **"Bitcoin Creator Satoshi Nakamoto":** Paul Vigna, "Bitcoin Creator Satoshi Nakamoto Could Be Unmasked at Florida Trial," *The Wall Street Journal*, November 13, 2021.

187 **"We are here today in this courtroom":** Transcript of Trial Day 1, November 1, 2021, KW.

187 **more than two hundred thousand documents:** Order, U.S. District Judge Beth Bloom, April 13, 2020, KW.

187 **1.9 million pages:** Order, U.S. District Judge Beth Bloom, June 24, 2020, KW.

187 **turned down all of W&K's research proposals:** Department of Homeland Security, letter to Kyle Roche (responding to Roche's FOIA request), March 22, 2018, Attachment 21 to Second Amended Complaint and Jury Demand, January 14, 2019, KW.

187 **he hadn't yet released the app:** Examination Before Trial of Jonathan Warren, July 24, 2019, KW.

187 **fonts that didn't exist on the creation dates:** Transcript of Evidentiary Hearing Proceedings, June 28, 2019, KW.

187 **he threw a piece of paper at Freedman:** Vel Freedman, interview.

187 **prompting the judge to threaten:** Transcript of Evidentiary Hearing Proceedings, June 28, 2019, KW.

187 **Wright's own lawyers:** Testimony of Dr. Ami Klin, Transcript of Trial Day 13, AM Session, November 19, 2021, KW.

187 **testified under oath that he had no involvement with W&K:** Affidavit of Craig Wright, attached to Motion to Dismiss for Failure to State a Claim, April 16, 2018, KW.

187 **Kleiman's lawyers surprised him with Australian court documents:** Attachments 4, 5, 11, and 19 to Amended Complaint and Jury Demand, May 14, 2019, KW.

187 **"I've got to be the man":** Deposition of Jamie R. Wilson, November 8, 2019, KW.

187 **"Dave intended to end his own life":** Dr. Craig Wright's Opposition to Plaintiffs' Omnibus Motion in Limine, May 22, 2020, KW.

188 **"possibility that Wright had David murdered":** Plaintiffs' Reply in Support of Their Omnibus Motion in Limine, June 2, 2020, KW.

188 **jury found Wright liable for conversion:** Blake Brittain, "Verdict Against Self-Proclaimed Bitcoin Inventor Balloons to $143 Mln," Reuters, March 10, 2022.

188 **He told the ATO:** Arthur van Pelt, "Craig Wright's Tulip Trust List Forgery—A Full History," *MyLegacyKit*, Medium, December 21, 2022.

188 **"facially incredible":** Transcript of Telephonic Motion Hearing, May 6, 2019, KW.

188 **"a bonded courier":** Transcript of Evidentiary Hearing Proceedings, June 28, 2019, KW.

188 **the courier was a lawyer for the Tulip Trust:** Hearing Transcribed from Digital Audio Recording Before the Honorable Bruce E. Reinhart, March 5, 2020, KW.

188 **questioned whether he even existed:** Order on Discovery, March 9, 2020, KW.
188 **a ruinous hack:** Jordan Atkins, "Dr. Craig Wright Stolen Bitcoin: Here's What Went Down," CoinGeek, May 14, 2021; Jon Southurst, "Craig Wright Hack Could See Bitcoin Rights Settled in Court," CoinGeek, June 15, 2020, WM.
188 **called a pineapple:** Arthur van Pelt, "'Your Honor, The Dog Ate My Homework!,'" *MyLegacyKit*, Medium, June 23, 2022.
189 **"very frail":** Australian Taxation Office, "Reasons for Decision" for C01n Pty Ltd, March 11, 2016, Attachment 7 to Plaintiffs' Response in Opposition to Defendant's Omnibus Motion in Limine, June 1, 2020, KW.
189 **"full of academic wankery":** Transcript of Trial Day 9, November 15, 2021, KW.
189 **"I exaggerated Dave's role":** Transcript of Trial Day 7, November 9, 2021, KW.
189 **the Second Man switched from Kleiman to Wright's uncle:** Dr. Craig Wright, deposition, March 16, 2020, KW.
189 **"That is one name he used.":** Wright, deposition, March 16, 2020, KW.
189 **Escapologists had tried more than four hundred times:** Josh Halliday, "MI6 Spy Found Dead in Bag Probably Locked Himself Inside, Met Says," *The Guardian,* November 13, 2013.
190 **"were you a super spy":** Wright, deposition, March 16, 2020, KW.
190 **national security issues were at stake:** Dr. Craig Wright, deposition, April 4, 2019, KW.
190 **a sealed court filing that was later unsealed:** Dr. Craig Wright's Motion for Protective Order, Filed Under Seal, April 18, 2019, KW.
190 **LeRoux's biographer:** Evan Ratliff, "Was Bitcoin Created by This International Drug Dealer? Maybe!," *Wired,* July 16, 2019.

Eat Sleep Hodl Repeat

192 **had given an interview to a Norwegian newspaper:** Magnus Newth, "'Trist og patetisk taper,' sa Røkkes tidligere bitcoin-guru om mannen som hevder han oppfant bitcoin. Så begynte jakten på hans identitet," *DNHelg,* September 9, 2022.
192 **"who needs objectivity":** @Silvercoinfox, Twitter, September 11, 2022.
192 **Norbert live-tweeted the trial:** @bitnorbert, Twitter, September 12, 2022.
193 **thirty-seven thousand tweets:** Fran Velasquez, "Pseudonymous Hodlonaut 'Very Confident' as Craig Wright Defamation Case Nears," CoinDesk, August 25, 2022.
193 **227-page forensic report by KPMG:** "Rapport: Bistand til datateknisk analyse ifm. rettstvist," KPMG, December 13, 2021, submitted in *Granath v. Wright,* Oslo District Court.
195 **15 million Norwegian krone:** Testimony of Magnus Granath, *Granath v. Wright,* Oslo District Court, September 14, 2022.
195 **2,600 contributors:** Testimony of Magnus Granath, *Granath v. Wright,* September 14, 2022.
196 **"I think" . . . "side of Craig":** Kurt Wuckert, Jr., "Satoshi Trial Norway Day 2: Craig Wright's defense | Granath "Hodlonaut" vs Wright | Livestream," CoinGeek channel, YouTube, September 13, 2022.

197 **talked about *Citadel21*:** https://www.citadel21.com.
199 **"proving ceremony" . . . "bamboozled" . . . "gobbledygook":** Gavin Andresen, deposition, February 26, 2020, KW.
199 **"paranoia":** Andresen, deposition, February 26, 2020, KW.

Alistair

201 **World War I military slang:** "'Hosed' Etymology—When Did This Phrase Come into Use?," Ask MetaFilter, May 17, 2013.
201 **"drinking water from a firehose":** "Hosed."
201 **who'd written about digital cash for the 'zine *Extropy*:** Mark Grant, "Introduction to Digital Cash," *Extropy* 7, no. 2, issue 15, 2nd–3rd Quarter 1995.
202 **Twice it was by the same person:** James A. Donald, "Phishers Defeat 2-Factor Auth," CR, July 11, 2006; James Donald, "Why self describing data formats," CR, June 11, 2007.
202 **first person on the list to respond to Nakamoto:** James A. Donald, "Bitcoin P2P e-cash paper," CR, November 2, 2008.
202 **"Definitive Proof":** Phinnaeus Gage, "Definitive Proof That Satoshi Nakamoto is James A. Donald," BF, May 28, 2014.
203 **declared that he was Canadian:** Gerald Votta, "I Know Who Satoshi Nakamoto Is," Medium, November 16, 2021.
203 **that he had died:** Matthew Cornelisse, answer to "Is Satoshi Nakamoto from heaven?," Quora, 2022.
203 **that "James A. Donald" wasn't his real name:** Richard_Kennaway, comment on "Rationality Quotes April 2014," *LessWrong* (blog), April 7, 2014; Jamie Redman, "Celebrating the Seminal Bitcoin White Paper Satoshi Nakamoto Published 13 Years Ago Today," Bitcoin.com, October 31, 2021.
203 **a British sleuth had described in vague terms:** "Who Is Satoshi Nakamoto—A Deep Dive Into the Creator of Bitcoin," Payment Coin (Pod).
203 **word Nakamoto had used once:** Satoshi Nakamoto, "Bitcoin P2P e-cash paper," CR, November 16, 2008.
203 **it appeared in a post by Donald:** James Donald, "RE: GPL & commercial software, the critical distinction (fwd)," CP, October 4, 1998.
203 **the sites linguists use to assess a word's rarity:** Corpus of Contemporary American English; Corpus of Global Web-Based English; News on the Web.
204 **in a quote about retail theft:** Tim O'Connell, "Tobacco Price Rises Cut Smoking but Some Pay More Than $40 a Packet," Stuff, January 27, 2017.
204 **He was Australian:** Tim Starr, Bob Hewitt, and Brian Martin, interviews.
204 **had lived in Silicon Valley for many years:** James Donald, comment on his post "Cathedral Imperialism Revealed," *Jim's Blog* (blog), February 8, 2014.
204 **"So guys, that is the plan":** James Donald, "Why does the state still stand," CP, May 12, 1996.
204 **"Eventually people will bypass the banks":** James Donald, "Re: Bank Fees and E-Cash," CP, August 12, 1995.
204 **"That is the big remaining battle.":** James Donald, "Re: Cypherpunks defeat?," CP, September 28, 1998.
204 **he also registered the domain Netcoin.com:** This had been discovered by Or Weinberger; @orweinberger, Twitter, September 23, 2022.

205 **he'd promoted a piece of communications encryption software:** James Donald, "Announcing Crypto Kong, Release Candidate Two," CP, January 8, 1998.

205 **I found an archived copy of the source code:** WM, https://web.archive.org/web/20020529104724/www.echeque.com/KONG/install.htm.

205 **"a lot of time off the grid":** James Donald, comment on his post "And Another One Bites the Dust," *Jim's Blog* (blog), August 25, 2018.

206 **"Not only should you disagree with others":** Nick Szabo, "More Short Takes," *Unenumerated* (blog), July 1, 2012.

206 **"a prototype that is prematurely being used":** James Donald, "Where We Go from Here," *Jim's Blog* (blog), January 23, 2021.

206 **"The bailout will fail.":** James Donald, "The cause of the crisis," *Jim's Blog* (blog), October 11, 2008.

206 **the London *Times* headline:** "Genesis block," Bitcoin Wiki.

206 **"the degeneration of Britain":** James Donald, "The degeneration of Britain," *Jim's Blog* (blog), February 25, 2009, WM.

206 **"a long and terrible illness":** James Donald, "What People Really Mean When They Say There Is a Lot of Rape," *Jim's Blog* (blog), June 17, 2016.

207 **"Satoshi's identity doesn't matter":** Ray Dillinger, comment, September 26, 2021, on "I Am Not Satoshi Nakamoto," Schneier on Security, September 24, 2021.

207 **a radical leftist:** James Donald, "Confessions of an ex commie," Jim's Liberty File Collection.

208 **a symbol of resistance to "oppression by the state":** James Donald, "Crypto Kong," WM.

209 **cowrote the paper:** J. A. Donald and B. Martin, "Time-Symmetric Thermodynamics and Causality Violation," *European Journal of Parapsychology* 1 (1975): 17–36.

209 **"one of those rare individuals":** Brian Martin, "Psychic Origins in the Future," *Parapsychology Review* 14, no. 3 (May–June 1983): 1–7.

209 **ended up dropping out:** James Alistair Donald, "Assumptions of the Singularity Theorems and the Rejuvenation of Universes," James Alistair Donald, *Annals of Physics* 110, no. 2 (February 1978): 251–73.

209 **"Sandy's Word Processor":** Kyle R. Ratinac, ed., *50 Great Moments: Celebrating the Golden Jubilee of the University of Sydney's Electron Microscope Unit* (Sydney: Sydney University Press, 2008), 229.

209 **a fast-disk operating system:** *NZ Bits and Bytes,* November 1984, no. 3-03.

209 **programmed videogames for Epyx:** James Donald, comment on his post "#gamergate," *Jim's Blog* (blog), September 21, 2014.

209 **database companies including Informix:** James Donald, "RE: GPL & commercial software, the critical distinction (fwd)," CP, October 4, 1998.

209 **"to database people it means":** Satoshi Nakamoto, email to Hal Finney, January 13, 2009 (published with Paul Vigna, "Hal Finney and Bitcoin's Earliest Days," *The Wall Street Journal,* August 29, 2014).

209 **"Institutional momentum is to stick with the last decision.":** Satoshi Nakamoto, "Re: They want to delete the Wikipedia article," BF, July 20, 2010.

209 **Donald had been a Wikipedia contributor.:** "User: James A. Donald," Wikipedia.

210 **"I know who Nakamoto was":** James Donald, comment, August 17, 2023,

on his post "Enormous Move in Bitcoin Coming Up," *Jim's Blog* (blog), June 29, 2023.

210 **internet ideology called neoreaction:** Rosie Gray, "Behind the Internet's Anti-Democracy Movement," *The Atlantic,* February 10, 2017.

210 **what they called the Cathedral:** Curtis Yarvin, "A brief explanation of the cathedral," Gray Mirror, January 21, 2021.

210 **attributed the covid pandemic to a Jesuit conspiracy:** James Donald, "Covid 19 and the Faith," *Jim's Blog* (blog), February 28, 2023.

210 **the extropians listserv had kicked him out:** Harry Shapiro, "Meta: Judgement," EX, November 11, 1993.

210 **In 2014, *Slate Star Codex*:** Scott Alexander, comment on "Typical Mind and Disbelief in Straight People," *Slate Star Codex* (blog), March 20, 2014.

210 **"whipping a woman on the buttocks":** James Donald, "The Cervix and Rape," *Jim's Blog* (blog), November 3, 2015.

210 **"very few rape accusations are true":** Donald, "What People Really Mean."

210 **"The problem is young girls":** James Donald, comment, August 26, 2020, on his post "The Three Magic Words," *Jim's Blog* (blog), August 7, 2020.

212 **"let's not elevate him to sainthood just yet":** @bergealex4, Twitter, June 12, 2020.

212 **"Nuke the nym from orbit":** @adam3us, Twitter, June 13, 2020.

212 **raging about election fraud and Black Lives Matter:** @NickSzabo4, Twitter, November 5 and December 18, 2020.

212 **"The decline of Nick Szabo":** @VitalikButerin, Twitter, August 6, 2020.

212 **lived alone with his cat—Nietzsche:** Andy Greenberg, *This Machine Kills Secrets: Julian Assange, the Cypherpunks, and Their Fight to Empower Whistleblowers* (New York: Plume, 2013), 56, 58, 82.

212 **and a large gun collection:** Lucky Green, remembrance, Facebook, December 15, 2018.

212 **in the foothills of the Santa Cruz Mountains:** Nathaniel Popper, "Timothy C. May, Early Advocate of Internet Privacy, Dies at 66," *The New York Times,* December 21, 2018.

212 **"need a trip up the chimneys":** Tim May, "Commie Rag praises MLK," scruz.general, Google Groups, 2005.

212 **conspiracy theories about the CIA:** May, "Commie Rag praises MLK."

212 **online reviews of local taquerias:** E.g., his review of "Los Perricos" on TripAdvisor, by tcmaycorralitos.

212 **drank himself to death:** Autopsy report for Timothy C. May, December 19, 2018, Sheriff-Coroner, County of Santa Cruz, CA.

213 **an obituary for "Satoshi Nakamoto," a veteran of World War II:** Obituary for Satoshi "Johnny" Nakamoto, *The Honolulu Advertiser,* June 19, 2008.

214 **"Unfortunately, I can't receive incoming connections":** Satoshi Nakamoto, email to Hal Finney, January 12, 2009 (published with Paul Vigna, "Hal Finney and Bitcoin's Earliest Days," *The Wall Street Journal,* August 29, 2014).

214 **a recognizable range of emotion:** "many thanks" ("Bitcoin 0.2 released," [bitcoin-list], December 17, 2009); "poor thing" ("Faster initial block download [5x faster]," BitcoinTalk, July 23, 2010); "my apologies" ("Re: Development of alert system," BitcoinTalk, August 26, 2010); "I'm better

with code than with words" ("Bitcoin P2P e-cash paper," CR, November 14, 2008).

Meh

215 **which he'd proposed in 1999:** Ben Laurie, Lucre license, 1999.

216 **a vocal critic of proof of work:** Ben Laurie and Richard Clayton, "'Proof-of-Work' Proves Not to Work," Third Annual Workshop on Economics and Information Security, 2004.

216 **"Bitcoin. Meh.":** @BenLaurie, Twitter, May 17, 2011.

216 **"A friend of mine alerted me":** Ben Laurie, "Bitcoin," Links, May 17, 2011, WM.

216 **and a follow-up:** Ben Laurie, "Bitcoin 2," Links, May 20, 2011, WM.

216 **Later, Ben elaborated on his critique:** Ben Laurie, "An Efficient and Practical Distributed Currency," Links, July 23, 2011, WM.

217 **Satoshi Nakamoto had warned about the danger of a so-called 51 percent attack:** Satoshi Nakamoto, "Bitcoin: A Peer-to-Peer Electronic Cash System," section 6, Bitcoin.org.

Brian

219 **"scary" person:** James Donald, "Hitting Your Woman with a Stick," *Jim's Blog* (blog), September 17, 2016.

219 **with guns:** James Donald, comment on his post "The End of Gold," *Jim's Blog* (blog), November 20, 2021.

219 **"Is it possible that you are, in fact, Satoshi Nakamoto?":** Lex Fridman, "#192—Charles Hoskinson: Cardano," *Lex Fridman Podcast,* June 16, 2021.

219 **"a lovely paper":** Aylin Caliskan-Islam et al., "De-anonymizing Programmers via Code Stylometry," in *Proceedings of the 24th USENIX Security Symposium, August 12–14, 2015* (USENIX Association, 2015), 255–70.

220 **An Iranian programmer:** Saeed Kamali Dehghan, "Iran confirms death sentence for 'porn site' web programmer," *The Guardian,* January 18, 2012.

220 **I was able to find samples:** Those I sent to Brian Timmerman, besides Satoshi Nakamoto (bitcoin-nov-08), were Adam Back (hashcash), Pr0duct Cypher (pgptools), Wei Dai (crypto++), James A. Donald (kong), Hal Finney (rpow), Mark Grant (privtool), Ben Laurie (lucre), Paul LeRoux (e4m), Bram Cohen/Zooko Wilcox/Greg Smith (mojo nation), Colin Plumb (bignum), and Len Sassaman (mixmaster). The authorship of mixmaster is ambiguous, because it was originally coded by Lance Cottrell, but Len Sassaman became its lead maintainer.

222 ***adult site*:** Satoshi Nakamoto, "Bitcoin v0.1 released," CR, January 16, 2009.

223 **written a cult book:** Peter Laurie, *Beneath the City Streets: The Secret Plans to Defend the State* (London: Allen Lane, 1970).

223 **a secure-internet-hosting business called the Bunker:** "Top British Firms Retreat into Bunker to Ward Off Anarchists," *New Zealand Herald,* June 10, 2001.

223 **nine-ton blast doors:** Alex Miller, "The Bunker: Keeping it safe," AccountancyAge, January 4, 2002.

223 **published a revision of his Lucre white paper:** Ben Laurie, "Lucre: Anonymous Electronic Tokens v1.8," October 30, 2008.

223 **"There is no limit to what a man can do":** E.g., Ben Laurie, "Re: [dix] on the dix: URI scheme for DIX/SXIP," uri@w3.org mailing list, March 18, 2006.

224 **"My grandfather once told me":** E.g., Ben Laurie, "Re: STANDARD20_MODULE_STUFF," dev@httpd.apache.org mailing list, September 7, 1999.

224 **"Not content with destroying the world's economies":** Ben Laurie, "More Banking Stupidity: Phished by Visa," Links, March 28, 2009, WM.

Bacula

226 **"Ben Laurie wrote the code, but hates the idea.":** socrates1024, "My Useless Who-Is-Satoshi theory," BF, July 13, 2014.

I Support the Current Thing

231 **"the court believes that Granath had sufficient factual grounds":** Cheyenne Ligon et al., "Hodlonaut Wins Norwegian Lawsuit Against Self-Proclaimed 'Satoshi' Craig Wright," CoinDesk, October 20, 2022.

231 **Wright had filed an appeal:** Jon Southurst, "Craig Wright's appeal against Hodlonaut given permission to go ahead in Norway," CoinGeek, December 23, 2022.

232 **"I have been too angry for too long":** @Dr_CSWright, Twitter, December 21, 2022.

233 **announced that he'd be holding a series of workshops:** @Dr_CSWright, Twitter, December 18, 2022.

233 **If conferences were going to disinvite him:** Dan Milmo, "Another court case fails to unlock the mystery of bitcoin's Satoshi Nakamoto," *The Guardian,* August 6, 2022.

233 **or not invite him in the first place:** Milmo, "Another court case."

234 **Craig and nChain continued to amass patents:** "Q1 2024 update: blockchain related patent activity in the technology industry," Verdict, April 24, 2024.

236 **claimed it would eventually be able to handle 1.1 million transactions per second:** "BSV Association begins technical testing of Teranode," press release, February 22, 2024.

236 **Bitcoin's paltry maximum of seven:** "Transactions Per Second (TPS) Meaning," Ledger website, December 16, 2022.

His Excellency

238 **taken over his debts and bankrolled his life:** Andrew O'Hagan, "The Satoshi Affair," *London Review of Books,* June 30, 2016; @agerhanssen, Twitter, May 21, 2024.

238 **"I don't believe in rewriting history":** New headnote (added February 2023) to Gavin Andresen, "Satoshi," *Gavin Andresen* (blog), May 2, 2016.

239 **son of a pig farmer:** "How a pig farmer made billions in online gambling," CTV News, March 13, 2010.

239 **convicted of marijuana smuggling:** Timothy Taylor, "Casino Risqué," *The Globe and Mail* (Canada), April 27, 2007.

239 **various stock violations:** Settlement Order, British Columbia Securities Commission, October 3, 1996.

239 **appeared on the cover of *Forbes*'s "Billionaires" issue:** Stephen Ripley, "Early bet on Internet gambling paid off for former farm boy Calvin Ayre," *Regina Leader-Post,* April 12, 2017.

239 **Goldfinger, as photographed by *Maxim*:** Matthew Miller, "Catch Me If You Can," *Forbes*, May 11, 2006; Simon Bowers, "Billionaire Bookie Who Went from Farmboy to Playboy," *The Guardian,* February 7, 2008; John Gray, "Calvin Ayre—The Dealer," Canadian Business, October 24, 2005, WM.

239 **bulletproof Hummer:** Timothy Taylor, "Crypto kingpin," *The Globe and Mail,* November 24, 2017.

239 **submarine of sorts:** Rebecca Liggero, "A Calvin Ayre and Bodogbrand.com Education in Antigua, CalvinAyre.com Style (Ya, I Thought He Was Retired Too)," GWPA website, July 30, 2009.

239 **go down ninety feet:** Gay Nagle Myers, "Submarine tour introduces visitors to underwater Antigua," Travel Weekly, April 2, 2009.

239 **a pay-per-view Lingerie Bowl:** "Supermodels in Lingerie, or 60-Year-Old Rock Retreads? Bodog Lingerie Bowl is Back On Super Bowl Sunday," Doc's Sports Service, January 9, 2006.

239 **used the words *billionaire playboy*:** Josh Dean, "Last Call," *Fast Company,* July/August 2008.

239 **one of his inspirations:** Dean, "Last Call."

239 **indicted in Maryland on money-laundering and other charges:** "Bodog and Four Canadian Individuals Indicted for Conducting Internet Gambling Business Generating over $100 Million in Sports Gambling Winnings," U.S. Attorney's Office (Maryland), news release, February 28, 2012.

239 **Eventually, he pled guilty:** Nathan Vardi, "Former Online Gambling Billionaire Calvin Ayre Pleads Guilty to Misdemeanor Charge," *Forbes,* July33314, 2017.

239 **one of his publicists sent me two documents:** Lindeborg Counsellors at Law, "Legal Opinion in Respect of the Good Standing of Mr Calvin E. Ayre," October 11, 2017; Patrick Basham, "'Do As I Say, Not As I Do': How the WTO, Antigua & a Canadian Overcame American Hypocrisy on Free Trade," Democracy Institute Series Report No 1, September 2017.

240 **a book about Craig by two foreign journalists:** Byron Kaye & Jeremy Wagstaff, *Behind the Mask: Craig Wright and the Battle for Bitcoin* (Melbourne: Affirm Press, 2020).

240 **only to be cancelled a week before its release date:** Jon Southurst, "Craig Wright Responds to Affirm Press Dropping Book," CoinGeek, January 21, 2020, WM.

241 **at whose company Seetee Magnus had worked a few years earlier:** "Aker ASA Seetee to invest in Bitcoin and blockchain technology," Aker ASA website, March 8, 2021.

243 **"early version" [footnote]:** Approved Judgment, *Crypto Open Patent Alliance v. Craig Steven Wright,* High Court of Justice, Business and Property Courts of England and Wales, Chancery Division, Intellectual Property List, May 20, 2024.

243 **"a barefaced lie" [footnote]:** Approved Judgment, *Crypto Open Patent Alliance v. Craig Steven Wright,* High Court of Justice, Business and

Property Courts of England and Wales, Chancery Division, Intellectual Property List, July 16, 2024.

244 **Eight months later, Calvin would fire Craig:** Arthur van Pelt, "The Tale of a BSV Culture Shock: Why Both Craig Wright And Christen Ager-Hanssen Have Left nChain," MyLegacyKit, Medium, October 5, 2023.

244 **"I am on a beach in southern Spain":** Calvin Ayre, email to Craig Wright, reproduced in @agerhanssen, Twitter, October 1, 2023.

245 **the most definitive declaration by a court yet:** "Justice James Mellor's Ruling on Craig Wright, COPA Trial, in His Own Words," CoinDesk, March 14, 2024.

245 **"W," Jack Dorsey crowed:** @jack, Twitter, March 14, 2024.

245 **"I know he is Satoshi":** @CalvinAyre, Twitter, March 14, 2024.

245 **"Goodbye everyone":** @CalvinAyre, Twitter, March 15, 2024.

245 **a humiliating statement:** Approved Judgment, *Crypto Open Patent Alliance v. Craig Steven Wright,* High Court of Justice, Business and Property Courts of England and Wales, Chancery Division, Intellectual Property List, July 16, 2024.

Florian

246 **an operatic tenor:** "DALLA – Caruso – Florian Cafiero – MEF 2019," Classical HD Live, YouTube, February 25, 2020.

246 **who'd written disputed plays by Molière:** Florian Cafiero and Jean-Baptiste Camps, "Why Molière Most Likely Did Write His Plays," *Science Advances* 5, no. 11 (2019).

246 **who was behind the Q of QAnon:** David D. Kirkpatrick, "Who Is Behind QAnon? Linguistic Detectives Find Fingerprints," *The New York Times,* February 19, 2022.

247 **"The creator of Bitcoin is Travis Hassloch":** Comment by Dimitrios4615, on Cyrus Farivar, "Man who claims he created bitcoin committed perjury, lawsuit says," Ars Technica, May 15, 2018.

248 **the sixty-ish thousand words of Nakamoto text:** These include the white paper, emails, and forum posts.

248 **Adam Back had finally made public:** Pete Rizzo, "Read Adam Back's Complete Emails with Bitcoin Creator Satoshi Nakamoto," *Bitcoin Magazine,* February 23, 2024.

248 **Martti Malmi:** "Satoshi—Sirius emails 2009–2011," GitHub.

248 **120 pages of private emails:** Pete Rizzo, "The New Satoshi Emails: Early Developer Sirius Releases 120 Pages Detailing Work on Bitcoin," *Bitcoin Magazine,* February 23, 2024.

248 **"absolutely disgusting":** @TheBlueMatt, Twitter, February 24, 2024.

248 **"immoral":** @btc_penguin_0x, Twitter, February 24, 2024.

248 **"so fiat":** Jack Mallers, "Who Is Satoshi Nakamoto? Who Cares," *The Money Matters Podcast,* February 26, 2024.

248 **"a massive asshole":** @lopp, Twitter, February 23, 2024.

249 **much of his career:** Hassloch's LinkedIn page.

249 **"privacy fanatic":** Solinym, Amazon review of Michal Zalewski, *Silence on the Wire: A Field Guide to Passive Reconnaissance and Indirect Attacks* (San Francisco: No Starch Press, 2005), October 1, 2005.

249 **"Solinym":** See URL of "TRAVIS HASSLOCH, Computer Security Professional," Stanford Splash.

249 **"Shugenja":** @shugenja on Twitter.

249 **attended Burning Man:** Travis D Huzzah, Facebook page.

249 **he'd previously been a libertarian:** Travis D Huzzah, Facebook comment, February 2, 2022.

249 **"Nothing banks do hurts me more":** Travis D Huzzah, Facebook comment, October 12, 2019.

250 **In 2020, after the pandemic began:** Cryddit (Ray Dillinger), "Re: Did this guy just find the founder of Bitcoin?," BF, March 24, 2020.

252 **turned out to have made the same assertion elsewhere using his full name:** This was a May 15, 2018, Facebook post by Dimitrios Tsoulogiannis, consisting of the two-word comment "Travis Hassloch" and a link to the Ars Technica article.

252 **"Pope of the Church of Satoshi":** Dimitrios Tsoulogiannis's LinkedIn page.

253 **I couldn't talk to Stowe, because he'd died in 2022:** "Thomas Christopher Stowe: 1981-2022," *San Antonio Express-News*, July 27–28, 2022.

Numero Uno

Details of the Finney swatting come from Giana Magnoli, "Call Reporting Shooting on Arroyo Road Near Goleta Deemed a Hoax," *Noozhawk*, May 29, 2014; Robert McMillan, "An Extortionist Has Been Making Life Hell for Bitcoin's Earliest Adopters," *Wired*, December 29, 2014; and Dustin Dreifuerst, "Episode 73: Fran Finney," *Did You Know* (podcast), February 20, 2020.

254 **made his first post to BitcoinTalk in November of 2010:** Hal Finney, "Re: Price vs. Difficulty Graphs," BF, November 30, 2010.

254 **a month before Nakamoto made his last post there:** Satoshi Nakamoto, "Added some DoS limits, removed safe mode (0.3.19)," BF, December 12, 2010.

254 **After his death, former colleagues:** Phil Zimmermann, Gene Hoffman, and Jon Callas, interviews.

255 **"web of trust":** Philip Zimmermann, "PGP Marks 30th Anniversary," Phil Zimmermann website, June 6, 2021.

255 **Emin Gün Sirer:** Charlie Shrem, "Satoshi's Identity in the Bitcoin Code? Ava Labs' Emin Gun Sirer on Bugs, Forks, and Dapps," *The Charlie Shrem Show* (podcast), May 5, 2020.

256 **"I don't mean to sound like a socialist":** Satoshi Nakamoto, email to Laszlo Hanyecz, reported in Nathaniel Popper, *Digital Gold: Bitcoin and the Inside Story of the Misfits and Millionaires Trying to Reinvent Money* (New York: Harper, 2015), 42.

257 **which was doing work for Barclays Bank:** "Barclays Bank selects PGP encryption platform," The Paypers, May 26, 2008.

258 **he would only officially retire from the company in early 2011:** Hal Finney, "Bitcoin and Me (Hal Finney)," BF, March 19, 2013.

258 **"That means a lot coming from you, Hal":** Satoshi Nakamoto, "Re: minimalistic bitcoin client on D language," BF, December 11, 2010.

259 **"My bitcoins are stored in our safe deposit box":** Hal Finney, "Bitcoin and Me."

259 **calling himself Bitcoin Troll:** Dreifuerst, "Episode 73."
259 **ransom of one thousand bitcoins:** McMillan, "Extortionist."
260 **he'd murdered his wife and child:** Magnoli, "Call Reporting Shooting."
260 **a stabbing and shooting rampage:** Emma G. Fitzsimmons and Brian Knowlton, "Gunman Covered Up Risks He Posed, Sheriff Says," *The New York Times,* May 25, 2014.
260 **"Is anyone being attacked in your house?":** McMillan, "Extortionist."
260 **"I was just panicking":** McMillan, "Extortionist."
261 **And he wasn't done.:** McMillan, "Extortionist."
261 **He was never caught.:** Mike McCoy, Criminal Records Sergeant, Santa Barbara County Sheriff's Office, email to author, January 5, 2023.
261 **"it took away some of the peace":** McMillan, "Extortionist."
261 **started an annual half-marathon:** Namcios, "Join the 'Running Bitcoin Challenge' to Fight ALS in Honor of Hal Finney," *Bitcoin Magazine,* December 28, 2021.
261 **a nearly three-and-a-half-minute speech:** Jon Callas, "Blockchain!," talk at Crypto 2018 conference, October 5, 2018.
262 **a ten-mile race in Santa Barbara:** Jameson Lopp, "Hal Finney Was Not Satoshi Nakamoto," *Cypherpunk Cogitations* (blog), October 21, 2023.

Occam's Razor

265 **a trio in England:** Steven Levy, *Crypto: Secrecy and Privacy in the New Code War* (New York: Penguin, 2002), 313–30; Simon Singh, *The Code Book: The Evolution of Secrecy from Mary, Queen of Scots, to Quantum Cryptography* (New York: Doubleday Anchor, 2000), 279–92.
265 **mentioning COINTELPRO:** Mark Mazzetti, "Burglars Who Took on F.B.I. Abandon Shadows," *The New York Times,* January 7, 2014.
266 **Only forty-three years after the burglary:** Betty Medsger, *The Burglary: The Discovery of J. Edgar Hoover's Secret FBI* (New York: Knopf, 2014).

Valley Boy

267 **an early-'90s email exchange:** Tim May, "Textual Analysis," CP, March 2, 1993.
267 **"Take this pretentious word 'nym'":** Graham Toal, "ID of anonymous posters via word analysis?," CP, November 1, 1993.
267 **mentioned how frequency analysis:** Murdering Thug, "Re: Textual Analysis," CP, March 2, 1993.
268 **build a "nymalizer":** Tim May, "The 'Nymalizer' and Shannon's Information Theory," CP, November 8, 1993.
268 **machine-translating a message:** Dark, "Style Analysis," CP, October 29, 1993.
268 **"randomly modify spacing":** Alexander Chislenko, "Textual Analysis," CP, March 2, 1993.
268 **"These are pretty amusin'":** Hal Finney, "REMAIL: Filters for copyright?," CP, March 31, 1993.
268 **he'd combined it with BitTorrent:** Hal Finney, "Cypherpunk help with Hal Finney demo," CP, February 11, 2005.

268 **"a P2P gambling game":** Hal Finney, "Your source code, for sale," CR, November 5, 2004.
268 **the original Bitcoin software included code for a poker game:** Jamie Redman, "Satoshi's Pre-Release Bitcoin Code Contains Fascinating Findings," Bitcoin.com News, March 14, 2019.
268 **who'd flown within California many times:** Giana Magnoli, "Local Software Developer Hal Finney Dies After Five-Year Battle with ALS," *Noozhawk,* September 11, 2014.
269 **"I'm comfortable with my legacy.":** Hal Finney, "Bitcoin and Me (Hal Finney)," BF, March 19, 2013.
269 **"Lois Lane":** Hal Finney, "Another *Potential* Identifying Piece of Evidence on Satoshi," BF, June 15, 2013.
269 **"the kind of elaborate prank Hal would have loved":** WalterBright, comment on "Len Sassaman and Satoshi," Hacker News, February 23, 2021.
269 **promissory notes and negotiable instruments:** Hal Finney, "Promise her anything . . . ," CP, March 22, 1994.
270 **"we will miss you Hal Finney":** @NickSzabo4, Twitter, August 29, 2014.

Vincent Adultman

272 **Gwern Branwen had speculated about Elaine Ou:** Gwern Branwen, comment on "Bitcoin may have a fixed supply only because Wei Dai didn't get back to Satoshi with comments on the white paper in time," Reddit, r/Buttcoin, February 12, 2021.
272 **experienced C++ coder:** Elaine Ou's CV, WM.
272 **wife of Nick Szabo:** Tim May, "JW Weatherman Interviews Cypherpunk Legend Timothy C May—Author of the Cyphernomicon," *Under the Microscope* (podcast), June 9, 2018.
272 **"Working on something fantastic.":** @eiaine, Twitter, February 20, 2009.
273 **four mining pools controlling more than 75 percent of the network:** Blockchain.com Charts—Hashrate Distribution.
273 **"an embarrassment" and "a ghetto of criminality and fraud":** Dustin Dreifuerst, "Episode 34: The Legend Phil Zimmermann," *Did You Know* (podcast), May 5, 2019.
273 **"an experiment" that had "failed":** Mike Hearn, "The Resolution of the Bitcoin Experiment," Medium, January 14, 2016.
273 **"a failure" and "a disaster":** Ray Dillinger, "Bitcoin is a disaster," CR, December 28, 2020.
274 **"I think Satoshi would barf":** Tim May, "Enough with the ICO-Me-So-Horny-Get-Rich-Quick-Lambo Crypto," CoinDesk, October 19, 2018.
274 **lamenting Bitcoin's lack of anonymity:** James Donald, "Bitcoin as a speculative bet," *Jim's Blog* (blog), April 14, 2013.
274 **and relative centralization:** James Donald, "Bitcoin failure," *Jim's Blog* (blog), June 15, 2014.
274 **"money laundries":** Donald, "Bitcoin as a speculative bet."
274 **enhanced privacy:** James Donald, "zeek rollups can enable full blockchain scalability and full blockchain privacy," *Jim's Blog* (blog), August 17, 2022.
275 **enabled faster transactions:** James Donald, "Bitcoin time," *Jim's Blog* (blog), October 23, 2021.
275 **"a shitcoin":** @NickSzabo4, Twitter, October 16, 2019.

275 **"Multitudes and charlatans":** @NickSzabo4, Twitter, October 16, 2019.

275 **"digital gold for the next millennia":** @adam3us, Twitter, September 21, 2013.

275 **"I know who Nakamoto was":** James Donald, comment on "Enormous move in bitcoin coming up," *Jim's Blog* (blog), June 29, 2023.

278 **"old and beautiful buildings bulldozed":** James Donald, "Georgia color revolution," *Jim's Blog* (blog), June 13, 2024.

282 **"Satoshi will be, or already has been, de-anonymized":** @zooko, Twitter, December 6, 2013.

282 **"Watergate moved history":** Bob Woodward, *The Secret Man: The Story of Watergate's Deep Throat* (New York: Simon and Schuster, 2005), 217.

A New Life Form

283 **a list of pessimistic predictions that turned out to be wrong:** Ralph Merkle, "Incorrect Negative Forecasts," https://www.ralphmerkle.com.

284 **he wrote a paper on how electron microscopy:** Ralph Merkle, "Large Scale Analysis of Neural Structures," Xerox Technical Report CSL-89-10, November 1989.

284 **He was further convinced:** K. Eric Drexler, *Engines of Creation: The Coming Era of Nanotechnology* (New York: Anchor Books, 1987).

284 **trouble with the Riverside coroner and health department:** Louis Sahagun and T.W. McGarry, "Judge Bars Coroner From Thawing Frozen Heads and Body at Lab," *Los Angeles Times,* January 14, 1988; and Max More, interview.

285 **had his daughter Luna's brain cryopreserved:** Art Quaife, "Patricia Luna Wilson," Cryonics website, WM.

287 **DJ Steve Aoki has said he's a member:** Jonah Weiner, "Inside Steve Aoki's Quest for EDM Immortality," *Rolling Stone,* August 24, 2016.

287 **Peter Thiel has been reported to be a member:** Steve Mollman, "Billionaire Peter Thiel Says He's Signed Up to Be Cryogenically Preserved When He Dies So He Can Be Revived in the Future—but He's 'Not Convinced It Works,'" *Fortune,* May 4, 2023.

287 **A milestone for the field:** Robert C.W. Ettinger, *The Prospect of Immortality* (New York: Doubleday, 1964); the book was published privately in 1962.

288 **head and body of Ted Williams:** Stephanie Innes, "Scottsdale cryonics facility, the home of Ted Williams' head, hopes frozen dead people will live again," *The Arizona Republic,* June 11, 2019.

288 **Marvin Minsky:** "Ray Kurzweil Remembers Marvin Minsky," Sentient Technologies channel, YouTube, April 4, 2016, WM.

289 **"network states":** Balaji Srinivasan, *The Network State: How to Start a New Country* (N.p.: Amazon Kindle, 2022).

289 **a "distributed," blockchain-coordinated "city":** Danny Nelson, "Coliving Project Cabin Wants to Put Digital Nomads in Nature," CoinDesk, May 23, 2023.

289 **signed up with Alcor when he was twenty:** Andrew Fenton, "Roger Ver's Next Life: Cryonics Meets Crypto," *Magazine by Cointelegraph,* April 28, 2021.

289 **Vitalik Buterin had donated crypto to life extension organizations:** Kelsie

Nabben, "Crypto Leaders Are Obsessed with Life Extension. Here's Why," *Magazine by Cointelegraph,* August 11, 2021.

289 **Brad Armstrong made the largest gift yet to Alcor:** "Unprecedented $5 Million Contribution to Cryonics Research!," Alcor, announcement, May 15, 2018.

289 **a currency called Stellar:** "Please donate appreciated cryptocurrency to Strengthen Alcor," Alcor, June 17, 2021.

289 **"the study of the economic problems of immortal existence":** "Futique Neologisms 2," *Extropy: The Journal of Transhumanist Thought* 3, no. 2, issue 8 (Winter 1991–92).

289 **"the first example of a new form of life":** R. Merkle, "DAOs, Democracy and Governance," *Cryonics Magazine,* July–August 2016, 28–40.

290 **"a sewer rat":** Mark Frauenfelder, "Bitcoin Is the Sewer Rat of Currencies," Medium, February 24, 2016.

290 **inoculating Bitcoin against even the death of the internet:** Gregory Barber, "The Cypherpunks Tapping Bitcoin via Ham Radio," *Wired,* June 27, 2019.

290 **an ASCII portrait of his bearded face:** https://pastebin.com/raw/BUB3dygQ

290 **Fidelity now advised retail clients:** Teuta Franjkovic, "Fidelity All-in-One ETF Allocates Up to 3% in Bitcoin as Institutional Crypto Investing Normalized," CCN, February 8, 2024.

Acknowledgments

I could only write this book thanks to a serendipitous assignment in 2011 by Jason Tanz, then an editor at *Wired*. At *New York*, my professional home for many years, I was lucky to receive crypto-adjacent assignments from Noreen Malone, Genevieve Smith, and David Haskell.

Thanks to Maciej Eder, creator of Stylo, for putting me in touch with Joanna Byszuk, and to Joanna for fielding my Stylo-related questions. My stabs at DIY stylometry provided a useful reminder that some things are best left to the pros. I am fortunate that Florian Cafiero and Jean-Baptiste Camps were willing to lend their time, expertise, and goodwill.

Code stylometry is new enough that practitioners are few. I thank Brian Timmerman, a machine-learning engineer, for gamely tackling the Nakamoto problem.

Ben Kalin fact-checked this book with rigor and care. Dan Novack offered FOIA savvy. Clive Thompson gave encouragement to a novice coder. I am thankful to Karen Brown for years of wise counsel.

For help of all sorts, I acknowledge Gavin Andresen, Gary Berman, Gwern Branwen, Eileen Brown, Andrea Chang, Fran Finney, Robert Graham, Matthew Householder, Mills, Justin Posey, Daniel Quinn, Marcia Stornetta, and Sam Teller.

Larry Weissman and Sascha Alper, my extraordinary agents, were quick with enthusiasm for this book and steady advocates in seeing it through.

At Crown, Kevin Doughten was generous with his thoughts and attention, pushed me in the best possible way, and made the book better. I also thank Gillian Blake and the ace team at Crown, most especially Dustin Amick, Christina Caruccio, Julie Cepler, Mason Eng, Anna Kochman, Amy Li, Elisabeth Magnus, Dyana Messina, Dan Novack, Amani Shakrah, Ojasvinee Singh, Stacey Stein, and Serena Wang.

I'm blessed to have friends who helped me think through various aspects of this story. Thanks to Chris Buck, David Fields, Eric Liftin, Andrew Rice, Steve Rinella, and Andy Sack. Max Potter made a dam-busting suggestion at a crucial moment. Eric Konigsberg was a stalwart adviser, early draft reader, and ready source of journalistic wisdom and literary intelligence.

Thank you, finally, to my always supportive parents, Don and Daphne Wallace, sisters Alexandra and Sarah, extended Wallace family, and Dooskin in-laws, particularly Tyler, fellow student of things crypto. And endless love and gratitude to my wife Nicole and daughter Lucinda, who shared their home, husband, and father with this project; they are my center.

ABOUT THE AUTHOR

BENJAMIN WALLACE is the *New York Times* bestselling author of *The Billionaire's Vinegar*. He has been a features writer at *New York* magazine and a contributing editor at *Vanity Fair.*